CHINA'S EDUCATION AND THE INDUSTRIALIZED WORLD

*A Publication of the Ontario Institute for
Studies in Education*

CHINA'S EDUCATION AND THE INDUSTRIALIZED WORLD

STUDIES IN CULTURAL TRANSFER

Ruth Hayhoe and Marianne Bastid, Editors

M. E. Sharpe, Inc.
ARMONK, NEW YORK/LONDON

The Ontario Institute for Studies in Education has three prime functions: to conduct programs of graduate study in education, to undertake research in education, and to assist in the implementation of the findings of educational studies. The Institute is a college chartered by an Act of the Ontario Legislature in 1965. It is affiliated with the University of Toronto for graduate studies purposes.

The publications program of the Institute has been established to make available information and materials arising from studies in education, to foster the spirit of critical inquiry, and to provide a forum for the exchange of ideas about education. The opinions expressed should be viewed as those of the contributors.

Library of Congress Cataloging-in-Publication Data

China's education and the industrialized world.

> Bibliography: p.
> Includes index.
> 1. Education—China—Foreign influences.
> 2. Education—China—History. 3. Comparative
> education. I. Hayhoe, Ruth. II. Bastid, Marianne.
> LA1131.C53   1987   370'.951   87-4744
> ISBN 0-87332-425-0
> ISBN 0-87332-428-5 (pbk.)

Canadian Cataloguing in Publication Data

> Main entry under title:

China's education and the industrialized world.

> Bibliography: p.
> Includes index.
> ISBN 0-7744-0307-1

> Education—China—Foreign influences.
> 2. Education—China—History. 3. Comparative
> education. I. Hayhoe, Ruth. II. Bastid, Marianne.

> LA1131.C45   1987   370'.951   C86-094999-0

Printed in the United States of America

Contents

Preface

In July of 1984, the World Society of Comparative Education held its Fifth Congress in Paris, focusing on the theme of Dependence and Interdependence in Education. It was the first occasion on which scholars of education from the People's Republic of China had participated in such a congress and during that week the Chinese Comparative Education Society was accepted as a full member of the World Society.

For those of us who had been studying recent and contemporary Chinese educational history, this was a happening of the greatest significance. At last we were able to sit down with Chinese colleagues in a scholarly forum and discuss China's experience in educational development. As a part of the World Congress, I had been invited to organize a workshop on the subject of China's educational relations with foreign countries. I was delighted when Marianne Bastid-Bruguière agreed to the role of senior scholar and advisor to this workshop, and her many years of research on Chinese educational history from the late Qing to the present have provided the essential foundation for subsequent developments.

The workshop itself was a stimulating event, enhanced by the surroundings of a beautiful seminar room overlooking the Square of the Pantheon. However, after it was over we decided against the publication of the conference papers in favor of planning for a new publication that would present in a more comprehensive and ordered way the history of China's educational relations with the industrialized world. The conference theme of dependence and interdependence drew on concepts and issues thrown up by Dependency Theory. Following this cue, we decided to test the view that educational transfers have been used to consolidate political domination and economic exploitation between developed and developing countries by a careful look at China's historical experience with Japan and the Soviet Union, as well as with Western industrialized powers. Furthermore, we felt that a thorough and analytic explication of China's historical experience in this regard was important for a balanced understanding of both the possibilities and the dangers inherent in China's present open door to educational ideas and patterns from outside. Three chapters of the book are therefore devoted to aspects of contemporary educational policy and practice in China. Finally, we judged that a study of this type would be incomplete without some recognition of the fact that Chinese educational ideas and patterns have also made their impact on the industrialized world. While the scope of the book did not allow for this topic to be treated as fully as it deserves, we were pleased to be able to commission two chapters which depict the European perspective on Confucian education in the seventeenth and eighteenth centuries and the French fascination with Maoist educational thought in the sixties of this century.

I would like to comment on the special qualities which each contributor has brought to his or her chapter, but I will leave this for the reader to discover. Many are already well known names in Sinological and Comparative Education circles; others are younger scholars just beginning to make their mark. All have cooperated in linking their analyses to the overall theme of the book, and in undertaking the revisions and adjustments requested of them. I'd like to thank each one for the pleasure I have had in working together on a topic far too large for any one researcher to take on alone. In addition I must thank Sun Yilin for preparing the glossary of Chinese terms, Sharon Richmond and Sheila Barnard at OISE Press, for their professionalism in all aspects of preparing the final manuscript, and Douglas Merwin, editor at M. E. Sharpe, for his encouragement and cooperation in the project. I must take personal responsibility for the translations of chapters 1, 2, 5 and 11 from French into English, and for the preparation of the select bibliography on Chinese education and its international relations, which I hope will be a useful research tool.

R.H.

List of Contributors

Hiroshi Abe is Head of the Section of Asian Education, National Institute of Educational Research, Japan, and lecturer in the Graduate School of Education, Tokyo University. Author of numerous articles on aspects of Korean and Chinese educational history, he also translated, with W. Watanabe, a *History of Modern Education in Korea* (Koma Shorin, 1979), and edited *Educational and Cultural Exchange between Japan and China and Its Conflict: Japanese Educational Activities in Pre-War China* (Daiichi Sobo, 1983) and *U.S.-China Educational Exchanges: Historical Lessons in International Cultural Cooperation* (Kazankai, 1985).

Marianne Bastid is Directeur de Recherche at the Centre National de la Recherche Scientifique, Paris. She is the author of *Aspects de la réforme de l'enseignement en Chine au début du XXe siècle, L'Evolution de la société chinoise à la fin de la dynastie des Qing,* and other publications on the political, social and cultural history of the late Qing period and the People's Republic of China.

Hubert O. Brown is a Senior Lecturer in the Department of Education, University of Hong Kong. Specializing in Chinese educational thought, he has written on Dong Zhongshu, Tao Xingzhi, educational research in the People's Republic and rural education in China. He holds degrees from Columbia University, the University of Chicago and Stanford (Ph.D), and taught in the Chicage Public Schools, St. Mary's College, California, and University Sains Malaysia before going to Hong Kong.

Delia Davin taught English in Peking for two years in the 1960s and went on to do Chinese studies at Leeds University. Her doctoral thesis was on Chinese women's history and she has subsequently worked on family reform and population policy in China. At present she is co-editing a translation of a volume of life histories written by Zhang Xinxin and Sang Ye. She is a lecturer in Economic and Social history at the University of York, England. Her publications include

Womenwork: Women and the Party in Revolutionary China (OUP, 1976) and (joint editor), *China's One-Child Family Policy* (Macmillan, 1985).

Roland Depierre was formerly a professor of the philosophy of education at the Ecole Normale, Le Mans, France. His research has been concerned with psychometry and social models. From 1976 to 1983 he taught French literature and civilization at universities in Shanghai and Guangzhou. He is at present a teacher of philosophy in Nantes, France.

Ruth Hayhoe is assistant professor in the Higher Education Group, Ontario Institute for Studies in Education. She teaches courses in Comparative Higher Education and does research on aspects of Chinese higher education and its international relations. She is editor of *Contemporary Chinese Education* (Croom Helm and M. E. Sharpe, 1984) and author of numerous articles on Chinese universities. For thirteen years, she was privileged to teach Chinese students in Hong Kong and Shanghai.

Jürgen Henze is a researcher at the Institute of Comparative Education, Ruhr University, Bochum. He is the author of *Bildung and Wissenschaft in der Volksrepublik China* (Institut für Asienkunde, 1983), *Hochschulzugang in der VR China* (Böhlau, 1987) and numerous articles on aspects of education and science in China.

Huang Shiqi is Director of the Information and Documentation Unit, State Education Commission, Beijing, and Vice-president of the Chinese Educational Association for International Exchanges. He has held leadership positions in the fields of civil engineering, engineering education and comparative education, and was Deputy Director of the Bureau of Science and Technology, Chinese Ministry of Education in 1981-82. He is the author of *Education in China — The Past Five Years,* a book prepared for the UNESCO Regional Office for the Pacific and Oceania in August, 1982, and of numerous articles on aspects of higher education in China.

Francoise Kreissler pursued studies in German language, literature and history at the University of Paris 3, Munich and Vienna and has an M.A. in German History (1967-72). Subsequently she studied Chinese language, literature and history at the University of Paris 7, the Beijing Language Institute and Fudan University (1969-75). She has a doctorate from the Ecole des Hautes Etudes en Sciences Sociales (Paris) with a thesis on German cultural activities in China from the late nineteenth century to World War II (1983). Since 1984 she has been a lecturer in the German department of the University of Paris 3, and she does research on Sino-German relations in the first part of the twentieth century and foreign communities in Shanghai during World War II.

Isabelle Llasera is a teacher of French as a foreign language and currently works in the Cultural Department of the French Embassy in London. She has spent nearly four years in China, teaching at Fudan University in Shanghai and training teachers of French in Beijing. She has published articles on linguistics and on teaching in the seventeenth century.

Karen Minden is a professor of Political Studies at the University of Manitoba in Winnipeg. She specializes in the study of Chinese politics, with an interest in the transfer of technology and Canadian-Chinese relations. A student of the Beijing Language Institute in 1974, she received her M.A. from the University of California at Berkeley and her Ph.D. from York University in Toronto. She has completed a study on the politics of the Canada-China wheat trade and is currently working on a project examining the historical role of missionaries in the modernization of China.

Born in the Soviet Union and raised in China, Leo A. Orleans spent most of his professional career as a China specialist at the Library of Congress, Washington, D.C. He is the author of several books and numerous articles and monographs on population, education, science and technology and other aspects of China's social and economic development. Since his retirement, Orleans has continued to pursue his research interests in a consultant capacity.

Ronald F. Price has taught English in technical colleges, a secondary school in Bulgaria and teacher training institutions in Beijing (1965-67) and Xi'an (annually since 1980) Currently he teaches Comparative Education at La Trobe University, Melbourne, Australia. He is the author of *Education in Modern China* (1970, 1979) *Marxism and Education in Russia and China* (London: Croom Helm, 1977), *Marx and Education under Late Capitalism* (London: Croom Helm, 1985) and numerous articles on aspects of Chinese education.

CHINA'S EDUCATION AND THE INDUSTRIALIZED WORLD

1

Servitude or Liberation? The Introduction of Foreign Educational Practices and Systems to China from 1840 to the Present

Marianne Bastid

Introduction

> If a sage-prince wishes to transform the people, to improve their morals and manners, should he not pay attention first to the schools? When sovereigns of old set up their states and regulated the government of their people, they made education and the schools a priority.[1]

These maxims from the Book of Rites, one of the Five Classics, underline the essential responsibility over education which the Chinese have accorded to the State since ancient times. In China education has also always been explicitly integrated within a set of political and social conceptions. Whether it aimed at fostering virtue or at forming men of affairs for leadership, it had a function within the State. It was to ensure a certain social order. In this role it was recognized as a state function in which practical tasks could eventually be shared with various non-government agencies or individuals, but which always preserved the state's sovereign authority.

This prerogative of the state and these traditional ideas about the role of education have had considerable importance in the history of Chinese educational interaction with the outside world. They explain Chinese awareness of the political and social risks of the introduction of foreign beliefs and practices at an early period, and the fact that the success or failure of these educational transfers was closely linked to the transformations undertaken by the Chinese state itself.

I will limit myself here to a description of the different phases of the penetration of foreign educational ideas into China and an attempt to identify the characteristic features of each phase. The intention is to illuminate the discussion of contemporary aspects of the opening of the Chinese education system to interaction with foreign countries.

Four periods can be distinguished since the Opium War in 1840. Foreign education was first viewed solely as the vehicle of new knowledge in specific fields. Then, from the 1890s to 1925, came the adoption of one foreign model that served both to liberate and to unify. The years from 1925 to 1949 were a period of eclectic educational borrowing. From 1949 to the present day, past experience in educational transfers has been repudiated and played back in a novel sequence of recantations, while inside and outside developments changed the impact and significance of old patterns.

Foreign Education as the Vehicle of New Learnings

The earliest reports on educational practices in Europe were taken to China by the Jesuits of the seventeenth and eighteenth centuries. However, the fathers of the Society of Jesus never founded any educational institutions in China, though they did put their scientific and technical expertise at the service of the Emperor. They were concerned to communicate their knowledge in specific areas to the Chinese literati, yet they did this without recourse to any formal mode of instruction. At the Chinese Bureau of Astronomy, where they were employed, they gave assistance to their collaborators without ever forming a school for scientists. As for the training of indigenous priests — only 45 were ordained between 1581 and 1740[2] — this was carried out in seminaries outside of China. The Jesuits were accorded attention not for any originality in their educational principles and methods, nor indeed for their style of reasoning, but simply for the content of their knowledge. For the Chinese literati of the late Ming dynasty, this knowledge, moral, philosophic, scientific and technical, formed an integral whole which was almost unanimously admired under the designation given to it as "heavenly learning" (*tianxue*) or "western learning" (*xixue*).[3] However, from the mid seventeenth century it became common to distinguish between two aspects of missionary teaching: science and technology, which deserved consideration, and religious doctrines, which were to be rejected.

Even scientific technical imports did not escape criticism. There was reservation over the way in which they depicted the universe, as well as a sense of their deficiency and uselessness for the task of moral improvement, which was the final aim of all human activity. The denunciation of religious doctrines did not confine itself to the exposure of their inconsistency and irrationality, but cast them in the light of an enterprise of political subversion. It was as spies in the employ of foreign nations that Adam Schall and other missionaries were arrested and held in 1661. When expelling the missionaries in 1723, the Emperor Yongzheng said to them:

> You wish all Chinese to become Christians, and your religion demands this,
> I know it well. But in such a case, what shall we become? The subjects of
> your king?[4]

In this period of the first religious missions in the seventeenth and eighteenth centuries, the current of educational exchange almost certainly flowed from China to Europe rather than the other way around. (See the next chapter by I. Llasera.) The institution of competitive written examinations for the civil service, which has been central to the conception of modern educational systems in various western countries, can be attributed to the Chinese Empire,[5] whereas the education practised in China over this period underwent no changes at all. However from this contact of the Chinese literati with an intellectual tradition totally different from their own, two ideas took shape which constantly reappeared in the subsequent history of Chinese educational relations with the outside world. One is the notion that influences coming from other civilizations constituted a risk of moral alienation and political subjugation. The other is that a distinction can and should be made among the elements which make up another culture, so that a selective assimilation is possible of those elements pre-judged as capable of enriching Chinese civilization. These two interlinked ideas were rooted in a vivid sense of the originality and historical coherence of Chinese culture and in the conviction that this culture was the very foundation of the existence and unity of the Chinese Empire.

Does the proselytizing spirit of the missionaries suffice to explain this reaction of distrust and defensiveness? In their earlier contacts with different civilizations, whether Arabic culture or that of the people of the Steppes, the Chinese had shown less prejudice and a greater degree of indifference and contempt. It was not so much the militant spirit of the missionaries, a characteristic not shared by all of them, as the pretensions to universality of European Christian civilization which shook the Chinese literati. They had been accustomed to regarding their own culture as the only one capable of controlling and sustaining the universe. Since Ming times and more strongly so under Qing rule, the authority of neo-Confucianism, its establishment as the leading ideology and its institutionalization in the examination system also set an environment less conducive to intellectual flexibility.

If the seventeenth and eighteenth century Catholic missionaries passed on to the Chinese literati a certain view of what made up the intellectual baggage of the educated classes in Europe of that time, no precise knowledge about educational practices in Europe reached China until much later, when schools were founded by foreign missionaries, first of all by Catholics. The first seminary was set up by Lazarists in Peking in 1786. In subsequent years some schools for boys were opened in Peking and in several communities elsewhere.[6] They had to close in 1805, as did the seminary in 1820. Another initiative was taken in 1835 and this time included educational provision for girls, a significant innovation in view of Chinese custom during that period. In 1837 the school of the village of Xiwanzi, near to the city now known as Zhangjiakou, beyond the Great Wall, had sixty girls aged from eight to sixteen years.[7]

Protestant missionaries took their cue from these Catholic exemplars, not from the beginning of their evangelistic activity in China which dates back to the arrival of Robert Morrison of the London Missionary Society in Canton in 1807, but after the First Opium War. Their first school for boys was opened in Hong

Kong in 1842, and the first school for girls in Ningbo in 1844.

No matter what their creed, these first schools were foreign implants introduced into Chinese society. It was not at the demand either of Chinese families converted to Christianity or Chinese clergy that the missionaries opened these establishments, but of their own accord for the needs of their work. Nor was it the purpose of these schools to provide an education suited to the needs of Chinese society, although the Catholics took great care to entrust the education of girls to women or to very old teachers in order not to offend Chinese sensitivities. The purpose rather was to implant a new mode of life and new mental attitudes. What the missionaries meant was only a moral and spiritual transformation. The core of the teaching given in these first religious schools added to that simple lessons in English and arithmetic. The Catholics, however, only taught Chinese, reserving Latin for those who were to become priests. Whatever may have been the later efforts, especially after 1870, to integrate into these educational programs more teaching relating to the material needs of the Chinese social environment, (see chapter 3 by D. Davin), the original sin was to have intended to detach the youth from the moral system which for the literati formed the Chinese identity. This weighed heavily against the general influence of religious missions in China and against their educational activity in particular.

Exemplified in the parish school, foreign education appeared first of all as a channel for knowledge that was harmful, either futile or actually pernicious. Among the Chinese educated classes, there was an explosion of anger against the religious and moral teachings propagated by these establishments and by extension against everything that might be done in them. The points of criticism raised first in the seventeenth century now reappeared, mingled with new themes inspired by the current political situation. The deep-rooted hostility of the literati towards religious sects, which they regarded as guilty of leading the credulous and weak masses into heresy and rebellion, was sharpened due to the fact that the Taiping rebels had borrowed a part of their ideology from Christianity, and had gained active sympathy from Protestant missionaries over some years. The links of Chinese converts with foreign political interests became more obvious in that interpreters for invading armies were recruited from among them and foreign legations were constantly intervening to protect their interests. Long before the Marxist concept of religion as the opium of the people had been translated into Chinese, Chinese pamphlets written by the literati linked religious propaganda with the cargoes of drugs coming into China in the same boats that transported the missionaries, and made the latter responsible for this double poison.

Thus the first attempts of the religious missions to promote education were confronted with this total repudiation by the majority of the Chinese literati, elicited in response to the treaties extracted from China under force of arms. These guaranteed freedom of movement to foreign missions in the open ports from 1844 and throughout all of China from 1858. The idea that everything exterior to China was wholly perverse persisted for a long time and seriously impeded the course of educational exchanges, since education was the area in which Chinese tradition had developed an intellectual and political vigilance of particular intensity.

Nevertheless, the exigencies of political relations with foreign powers led certain high officials and some of the literati surrounding them to accept the utility of some of the knowledge transmitted to China by the Barbarians. Significantly, it was less the educational programs of missionary schools that drew their attention than the way in which certain foreigners by their knowledge of the Chinese language, their study of Chinese culture and the methodical collection of data on all that concerned China, gained substantial advantages for the activity of their own government with regard to China. It was this practice which the Chinese literati set themselves to imitate. This involved building up a certain amount of knowledge about the barbarians which would make it possible to interact with them from a position of strength and to control them. It was thought possible to isolate this specific knowledge from its general context and to master it in order to liberate themselves from foreign domination.

This approach is illustrated by the efforts of the Commissioner Lin Zexu of Canton to collect, have translated, published and eventually make use of information concerning western political and technical activity. It resulted in two notably different educational developments. The first consisted of the addition of certain new subjects, mainly foreign languages and various sciences, to the study of classical texts. Such a broadening of the horizons of intellectual curiosity scarcely differed in kind from the traditional practices whereby the literati eventually took up instruction in new philosophical researches, medical discoveries and other areas of scholarship alongside of their rigorous preparation for the official examinations. The other development was the creation of adhoc institutions, quite separate from the general organization of study, intended for teaching the new learnings.

The first development, which has been given very little attention by historians, was only slowly consolidated after 1860-1870, simultaneously and proportionately with the publication of translations from western languages either by missionaries or by the Chinese authorities. Modern subjects were introduced in the programs offered by the best classical academies, such as Nanqing, founded in 1884 in Jiangyin in Jiangsu province, which included an observatory, or Lianchi in Baoding prefecture in the northern province of Zhili. Many diaries kept by younger and older scholars in the 1870s and 1900s also give evidence of a widening range of reading and discussion on foreign subjects with their friends and colleagues. Their information was gathered mostly from books and newspapers rather than from direct contact with foreigners in China. Such contact provided indeed one source for those scholars employed in certain government offices involved in foreign relations or working on the private staff of high provincial officials, but was generally not keenly sought after by others. This kind of individual reading resulted in the dissemination of knowledge concerning the outside world among the educated classes of various provinces and, more importantly, in the assimilation of political and scientific ideas from Europe which opened the way for the sudden launching of the movement for political reform starting from 1894-95.

On the other hand, the history of the special institutions intended for education in western learning is much better known. The first school of this type, known as the *Tongwenguan* or College of Languages, was set up by the Imperial Government in Peking in 1861 for the purpose of training interpreters. The treaty of 1858 had made it obligatory for the Chinese authorities to communicate in English with British government representatives from that time onwards. Similar establishments were opened in Canton and Shanghai in 1863. Scientific teaching was introduced into the school in Peking in 1867, and a bureau for translation was subsequently added. This pattern was followed in Shanghai. Other official institutions designed to prepare the administrative personnel needed in foreign relations were founded in several provincial capitals, as well as various technical schools for training the cadres necessary for modernization projects in the navy and the army, for the development of a telegraph system and of mining and metallurgical industries. By 1895 there were in existence 22 establishments dedicated exclusively to the teaching of specific branches of western knowledge. One must add to these the system of educational missions abroad started in 1872, by which the imperial government had arranged training either fully or partially for several carefully chosen groups of Chinese students in the United States, France, England and Germany. The total of the students sent abroad scarcely exceeded 300 up to the Sino-Japanese War of 1894.

All of these diverse institutions took specific precautions to ensure the loyalty of their students to the motherland. Some obliged them to sit for the imperial examinations, others recruited only Chinese from the Eight Banners, who were more loyal to the reigning dynasty. Substantial teaching in the Chinese language and Chinese classics was imposed in all cases. It was precisely the fear that Chinese students were becoming Americanized that decided the government to suddenly terminate the educational experience of young Chinese in the United States in 1881.

The utilization of the knowledge acquired from outside was further limited to carefully demarcated sectors of activity. In fact even those graduates of the new schools who had mandarinal titles were given only technical employment and had no access to the opportunities for politically responsible positions reserved for graduates of the traditional system. The western education dispensed by these official institutions was thus a kind of appendix to the traditional education system, without ever being properly integrated into it or being able to substitute for any of its functions. The creation of the new schools was inspired by a principle developed by the Chinese literati in the beginning of the seventeenth century, the principle that it is necessary and possible to separate that which is useful from that which is harmful in foreign culture. But it put a new idea into action, one which was important for the future: that effective learning of the useful elements of a foreign culture can only take place within a specific education system. All religious propaganda was forbidden in these institutions. Foreign teachers were appointed by the Chinese authorities and were under their strict control. Still the teaching style was more lively than in the traditional system, the learning process was more carefully graded and exercises and practical work of a type otherwise completely unknown were included.

One Unifying and Liberating Model

The development of government schools, as well as the bloody popular uprisings elicited by the extension of missionary activity into the provinces from the time of the Second Opium War, pushed the missions to give greater importance to their teaching activities and to increase the proportion of general knowledge as well as scientific and technical training in the curricula they offered. This was particularly evident after the massacre of Tianjin in 1870. In 1877 the Protestant schools had 6,000 pupils and by 1890 the enrollment reached 16,836.[8] At that time the Catholics had about 25,000 pupils. Several establishments for higher education were opened, first for the needs of the apostolate. A large Jesuit seminary was founded in 1843 and reorganized in 1858. The Protestant College of Dengzhou in Shandong was founded in 1864. However during the 1880s others appeared with more general educational aims.

Specialist studies were published describing in detail various European systems of education. The first of this type, and one which had considerable influence, was published in 1873 under the title *An Overview of German Schools (Deguo xuexiao lunlüe)*. The author was a well known German missionary, Dr. Ernst Faber (Hua Zhian). In a preface written by the noted mathematician Li Shanlan, it was observed that Prussia owed her recent military victories to the education received by her soldiers, which had inspired them to fight for an ideal and for certain principles. It underlined the importance of compulsory education and of the number of schools, especially professional schools, spread throughout the country.

In 1880-82 the American missionary W. A. P. Martin, who was Director of Studies at the College of Languages (*Tongwenguan*) in Peking, was sent by the Chinese government to seven foreign countries to collect materials on their education systems. The results of his study were published in Peking in 1883 under the title *An Enquiry into Education in the West (Xixue kaolüe)* and became an important reference work. The commissioning of this mission by the Chinese authorities evidences a general concern to go and acquire information directly from the sources of foreign thought. The difficulty experienced by the Imperial Government in suppressing the large popular uprisings which disturbed the Empire from 1850 to 1872, and its incapacity to stand up to foreign military threats and the growing demands of foreign powers on its borders and within its own territory, made many Chinese officials and scholars aware of China's internal weakness. They sought to penetrate the secret of foreign strength, to understand its foundations as well as its means and the intricacies of how it worked. In this quest, precipitated by the anguish of defeat and intensified by the Japanese victory of 1894-95, foreign education was no longer viewed as a simple collection of various kinds of knowledge, some of which could be usefully selected and introduced into China. It was seen as an instrument of intellectual and moral formation which enabled individuals to construct a nation.

Rather than looking solely at the content of foreign education, as had been done in the past, the importance of studying its methods, its organization and its patterns became evident. During the 1880s a few rare individuals had advocated a reform of the imperial examination system and eventually its abolition and the establishment of schools on a European model. After 1895 conviction grew that the whole education system must be reformed; it was no longer satisfactory to create innovative institutions alongside of the traditional ones. This point was so well accepted that when the examinations were abolished in 1905, not a word of protest was raised, although they had been the keystone of the traditional system and long the object of jealous protection.

The debate among the educated elite now centered on which model to follow, which foreign system had an approach to knowledge which was best suited to China. For the whole period from 1895 to 1925 Chinese borrowing from foreign educational institutions was clearly a coherent part of a national and social program. A certain conception of what shape China's new political and social organization should take motivated reformers to select a system of education coming from a particular country. These implants were in no way imposed by foreign powers, which were vying for a predominant role in China. Rather they were desired and sought after by the Chinese on their own initiative.

This point is not intended to underplay certain evident facts. It is certain that foreign penetration and domination undermined the values and institutions on which the Chinese Empire rested and forced the Chinese to seek new ones. It is also certain that each of the foreign governments which had diplomatic representation in Peking did all they could to persuade the Chinese authorities that their culture and institutions, not to mention their industrial products, were superior to those of other nations and merited sole recognition and acceptance by the Chinese. All hoped for a lasting increase in their influence in China. (See especially chapter 5 by F. Kreissler.) It is also true that neither the missionary institutions nor the secular educational projects financed by various foreign governments from the late nineteenth century (schools, scholarships, professorships, and gifts of books) were initially solicited by the Chinese nor ever placed fully under their authority. One should note, however, that the major thrust of this educational activity initiated by foreigners came after 1902, the date at which the imperial government established the first complete educational system to replace the traditional system with its literary academies (*shuyuan*) and official schools (*ruxue*) enrolling students with various levels of qualification in the imperial examination system. Furthermore, even at the height of its development, just before the crisis of May 1925, this foreign controlled educational provision never represented more than a meagre percentage of the pupils enrolled in the education system: it had reached barely seven percent of the overall enrolment,[9] and more than two thirds of the teachers in these schools were Chinese.

It is probably true that the presence of foreign domination had forced the Chinese to look outwards, yet it never dictated the choices they made in their educational borrowing. When the imperial government and the gentry rivalled one another in their zeal to open modern schools from 1904 to 1911, they looked for models or for general inspiration to guide their reform efforts. They went directly to foreign countries to draw their information. They collected materials with an extraordinary avidity without excluding anything. These materials were studied, discussed, compared and criticized. From 1895 to 1911, the central government and the provincial authorities sent numerous missions to collect information in many countries. The publication of official reports, generally written with meticulous precision and care, was complemented by reports which scholars, gentry and young intellectuals had managed to compile and disseminate through their own channels.

It was first of all the Japanese model which shaped the education system set up by the imperial reforms of 1902 and 1904. (See chapter 4 by Hiroshi Abe.) In spite of provisional adjustments made in 1912 in the first months of the Republic, and again in 1917 on the death of Yuan Shikai, it remained in place until 1922. It was well suited to the authoritarian spirit adopted by successive governments and given considerable support by public opinion as appropriate to the task of re-building the state, reorganizing society and imbuing the people with a spirit of public service.

The reforms of 1922, carried out more by educators than by politicians, saw the victory of the American model. Its liberalism suited the aspirations of many university scholars and intellectuals. In the wake of the May Fourth Movement of 1919 they had become convinced that the strength of the modern state must rest on the intelligence and individual conscience of its citizens rather than on a superficial militarization imposed from above. In their view education should not be an instrument of the state, but it should create the state in the sense that it was to form citizens capable of self-government. The new system thus focused on children themselves, no longer on concerns external to the school.

Those opposed to these reforms did not lose the opportunity of denouncing them as evidence of enslavement to foreign interests. In fact, however, the adoption of the Japanese model preceded the period of overwhelming Japanese political and military domination in China. The threatening demands of Japanese imperialism during the First World War actually precipitated the abandonment of the Japanese model. Similarly, the conversion to the American model in 1922 did not coincide with the height of American political and economic influence in China, and in its pure form it lasted a very short time.

For its partisans, the foreign model, whether Japanese or American, was regarded as a liberating force. It was to emancipate from the past, making possible what they saw as a complete break with old ways. Entirely new structures would be created rather than some reshuffling of the parts of the old system. In this way new methods of work and a new spirit might grow unimpeded. The foreign model was also meant as an instrument of unity and unification. It should make possible the summoning and channelling of reform aspirations as well as the stemming and marginalization of divergent ideologies.

The promoters of the foreign models never lacked awareness of the risk of dependency involved in the adoption of one model. As early as 1901, Luo Zhenyu, then already one of the most fervent advocates of the Japanese model, penned vivid warnings against the dangers of cultural alienation, citing as examples the russification of Poland and the Americanization of the Philippines.[10] His friend Zhang Yuanji also predicted a brain drain if China was not vigilant in keeping the whole initiative and direction of education under her own control.[11] In the eyes of Chinese intellectuals and politicians of the early twentieth century the necessary counterbalance to this danger of alienation was that education remain a national enterprise, exclusively administered by the Chinese, that all instruction be given in Chinese, that literary disciplines had their basis in knowledge of China, and finally that a national ideology (then termed *guojiao*) should be inculcated through the schools. There was some difference of opinion about the content of this national ideology: for some it meant submission to imperial authority, for others a regeneration of Confucian morality, and for others a militant nationalism.

However, alienation was then seen basically in terms of political loyalty to the interest of the country at large, even by those who identified such interest with imperial rule. What underlay this idea of the country's interest was not the blind maintenance of a set of traditional moral and social values, but a thorough acquaintance with and understanding of the country's conditions and characteristics. This was a departure from the *ti-yong* approach to cultural change which had earlier appealed to many scholars and whereby ''Chinese learning,'' narrowly equated with Confucianism, should remain the core (*ti*) both of studies and of accepted values, while Western sciences and techniques would be cultivated as a complement for practical use (*yong*).

The adoption of a model was like taking a frame within which it was possible to modify the content in certain cases. The Japanese model fitted this situation admirably, since it itself had been constructed to cope with the same difficulties that were now facing the Chinese. It was thus possible to replace the cult of Japan and of Tenno with that of China and on occasion of the Son of Heaven. The American model adopted in 1922 was more strongly attacked than had been the Japanese model in its beginning, precisely over the question of the place of national culture and traditions within the new education. Its call for independence from politics and its ideal of a disinterested individual development of the human personality were denounced as antithetical to Chinese culture and to China's needs. This form of education was accused of destroying the communal traditions on which Chinese unity had rested for centuries and that should now primarily be strengthened by fostering an esprit de corps and a sense of duty to the state.

Whereas the danger of cultural alienation in the form of political subjugation to foreign interests and of the destruction of national autonomy had been constantly recognized from the beginning by the same Chinese who introduced foreign systems and practices into China, they were slower to become aware of the political and social divisions that resulted from the adoption of foreign models. More costly both in terms of material and personnel than the traditional literary education, and more oriented to groups than individual pedagogy, the new education took institutional root in the important cities and developed more rapidly in the prosperous provinces of the center and east of China. This urbanization of the modern elite and their geographical concentration contrasted strongly with the more even distribution of the educated class in traditional society and their closer links with local rural realities. The latter had fostered a system of study centered on books rather than on the school, a regional allocation of examination quotas and several administrative rules that helped to provide talented people from wider areas and to keep them less estranged from the countryside.

The characteristics of the new elite formed in these modern schools distanced them not only from the peasantry, as was deeply felt by the students of the May Fourth generation, but also from members of the traditional gentry. The latter continued to oversee daily life in the large villages, medium sized towns and even in important sectors of the large metropoles. These divisions favored the emergence of local military powers which came into their own after the fall of the Monarchy in 1912. The education system nurtured a social and political fragmentation which was the more complex, since it had never been fully shaped on a single foreign model nor had the quality of its teaching ever attained the level of the model emulated except in a minority of institutions. Between official legislation or the aspirations of educators and the reality of what went on in the schools there was often a gaping disparity. Up to the death of Yuan Shikai in 1916 the spirit of education had been generally rigid and authoritarian, yet there had always been some establishments which had followed differing teaching methods and curricula, drawn from Anglo-Saxon rather than Japanese sources. On the other hand, the authoritarianism itself was often less related to Japanese practices than to the persistence of traditional educational methods. In spite of several changes in terminology and other adjustments, primary education continued to be provided to a large proportion of children by traditional-style private schools (*sishu*) where old manuals were recited by heart and the Classics were taught.[12] This type of pedagogy was also frequently found in secondary schools and universities, where the curricula supposedly followed official directives. There it was the inadequate training of teachers, specially in the sciences, and the lack of equipment, which necessitated a style of teaching that was formal, bookish and speculative.

The American model had already replaced the Japanese militaristic model in the provincial schools of Guangdong and Jiangsu before the promulgation of the law of November 1922. Subsequently its application scarcely reached beyond regions of the North near to the capital where the Peking Government was able to exercise some authority.

All in all, the new education brought about heterogeneity in the Chinese elite, both in terms of social status and function and in terms of economic interests and intellectual formation to an extent that was unknown to the ruling classes of the imperial period. However, it also provided a channel for ideologies capable both of unifying and of mobilizing the people. Its contribution to the rise of nationalism matched its concessions to foreign culture. And it was a particularly touchy and obdurate type of nationalism because Chinese consciousness had to reassert itself when the suppression of monarchy in 1912 wrecked the legitimacy of the Confucian moral, social and political system with which national identity had been confounded over long centuries.

Eclectic Borrowing: Enriching or Explosive?

It was precisely the exigencies of nationalism which led to abandonning the use of any single foreign model in educational policy. The last attempt made, which was brief and fruitless, was that of Cai Yuanpei to adapt the French system of educational administration between June 1927 and August 1928. The idea was that educators should have the sole prerogative in determining educational policy.

The antagonism towards the adoption of any one model was at first a political sentiment. The Chinese did not wish to be linked to any one country or to become dependent on anyone. The growing movement for the abolition of the unequal treaties was directed against all foreign implantations in China, and most notably educational establishments. The first wave of demonstrations was unleashed in 1922. It was revived with greater intensity in 1924 with demands that all foreign schools be placed under the control of Chinese authorities. Many of these establishments were forced to close down because all of their students had left. The march of the Nationalist troops from the south to the north between 1925 and 1927 was marked by many serious incidents. In July 1927 only 500 of a former 8,000 missionaries were left in China. Once installed in Nanjing, the Nationalist government imposed regulations on all foreign schools which ensured that the Chinese had the upper hand from that time on.

The American system of education was now criticized, as had been the Japanese one earlier, by the very people who knew it best and had been instrumental in its wide recognition in China, Tao Xingzhi for example. (See chapter 7 by H. Brown.) However, the argument was no longer simply over the unacceptable features of one or another foreign system but over the principle itself of the adoption of any foreign model. In effect, the situation had changed considerably within the educated classes. Chinese cultural traditions no longer weighed heavily on their spirits as had been the case in the beginning of the century. After the May Fourth Movement of 1919, the break with the cultural enslavement of the past was felt to be completed. The foreign model therefore no longer had the function of liberator from the past, which it had assumed in the last days of the monarchy. Rather there was a desire to brush away all exterior influence which might impede or divert the flowering of a new Chinese culture. It was not a refusal to borrow any elements from outside rather a desire for eclecticism in the selection of elements to be introduced, without favoritism toward any one foreign culture, and most of all a desire for these elements to be integrated within the efforts actively undertaken by Chinese educators to promote local educational development.

The criteria for selection of actual borrowings appear to have been a matter of individual persuasion within educational circles rather than borne out by some unified view concurring with one single well-defined aim. Prompted as it was by considerations pertaining to specific situations, the choice resulted in an apparently erratic and contrived collection of foreign devices, each serving its own end, but a multifarious and flexible one.

The years from 1920 to 1930 were remarkably rich in their educational thought and practice. This was also true of general intellectual life in China. Innovation and experimentation flourished, upheld as they were by the movement of national revolution which made possible the reunification of the country and the construction of a modern state under the aegis of the Nationalist Party after 1927. The educational system enacted in 1928, and later filled out by acts of 1929, 1932 and 1933, was the first to be conceived in relation to China itself, without reliance on any foreign model. The educational activity of Tao Xingzhi, Liang Shuming and James Yan in the rural regions was further evidence of the autonomy exercised by Chinese educators as they responded to educational needs. At the same time copious information about foreign educational beliefs and experiences was widely available. A variety of transfers were taking place, in many cases contradictory to one another. (See chapter 6 by R. Hayhoe.) This was at the initiative of individuals, associations, overseas Chinese, but very rarely included the direct involvement of foreigners. Their educational activity was restricted by the regulations which had been enacted. (See chapter 8 by K. Minden.)

The government set itself first to unify educational practices and then above all to control them. In addition to its nationalist concerns, the campaign which it undertook against communism made it soon very suspicious of all innovations. If it sought to make China's progress in developing a public education system known to the outside world, it scarcely thought of exporting the most significant achievements. Its cultural policies towards foreign countries made more of Chinese antiquity than of rural reconstruction. During the second quarter of the twentieth century, Chinese education became truly liberated from any specific foreign domination, whatever one might write subsequently to condemn the Guomindang regime. But its proper course was yet unsettled. It was torn between different needs and aspirations: those of self-cultivation and disinterested study, upheld by an important current of Chinese literary tradition and revitalized by certain elements drawn from European philosophic and scientific culture, notably French, Italian and German thought; the preoccupation with social utility and the practical application of knowledge, also a vigorous part of Chinese tradition, now fortified and expanded by familiarity with the technical civilization of Japan and the West, and the currents of thought that sustained it, Ango-Saxon pragmatism, utilitarianism, and socialist ideas of holistic education; finally the desire to set up a regime of a type unprecedented in Chinese history, that of the hegemony of one political party, organized as a body separate from the state and guiding the whole life of the country by the use of methods of constraint.

This hesitation over the basic aims of Chinese education may explain how it was that many foreign transfers remained poorly integrated into the education system. In one place the Dalton plan was adopted, while the criterion of knowledge accumulation persisted in the examinations used. In another place, the system of psychological testing was introduced, yet in fact the Nationalist Party cell had complete control over the promotion of students. In such a situation the diversity of foreign ideas and practices brought in under the principle of eclectic foreign borrowing might be regarded as a factor of disruption rather than enrichment, might it not?

The Japanese invasion gradually silenced these controversies without really

reconciling the divergent points of view. The ravages and havoc that ensued depriv-
ed the country of even the meagre resources it had for the development of a
technical and vocational education suited to its needs. Whether in the regions under
Nationalist government or in those held by the Communists, the war gave the
party in power an opportunity to tighten its control over schools. Difficulties of
communication resulted in isolation from the outside world. It was in primary
education that the most spectacular progress was achieved. If Communists and
Nationalists indulged in reciprocal accusations of using this means to rouse the
people against the propaganda of the adversary, the reality was nevertheless a
whole new stage in the diffusion of modern education for the ordinary people,
a stage vital not only to autonomy but also to effective national development.
In the aftermath of the war, the priority in educational circles was to be useful
to the country and particularly to contribute to its economic reconstruction. The
unequal treaties had been abolished. China had taken its place as an equal partner among the victorious powers. The memory of recent humiliations kept alive
a certain distrust towards any form of dependence, yet the international recognition then being gained by Chinese scientists, artists and literary figures increased
national self-confidence and opened up more serene prospects of genuine cooperation with foreign countries.

In spite of the close links binding education and the world of politics in China,
it is hard to sustain the view that China ever experienced an intellectual dependence
comparable to the limits foreign domination placed on its political sovereignty
or the exploitation of its economic resources. The only exception to this is the
region of North East China which fell under strict Japanese tutelage after the creation of Manzhuguo in 1932. Elsewhere the control of education always remained
the exclusive prerogative of the state, without any participation by foreign experts or advisors. Education was also given solely in the national language at
the primary and only incidentally in a foreign language at the secondary and tertiary level, a practice mainly found in missionary institutions. The editing and
use of textbooks consonant with the new curricula and adapted to Chinese realities
had accompanied the opening of modern schools in 1904 and always followed
closely on subsequent reforms, even though good quality at college level was
reached only in the early 1930s with the University series published by the Commercial Press. When these works were not made use of, it was rarely because
recourse was taken to simple translations of foreign textbooks, rather due to the
fact that material deprivation made them inaccessible. Older Chinese texts were
relied upon that were more easily available and cheaper. The number of foreign
teachers also remained very low. At their height of influence in 1922, the missionary schools which recruited the most had only twelve hundred as against eleven
thousand Chinese teachers on their staff.[13]

Attention is often drawn to the insidious dependence created by the sending
of students overseas for study. From 1872 to 1949 about three hundred thousand
Chinese students obtained a higher degree, and of these about one seventh were
holders of foreign degrees.[14] Of the one million students who had some exposure
to higher education, about a hundred thousand spent time abroad. Even if the

proportion of the elite educated abroad remained small, it must be admitted that this group occupied strategic positions. In 1932, for example, of the 45 highest posts in the Nationalist government, only 14 were held by persons who had never studied abroad, 18 by those who had studied in Japan, six by returnees from the United States, one respectively by returnees from France, England and Germany, and four by persons who had studied both in Japan and the West. Yet among the 322 best known authors in 1937, more than half had never studied abroad, and this proportion was stronger among literary authors, where it was 167 out of 217.[15]

In the scientific disciplines higher degrees had almost always been gained in the outside world, because it was only from 1935 that postgraduate programs could be followed in China, and the war greatly limited the numbers participating. Yet in spite of the meagre resources available, a national scientific research venture took shape, first by the establishment of learned societies, then by the organization of the Academica Sinica in 1928, finally by the creation of university research centers. If these agencies depended on foreign cooperation for their equipment and their scientific documentation, they were by no means simply appendages to foreign institutions, but decided on their own program of research. They proved able to create their own methods in certain fields and to gain results which subsequently contributed to foreign research.

Finally, the period of study abroad, especially in the United States, certainly made it easier to gain employment in the Chinese university system in certain periods and so aroused fierce resentment. However it would be simplistic to regard studies abroad as implying subservience to the interests of the host country. The example of Zhou Enlai, who studied in Japan, France and the Soviet Union, gives evidence of this as much as that of Jiang Jingguo (son of Chiang Kai-shek), who studied in the Soviet Union. The most fiery nationalists were usually found among those who had returned from study abroad. In addition, precautions against those elements formed abroad always remained strong in certain influential groups. During the war, within the Nationalist Party itself, the distrust of the Chen clique towards those who had studied in the United States was no less intense than the suspicion in Yan'an against young Communists who had been educated abroad.

In the first half of the twentieth century a world of education took shape in China which had both autonomy and a personality of its own. It succeeded in integrating China within international education currents without subordinating it to any one dominant influence. But in the aftermath of the World War II this educational world was unable to escape the internal confrontation between the Nationalist and Communist Parties, even though the majority of the teaching corps itself identified with a political stance somewhere between these two extremes.

Recanting the Educational Past in People's China

The first concern of the People's Government of China in the realm of education was to repudiate the reactionary and imperialist influences which in their view had perverted both educators and the educational system. This collective denunciation organized in the schools took as its main targets Anglo-Saxon pedagogy, the ideas inherited from Chinese and European tradition about the transcendance of knowledge and its independence from political and social realities, and finally the place given in the curriculum to Chinese classical culture as well as Western and Japanese civilizations. By a series of administrative measures taken in 1951 and the beginning of 1952, the management of the schools and the control of the whole education system was taken out of the hands of educators and entrusted to the party machine.

It was in these conditions that the Soviet model of education was actively promulgated. (See chapters 9 and 10 by R. Price and L. Orleans.) This return to the emulation of a single model has striking parallels with the situation between 1900 and 1925. As at that time, the model had the role of liberator. It made possible a clear break with previous practices, emancipation from the enslavement of the past and the creation of a determinedly new system. This model also had a unifying function: authoritarian and centralized, it erased regional differences, favored the consolidation of political power and the diffusion of one sole socialist dogma. In the field of education, the years from 1952 to 1957 might well be regarded as a delayed continuation of the first quarter of the century. Among the foreign systems of influence, the Soviet system was the only one which China had not had occasion to experiment with, since by the time it had been fully constituted in the late twenties, the Nationalist government had already broken its special links with the Soviet Union, and the Communist party, for its part, scarcely had the means to apply the Soviet model in the impoverished rural areas to which they were forced to retreat.

The ardor with which the Chinese government and educators promulgated Soviet curricula, teaching methods and Soviet-style educational organization, the use of Russian as the language of scientific communication, the presence of Soviet teachers and advisors in greater numbers than any foreign contingent in the pre-1949 period, and finally the cooperative ties binding Chinese and Soviet institutions in teaching and research, might make one believe that the Communist revolution had overcome the political apprehensions and psychological obstacles which up to then had restricted the application of foreign models and undermined the efficacy of their contribution. However the Soviet model did not actually extend its influence beyond higher and secondary education, where it left its imprint in the notion of specialization, the importance given to mathematics, and the control over educational quality. It only affected primary and pre-primary education in a small minority of urban establishments. Furthermore, it became the object of partial criticism in 1957, then of official repudiation after the break with the Soviet Union in 1960, finally of violent attacks during the Cultural Revolution of 1966 to 1976.

In spite of these attacks to which it was subjected, the Soviet model still had a lasting influence. In fact there are several variants — Stalinist, post-Stalinist, and pre-Stalinist — from which the Chinese successively drew their inspiration. Even while the rigidity of the Stalinist model was being criticized, the educational reforms of the Great Leap Forward of 1958 would be given justification from recently promulgated ideas of Kruschev on mingling mental and manual labor. His ideas were also appealed to in the attempt to institute a period of compulsory productive labor between the completion of secondary education and entry into higher education. When this arrangement was actively revived during the Cultural Revolution, there was absolute silence about its origin, so that it could be promoted as a living expression of Mao Thought. Other ideas assumed at this time, the suspicion of examinations and of the whole formal education system, and the notion of the involvement of the masses in the teaching process, may have had their source in Soviet pedagogy also, that of Lunacharski and Shul'gin during the first years of the Russian revolution. It is unlikely that the Red Guards themselves were conscious of this source, but highly possible that some of their older mentors were. During the brief periods of calm in the revolutionary tempest, the years of 1972 and 1975, as earlier in 1961-62, attempts were made to restore the Stalinist education system without openly giving recognition to this model.

In sum, the Chinese government deliberately reactivated the old reflexes of fear and defensiveness in face of the moral and political implications of a foreign cultural influence, not because they regarded this as a serious danger, but because it was useful to them in their internal political struggles. However the grafting of foreign practices into the Chinese educational body was not rejected at this time, as it had been in the past. The anti-Soviet campaign only succeeded in condemning Soviet implants to anonymity, not in uprooting them. This progressive trivialization of educational transfer into China is a significant phenomenon. It is the corollary of the consolidation of Chinese power in the second half of the twentieth century. More self-assured within themselves, the Chinese have less reason to fear that cooperation will bring dependence in its train.

China's recent re-entry into world educational currents succeeded a phase of almost total repudiation of all outside influences from 1966 to 1971. This spell of estrangement also witnessed an amazing revival of China's influence on Western academic life. (See chapter 11 by R. Depierre.) It might be viewed as a return to the period when the Chinese literati considered that there was nothing of value to China outside of its borders beyond some carefully circumscribed areas of technical knowledge. In fact, however, this total repudiation, imposed from above rather than genuinely felt by the educated classes in this case, resulted in recourse being taken to anonymous transfers and contributed more to destroying prejudice than nurturing it.

The openness to the outside world which the Chinese government has adopted as educational policy since 1978, as in other areas (see chapters 12 and 13 by Huang Shiqi and J. Henze), brings to mind the eclecticism of the 1930s. It is not without fragility, as was demonstrated in 1983 by the vigorous campaign against spiritual pollution introduced through Western philosophy and literature. But this time those who seek for political ends to invoke the spectre of subversion and enslavement have found less popular resonance than in the past. The problem is rather to estimate how far the new eclecticism will achieve a better integration of borrowed elements than in the past, and assure greater effectiveness of the overall education system than resulted from the emulation of a single foreign model. On the first point, it is notable that the national identity of specific transfers is far less obvious than at the beginning of the century, since the system of education and research in developed countries, to which China is looking, has become more and more internationalized. For this reason the assimilation of various transfers and their integration within a coherent whole should present fewer difficulties. On the other hand, the question of the effective use of what is borrowed is more complex. As far as pedagogy, teaching methods, curricula and educational and laboratory equipment are concerned, China's geographical immensity and the size of its population militate against the swift diffusion of innovations. The lag in development of the interior requires certain delicate adjustments. The natural temptation to speed up the progress already taking place in the advanced sectors could cause no less frustration than the concentration of resources in the most backward sectors.

The Chinese had a vivid consciousness of the risk of dependence implied in the adoption of foreign cultural practices long before China fell prey to contemporary imperialist aggression. This vigilance, rooted in a sense of the originality and value of their civilization, is doubtless one of the reasons why the Chinese were more successful than many other nations in resisting the compulsions that borrowing foreign educational systems and patterns may involve. However the real mastery of the transfers which have taken place, making it possible for them to effectively serve national development, appears to have been a slower process in China than in other Asian countries, such as Japan. Neither the sole authority of the government nor the convictions of an educated elite, nor indeed the conjunction of these two, has been able to overcome the problems of China's vast dimensions. If in recent years more encouraging results seem to have taken form, this is probably because a large part of the population has received basic education and is now in a position to become involved in this domestication of foreign implants.

2

Confucian Education Through European Eyes

Isabelle Llasera

When the Jesuit father Matteo Ricci arrived in South China in 1582, he first wore a Buddhist robe in order to integrate himself with the Chinese way of life and to prepare for his task of evangelism. With the passage of years, he became aware that the religious habit did not aid his enterprise. So it was that he arrived in Peking in 1601 dressed as a member of the ruling class in the civil robes of the literati and he was received by officials.

The Jesuit missionaries continued this tradition which had been initiated by Matteo Ricci.[1] They studied the language and history of China, translated European scholarly works into Chinese and Chinese writings into various European languages, performed their services partly in Chinese and integrated into their evangelization certain rites which were hardly congruent with Christian doctrine. They dressed in literati robes and had their portraits drawn as literati, and eventually as officials. They even adopted Chinese names. In so doing, they transformed themselves into those whom they had come to transform. Accepting posts of responsibility within the imperial court,[2] they chose to associate with and actually became a part of the elite within Chinese society, the very representatives of Chinese virtue. Evidently they preferred the temporal power of the mandarins to the spiritual power of the Buddhist monks.

Once they had come close to the imperial court, the Jesuits changed and even reversed the expected play of influence as an exterior group bringing its superiority to bear on another group and so transforming it. They were led to write about those whom they had learned to emulate and even imitate in a way quite unexpected. Forced to reflect on their situation in order to give account to their superiors of their unusual practices, the missionaries published works in Europe which provided the foundation for the first ''objective descriptions'' of China composed by European scholars. These works became also a reference point for the political and moral musings of Enlightenment philosophers. They created an image of China which persisted until the end of the eighteenth century.[3]

A certain degree of sinification seemed necessary to the missionaries if they were to make themselves heard among the Chinese, yet that in itself did not imply that they had to respect Chinese superiority. Nevertheless, on reading what they wrote, it becomes clear that this fashioning of themselves in the Chinese mode was not merely a temporary ploy for the purpose of penetrating Chinese society. It was evidence of an attitude of interest, in both senses of the word, and a respectful admiration. This borrowed mode of life led them to reflect on the power which they sought and sometimes succeeded in attaining. It obliged them to give account of themselves, lest they be viewed as traitors.

The Most Exalted Prince of the Orient

The most powerful monarch of Europe and the most exalted prince of the Orient.[4]

The missionaries formulated some kind of equivalence between the power and the greatness of oriental and occidental authority. In his *Historical Portrait of the Chinese Emperor* [Kang Xi], Bouvet made these comments to the French King, Louis the XIVth: "The Jesuits were astounded to find at the ends of the earth, what they had never seen before outside of France — a Prince, who, like your Highness, combines a spirit both sublime and sound with a heart still more worthy of Empire . . equally adored by his people and respected by his neighbors . . . in a word, a Prince who would be the most accomplished monarch the world has seen for a long time, if his rule did not coincide with that of your Majesty." Bouvet went on to describe Kang Xi as "a monarch who, having the happiness of resembling you in many ways, has the same advantage over pagan princes as Louis the Great has over the Christian princes."[5]

This recognition of the validity of the authority they found manifested in China and its comparison with the power of occidental authority justified the Jesuit attitude of submission towards the Chinese Emperor and their actions in becoming mandarins, and thereby agents of a foreign state. If Jesuit mission principles encouraged observation of and adaptation to foreign conditions, in order to understand the context in which their mission was to proceed, the choice of imitating the mandarin rather than the monk was certainly a clever manoeuvre. Yet even more, it reflects the Jesuit tradition of participation in the power of state. The occidental elite identified the oriental elite and integrated themselves into this group. Great respecters of order, in their case a military order which was thought to represent heavenly order, the Jesuits found in China an ordered state. Their assimilation to this state was allowed by the comparison they made between two forms of power. Furthermore, they found the Christian attitudes of loyalty and submission to hierarchy echoed in Chinese rites.

Required to give account to their superiors and their opponents in Europe for practices which were strongly criticized,[6] the Jesuits described and praised the social order which they had become a part of. In the process they became propagandists. Their participation in a foreign bureaucracy and their tolerance towards such rites as ancestor worship and homage to Confucius would elicit understanding, if not justification, by showing, on the one hand, that submission to the Chinese

Emperor expedited the work of evangelism and, on the other, that this imperial order, far from being barbarous, was in fact the result of a comparable, even superior, authority to that of Western monarchs.

The fact that this order was not considered essentially religious but secular in no way interfered with this submission, since it supposed the same type of attitude raised to a level of perfection:

> Among the several models and plans of government which the ancients framed, we shall perhaps meet with none so perfect and exact as is that of the Chinese monarchy . . . as though God himself had founded their empire, the plan of their government was not a whit less perfect in its cradle that it is now after the experience and trial of 4,000 years.[7]

Was this a sincere expression of admiration or a ploy to defend themselves from criticism? Jesuit motivation is really not the fundamental question here. In their actions of imitation and integration, a missionary, or more accurately a Jesuit, practice was initiated which moved beyond the strict boundaries of religious practice revealing a mode of thought which was inscribed in the history of ideas in the seventeenth and eighteenth centuries. In these texts, parallel with the actions depicted in memoires, reports and pastoral letters, certain facts were recorded, clarified and discussed. At first glance, the approach was surprising, if one thinks of the missionaries' intention to transform and evangelize the Chinese. In fact it contributed to the evolution of new European modes of approach to the social world and was to serve as a reference point for enlightened thinkers of the eighteenth century.

Peace and Good Order

> *In the belief that peace and good order are the basis of all society, the Chinese devote themselves particularly to that form of study which produces these two fruits.*[8]

At a time when Europe was seeing its social foundations crumbling and was seeking means to strengthen them or establish new ones, the missionaries discovered and made known an empire that offered the spectacle of order and permanence. They started to describe the government, the customs, the ceremonies which seemed to them to assure this good order, peace and permanence and to make it known that these qualities derived from a bureaucracy whose officials were only accepted after long years of study and submission to a lengthy series of examinations.

The methods of attaining governmental posts — the examinations and the unremitting study of Classics which they required — the way in which the mandarins functioned officially and the role they played in Chinese society became the objects of lengthy descriptions and commentaries in chapters they devoted to the government and the customs of China.

A questionnaire was prepared by the Academy of Sciences at the request of Louvois and given to Father Couplet, when he returned to China in 1692.[9] The purpose of the questionnaire was to make possible a deeper knowledge of China, yet it mentioned neither education nor examinations, nor the means of recruiting officials to the government. There was a simple reason for this. A society ruled by officials who had been selected by competitive examination was as yet inconceivable in the West.[10] Yet the Jesuits, who were themselves educators and founders of colleges[11] and who participated actively in affairs of state, could not fail to be struck by the importance which the Chinese gave to education, by the role played by scholars in Chinese society and by the moral, social and political consequences of a system in which the official elite had been recruited by competitive examinations.

The Most Important Affair of the State

One must assume that these examinations form the most important affair of the state, because they are concerned with posts of responsibility, with prestige, honor and riches. They are the one object watched by all with attention, to which all give the greatest care and thought.[12]

The imperial examination halls were of great size and splendor,[13] the invigilation was conducted with severity,[14] precautions were taken in the correction of scripts, selection being extremely rigorous, banquets and ceremonies in honor of Confucius followed the publication of results[15] and the Emperor himself was present for the conferral of degrees at the highest level. All of the dignity and solemnity that surrounded the imperial examinations gave the Jesuits the vision of a power acceded to through merit. Entrance into governmental posts was a serious matter. The Emperor himself selected the subjects of the compositions for the examinations leading to the highest degree of doctor (*jinshi*). The importance accorded by the government to the examinations was evidenced not only in the ceremonial accompanying them, but also by the fact that all the financial costs were born by the government.

> . . . as for doctors they commence only at Peking: but because some who deserve this Degree have not wherewith to defray so expensive a journey, what is necessary for it, is bestowed on them gratis, that so poverty may not deprive the State of the service of those men who may prove useful and beneficial to it.[16]

The government desired to see schools under its charge founded in all corners of the Empire:

> In order to make it possible for all sorts of persons to study, also in order to keep a watch over the progress of students, the legislators established schools in all the cities of the Empire, where young people brought up at the expense of the government took rigorous examinations in order to attain those literary degrees which gave the right to honors and the highest social positions.[17]

It was a true system of public instruction which the missionaries presented to

Europe. In his *Description de la Chine,* Du Halde included a lengthy excerpt from a Chinese book entitled "The Art of making the people happy through establishing public schools."[18] Education and the civil service examinations constituted an affair of state:

> The state takes upon itself responsibility for those who work for the state and defend it. It offers magnificent rewards to those who serve it.[19]

Finally, study is a permanent occupation.[20]

> As the fortunes of the Chinese do wholly depend upon their capacity and understanding, so they spend their whole life in study: Composition, Eloquence, Imitation, Knowledge of their ancient Doctors and the delicacy and politeness of the modern ones, from six to sixty are their constant employ.[21]

If the theatricality of the imperial examinations, the state's financial support for education and the length of study aroused the admiration and astonishment of the Jesuits, it was the moral values which the scholars represented and the posts they held in Chinese society that were described and discussed at the greatest length.

The Political and Civic Being

> *In a word, the scholars are that part of the nation which is like the soul, since it is wholly and exclusively on them that the rest depend for their moral existence and their whole political and civic being.*[22]

Chinese society appeared to the Jesuits to be indestructible. Its frame consisted of moral principles which gave it existence and its flesh of ceremonies which made possible movement in regulating social relations.

By virtue of their education and their success in the examinations, which made them into models, the scholars were the pillars of the state. They made up this ideally loyal and devoted community which made the machine of state function in the exercise of the power conferred on them. Recognized as the depositories of principles and rites which governed both public and private life (the former reflecting the latter), they had always been the guarantor of its survival.[23]

As providers of the "moral existence" and the "political and civic being" of the state, the community of scholars stood for China itself. They had become the "soul of the nation," the "light of their country,"[24] through the lengthy and slow implantation of moral principles drawn from the classics and the rule of civility that took place throughout their studies. "The Chinese are not permitted to cast their eyes on other books before they have committed to memory those that contain the teachings of Confucius."[25]

This intimate knowledge of the Four Books and Five Classics which contained the morality, history, laws and principles of human relations was spread throughout the Empire. It ensured a remarkable social homogeneity. The moral unity, even conformity, of the nation was assured by the standardization of study programs, and its social cohesion was assured by the application of the principles that had been learned to government. The sayings of Confucius formed a state doctrine to which the scholars, as state officials, had the duty of giving life. Through the functions they carried out, they were both mediators between the emperor and the people and guarantors of the moral laws of the Empire. Leibniz wrote in this way on the subject of morality in China:

> Our circumstances seem to me to have sunk to such a level, particularly with regard to the monstrous and increasing breakdown of morality, that one could almost think it necessary for the Chinese to send missionaries to us to teach us the purpose and use of natural theology, in the same way as we send missionaries to them to instruct them in revealed theology.[26]

They had the duty of serving the Emperor and honoring the Ancients in order to assure peace and and good order. They were subjected to regular inspection in the provinces where they were assigned, and recalled,[27] if any disturbances, disorders or excesses were found among the people. Such problems revealed a flaw in the social cement which the mandarinate constituted. When a mandarin lost the favor of the emperor due to such problems and was removed from his post, he had to return to the study of the classics, whatever his age, and once again put himself through the test of the imperial examinations. The mandarinate provided central authority with a loyal civil service which was supposed to be unaffected by political change, since it obeyed principles of a moral philosophy which were themselves unchanging.

Furthermore, the scholars were a nobility which did not inherit this role but owed both their function and their reputation to their own merit:

> Nobility is only granted on the basis of merit. One may inherit the material possessions of one's father, but one may not inherit his posts or his reputation. One must raise oneself in society through the same imperial degrees as one's father. It is for this reason that they accumulate their capital by constant studies.[28]

Du Halde gave a vision of Chinese society which was almost egalitarian:

> Since it is on the basis of merit alone that these appointments are made, a scholar who is the son of a peasant has as much hope of attaining the post of Viceroy or minister as the children of well-positioned persons.[29]

In an almost lyrical manner, Semedo wished to offer this ''true nobility'' as an exemplar:

> If this practice were followed in other kingdoms, we would not see so many sons of lords and nobles so ignorant; as if true nobility did not consist of knowledge and a beautiful quality of spirit.[30]

In his *Essais sur les Moeurs*,[31] Voltaire was also deeply attracted to this elite, whom the Jesuits described as being recognized on the basis of reason rather than by an accident of birth. Yet if success in the imperial examinations sanctioned knowledge and created the Chinese nobility, it also conferred a power which, in association with a duty to act according to the principles that had been learned, could be called into question. It was precisely through action that this power was preserved. Since the power of the ruling elite went together with duty, it assured a government which would not be arbitrary or despotic. These are Voltaire's comments:

> The human mind cannot imagine a government better than this one where everything is to be decided by the large tribunals, subordinated to each other, of which the members are received only after several severe examinations. All matters are handled by these tribunals. Under such an administration, it is impossible for the Emperor to exercise power in an arbitrary way . . . if there has ever been a state in which the life, honor and welfare of people have been protected by law, it is the empire of China. The more there are these great depositories of law, the less possible is it for administration to be arbitrary. . . . Everywhere a certain restraint is imposed on the arbitrary use of power by the law, the customs and the morals.[32]

The Greatest Scholar

> *Occupied without respite in serving all the various concerns of an admirable government, the greatest potentate there could be in the universe is at the same time the greatest scholar in the Empire.*[33]

In describing the birth of a "raison d'état" in the seventeenth century, M. de Certeau comments that it "mobilized the preachers and the men of letters in the service of government."[34] One might believe that this was a reference to China, to that ancient characteristic of Chinese society which had been discovered and admired by the Jesuits: the service of power. "What is astonishing," continues Certeau, "about the fact that tasks which concern morality and knowledge are centered around the Prince, the kernel in whom all meaning originates? Why should we be surprised if the education of the Prince becomes the practice of greatest significance, the practice through which a new political order focuses on formulating a new language of reference for society?"[35] Here is described a movement which makes the Prince a center on whom morality, knowledge and education are concentrated. The Jesuits described the imperial palace as the microcosm of the Empire, where the imperial prince was educated by those doctors who had ranked highest in the imperial examinations and were part of the Hanlin Yuan, the Academy of Science, which was composed of the leading lights of the Empire. An educated prince proved by his government the justice of those virtues and principles which he had learned, and so became the model to be followed by each prefect in administering his prefecture and by each scholar facing a post of responsibility.

The Palace from which the Son of Heaven, philosopher prince who had been nourished in the best of Chinese moral sciences, governed like a father owing respect to his parents and watching over his family, was the place where the rule determining human and social relations was expressed at the highest level. It was these customs and practices which Voltaire had seen as constituting a restraint over the arbitrary use of power:

> It is not difficult to guess that a people who are so gentle have in their education certain principles relating to moral gentility and civility. . . . The Chinese are convinced that attention given to developing the duties of civility do much to purge human character of its natural harshness. They help to form a certain gentleness of character, also to maintain order, peace and subordination. The proprieties, public and private, are not merely formalities which have been established by custom, they are laws which one cannot set aside. The nobility, the princes, even the emperor himself, are subjected to them.[36]

The knowledge of the place held by each individual in the private or familial domain and in the public or social domain, also the process of learning what behavior is appropriate to this place, formed one of the fundamental elements in Chinese education and had the force of law. This education was all-embracing insofar as it implied the internalization of moral laws and rules of civility,[37] which set up obligations rather than imposing interdictions.

Discerning Judgement Over All Matters

> *The reputation of those who excel in moral philosophy, the scholars, is so great among the Chinese that they judge these men to be fully capable to exercise discerning judgement over all matters, however far removed these may be from their profession.*[38]

Magistrates, prefects, administrators, chroniclers of the empire, examiners, instructors of princes — these were the posts to which the successful candidates in the imperial examinations were appointed. The education which they received, like the instruction they imparted in the carrying out of their duties, consisted less of the transmission of pure knowledge than an apprenticeship in a capacity for action based on the classical precepts. Their functions required of them the application of such laws as presupposed neither scientific nor military knowledge.[39] In other words, peace and order were maintained by a respect for moral principles and rules of civility, not by force nor by the mastery of technical skills, which were reserved for the non-elite of Chinese society. No value at all was attached to those forms of knowledge which did not have an immediate and demonstrable relation to the public good. Intimacy with the teaching of the masters was in itself adequate for a "discerning judgement over all matters" and one was judged by the quality of one's practical application of classical principles. It was in this way that the honors conferred after success in the imperial examinations were confirmed.

The Public Good

There is no empire on earth where the sciences are more valued than in China or where they touch more closely the realm of government. Nevertheless, the Chinese are only interested in the sciences insofar as they offer something to the public good. To all that is strange or useless in the sciences they accord little attention, without at the same time regarding it with contempt.[40]

No "pure" science was taught, and the knowledge of technology was only a hand-maiden to other disciplines. History was learned in the Book of Annals and only the rites and moral sciences transmitted through ancient texts illuminated the political and civil practices which governed the country. In the eyes of Confucians, these were the only matters of importance. Neither a hereditary nobility nor the depositary of a mere theoretical knowledge, nor specialists in science or technology, the elite of China was the body politic which, in ensuring its own perpetuation through education and the imperial examinations, thereby ensured the very existence of the Chinese state. Thus the Jesuits could present China as a state whose cohesive strength over the centuries emanated from the repetition of principles and the observation of ceremonies which regulated social and political life.[41] These principles and ceremonies were both the backbone and the moving force of the state, assuring to it stability and permanence. Education, as an affair of state and a permanent process throughout one's life was thus organized through public instruction which gave a formation in morality and civility that permeated every pore of Chinese society and constituted the principal and essential factor in the reproduction and conservation of the models drawn from the Classics.

In the Jesuit colleges in Europe, which represented 64% of secondary educational establishments in 1626 (52% in 1710),[42] considerable attention was nevertheless given to astronomy, arithmetic and music. The study of the sciences in Europe gave entrance to a new way of understanding the world and of acting upon it. Deeply impressed with European scientific discoveries, the Jesuits did not hestitate to carry out secular work in order to gain admittance to the imperial palace. They were certain that the Chinese would defer to the power which the knowledge of science gave, and they made themselves geographers, astronomers, clock-makers, musicians and even makers of canons. However, even if they were sometimes asked to fulfill these roles, they proved to be objects of curiosity, even of amusement, rather than of genuine interest for the most part.

In the period of their first encounters with the otherness of China, some of the early writings of the missionaries reveal attempts at finding the link between Confucian principles and the purity of Christian principles,[43] and even between the Chinese language and the language used before Babel,[44] which provided a special connection between word and reality. These interpretations were the last manifestations of a way of thinking that was dying out and they soon disappeared.

The Jesuits soon relegated the Chinese religions of Taoism and Buddhism to the category of idolatry and superstition. But above all, they dissociated Confucianism from religion. They described a state where the spiritual effaced itself before the political, where ethics were valued above science and where education played a central role as a way of learning how to act. All of this necessarily proceeded from the internalization of the classical principles rather than from a practical learning separated from knowledge itself. This interest of the missionaries in a form of education which made up the canvass on which the motifs of Chinese society were interwoven was not merely the effect of a certain objectivity in Jesuit thought. Their texts were situated within the intellectual currents of the century in which they lived.

Morality Rather than Faith

Religion was progressively led over the terrain of practice throughout the seventeenth century. What became decisive was morality rather than faith. [45]

In the educational formation of the colleges of Europe, and in particular the Jesuit Colleges, "what came to be more and more important were socio-cultural and economic virtues, such as politeness, bearing, output (the student condition aimed at social utility), competition (knowledge was ordered through a struggle for advancement), civility (the established order of social conventions)." [46] The Jesuits were teachers more of these "virtues" than of theology due to their desire to give over-riding importance to social know-how. They did not renounce faith, but religion gradually lost its central place and became an individual matter. The sciences were not neglected. They gave a power over the world, but the moral virtues, linked with social practices, gave evidence of belonging to the world.

Chinese education, as discovered and described by the Jesuits, fitted exactly the principles which governed their own education. It should be made a priority, it should have social utility and it should give each student a sense of respect for temporal power and for the conventions that govern the social order.

These great principles were inscribed in the currents of ideas of the epoch which removed religion from being the necessary and universal frame of reference to being an individual and personal matter. "The socio-cultural changes taking place in the seventeenth and eighteenth centuries affected the very frames of reference. They brought about a shift from a religious organization to a political and economic ethic." [47] During the sixteenth century religion "still held a unifying control over behavior. In the seventeenth and eighteenth centuries that unity cracked, then burst open." [48] Debates about morals replaced the great theological debates; action replaced belief. [49]

This displacement of religion from the public to the private domain opened the way for a judgement of the public domain based on criteria drawn from temporal matters, in sum, from politics. Given the situation and the fact that the Jesuits were a part of the intelligentsia of this period and affirmed the supremacy of temporal over spiritual power,[50] is there anything surprising in the fact that they were attracted by Chinese education and its functions? It was as if China offered an ideal exemplar of some of the principle elements of the models of society which were just beginning to be elaborated in the West.

Certainly it was in the interest of the Jesuits to be apologists of the social system of a country into which they had sought to become integrated in order to defend themselves against the attacks which they were subjected to in Europe.[51] Yet even more, their admiration was due to the distinction which had been established and which they affirmed between religion and politics. This made possible a non-religious interpretation of facts, it was based on a quest for a social ethic and took into account the behaviors and facts of society. Their association with power and with the intellectual elite and their role as educators at a time when ways of action more than ways of belief were a central preoccupation, made it possible for the Jesuits to note certain specific aspects of Chinese society, even though the Chinese social system was profoundly foreign to them. Equally, these factors made them mediators of a scientific approach that began to perceive human persons in their social context.

In the seventeenth century, "science imposed its criteria upon all, whether believers or not. It removed religion from the scientific realm."[52] In affirming the separation between the individual, subjective and private affair which religion had become and public affairs which meant participation in the events of the time, the Jesuits adopted a way of thinking suited to the progress of science which wished to see all facts described outside of religious interpretation. Their descriptions of China were organized in chapters entitled philosophy, customs, religion, administration, sciences etc.

A Great Reservoir of Utopias

> *A clearly demarcated region, whose name alone constitutes for the West a great reservoir of utopias. . . . For our system of imagination, Chinese culture is the most fastidious, the most hierarchical, the one least affected by passing events.*[53]

Having no access to the diverse currents of Chinese thought and not being able to recognize the part played by religion in what they observed, the Jesuits presented a picture of China as a society whose principles of organization were founded on a morality and an approach to political life which was echoed in Europe of the Enlightenment, as it reflected on its history, its religion and its morals, on the inter-relation among these three areas and as it sought a "raison d'état."

Admirers of a system which they regarded as the best guarantor of stability and permanence, the Jesuits were paradoxically nurturing and vitalizing in Europe an unfolding political and moral consciousness which was actually antithetical to permanence. Furthermore, it would scarcely benefit their company.[54] "The

King never suspected that these very narratives could give birth to ideas capable of undermining the beliefs most necessary for the maintenance of his authority,''[55] wrote Paul Hazard with reference to the narratives published by the missionaries at the end of the seventeenth and the beginning of the eighteenth centuries.

The texts of the Jesuit fathers concerning Chinese education and society certainly did not of themselves change western thought, but they fertilized it by providing real information to dress an image which was beginning to take shape, the image of a civil state, stable, secular and founded on reason. These texts both revealed the evolution of western thought and were instruments of that evolution. They served to create a Chinese utopia on which those who questioned their own age and searched for new points of reference could draw. These texts declared ''Another form of society is possible, which is eminently civilized. It exists on the other side of the world.''

In a period of crisis of conscience,[56] Europe turned, dazzled, towards ''this place which is a paradise,''[57] this China of the Jesuits, a republic of letters in which education was both the foundation and the preserver of order and peace, this state whose origin was lost in the mists of time, where people were made blessed by the government, this state which was founded upon an ethos rather than a religion, which was jointly sustained by a philosopher prince and a ''true'' nobility, enlightened and continuously controlled. The creation of a Chinese utopia was necessary as a symbol for Europe that a new world was possible. But the Chinese themselves did not inhabit this utopia. The Chinese intelligentsia had never tried to export the currents of their thought, they had never sought to convert, to conquer or to convince the West. China remained innocent of this innoculation of the Chinese spirit. Nevertheless, this China of the Jesuits, crucible of the intellectual ferment of the period, came to be one of the most powerful utopias created by the Occident. Out of the cinders of chinoiserie, of exoticism, of romanticism and colonization, it was reborn two centuries later in the mid-twentieth century.

3

Imperialism and the Diffusion of Liberal Thought: British Influences on Chinese Education

Delia Davin

Introduction

Upon first examination at least, the most noteworthy feature of British educational influence in China is that it was unexpectedly slight. Britain of course took the leading part in the forced "opening of China" in the nineteenth century and the Treaty Port System was, to a large extent, shaped under military and diplomatic pressure from Britain. Throughout the second half of the nineteenth century, Britain remained the dominant power in East Asia with considerable colonial territories, military and naval commitments and, of course, great commercial and economic interests.

In China, Britain's commercial and banking interests were greater than those of any other foreign nation. Even in the early twentieth century she held more significant mining and railway concessions than any other power, while in 1910, 38% of China's foreign and interport trade cleared through customs was still carried in British vessels. The British were the most numerous of all foreign residents until about 1904. The British navy patrolled and to a large extent controlled both the China coast and the Yangzi River. The Imperial Maritime Customs was directed by an Ulsterman and the British were the largest group among its multinational staff. The English language quickly became, and except for a brief eclipse in the 1950s has remained, the leading foreign language in China. Once it was established as the main business language of the Treaty Ports, an insatiable demand for English-language instruction quickly developed.[1]

British intellectual influence on educated Chinese in the last years of the nineteenth century was far from negligible. Englishmen, Scots, and Ulstermen played a role both as advisors and as teachers in government-sponsored "schools of Western learning." Later the classics of British liberal thought helped to shape the ideas of leading members of the Reform Movement. Even the conviction that the power and wealth of western nations was associated with their economic and political evolution and that the key to a similar achievement for China was Western learning was to a large extent brought about through contact with the British.

Yet when the Chinese government began its search for a system of national education it was to the Japanese, German and French models which it turned, rather than the British. Later, U.S. pedagogical theory had an influence far beyond that which British educational ideas achieved. Chinese students who studied in Japan and the U.S. greatly outnumbered those who went to Britain. British-returned students distinguished themselves in academic fields as varied as engineering, medicine and anthropology, but their influence on China tended to be limited; certainly they never acquired the control over the structure and organization of education which some U.S.-returned students were to have under the Republic.

If we turn to the missionary sector of education, an extremely important vehicle for the transmission of Western culture and education, again the British influence was weaker than might have been expected. Even when the British outnumbered the Americans among missionaries, the U.S. contribution to mission education seems to have been greater. In the twentieth century, for reasons I will examine later, the gap widened further and American missionaries and mission funds came to dominate the China field. This was especially noticeable in tertiary education. With the exception of Hong Kong University, no university in China was ever explicitly run on the British model.

Given this dearth of structural or institutional imitation or transfer, how can British influence be studied, indeed, is the subject worthy of research? The answer, I think, is that British influence was far more pervasive than it appears upon first examination, but was so diffuse that it is often hard to identify. As this influence came about through contact with a great variety of institutions, a rather broad focus must be maintained to encompass its extent and significance.

Another complicating factor is the closely interconnected nature of British and American influence. Although the British and the Americans sometimes saw themselves as rivals in the China, they also co-operated a great deal, especially in the missionary context where denominational loyalties might be more significant than national ones. Missionary teachers often moved freely between American and British schools and colleges. British and American teachers were very aware of their differences, but they had, of course, a common language and, broadly speaking, a culture from common origins. For the Chinese ''the West'' meant above all the United States and Britain, but the two were not always easily distinguishable.[2] For these reasons this article inevitably contains some discussion of the American presence in China.

In my first section I attempt to show why British education did not attract the Chinese government in its search for an appropriate model. I then examine British influences on the early schools of Western learning and on the introduction of Western science to China. Some of the leading advocates of reform whose ideas and activities opened the way to a national system of education in China had contacts and friendships with Britain and her nationals. After a general look at these, I focus on the lives of the Englishman John Fryer and the Welshman, Timothy Richard, two men deeply committed to education, whose careers linked the missionary endeavour and the Reform Movement. I then turn to a more general consideration of British participation in missionary education. In my next section I examine the indirect influence which Britain had through colonial institutions in Hong Kong, Singapore and the Treaty Ports. Finally, in a brief survey of British influence in the twentieth century when it was clearly on the wane, I look at the failed United Universities scheme, the use of British Boxer Indemnity funds, and some of the activities of the British Council.

England, the world's first industralized nation, was yet rather backward in education. Until 1870, England had no national school system and no public control of education. Schools were run privately or by religious bodies although many were financed by government grants-in-aid. The Education Act of 1870 provided for public elementary schools to be established by local school boards, but preserved also denominational schools which continued to receive public funds.[3] Secondary schooling was less developed than elementary education. "Public schools" providing a gentleman's education for the privileged few had been rescued by reformers whose interests lay in character building rather than a modern curriculum. Grammar schools, until the effects of the Commission of 1868 began to be felt, were on the whole inefficient, and tied to an impractical classical curriculum. It was not until the twentieth century that England developed a national system of secondary education. University education, which was not in the hands of the state, was provided, roughly speaking, at Oxford and Cambridge for the upper class, and at provincial universities for the middle classes. Teacher-training colleges, a far more accessible form of higher education, were becoming more numerous but their status was low.

It is worth noting that Scotland, which had a different pattern of educational provision, was better-off on some counts than England. However, Scotland was a small remote nation, unlikely to draw the attention of investigators from afar. It was the English system which would have attracted, or fail to attract, Chinese searching for a model.

That system was, as we have seen, a decentralized one in which schools maintained a high degree of autonomy. Although English educational reformers often looked wistfully towards Prussia, the ethos of the English education was profoundly different. J. S. Mill in his essay *On Liberty* warned of the dangers of what he called "a general state education" allowing the government to establish a despotism over people's minds.[4] Opposition to state regulation ensured that great variety was preserved. English educational provision evolved from a long series of historical compromises between central and local authorities and the various interested religious bodies. Its complexity would have made it difficult for an outsider even to understand, and its roots in a specific history made it unsuitable for transplantation. The one common characteristic of all English schools, the prime place they give to religion, also disqualified them. It is hardly surprising that the centralized systems of the German type, widely regarded as superior even by many English educationalists, found favor with those searching for an educational structure to unify and modernize China. Finally, certain similarities between the Chinese and English systems in the nineteenth century would surely have encouraged reformers to look elsewhere. Sally Borthwick has pointed out that they shared:

> a combination of restriction to a wealthy elite of access to the higher educational process, of a classical, formalistic, literary moralistic curriculum, and of competitive entry into the bureaucracy by examination in familiarity with this body of literature.[5]

Education at all levels in England was intended to train the character. Both in schools for the elite and in establishments for the lower classes, moral values were emphasized over academic attainment. The primary objective of elite education was the production of English gentlemen, as in China it was the training of Confucian gentlemen.[6] Only later, when the prestige-seeking nouveaux riches of the Treaty Ports were drawn by the social pretensions of elite schools of the British type did this aspect of the British educational tradition hold any attraction for the Chinese.

Self-strengthening and Reform: The British Influence

Prior to 1904, official Chinese involvement with the promotion of Western learning was limited to a small number of modern schools. Important among them were establishments such as the *Tongwenguan* or Interpreters College in Peking (1862), the School of the Jiangnan Arsenal at Nanjing (1865), the Fuzhou Shipyards School (1866), the Tianjin Telegraph School (1880) and the Viceroy's Hospital Medical School at Tianjin (1881).[7]

All of these were associated with "self-strengthening," that is the attempt by Chinese officials to obtain for China sufficient Western knowledge in military, naval technical and diplomatic matters for her to resist the threat of the West. In the 1860s at least, this attempt enjoyed some foreign diplomatic cooperation, notably from the British.[8]

In no sense did these schools constitute a recognition of government responsibility for education or a general need to change the traditional syllabus. Their objective was to impart specific skills in language and technology to a very small number of selected students. In that they offered instruction in Western languages, science and technology under government auspices, they represented a new departure for China, but the experiment was under tight control. Where possible, foreign staff appear to have been kept in the position of "foreign experts," there to teach, but not to determine the basic organization of the school, nor to make the final decisions.

Qing officials avoided their schools becoming too closely associated with any single foreign power. Most had teachers of more than one nationality although an all-Danish staff was allowed to run the Tianjin Telegraph School. [9] The Fuzhou Navy Yard School had a French division for the study of French, engineering and shipbuilding and an English division which trained deck and engine officers for the Chinese navy.[10] Many of the first Chinese to study in Britain were naval personnel or technicians.

The Peking *Tongwenguan* had strong British connections from its inception. The officials who first pressed for its establishment were partly motivated by the need for Chinese translators and interpreters to assist in diplomatic communication with British and French officials who, under the 1858 treaties of Tianjin, had begun to use their own languages. The school might have had a less secure existence if it had been dependent on central government for finance. Instead it received regular support from Sir Robert Hart, the Ulsterman who headed the Chinese Imperial Maritime Customs from 1863 to 1911.[12] Hart's support for the school continued for over 30 years. In 1866 when he returned to Ireland to get married, he took with him three of the school's most able students for whom he arranged a three-month tour of Europe, visiting factories and museums. He took advantage of this tour to recruit professors of English, French and astronomy.

Despite Hart's relationship to the school, foreign influences in it were never exclusively British. The first two professors of English, J. S. Bourdon and John Fryer, each left after a year in the job, to be succeeded in 1864 by an American W. A. P. Martin. Martin became head of the school in 1869, a position which he retained for 25 years. The staff was always multi-national. Chinese professors were employed for Chinese studies, while from 1869 mathematics was the responsibility of the distinguished Chinese mathematician Li Shanlan. Additionally there were on the staff in the mid-1890s, two Germans, two Scots, an Irishman, a Frenchman and a Russian.[13]

Sir Robert Hart's promotion of Western learning was not limited to the *Tongwenguan*.[14] He also favored the establishment of the Fuzhou shipyard and its school which received funds from the maritime customs revenue. He had close relations with the Zongli Yamen which was central to the self-strengthening movement. He supplied prizes for essay competitions run by missionaries to promote Western learning.[15] Yet he maintained the Customs Service as a foreign-led operation. Although he insisted that Western customs officials should respect their Chinese masters, and claimed to recognize that the service should one day become Chinese, he did little to hasten that day. No Chinese even attained the grade of assistant in the Indoor Staff while he was Inspector General, although 60 had attained that rank by 1915, four years after his death.[16] The Customs School was set up in Peking in 1908 only after years of difficulty in recruiting Chinese staff with adequate English who had frequently to be brought in from Hong Kong.[17]

As the self-strengthening movement lost its original impetus and its limitations became clear, a new generation of thinkers emerged who advocated more thorough-going reform as the only way to save China. One of the earliest of those was Guo Songtao, China's first minister to Britain and France (1876-78). His experience abroad convinced him of the need for root-and-branch change in China's political and social institutions, including her educational system.[18] Unfortunately his progressive ideas virtually ended his official career and thus he had little influence. Another reformer, Wang Tao, was brought both by his residence in Hong Kong from 1862, and by the two years he spent in Scotland assisting James Legge with his translations, to believe that China should, like Japan, adopt such Western institutions as would be useful. [19] As a journalist based in Hong Kong from 1870, he was able to reach a growing readership.

An important intellectual basis for the reform school came from the work of Yan Fu, scholar and translator. Yan had received a classical Chinese education followed by five years at the Fuzhou shipyard and two at the Greenwich Naval Academy. In England he encountered the ideas of political liberalism and social Darwinism. In these ideas he began to see an explanation both for the wealth and power of Britain and for the weakness of China. He believed that Western culture encouraged assertiveness, initiative and struggle while Western governments, and the British government in particular, left the individual's energies free to achieve their maximum potential. China, he asserted, was enfeebled by a system of government which kept people ignorant and weak. The only way for her to survive in the modern world was to discard the burden of tradition.

Among Yan Fu's translations were T. H. Huxley's *Evolution and Ethics* (1896), *Wealth of Nations* (1901), J. S. Mill's *On Liberty* (1903) and Herbert Spencer's *Sociology* (1909) all published with Yan's introductions. His elegant but difficult style helped to make his ideas acceptable to the gentry, although it limited his audience to the privileged few. The impact of Yan's translations was, however, greater than this would indicate. Simplified versions of their ideas, especially of social Darwinist theory, became current among people who had not themselves read them. Nor was their impact limited to the coastal cities. Mao Zedong appears to have read some of them in Changsha in 1911-12. [21]

Like other major figures of the reform movement, Yan's importance to the history of education lies not in a direct contribution, but in the way he helped to form a new view of the West and what it had to offer. In 1902 he wrote:

> Of all the evils which confront China, ignorance is the most dire, since it is only knowledge which can overcome all of China's ills, and more specifically, it is only Western knowledge which can overcome the particular forms from which China suffers. [22]

Yan Fu himself was powerless to change China. Yet, as his biographer Benjamin Schwartz has written, "his preoccupation with wealth and power remains a fundamental feature of the consciousness of the Chinese intelligentsia."[23] This preoccupation was often the motivating force of twentieth century efforts to transform education.

Like Wang Tao, Yan Fu was aware of the existence of secular thought in eighteenth and nineteenth century Europe. The first book which he translated in the 1890s, Alexander Mitchie's *Missionaries in China,* contained forceful criticisms of missionary practice.[24] Formerly, the difficulty of distinguishing between Christian teaching and other elements of Western learning had held up the spread of the latter.[25] Yan's work informed Chinese that not all foreigners approved of missionaries, some were themselves not Christians and Western learning was not inseparable from Christianity. The discovery was important because this was not a message which Western missionaries, then still the main purveyors of Western learning in China, were likely to spread. A generation later, some Christian educators were opposed to sending Chinese students abroad precisely because they feared their pupils might come under atheistic influence and they deplored Bertrand Russell's presence in China for the same reason. [26] For the Chinese, the realization that religious and secular learning could be separated was tremendously important since it allowed them to accept the universality of science while rejecting the Christian message so often packaged with it.

John Fryer and Timothy Richard

John Fryer and Timothy Richard, despite many differences of personality and life history, both through their careers linked the self-strengthening and reform movements with missionary educational endeavour.

Fryer, the son of a poor clergyman, gained his early education as a pupil and then a pupil-teacher at a church-run elementary school in Bristol. [27] From this inauspicious beginning, he progressed via a scholarship to a teacher training college in Highbury, London, and thence to a post at a mission school in Hong Kong where he arrived in 1860. His next move was to the *Tongwenguan* in Peking in 1863, at which he spent only a year before moving to Shanghai. There he taught at a Church Missionary Society School for three years and then abandoned teaching to become editor of the Mission News *(Jiaohuibao),* a post which he held for two years. Finally, in May 1868, Fryer was engaged as a translator at the Jiangnan Arsenal and embarked on the work he was to continue for 28 years.

Fryer's appointment to the Arsenal marked his rejection of evangelism as his mission in life. However, he devoted himself with equal dedication to another cause, the introduction of Western ideas at first in science and technology, and later in the social sciences, to the Chinese in their own language. Of course important translations had already been made and continued to be made by other people. For example as early as the 1850s, Alexander Wylie, a Scot who later joined Fryer at the Arsenal, had, together with the mathematician Li Shanlan, completed a translation of Euclid's *Elements of Geometry* first began by the Jesuits in Peking early in the seventeenth century.[28] It is the scope and quantity of Fryer's work which makes it such an impressive achievement. Among his 75 translations for the Arsenal were works on maths, pure and applied sciences, medicine and social science. When the reformer Liang Qichao compiled a list of 329 recommended works on Western topics, 119 of them had been translated by Fryer. This alone demonstrates his importance in the transmission of Western ideas to China.

Fryer's other activities include the establishment of a public library, the grandly named Shanghai Polytechnic Institute in 1875, the editing of a scientific magazine containing extracts from British and American educational and scientific journals and the establishment a book depot to market Chinese-language books introducing Western knowledge. The Polytechnic Institute which consisted of a reading room and exhibition rooms, seems to have been very much in the Victorian British tradition of self-improvement. Unlike the museum of the Royal Asiatic Society, also set up in Shanghai in the 1870s, it was intended to inspire curiosity among Chinese about Western education. (The Royal Asiatic Society by contrast was open to Chinese only on Monday and Tuesday afternoons because it had suffered from ''an excess of Chinese visitors.'')[29] Exhibitions were put on by the Polytechnic on subjects as varied as needle and fishhook manufacture and the use of globes and other educational equipment. From 1894 it had a program of public lectures and magic lantern shows.[30] Another of the Polytechnic's undertakings was the organization of essay competitions on ''reform topics'' such as:

> What ought China at the present time to regard as of foremost importance
> in her endeavor to improve wealth and power?[31]

Finally it seems worth noting that Fryer financed some of the first schools for the handicapped in China, an interest taken up by his son who was for many years superintendent of a school for the blind in Shanghai.[32] In this very specialized area he was also then a pioneer.

Fryer's conviction that scientific ideas could be spread and studied through the medium of Chinese was hotly contested in his time. As late as 1893 some Western missionaries still argued that the Chinese language was not adequately developed for the discussion or study of science and that scientific education had therefore to be in a Western language.[33] Through his translations, his role in the creation of a scientific vocabulary and his forceful speeches at missionary conferences on education, Fryer helped to refute this claim, and thus to make a modern education more accessible to the millions of literate Chinese who never mastered a foreign language.

Liang Qichao's appreciation of Fryer has already been mentioned. His mentor, Kang Youwei, passing through Shanghai in 1882, brought all the available Jiangnan translations. Another leading reformer, Tan Sitong, is known to have read some of them. The circulation of the translations was poor, a sale of one thousand copies being accounted a success, but sales did rise with the mounting popularity of Western learning in the 1890s, and a few works were even popular enough to be pirated.[34]

In time, of course, both the books which Fryer translated and his translations themselves were superseded. More up-to-date works were translated by Chinese scholars from Japanese and from Western Languages.[35] But Fryer must be credited with two major achievements. He made available to that first generation curious about Western learning an impressive range of texts, and helped to give reality to his conviction that Chinese was perfectly capable of becoming a vehicle for the study of science.

Timothy Richard, a Welshman born in 1845, went to China in 1869 under the auspices of the Baptist Missionary Society. The youngest son in a farming family with nine children, he had to struggle to gain an education and financed himself through Swansea Normal School with savings from his teaching job. He was converted at the age of fifteen in the course of one of the great revivalist movements sweeping Wales at the time, and soon afterwards developed an interest in the mission field.[36]

In 1865 he entered Haverford West Theological College in West Wales. The curriculum was unrelievedly classical, consisting of ancient languages, theology and history. Despite Richard's talent for such subjects — he won the college prize for Hebrew — he joined other students in demanding reform of the syllabus. They wanted to substitute modern languages for Greek and Latin, to add world history to European history and to be taught science. The students insisted that they would rather be expelled than back down and in the end they won. The story is obviously relevant to Richard's subsquent career, showing as it does that he came from a society where, as in China, there was a struggle between old and new studies and that, despite a real interest in both, he felt the practical need for new studies.

Unlike many missionaries of his day Richard acquired an impressive mastery of both spoken and written Chinese. He travelled widely and developed a sympathetic understanding of many aspects of Chinese culture. He was in Shanxi for the severe famine years of 1876-8, an experience which proved a turning point for him.[37] He came to believe that the only way to save China from such suffering, was to win over the officials and gentry to the cause of Western education. He began to argue that education was as much Christian work as any other. Although unlike Fryer he did not turn wholly away from evangelism, his energies subsequently went into education and into convincing the Chinese elite of the need for Western learning.[38]

In 1878, Richard married, having decided according to his memoirs that he would do more efficient mission work with a wife.[39] Mrs. Richard had come to China under the auspices of the United Presbyterian Mission and their interdenominational marriage was typical of Richard's attitude to divisions within the mission movement. Not only did he urge cooperation between Protestant groups, he maintained friendly relations with Catholic missionaries. Mrs. Richard even taught the use of the sewing machine in a Catholic orphanage in Taiyuan as there were, at that time, no sisters so far inland.[40] Richard's interest in all forms of Christian belief and even in Chinese religious belief and practice would seem unremarkable today, but they scandalized some of his colleagues and led in time to formal accusations that he taught a "mixture of science, popery and heathenism."[41] However, his liberal attitudes and his command of the Chinese language allowed him to exchange ideas with Chinese officials in a way that was rare for a missionary.

In Taiyuan, Mr. and Mrs. Richard ran a school for sixty boys. They also supervized seven elementary schools in nearby villages.[42] Richard was always conscious, however, that missionaries could achieve little, given the great size of China, without Chinese cooperation. He gave public lectures to inform the local gentry of the achievements of Western science. He and his family lived and ate as cheaply as possible in order to have money for books and equipment. Among his purchases were a telescope, a microscope, a spectroscope, a dynamo, a voltmeter, an electrometer and a sewing machine, all of which he demonstrated at his lectures.[43] He used a magic lantern, and instructed and equipped a photographic assistant who became the pioneer photographer of Shanxi. These popular lectures helped him make gentry contacts and were still remembered in the city 20 years later in 1906.[44]

On his first home leave in 1884, Richard took courses at South Kensington in order to improve his knowledge of science. Anxious to learn more about systems of education which might have relevance to China, he visited educational authorities in both Berlin and Paris.[45] Later he wrote up these visits in a pamphlet for circulation among Chinese officials.[46] True to his idea that China would be changed through her leaders, Richard always took any chance to talk to high officials. At different times he became acquainted with most of the great provincial leaders. In 1880, at an interview with Zuo Zongtang, he discussed the viceroy's self-strengthening enterprises and pressed his own causes: religious toleration and mission schools. He presented Zuo Zongtang with a typically imaginative gift, a wall-chart, designed by Richard himself, showing the comparative history of the world.[47]

In 1891 Richard moved to Shanghai to run the Society for the Diffusion of Christian and General Knowledge (SDK) as its only full-time member of staff.[48] By the time he retired 25 years later, it had a staff of six foreign and 18 Chinese workers and assets of nearly one quarter of a million dollars. He himself had published one hundred original works or translations among which a few were influential volumes. The most important of these was a translation of Mackenzie's *History of Christian Civilization in the Nineteenth Century,* a dull tome presenting a narrow culture-bound view of history.[49] However, its progressivist approach had great appeal to Chinese intellectuals appalled by the catastrophies which befell China in the 1890s. The SDK edition sold well, and it was also extensively pirated. In Hangzhou at one time six different pirated editions were available and it was estimated that a million pirated copies circulated throughout China.

It is consistent with Richard's faith in the leading role of the gentry that he saw a great need in China for higher education. This he believed would win China's leaders to Christianity and they would then convert the common people. On his first home furlough in 1884, he proposed to the Baptist Society that future mission efforts should be chiefly directed to education, and that the mission societies should found one good college in each of the eighteen provinces of China. [50] The Society's reaction was polite, but his plan was rejected on the grounds of expense. Richard's disappointment was bitter. He never abandoned hope of setting up a college, however. Like other British educators in China he was very aware that the majority of modern colleges in China were American foundations.[51] He tended to be critical of such establishments complaining that they were so Western as to make students "almost foreigners in thought and habits and largely out of touch with native thought and feeling."[52]

Richard's chance to realize a small part of his plan came in 1901 when he was invited by Prince Qing and Li Hongzhang to return to Shanxi to assist in the settlement of the aftermath of the Boxer Uprising. As early as 1894, he had conceived a plan to use some U.S. indemnity money for educational purposes in China but it came to nothing.[53] Now he negotiated the payment over ten years of about £100,000 compensation for missionary lives and property to be devoted to the cause of education in Shanxi. A university was to be established in Taiyuan offering a modern education to the ablest young men of the province. The staffing, the arrangement of the curriculum and the finance of the university were to be Richard's responsibilty for the first ten years, after which management would revert to the Shanxi government.[54]

Richard appointed Moir Duncan, a Baptist missionary and Oxford graduate, as principal of the college in 1902. He was succeeded by W. W. Soothill, later to become professor of Chinese at Oxford. An early dispute over a rival plan for a Chinese university in the same town was resolved by a merger.[55] Over the years, Shanxi University developed into a modestly successful institution offering a range of courses in law, languages, literature, history, mathematics, physics, chemistry, mining and civil engineering. An early problem was the difficulty of recruiting students who knew enough English to read or study in the language or finding staff able to teach in Chinese. This was solved by the use of interpreters brought in from the Treaty Ports.[56] Standards were probably not high. Like other mission colleges in China, but unlike universities in Britain, pre-degree level courses were offered. This is interesting because it was an aspect of the American-run mission colleges' work about which British educationalists were later extremely critical.[57] Shanxi University was obviously not following the British model rigidly, even at the onset. The three-year preparatory course was of a slightly higher standard, according to Soothill, than London University matriculation.[58] Students then went on to do four years in a specialism which brought them to B.A. standard. They were then considered qualified for post-graduate study abroad. Twenty-five went to England to study railway and mining engineering and at that time there were more Shanxi university graduates in Britain than students from any other Chinese educational establishment.[59]

It was typical of Richard's attitudes towards the Chinese that he was anxious to hand the university over to them as soon as possible. It reverted in June 1911, a little ahead of schedule.[60] The chaos which followed the outbreak of the 1911 revolution brought a halt to studies. Inexplicably, in his account, Soothill implies that this was the end of the university. In fact, it continued as Shanxi Government University. No foreign staff remained (G. E. Morrison claimed that the German-trained Chinese principal had got rid of them all)[61], but a high proportion of the 18 Chinese staff had British degrees.[62] It is listed in the 1918 Educational Directory for China as an establishment with 760 male students, making it larger than the largest of the mission establishments, the Peking (Methodist) University which that year had 600 students.[63] It was larger also than the two other government universities in China, the Peking (Government) University which had grown out of the old *Tongwenguan* and Beiyang University in Tianjin, another creation of official effort in the last years of the nineteenth century. These had 676 students and 300 students respectively.[64] The university had as feeders a network of government schools in Shanxi which several sources comment on as extraordinarily good for an inland province.[65]

Perhaps because the university was quickly sinified, unlike the mission colleges which remained conspicuously foreign in their ethos even when under pressure from the Chinese in the 1920s they registered with the government and appointed Chinese heads, Richard's achievement in Shanxi has largely been forgotten. In any modern evaluation of his contribution, the rapid integration of the university into the Chinese system should surely be seen as a mark of its success.

The British Role in Mission Education

The great historian of the missions in China, Kenneth Latourette, considered that the period 1856-97 was mainly one of evangelism and was marked by British dominance in the mission field.[66] He wrote:

> As was to be expected from the wealth and commerce of Great Britain and the part which the British played in the foreign relations of China, the majority of outstanding pioneers were British. The continent of Europe had as yet few representatives and Americans did not have as important a place as they were to win after 1900.[67]

Numerically, Americans surpassed the British for a time in the Protestant mission as early as 1874 when numbers were still very small, but later the British regained the lead and seem to have held it until the twentieth century (see Table 3.1).

There were reported to be 80 Protestant missionaries in China in 1858, resident only in the coastal provinces. By 1876 there were 473 and by 1889, 1,296.[68] In 1910 the figure was over 5,000.[69] A peak of 8,000 was reached in the mid-1920s when a fall began. By 1936, under 5,000 missionaries remained.[70]

Table 3.1
Nationality of Protestant Missionaries in China (in percentages)

	British	U.S.	German	Other Europeans
1874	44.5	48	7.5	
1889	56.5	39	?	4
1905	50*	33	?	20
1920	33	50	?	?

*includes U.K., Canada, Australia and New Zealand

Sources:
Latourette, *A History of the Christian Missions in China*, p. 406.
Feuerwerker, *The Foreign Establishment in China in the Early 20th Century*, p. 42.

Obviously not all missionaries were involved in education. Indeed, there was much disagreement as to the effort they should expend on it. Nor were all mission schools alike. The first ones were founded in order that converts might be taught to read the Bible and preachers and Biblewomen trained. Then it was felt that the children of converts must be offered a Christian education. After years of evangelism with little to show for it, however, some missionaries began to see education as a way to reach the unconverted. Offering non-Christian Chinese an education attractive enough to draw in pupils often involved compromises. For example many early elementary schools run by missions used the ancient primer from which children in indigenous schools also learnt their characters.[71] It might be part of Confucian culture, but it was what people expected of education and it worked. As the commercial demand for English grew, mission schools which offered it experienced a growing demand for places. Yet many missionaries felt that this sort of instruction was no part of their duties. In 1877, the Welsh evangelist, Griffith John voiced their concern when he asserted:

> We are here, not to develop the resources of the country, not for the advancement of commerce, not for the mere promotion of civilization, but to do battle with the powers of darkness, save men from sin and conquer China for Christ.[72]

The founder of the China Inland Mission, the Yorkshireman Hudson Taylor, declared that secular work could be justified only if "it enables us to bring a soul to him."[73] At the other end of the spectrum Timothy Richard who, as we have seen, came to regard education as essential work for the missionary, declared that "those who did the best to improve this world were best fitted for eternal bliss thereafter."[74]

Such differences affected many aspects of mission work. In recruitment for example, Hudson Taylor, whose China Inland Mission's educational work was mostly confined to primary schools run for the children of converts, wanted "fundamentalist faith, physical fitness and an absence of racial pride" from his missionaries; he did not insist on theological training or indeed on any formal qualifications.[75] Richard wanted the missions to chose "the best men from our universities." He thought a good missionary should have received a secular education and have a thorough knowledge of comparative religion.[76] It was his wish that prospective missionaries should be obliged to take an exam in Chinese language and culture and to prove that they could get on with non-Christian Chinese. Such different attitudes were reflected in great differences in the missions' involvement in educational work. With a staff of 366 missionaries in 1890, the China Inland Mission had 182 pupils in their schools. The smaller London Mission Society with 65 foreign missionaries had 2,214.[77]

While British influence was paramount, the zealot missionary was the norm. British missionaries were seldom university-educated and some had never had any kind of higher education.[78] From the 1890s, this began to change. Partly this was because of the growing numbers of Americans, most of whom were college-educated, but some British societies also began to require higher qualifications.

The missionaries' most important contribution to modern education came in the last two decades of the Qing dynasty when demand was greater than the government system could supply. This growth occured in the period when the older zealot was largely giving way to the college-educated missionary who could accept a vocation in education and when the Americans were begining to catch up the British in what missionaries so unfortunately termed the "Christian Occupation of China." However, the greater American commitment to education can already be seen in figures presented to the first conference of Protestant Missions in 1877. These show that the Americans had more pupils in both their boys'and girls' boarding schools, and in their girls' day schools, while pupils in British-run boys' day schools and theological colleges were more numerous. In all, the Americans had almost one thousand more pupils.

Table 3.2
America, British and Continental Missionary Society Schools and Students in 1877.

Missionary Society Schools

	U.S.	Br	Continental	Total
Boys' Boarding Schools	19	8	3	30
Girls' Boarding Schools	24	12	2	38
Boys' Day Schools	93	70	14	177
Girls' Day Schools	57	24	1	82
Theological Schools	9	9	2	20
	192	123	22	347

Numbers of students

	U.S.	Br	Continental	Total
Boys' Boarding Schools	347	118	146	611
Girls' Boarding Schools	464	189	124	777
Boys' Day Schools	1255	1471	265	2991
Girls' Day Schools	957	335	15	1307
Theological Schools	94	115	22	231
	3117	2228	573	5917

Source: Alice Gregg, *China and Educational Autonomy: The Changing Role of the Protestant Educational Missionary in China, 1807-1937* (Syracuse: Syracuse University Press, 1946).

The difference continued. Forty years later, the 1917 *Educational Directory of China* listed all U.S. and British mission secondary schools and colleges with the numbers of students enrolled. The U.S. total came to 3,776 students in 14 institutions while the British total was 2,217 students in 13 institutions. (If Hong Kong is included this becomes 3,767 students in 19 institutions.)

In addition another nine union colleges were listed with a total of 1,949 students. Union colleges were so called because they represented a pooling of resources between several mission societies. In some cases there were British schools among the institutions which merged to form these unions but this identity tended to become submerged once they joined larger, richer American schools.

The great survey of missionary strength in 1922 showed that the British were more involved with medical work and the Americans with educational work.[79] The British were more scattered, having extended into one half of China's land area whereas the Americans had only reached one third. The survey listed 31 British mission societies to 80 American ones.

The fact that the schools maintained by British missionary societies were at elementary or secondary level inevitably give them a lower profile and less influence than the sixteen universities and colleges maintained with funds from the U.S.[80] The focus of interest in mission education tended with time to shift from elementary schooling to the schools run for the better-off classes in urban areas and above all in the Treaty Ports when Western learning was so much in demand.

Although British missionaries did not set up tertiary-level institutions, they did establish a number of elite secondary schools where a British "public-school" style education was offered.[81] They were financed by high fees and by business including the British Chambers of Commerce of the main treaty ports. Boys in these schools worked for the Oxford or Cambridge local exams or London University matriculation until Hong Kong University set up its own exams. The syllabus offered was based on British norms except that in the Hong Kong examinations classical Chinese and its literature was accepted in place of Latin and Greek. Special provision was also made for candidates "from the interior and out-ports of China" who did not pass in English at their first attempt.[82]

These, however, were the only concessions made. All subjects except for Chinese itself were examined through English and, most strikingly of all, the history syllabus concentrated entirely on British and European history.

The best known of these elite colonial-style establishments was probably the Anglo-Chinese college at Tianjin, founded in 1902. It was used by wealthy Treaty Port families, particularly those which already had British or Hong Kong connections. It developed links with the University of Hong Kong after 1912, sending a number of students there despite the distance. Others went straight to England for the first degrees, a few to Oxford or Cambridge where many of the college masters had studied. Its professed aim was "not so much to give instruction to a large number, as to bring the highest influences to bear upon those over whom it has charge" and thus to make the school "a training ground for men of character."[83] The emphasis on character building is interesting as it highlights what British educational experts seem to have regarded as the British strength. Other countries, they were sometimes prepared to admit, might make a better job of imparting knowledge, but the British "public school" produced leaders.[84]

One major achievement of the missions was that they pioneered girls' education in China. Like other early mission schools, the first schools for girls catered for the poor, indeed they were sometimes scarcely distinguishable from foundling homes. The process of attracting fee-paying pupils was especially slow for girls' schools since the parents had to be convinced not only that the education was worth paying for, but that their daughters were worth educating. The syllabus of girls' schools tended to reflect the preoccupation with producing "good wives and mothers" which also characterized girls' education in the West at the time. Sewing, embroidery and hygiene feature heavily.[85] The bias probably reflected both missionary attitudes and parental demand.

Before the reforms of the May Fourth movement, although there were government normal schools and normal colleges for women, they were not admitted to the three government universities. Most of the mission colleges also excluded them but there were some American and union institutions open only to girls while a few were co-educational.[86] British establishments were more conservative. Outside Hong Kong none of their schools even offered advanced secondary work for girls. There were girls' secondary schools in Hong Kong but Hong Kong University admitted women only from 1921.[87]

Although the British missionaries were slow to promote advanced education for girls, the credit for the very first girls' schools must go to them. Elementary schools for boys run by the missions emphasized graded work and regular attendance more than the traditional *sishu* or private schools of China had done, but essentially they were performing the same task of teaching small boys to read and write. Few girls could read and write in the past and fewer still had learnt to do so outside a family setting. In this sense, the mission schools for girls, even though most were at the elementary level, were a revolutionary departure. Although more girls were registered in government schools than in mission schools as early as 1908,[88] in relative terms, mission schools offered better provision for girls. Even in 1922, less than 7% of the total enrollment of government primary schools was female, against about 30% for mission schools.[89]

British mission schools were always handicapped by a lack of funds. The British gave less generously to the China missions than the Americans and home boards were harder to persuade of the benefits of education. British missionary resources went to British colonies throughout the world, especially in Africa and India. In the colonies, however, their schools were often maintained by grants-in-aid from the colonial government. The British government tended not to favor missionary activity in China. It was the French action which obtained for missionaries the right to reside and evangelize.[90] Whereas U.S. missionaries were sometimes appointed to the American legation in Peking,[91] British officials often showed a patrician distaste for the zeal of their compatriots. An English officer of the 1880s described missionaries as being "one grade below the rank of gentlemen," accused them of living better in China than they would have done at home, and claimed that some of them were deficient in clean linen and aitches.[92]

Outside the Treaty Ports, with a few exceptions like that of naval training, British interest in education was the province of voluntary societies and individuals. In British colonies and concessions of course matters were different and it is to them that we now turn.

British Influence

The existence of Hong Kong as a British colony and the British presence in places with sizeable Chinese communities such as Singapore and Penang provided additional filters for British cultural and educational influence. In China itself, British institutions in the Treaty Ports, especially in Shanghai, played a similar role.

Yung Wing, the first Chinese to attend an American college had been at school in Hong Kong as had many of the boys he recruited to study in the U.S. in the 1870s.[93] The first Chinese students to study in Europe also seem to have been inhabitants of the British Colonies. One of them was Huang Kuan who accompanied Yung Wing to America but later went to Edinburgh and became the first Chinese to qualify as a doctor in Britain. Both the Chinese Customs Service and Treaty Port firms recruited employees from Hong Kong schools.[94] One quite simple role that Hong Kong played therefore was to provide boys whose English was good enough either for further study abroad, or for immediate employment in China.

We have already seen that Hong Kong helped to persuade Wang Tao of the need for reform, and other reform leaders like Kang Youwei and Liang Qichao also saw in the flourishing modern city evidence that China's backwardness must be attributable to her political system.

The most notable figure in Chinese history to have received a British education, Sun Yat-sen, also contrasted the modernity of Hong Kong with the backwardness of the hinterland of China and found it an inspiration to action. Despite his nationalism, Sun, who had been at a British mission school in Honolulu before going on to further study in Hong Kong, seems to have retained affection for the Hong Kong medical school to which he paid a last visit in 1923, after it had become a part of Hong Kong University. On this visit he made a speech to the students of the university from which the following remarks have been extracted:

> I feel as though I had returned home, because Hong Kong and its university are my intellectual birthplace.... Where did I get my revolutionary ideas from? The answer is, I got them in this very place, in the Colony of Hong Kong....
>
> More than thirty years ago, I was studying in Hong Kong and spent a great deal of my spare time in walking the streets of the Colony. Hong Kong impressed me a great deal because there was orderly calm....
>
> I compared Heung Shan (his home village) with Hong Kong and although they are only 50 miles apart, the difference of government oppressed me very much. Afterwards I saw the outside world and I began to wonder how it was that foreigners, that Englishmen, could do such things as they had done, for

example, with the barren rock of Hong Kong within 70 or 80 years while in 4,000 years, China had no place like Hong Kong.[95]

Hong Kong was, however, far from being an educational model for China. Its school system grew slowly, and like its English counterpart, developed as a hybrid public/private system. The grant-in-aid systems was introduced in 1873, benefiting 100 Confucian schools, 93 mission schools and 35 schools run by the colonial government. Despite the enthusiasm of some governors, educational provision remained limited, chiefly because Hong Kong taxpayers were not happy to pay for it.[96]

Hong Kong University, set up in 1912, also developed rather slowly. It graduated 28 students in 1922. By 1933 the student body had grown to 364 and by 1941, 600.[97] Its benefactors were mostly business men from Hong Kong and the Straights settlements and for many years it suffered from a chronic shortage of funds. Hopes for finance from the British Boxer Indemnity funds were not realized until 1931, but the University's worst problems were solved by a large grant from the Rockefeller Foundation in 1922.[98]

Part of the University's difficulty with finance was due to uncertainty about the role it was supposed to play. Sir Frederick Lugard, its first Chancellor, argued that the University should provide higher education not only for Hong Kong but for China as a whole, and that it should therefore be regarded as "an imperial asset and an imperial responsibility."[99] Local businessmen, doubtful anyway about Hong Kong's need for a university, were certainly unwilling to fund an institution intended also to serve China. The Hong Kong Government was prepared to cover a part of its expenses but not to pay the bill for university education provided in Hong Kong for the benefit of China. This it argued was the responsibility of the Imperial Government. Needless to say the Imperial Government did not agree.

Despite these disputes, the University authorities held to their wide view of the University's aims and influence. In 1921, Sir William Brungate, its third vice-chancellor, visited Peking, Shanghai, Hankou, Penang, Singapore and Java, all centers for the new Hong Kong matriculation exam. His vision of the University was as the head of a system of British mission schools in China and as a British university for China.[100]

The vision remained elusive. Yuan Shikai endowed some "President's scholarships" and the Canton provincial government also offered scholarships to Hong Kong University.[101] A steady trickle of students also came from British secondary schools in China and elsewhere in the Far East. But recruitment of students from China was inevitably limited by the language problem. Instruction at the University and at other prestigious schools in the Colony was in English, and most often by British lecturers. One professor wrote of his faculty:

> All of the lecturing is done by Englishmen. It is not the intention of the Faculty of Engineering to alter this rule because it is most desirable that Chinese students should be brought into intimate contact with Europeans during their training.[102]

Moreover, as student nationalism grew in the 1920s, some young Chinese doubtless rejected the idea of going to a colony for their education. If one adds to this the fact that non-Cantonese would not feel at home in a predominantly Cantonese-speaking city, difficulties of recruitment from China are easily understood.

Mission education in the Treaty Ports has already been discussed. Some Treaty Port Administrations also supported secondary schools. For example in the International Settlement of Shanghai in 1917, the Municipal Council controlled and supported eight municipal schools and made grants-in aid to another four run by religious authorities.[103] Perhaps the most striking aspect of this system was racial segregation. Elsewhere in China, the vast majority of schools catered only for Chinese. Foreign children were sent to boarding schools on the coast or in their home country. Shanghai's large resident foreign population made segregation conspicuous. Of the eight municipal schools, one was for boys and one for girls "of European parentage." There were four municipal schools for Chinese boys but none for girls. Finally there was one boys' school and one girls' school for Eurasians. Of the religious grant-in-aid schools, there was a Catholic school for girls, a Jewish school for boys and girls, a Catholic school for Eurasian girls and a Catholic school for boys of European, Eurasian or Chinese parentage.

British colonial education released into Chinese society, especially into business and the professions, a steady stream of Chinese who had passed through British schools and who tended to regard British ways as superior. For them, much more than for other Chinese, Britain *was* the West. The formal educational system in Hong Kong and the Treaty Ports was backed up by a host of other institutions from Boy Scouts' Associations to commercial training courses which tended to transmit or reinforce British values.[104] Although this sort of influence was largely limited to the Treaty Ports, it was important in that most modern sector of Chinese society. The final chapter in this process has yet to be written. When Hong Kong at last returns to China, in 1997, the last and perhaps the most powerful wave of British colonial influence will be felt throughout China.

British Influence in the Twentieth Century: Attitudes and Activities

In the twentieth century many British commentators began to express a regret at the paucity of British influence on Chinese education. Often this took the form of disdainful remarks about other rival influences, in particular that of the United States. "So much is China indebted to America for her educational ideas," wrote Lancelot Foster, professor of education in Hong Kong, "that one person long resident in China has asserted that for practical purposes, the educational system of China is controlled and guided from Columbia University."[105]

The correspondence of G. E. Morrison, China correspondent of the London Times from 1895-1920 contains various indications of concern. In January 1911 we find him telling Moberly Bell, manager of *The Times,* that Chinese students must be encouraged to come to England to study that they might "become foci of subsequent sympathy for England and for English things and . . . spread a knowledge of our language which at least is of great service to our commercial relations.''[106]

In December 1912, Morrison was bemoaning the fact that Shanxi University had fallen under German influence while in Peking he claimed British professors were being excluded in favour of the French. In 1920 the physician to the British legations, G. D. Gray, wrote to Morrison:

> As for the Educational Conquest of the Far East is concerned, America clearly leads the way. France is also making efforts to attract Chinese students. Our policy seems to be that they come to England if they like, otherwise they can stay away. Beyond Hong Kong University (which is not going ahead as it should) we British are doing very little and it is going to react on our trade and other interests later on.[107]

From an entirely different stance, Bertrand Russell who spent eight months in China in 1921-22, was also unhappy about American influence because he believed it was not in the best interests of the Chinese. In an ironical tone which surely betrays the disdain of the older culture for the brash energy of the new one, he wrote that if American influence prevailed ''it would no doubt, by means of hygiene, save the lives of many Chinamen but it would at the same time make them not worth saving. It cannot therefore be regarded as wholly and altogether satisfactory.''[108]

While he was in China, Russell met the American educationalist, John Dewey. Although Dewey was extremely kind to Russell during the latter's near-fatal illness in Peking, the two men did not like each other. Russell seems to have felt that Dewey's philosophy was an attempted justification of American imperialism.[109] As a conscientious objector he had been disturbed by Dewey's failure to oppose the First World War. Russell himself condemned the influence of all imperialism and of the missionaries. His radical views were of great concern to the British Foreign Office which tentatively explored ways of getting him out of China.[110] The missionaries were equally upset; it is said that when a false rumour of Russell's demise in Peking circulated, one missionary paper printed the line, ''Missionaries may be pardoned for heaving a sigh of relief at the news of Mr. Bertrand Russell's death.''[111]

There was certainly some cause for this alarm. Russell gave lectures in many Chinese cities and universities, attracting large audiences. His formal lectures were on philosophy but he also spoke of his atheism and made plain his anti-imperialist stance. He and his companion, the feminist Dora Black, lived together openly, flouting the strict conventions of the foreign community. Miss Black lectured at the Peking Women's Normal College and elsewhere on feminism, women's education, socialism and marriage, all subjects of great personal interest to the young intelligentsia struggling to free itself from the trammels of tradition.[112]

One of Russell's suggested titles for his book on China was *The White Peril*. Unfortunately the publishers preferred *The Problem of China*, the title under which the book eventually came out.[113] The earlier title aptly summarizes what Russell saw as the problem. Although he recognized that the influx of Western knowledge had provided China with a much needed stimulus, Russell strongly opposed the mechanistic imitation of the West and constantly urged young Chinese to preserve what was valuable in their own culture. He saw education as essential to industrialization but wanted China to adapt the educational institutions of the West to her own needs.[114]

Even after his return to England, Russell's interest in China continued. *The Problem of China* was published in 1922. In 1923, Russell was appointed by the Prime Minister, Ramsay MacDonald, onto a committee to consider the use of the British Boxer Indemnity Funds, only to be excluded after the fall of the Labor government later that year. In 1924 he published articles entitled "British Imperialism in China" and "British Folly in China" in the *New Leader*, giving great offence to the British China lobby.[115] In 1926 he was quick to express outrage at the shooting of unarmed demonstrators by British forces in China.[116]

The influence of Russell and Black on young educated Chinese and thus on education itself was effective because it was timely. In a time of growing nationalism it was an inspiration to many Chinese to realize that one of the leading intellectuals of the West had himself rejected Christianity, condemned imperialism and questioned capitalism. Russell and Black's relationship intrigued young people who were seeking greater personal freedom for themselves, while Dora was seen by some as the model of a modern emancipated woman.

In the 1930s a report by a joint European commission of the League of Nations contained strong criticism of American influence.[117] It paid tribute to American achievements but European distaste for the pedagogical science of Columbia was unmistakable. Teacher training was felt to concentrate on educational theory at the expense of knowledge of the specialism. The experts were concerned by the diffused, unfocused character of student courses which they attributed to the use of the credit system. The criticisms were echoed by Lancelot Foster, in a series of lectures on "English Educational ideals for Chinese Students" delivered at Peking University in 1935.[118]

Unease about other influences was expressed in a more facetious way by a British sinologist, Victor Purcell, who wrote:

> The semi-military uniform with a peak cap which is adopted many schools copied from the Germans via Japan is an eye sore. So long as Chinese parents send their children to school is this unseemly dress, there can be no serious improvement in Chinese education.[119]

Despite all this concern there was to be no great revival of British influence on Chinese education. For a time, there was a scheme known as the United Universities plan to build a "Chinese Oxford or Cambridge" in the Wuhan area to be attended by the best pupils of mission schools. It was hoped to use part of the British Boxer Indemnity Fund to finance it. One of the chief promoters of this scheme, the Reverend Lord William Gascoigne-Cecil, believed that it was necessary in order to save Chinese students from the insidious attacks of Western materialism.[120] (He was particularly upset at the detestable impression of Western

civilization that Chinese were likely to get from reading "erotic novels such as
La Dame aux Camelias."[121])

Gascoigne-Cecil argued that American missionary colleges in China were not
up to the standards of a British university and that it would be in the interests
of all missions to have one union university of real excellence in Central China.[122]
The scheme foundered because insufficient funds were forthcoming from Britain
whilst in the United States it proved hard to raise money for the interdenominational project.[123] Despite his concern for British influence in China, G.
E. Morrison proved no friend to the plan. In a letter of July 1914 to the university's president-elect, W. E. Soothill, he put forward what was probably a common British view:

> I have never been able to understand why we should, in a wealthy country
> like China, or in a country whose wealth is underdeveloped owing to her
> neglect of opportunity, found charities to assist in her education. It seems
> to me opposed to the national spirit which we ought to do our best to en-
> courage, that we should establish a university in Hankou. A university in
> Hong Kong is a good thing but I would wish to see the Chinese themselves
> take a hand in their education, with foreign help of course.[124]

When eventually a union of Christian higher education in Central China was
undertaken in the 1920s and Huazhong University was formed, it was a less ambitious establishment.[125] Most of its constituent parts were American and their
practice tended to prevail over that of minority British participants.

It is understandable that despite the hopes of British missionaries, the inter-
war period was not one of growth for their schools. The 1920s and 1930s were
difficult years for the British economy and for British self-confidence. There is
a certain weary resignation about some of the reports of waning British influence
in China. Furthermore Britain was especially handicapped by her imperial role
in an era of growing nationalist sentiment. Britain's political, military and commercial role made her the obvious target of anti-foreign feeling especially after
the May 30 incident of 1925 when British-officered police in Shanghai killed thirteen demonstrators in Nanking Road. This, together with the movement to restore
educational rights, made the 1920s a time of problems for all missionary education in China.[126]

By contrast, the British government began its first significant educational activity
through the return of the Boxer indemnity fund and later through the activities
of the British Council.

The long-delayed remission of the British Boxer funds to China finally got underway in the 1930s when the first grants were paid, but the indemnity installments
ceased to be absorbed into the British Treasury from December 1922 and were
instead accumulated in an account in the Hong Kong and Shanghai Bank.[127] When
remission was first mooted, the assumption was that, like the U.S. fund, the British
fund would be devoted to education. By 1926, when the Advisory Committee
on the use of the fund reported, it had been decided to invest the bulk of the money
in China, but to use £350,000 of the annual income thus generated to advance
education, science and agriculture. The committee consulted opinions as various

as the British and Chinese chambers of commerce in China, mission societies, the Chinese Government, the vice-chancellor of Hong Kong University and some well-known Chinese intellectuals as to how the money should be spent. Such establishment opinion was very disturbed by the radical student movement which was then so active and may well have felt that it was not the moment for a great expansion in education.

The committee appears to have been swamped with suggestions as to how the money should be used. Even missionary bodies like the London Missionary Society, which had in the past refused to accept reparation money for the loss of missionary life or property, announced that although they would not apply for grants from the fund, they would accept them if offered.[128]

Initially there was much disagreement about how the money might be divided between different levels of education. Eventually the committee decided to recommend against the funding of primary schools and to favor grants to British-run secondary schools, to the Christian-run universities and to Hong Kong University. It recommended the endowment of chairs in English literature, philosophy, history and political science in Chinese universities to be occupied wherever possible by invited British scholars. It was very interested by a proposal to set up a research institute for post-graduate work which would recruit from all the colleges and universities of China students who might otherwise have gone abroad.

Many of these plans never came to fruition or were put into operation only for a short time before the political situation forced their abandonment. In the event, the trustees also made grants for many uses which the committee could not have foreseen, for example for the support of teachers and students displaced by the war and for the evacuation of the treasures of the Palace Museum from Nanjing at the time of the Japanese invasion.[129] However, some of the earlier projects were implemented. In the 1930s, one hundred research fellows and seventy research assistants in the natural and social sciences were supported by the fund. Research institutes in sericulture and land survey were set up and two agricultural schools were established in Hunan. From 1933 to 1939, 148 students received "Boxer scholarships" to pursue higher studies in Britain. In 1939, of 350 Chinese students in Britain, 67 were supported by the Indemnity Fund.[130] After the establishment of the People's Republic in 1949, through the Universities' China Committee, money from the Indemnity Fund continued to be used in support of some very limited Sino-British educational and cultural exchange and in recent years this activity has greatly expanded.[131]

The British Council, founded in 1934 to promote a wider knowledge of British life and the English language abroad, began its activities in China in the 1940s.[132] Its first, and perhaps its most outstanding act was to send Dr. Joseph Needham, a British biochemist who had already made a study of Chinese, to China, an event hailed by Fu Sinian, director of Academica Sinica's History Institute, as "an event worth recording in the history of cultural intercourse between China and the west."[133] Needham spent three years as director of the Sino-British Science Cooperation Office which was financed by the British Council as part of an attempt to break the Japanese intellectual and technical blockade of China. This office brought books, journals, and apparatus to the beleaguered Chinese academic community and fostered the exchange of scholars between China and Britain even in difficult war-time conditions. A longer term benefit of this venture was that Dr. Needham was able to use the close links he forged in those years with a great variety of Chinese academics to visit China regularly and promote useful exchange after 1949 when such activity was unusual.[134] Finally, Dr. Needham's sojourn in China was a stimulus to work he had already begun and which was eventually to result in the publication of his magnum opus, *Science and Civilization in China.*[135]

In the 1940s the British Council set up libraries and reading rooms in many major cities as well as continuing to arrange working visits to China of outstanding British intellectuals. These activities came to an end, however, in the 1950s as the Council, seen by the new regime as an agent of British imperialism, came under pressure and decided to withdraw.[136] In the 1960s, British-educated Chinese, like others who were judged to have come under too much foreign influence, suffered greatly in the Cultural Revolution. Most of them ceased their professional activities and some lost their lives or left China.

The British Council began activities in Peking again in the 1970s. Today it plays a major part in Sino-British educational relations, fostering visits by scholars and students and promoting the teaching of English in China.[137] A notable contribution to the teaching of English arranged by the British Council was the showing of the BBC language program "Follow Me." It has been repeated many times and watched by an audience estimated at 20 million. Its presenter, Katherine Flower, enjoys star status in China. More Chinese students than ever before are now studying in Britain and a large number of British teachers are employed in China, mostly for language instruction.

Britain's educational influence in the nineteenth century reached China as a by-product of her imperialist role in the region. Missionary educators were present in China as uninvited guests. This fact informed the deep ambivalence of successive generations of Chinese towards foreign educational influence. It has resulted in much waste and human tragedy. Now China is once more interested in learning from other countries and is free to select what educational imports she wants from the rest of the world. This is surely a much better context for effective educational transfers.

4

Borrowing from Japan: China's First Modern Educational System

Hiroshi Abe

Introduction

It was only in the early twentieth century that a modern educational system came into being in China. Strictly speaking, the modern school system was officially established first by the passing of the School Regulations of 1904 (*Zouding xuetang zhangcheng*). In the period between 1904 and the revolution of 1911, nation-wide efforts were made to introduce a school system ranging from the elementary to the university level.

In the process of introducing and developing this first modern educational system in the late Qing, the Chinese regarded the experience of Japan as their model in the modernization of education. They copied Japanese education in all aspects, including the system, its purposes, contents, and methodology.

It is well known that Japan started the project of establishing a modern nation in the Meiji Restoration of 1868. For the purpose of enriching and strengthening Japan as a modern nation, the Meiji Government thought that the spread and development of education was one of the most important measures. Right after the Restoration, in 1871, they established the Ministry of Education to coordinate educational affairs throughout Japan. In the following year, 1872, they promulgated the Education System Regulations (*Gakusei*) to express the basic policy of developing a nation-wide modern school system from elementary school to university. After a period of trial and error, the establishment of the basic modern educational system was assured by the promulagation of various School Regulations (*Gakkorei*) in 1886. These regulations guided the basic structure of Japan's school system before World War II, characterized by the main pattern of elementary school, middle school, and Imperial University, with an additional separate track of normal schools for teacher training. Later the system was enlarged by adding various schools for vocational and specialized education.

Meanwhile, in the process of promoting education, the Ministry of Education placed the greatest importance on making it compulsory. By overcoming many problems such as indifference to school education among the people and the lack of finance, they gradually achieved universal education. The enrollment ratio for four-year compulsory education (elementary education), an average for both boys and girls, grew from 28% in 1873 to 40% in 1878, and then 50% in 1890. By 1902 the percentage surpassed 90%. Compulsory education was extended to six years in 1907.[1]

After China was defeated by Japan in the Sino-Japanese War (1894-95), some leaders realized that the remarkable achievement in developing a modern education system was the basic driving force of Japan's swift national enrichment and strengthening. This recognition stimulated Chinese leaders to start modernizing education on the model of Japan, when Japan gained a victory over Russia in the Russo-Japanese War in 1904-05. In 1905 the Civil Service Examination System, which was the backbone of the traditional educational system, was abolished and a Ministry of Education (*xuebu*) was established, along Japanese lines.

In the process of educational modernization in the late Qing, Japan cooperated with China directly and indirectly. They presented their experiences over the previous 30 years in educational reform as a model through various channels. They sent Japanese teachers to various places in China and supplied textbooks to be translated. Finally, they accepted more than ten thousand students from China.

This paper attempts to examine the ways in which Japan related to and influenced educational reform in China in the late Qing period.

The Establishment of a "Japanese-Style" School System in the Late Qing

The Establishment of Modern Schools

It was after the Second Opium War of 1860 that the Chinese government started to establish modern schools. This was done by pragmatic officials such as Zeng Guofan and Li Hongzhang in order to cope with incursions from the West. Thus they launched the so-called Westernization Movement (*yangwu yundong*), which attempted to strengthen the country by introducing advanced technology and military know-how from Western countries. In order to train personnel required for that purpose, they established various schools: first, the *Tongwenguan* of Beijing in 1862, and then the *Tongwenguan* of Shanghai and of Guangdong, the Fuzhou Navy Yard Training School, the Shanghai School of Engineering, the Tianjin School of Telegraph, the Tianjin Naval Academy, the Guangdong Naval and Military Academy, the Hubei Self-Strengthening School, and others.

These schools, however, were independent of the traditional education system which still led to the Civil Service Examination. They were established by a small group of officials only for the purpose of training experts in translation, mechanical engineering and military science. At that time, as traditional educational institutions, they had the *guozijian* in Beijing and *fuxue, zhouxue, xianxue,* and *shexue* serving as public schools at various levels. In addition, private schools such as *shuyuan* (old-style academies), *yixue, yishu, sishu,* also still existed. However, their function as educational institutions was limited by the Civil Service Examination for employment of government officials, and they were reduced to nothing but preparatory schools for the examinations by the late Qing. Given this situation, the modern schools mentioned above, which were established after the 1860s, did not make any contribution to Chinese educational reform in a broad sense.

A Systematic Introduction of Modern Education

After China lost the Sino-Japanese War of 1894-95, they started to introduce a modern educational system much more energetically. This trend was represented by the movement directed by Kang Youwei, Liang Qichao and others. These leaders were convinced that basic reforms in political, social, and economic systems (*bianfa*) were really needed, not just new technology, in order to enrich and strengthen their country. They made their opinions public through memorials to the throne, newspapers, and magazines. They considered that the wealth and strength of the West is not just due to advanced technology in machinery and weaponry, but to efforts made to enhance academic studies and popular education. They attempted to reform the traditional Civil Service Examination System and the educational system in general, which had been isolated from real life. They tried to establish modern schools in every corner of the country, taking other countries, especially Japan, as models. They also tried to establish academic associations, libraries and newspapers in every locality. Another point of emphasis was to enhance knowledge about the West by translating and introducing foreign publications. In order to develop persons talented in Western learning rapidly, they enthusiastically promoted plans to send students abroad, mainly to Japan. Among leading writings on educational reform of this period, we can find the *Datongshu* by Kang Youwei, the *Bianfa tongyi* by Liang Qichao, and the *Quanxuepian* by Zhang Zhidong.

The proposals made by these reformers were put to practice in the Hundred Day Reform of 1898. The reforms in education included the following measures:

(1) to reform the Civil Examination System, and to abolish ''eight-legged'' essays
(2) to reorganize the *shuyuan* (old-style academies) and Buddhist/Taoist temples of each province into modern schools
(3) to establish elementary schools and middle schools all over the country
(4) to establish an Imperial University in Beijing as a model for modern schools
(5) to establish a National Bureau of Translation
(6) to send students abroad, mainly to Japan

This reform of 1898 failed after only 100 days due to the coup d'état headed by the Empress Dowager. However, it is worth noting here that this was the first attempt at educational reform made by the Qing government in the modern history of China and that the model for reform was Japan.

The Establishment of a Modern School System

After the demise of the Hundred Day Reform, the reactionary policies of the conservatives of the Qing dynasty did not last long. In 1899, the Boxer Uprising occurred and Beijing was occupied by eight allied forces. The Qing Dynasty was forced to conclude a humiliating peace treaty, and to face the reforms which they had avoided two years earlier by means of a coup d'état. Upon request by the government, many high-ranking officials such as Zhang Zhidong (Viceroy of Huguang), Liu Kunyi (Viceroy of Liangjiang), Yuan Shikai (Governor of Shandong), presented their reform proposals. As prerequisites of their reform plans, all of them pointed out the necessity of training personnel. For the quick achievement of that goal, they emphasized the importance of establishing a modern school system, reforming the Civil Service Examination System, translating foreign publications, and sending students abroad, especially to Japan.

Responding to those proposals, the government announced a series of Imperial Ordinances on educational reform from August 1901 to January 1902. The major points of those ordinances were as follows:

(1)   The Reform of the Civil Service Examination System: "Eight-legged" essays will be abolished and replaced by elucidation of the Four Books and Five Classics, discussions of Chinese politics, and dissertations on the politics and arts of foreign countries. Traditional military examinations will be eliminated and military training given at modern schools.

(2)   Sending Students Abroad: Competent young people will be sent abroad by the sponsorship of provinces and employed as officials when they return, after taking a special examination. Also more experienced people will be sent abroad for observation, reflecting suggestions by Zhang Zhidong and others.

(3)   The Transformation of Old Educational Institutions into Modern Schools: All the examination bureaus and old-style academies in the provincial capitals will be made into modern universities. Those of prefectures will become modern middle schools. A number of elementary schools will be set up in each province. The major subjects to be taught at those schools are the Confucian classics, history, science, and Chinese and world politics. In establishing modern schools, the model will be the developments of Shandong province directed by Yuan Shikai.

(4)   The Reopening of the Imperial University of Beijing: The Imperial University of Beijing, closed after the Boxer Uprising, will be reopened as a model at the head of all modern schools.

Zhang Baixi was appointed Minister of Education and President of the Imperial University in January 1902. Zhang started with the preparatory schools, and three years later he worked on colleges. In order to supply necessary personnel promptly, a School of Officials and a Normal School were attached to the university for retraining currently-employed government officials and degree holders. Wu Rulun was appointed Vice President of the university and was sent to Japan to investigate the management and operation of the university and school system in general.

In order to establish a nation-wide system of modern schools, the School Regulations of 1902 (*Qinding xuetang zhangcheng*) were made public in August, based on the proposal of the Minister of Education, Zhang Baixi. In preparing the School Regulations, Zhang referred to those of Japan and other foreign countries. The school system consisted of infant schools, lower primary schools, higher primary schools, middle schools, higher schools, university preparatory schools, and universities. As far as legislation is concerned, this was the first attempt to introduce a modern school system in China. However, due to objections by conservative officials against Zhang Baixi and also due to the defects of the new school system itself, it was never put into practice. Instead, about one year later, in January 1904, new school regulations (*Zouding xuetang zhangcheng*), were prepared and made public by Zhang Baixi, Zhang Zhidong, and Rong Qing.

It was by the promulgation of the School Regulations of 1904 that the modern school system was finally established in China. After this, the government strongly encouraged establishing schools and modern school education spread to all regions. A partial picture of the establishment of modern schools is summarized in Table 4.1.

Table 4.1
The Number of Modern Schools in the Late Qing Period (1909)

	No. of Schools	No. of Students
Primary Schools	51,678	1,532,746
Middle Schools	460	40,468
Vocational Schools	254	16,649
Normal Schools	415	28,572
Universities/Higher Schools	111	20,672

Source: Chen Qitian, *Jindai Zhongguo jiaoyushi* (History of education in modern China), (1969), pp. 134-6, 147-8, 155-7, 164, 176-8.

The Regulations as the Basis of a "Japanese-Style" School System

Although it is officially said that the School Regulations of 1904 were prepared by Zhang Baixi, Zhang Zhidong, and Rong Qing, they were really drafted by Zhang Zhidong alone. The total system consisted of 21 years of education from lower primary to university. These 21 years were grouped into nine years of primary education, five years of middle education, and six to seven years of higher education. The system was completed by adding normal education and vocational education. It is depicted in Figure 4.1.

In addition, we should note that the Minister of Education was assigned, for the first time, as an independent agent to coordinate school affairs over the whole country, a role that used to be held by the President of the Imperial University of Beijing. In the same period as the School Regulations were promulgated, the three reformers proposed to gradually decrease the number of successful candidates in the Civil Service Examination, and this policy led to the abolition of the system in 1905. This contribution should be highly evaluated historically, because the traditional examination system was the most serious obstacle to developing a modern school system in China.

The first and foremost characteristic of the school system represented by these School Regulations is that it was totally modeled after the Japanese system of that time. The similarity of the two systems is apparent in Figures 4.1 and 4.2.

Zhang Zhidong, who prepared the School Regulations of 1904, was the leading person among educational reformers in the late Qing. In 1898, he wrote the famous *Quanxuepian,* in which he advocated the necessity of spreading modern school education in order to enrich and strengthen China, and he suggested that China should establish a school system ranging from primary school to university, modeled after the Japanese system. He also strongly recommended that China send many students to Japan and translate Japanese publications into Chinese. Later, he carried out various modernization projects of education in middle and southern China as viceroy of Liangjiang and Huguang. Among all these projects, the most famous were the new educational institutions opened in Wuchang, Hubei province. In pushing forward these modernization programs in education, he often sent investigators to Japan to study the educational conditions, and sometimes he invited experts as teachers or advisors from Japan. It is most likely that he referred to these materials from Japan when he prepared the School Regulations of 1904.

One such probable source of reference material was the magazine *Jiaoyu shijie* (The World of Education). This magazine was the first magazine of education published in Shanghai in May 1901 by Luo Zhenyu with the assistance of his follower, Wang Guowei. It came out twice a month, a total of 166 issues up till 1908. In the editing of this magazine, Takeo Tsuji, the chief writer of the leading educational magazine in Japan, *Kyouiku Jiron* (Current Opinion on Education) cooperated in all aspects. Actually, Zhang Zhidong and Liu Kunyi were also leading sponsors of *Jiaoyu shijie.*

This magazine included a broad range of articles: reports on foreign educational laws and conditions, educational theory, teaching methods, school administration, textbooks, child psychology, etc. However, especially in the beginning, it featured the translation of books and articles from Japan. For example, from vol. 1 (May 1901) to vol. 18 (February 1902), 84 Japanese educational laws and codes were translated serially. After that, the magazine was also responsible for translating more than 50 textbooks on various subjects, as well as books on education and educational history.[2] From around vol. 40, gradually more importance was placed on American and European education with the introduction of their educational theories, educational history, current educational conditions and educational philosophers.

For the preparation of the School Regulations, another source of information utilized might have been the record of observation of Japanese education, *Dongyou*

Figure 4.1
The Chinese School System of 1904

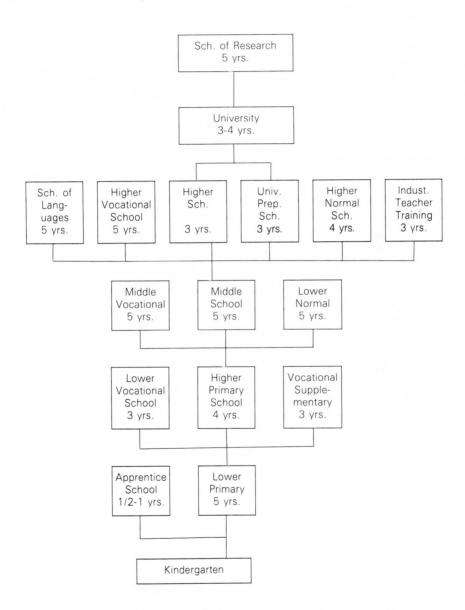

Source: Zhang Zhidong et al. *Zouding xuetang zhangcheng*, 1970, Reprint.

Figure 4.2
The Japanese School System of 1900 (for males)

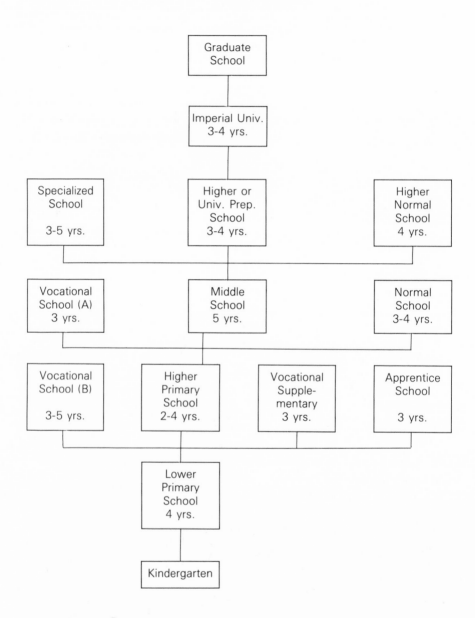

Source: Ministry of Education, Science and Culture, *Japan's Modern Educational System: A History of the First Hundred Years* (1980), pp. 436-437.

conglu, edited by Wu Rulun and published in October 1902. Wu was a prominent scholar and Head Master of Lianchi Academy in Baoding. In 1904, at the urgent request of Minister of Education Zhang Baixi, he took the position of Vice President of the Imperial University of Beijing. On taking office, he traveled to Japan for about four months, starting in June 1902, in order to survey the administration of the university and the educational system in general. During his stay in Japan, he energetically visited various types of schools, government offices, and cultural facilities. At the Ministry of Education, he was given 19 lectures on various subjects such as educational administration, outlines of schools of different levels, school management, teaching methods, school hygiene, school facilities, etc. He also visited many prominent educators including Minister of Education Dairoku Kikuchi, President of Tokyo Imperial University Kenjiro Yamakawa, and Principal of Tokyo Higher Normal School Jigoro Kano. Along with these visitations, he also corresponded with specialists all over Japan in order to exchange opinions on the educational reform in China.

All the information collected during this journey to Japan was precisely recorded, and documents such as statistical data, charts, and rule books were attached. On his return to China, these records were published and favorably received by educators and administrators.

Japan's Influence on Educational Ideas, Contents, and Methods

Japan's influence can be observed not only in the educational system but in educational ideas, course content, and measures to spread education. Zhang Zhidong was one of the opinion leaders advocating the idea of *zhongti xiyong*, that is stressing Chinese learning as the essence (*ti*), and Western Learning for its utility (*yong*).[3] He emphasized that Western learning was necessary for modernizing China, yet should be limited to practical areas; traditional Chinese learning and culture should be respected for their spiritual aspects and values. In education the people's spiritual roots should be firmly fixed in Confucian morality first, then other subjects from Western learning and basic technology should be added to make Chinese people modern. The introductory section to the School Regulations of 1904 (*Xuewu gangyao*) contains the following passage:

> The principle idea in establishing any school is a basis in loyalty and filial piety. In other words, traditional Chinese learning must be the basis of education to form students' character. After that, the importance of Western learning is emphasized to enrich knowledge and to give technical skills to students. . . .[4]

Given this basic idea, the unique Japanese style of education, combining a moral education that emphasized Confucian thought with modern sciences, appeared to be an ideal model for China. For example, Article One of the Elementary School Regulations of 1904 gives the following educational aim:

> . . . Children of seven years of age or older must attend schools for the purpose of enhancing the knowledge necessary in daily life, clarifying ethics, fostering patriotism, as well as physical protection and development.[5]

This was almost an exact copy of that of the Japanese Elementary School Ordinance. The school subjects at the elementary level were also organized with reference to those of Japan, but they were characterized by an even stronger emphasis on Confucian moral education.

These educational aims were clarified in the Decree on Educational Aims, promulgated in 1905 by the Ministry of Education, which stated that education should foster the following five qualities: loyalty to the emperor, reverence for Confucius, dedication to public welfare, admiration for bravery, and utility.

Measures for spreading education were also greatly influenced by those of Japan. As suggested above, educational reformers of the late Qing such as Zhang Zhidong had a common understanding that the driving force in Japan's modernization was the nation-wide spread of education over the past thirty years. They thought that spreading school education to all the nation with Confucian moral education at its core might correspond with the goal of enriching and strengthening China under the Qing dynasty. Thus they expected that the national educational system would be universalized in China after the model of Japan. "It is intended that henceforth universally (without any discrimination of class or sex) in each village there shall be no house without learning, and in each house no individual without learning." This passage in the Elementary School Regulation was taken directly from the Japanese Education System Ordinance of 1872, which was a landmark in Japan's modern educational history. In this Elementary School Regulation, they already promoted the idea of compulsory education, referring to the examples of other nations. In 1907 the Ministry of Education ordered all the provinces to implement compulsory education experimentally for children of seven years of age or older with penalties for parents who violated the regulation.

The establishment of an administrative system for education, headed by the Ministry of Education, was an important step in the nation-wide spread and development of school education. As mentioned before, on the occasion of promulgating of the School Regulations of 1904, a Minister of Education was specially appointed, distinct from the president of the Imperial University. The Ministry of Education was established on the Japanese model in 1905, reflecting the suggestion made by Baoxi, the Shanxi Provincial Director of Education (*xuezheng*), that they needed a central educational administrative organization with specialists as staff members, in order to promote modern education more efficiently. Rong Qing was appointed the Minister of Education.

On the other hand, in more advanced provinces such as Zhili and Hubei, Offices of Provincial Education had already been set up from around 1902 in order to coordinate education in the respective provinces. The Ministry of Education ordered all the provinces to set up Offices of Commissioners of Education (*tixueshisi*) in June 1906 in order to make the nation's education more standardized and efficient. Thus the old offices of provincial education were transformed. On appointing commissioners of education for all 23 provinces, the Ministry of Education sent them to Japan first in order to observe the conditions of school management and educational administration and to exchange opinions with Japanese educators.[6]

In December 1906, the Ministry of Education ordered the commissioners of education to establish Educational Exhorting Offices (*quanxuesuo*) as the lowest units of educational administration in each prefecture. This project was patterned on the experience of Zhili province. In 1904, they had opened Educational Exhorting Offices to establish schools and encourage people to send their children to schools in local areas, and they achieved tremendous success. This method of dividing each prefecture into several school districts, appointing superintendents, and making them work to establish schools and to encourage enrollment was also a reflection of Japan's local educational administration.

Japan's Cooperation in China's Educational Reform in the Late Qing Period

The Activities of Japanese Teachers in China
Under the circumstances described above, modern school education should have spread all over the country in early twentieth century China. In reality, however, there were many difficulties: financial problems such as shortages of funds to establish and run schools and to supply facilities; difficulties in securing and training teachers and school administrators; and a shortage of textbooks to be used in modern schools. Japan played an important role in solving these problems, especially the training of educational personnel and the supplying of textbooks. In this section, I will discuss the way in which Japan cooperated in training educational personnel in the late Qing period, by analyzing the activities of Japanese teachers in various regions in China and the conditions of Chinese students sent to Japan.

In the early twentieth century, when the number of Chinese students sent to Japan reached a peak, many Japanese were invited as educational advisors or teachers to play active roles in various fields of educational administration and school education. There were two ways in which Japanese educators contributed. One was to establish schools by themselves, and the other was to be invited as either teachers or advisors for the schools already established by the Chinese. In both cases, they depended on Japanese human resources in carrying out their modernization project in education based on the Japanese model. From Japan's perspective, there was a sense that Japan and China should cooperate in standing up to the power of the West. There might also have been some people who attempted to make use of this opportunity to send teachers and advisors to China as a strategy to penetrate China. Such an intention is evident in the following passage from the editorial of the leading magazine in education at that time, *Kyoiku Jiron*:

> While they are establishing various types of schools in many regions in China under the Qing dynasty these days, they face urgent problems in the shortage of capable teachers and appropriate textbooks. . . . In order to deal with this situation, they cannot avoid asking for help from foreign countries in supplying teachers. Japan also received requests from China to send teachers,

and now there are a number of cases where negotiation is under way. On this occasion, we should encourage and help them to invite as many Japanese as they wish, so that they can help develop the educational system in China. At the same time, we should make those Japanese introduce our culture to China and expand our power over there. . . ."[7]

According to Keishu Saneto, the number of Japanese who were invited by China to participate in educational programs in various regions surpassed the level of 500 or 600 at its peak in 1905-06.[8] Sakuzo Yoshino who had an experience of teaching at the School of Political Science of Beijing stated that the number of Japanese teachers who were working in China in those days was approxately 500, and he grouped them as follows:

(1)   those engaged in normal education .... about 125
(2)   those engaged in army training .... about 100
(3)   those engaged in general education .... about 95
(4)   those engaged in vocational education .... about 80
(5)   those engaged in law, politics, and economics .... about 45
(6)   those engaged in police education .... about 30
(7)   those engaged in medical education .... about 50
(8)   those engaged in Japanese language education .... about 10

The annual survey conducted by the Ministry of Foreign Affairs of Japan on Japanese people abroad gives us some insight into the situation. Table 4.2 shows the number of Japanese teachers and advisors over the period. A peak was reached between 1904 and 1909, then the number sharply dropped around the revolution of 1911, and did not recover to the peak level again, although engineers and advisors in fields other than education gradually increased again.

The provinces and the type of schools they were assigned to and the subjects they taught in 1909 are summarized in Tables 4.3, 4.4 and 4.5. Geographically, Japanese teachers were distributed to almost all provinces including farthest provinces such as Sichuan, Yunnan and Shaanxi as well as the coastal provinces of Zhili (with the greatest number of 114), Jiangsu, Hubei and Guangdong. They were assigned to all levels (from kindergarten to university) and all types of schools. It should be mentioned that a majority were assigned to normal schools, vocational schools and army academies. In addition to giving administrative assistance, many taught various subjects, especially science and vocational subjects.

Case Studies of Outstanding Japanese Educators in China

From the general picture given of Japanese teachers in China, I now turn to the particular activities of five leading people. The first is Saishi Nakashima, one of the Japanese teachers who played an important role in the early period. He went to China in 1892 to study under Head Master Wu Rulun of Lianchi Academy in Baoding, and then he was asked by Wu to teach Japanese language school, named *Dongwen xueshe (Tobun Gakusha)*, with the support of Wu, and taught general subjects as well as Japanese. At that time, this was the only modern school

Table 4.2
The Number of Japanese Teachers and Advisors Between 1903 & 1918

	1903	1904	1909	1912	1913	1918
Teachers/Educ. Advisors	99	163	424	63	84	36
Other Advisors/Engineers	49	71	125	96	93	394
Total	148	234	549	159	177	430

Source: Ministry of Foreign Affairs, Bureau of State Affairs, ''Shinkoku-kancho-kohei Honpojin Ichiranhyo'' (List of Japanese employed by the Qing government), 1903, 1904, 1909. ''Shinakancho-kohei Honpojinmei-hyo'' (List of Japanese employed by the Chinese government), 1912, 1913, 1918. These documents are in the official records of the Ministry of Foreign Affairs of Japan.

Table 4.3
The Provincial Distribution of Japanese Teachers in the Late Qing (July 1909)

Name of Province	Number of Japanese Teachers
Zhili	114
Hubei	38
Jiangsu	50
Shengjing	19
Sichuan	40
Guangdong	33
Hunan	19
Zhejiang	20
Fujian	12
Shandong	10
Shanxi	10
Guangxi	11
Shaanxi	7
Anhui	7
Jilin	3
Jiangxi	3
Guizhou	3
Yunnan	3
Henan	2
Xinqiang	1
Total	405

Table 4.4
The Distribution of Japanese Teachers According to Types of School

Level/Type of School	Number of Japanese Teachers
Kindergarten	7
Elementary School	26
Middle School	15
Higher/Specialized School	47
University	4
Normal School	105
Vocational School	78
Army Academy	58
Police Academy	13
Medical School	18
Foreign Language School	5
Women's School	5
Others	24
Total	405

Table 4.5
The Distribution of Japanase Teachers by Subject

Responsibility/Subjects	Number of Japanese Teachers
Administration (V.P.)	14
Japanese	16
Science	34
Vocational	39
Law	19
Military Science	10
Fine Art	8
Physical Ed./Music	11
Medical Science	8
Kindergarten Teacher Training	5
History/Geography	5
Mathematics	6
Education	5
Police	3
Handicrafts	2
Psychology	2
General	15
Uncertain	241
Total	443

in Beijing, and it attracted 180 students in the first week after its opening. He divided them into two classes. The specialized class (later called intensive class) was for older people with sufficient knowledge of the Chinese classics to learn Japanese intensively and focus on the translation of Japanese into Chinese. The regular class (later called middle class and teacher training class) was for younger students who were to learn Japanese and general subjects.

The number of students increased to 331 by 1902. They were divided into 17 classes, and 18 teachers taught them. The accumulated number of students in the first four years reached 1,470 and they constituted a considerable portion of educators in the education circles of China.[10] But the school was closed in 1907 due to Nakashima's illness.

Corresponding to the activity by Nakashima in the northern China, the activity of the members of *Toa Dobunkai*, including Kenjiro Kikuchi, in central China, should be mentioned. *Toa Dobunkai* was a private organization, established in 1898 for the purpose of enhancement of mutual understanding and cooperation between China and Japan through cultural exchange. It was first headed by Prince Atsumaro Konoe. As a part of its activities, the *Nanjing Dongwen Shuyuan* (*Dobunshoin*) was established in 1900 to educate both Japanese and Chinese students.

Later, the *Nanjing Dongwen Shuyuan* was moved to Shanghai, and renamed the *Toa Dobunshoin*. Their educational activity in Nanjing was led by Assistant Principal Kenjiro Kikuchi. Trusted by Prince Konoe, he played an important role in supplying educational information and selecting Japanese teachers, in cooperation with Zhang Zhidong who was devoting himself to educational reform in provinces in central China. In 1904, responding to a request by Zhang Zhidong, he went to work in Sanjiang Normal School in Nanjing as Vice President, together with ten Japanese teachers. Thus he assisted in the inauguration of normal education in central China.[11]

Next, we look at two people who played important roles in teacher training and educational administration: Unokichi Hattori, Associate Dean of the Normal School, Imperial University of Beijing; and Ryusei Watanabe, the higher councillor at the Office of Provincial Education (*xuexiaosi*) of Zhili.

As we noted earlier, on the introduction of a modern school system in 1902, the Minister of Education, Zhang Baixi, started by reopening the Imperial University of Beijing with an attached School of Officials and Normal School for intensive education. On that occasion, on request of the Qing government, Unokichi Hattori, an Associate Professor at the Liberal Arts College of Tokyo Imperial University, who specialized in Chinese philosophy, was sent to China as Associate Dean of the Normal School. For seven years he was to play an important role in the middle and higher school teacher training with the assistance of nine Japanese teachers including Tatsuto Ohta (mathematics, physics) and Keijiro Hoki (Japanese, education). In 1904, among 160 students who entered Normal School in the first year, 39 of the best were chosen as candidates to be trained for future college professors. Eight of them were sent to Europe and thirty-one to Japan.[12]

Zhili province was ahead of other areas in modern education in the late Qing period. Viceroy Yuan Shikai established an Office of Provincial Education for the modernization of education in the province. At the request of Yuan, Ryusei Watanabe, President of Tokyo School of Music, and also Professor of Ethics at Tokyo Higher Normal School, took the responsibility of advisor in October 1902 in Zhili province. When he went to China, he was accompanied by ten teachers including Kotaro Sekimoto (chemistry). With their cooperation, he assisted Chinese officials, who did not have any experience in establishing a modern school system. For seven years he helped them in educational administration, in compiling textbooks, in establishing and running schools including Zhili Normal School, and other educational activities.

The Office of Provincial Education, which later became the Office of the Commissioner of Education under the order of the Ministry of Education, was the first modern administrative organization of provincial education in China, and some of its activities were a model for establishing a nation-wide administrative system of education at that time. For example, as mentioned before, the establishment of Educational Exhorting Bureaus (*quanxuesuo*) and school district supervisors (*quanxueyuan*) as the smallest units of provincial educational administration was preceded by experiments and success in Zhili province, and then spread all over the country. Watanabe also took the office of Associate Dean at the Zhili Normal School, and worked in the intensive training of teachers, which was necessary for the rapid spread of elementary school education. In June of 1903, the Normal School was opened, and 600 students entered. Watanabe developed an original approach to teacher training which involved dividing 600 students into four groups, sending each group to local primary schools as teachers for half a year in turn, and also giving them basic knowledge and training in education at the Normal School.[13]

Besides those people, there were many Japanese teachers who played crucial roles in various fields. Among them, it may be worth mentioning the activities of female teachers in founding girls' schools and organizing pre-school education. Here, as an example, we look at the experience of Michie Tono who participated in the project of opening the Hubei Kindergarten.

Hubei Kindergarten was the first one founded by Chinese in Wuchang, the capital of Hubei province in 1904, based on the suggestion made by Zhang Zhidong, viceroy of Huguang. On Zhang's request for cooperation, three female teachers including Michie Tono, a teacher at the Tokyo Woman's Higher Normal School, were chosen. Tono ran Hubei Kindergarten for two years as the director, and she also took a part in founding Wuchang Woman's Normal School. The Hubei Kindergarten regulation, which are presumed to have been drafted on the suggestions of Tono, were almost an exact copy of Japan's Regulations for Kindergarten Nursing and Facilities which had been promulgated in 1899.[14]

The Historical Significance of Japanese Teachers in Chinese Schools in the Late Qing Period
In this way over several years in the late Qing period, a number of Japanese people played significant roles as advisors or teachers. They helped to introduce modern

systems at various administrative levels and educational institutions of various types, including the Imperial University of Beijing. However, their activities did not last long. After the peak of influence in 1905-6, they gradually declined in number. There are several major reasons for this decline.

First, the decline might have been due to the fact that the conditions of education in China, especially the training of educational personnel, had been successful, thanks to intensive training programs both in China and Japan. Thus, Chinese people began to take the place of Japanese in school management and educational administration as well as teaching. It might have been backed by the fact that one of the most popular professions that Chinese students pursued in Japan was normal education.

Secondly, we should point out the fact that the influence of the United States in Chinese education increased greatly and began to take the place of Japan in the early twentieth century. For instance, Protestant missioneries from the United States worked energetically for education by opening Yenching University and other Christian colleges and universities. They gradually took the leadership in higher education in China. The United States also remitted a part of the Boxer Indemnity in 1908, and used the money as a fund to establish Qinghua School and to start an official project to send Chinese students to the United States.

Third, we also have to admit the fact that some Japanese teachers themselves had problems. Some of them went to China to find new jobs after they were excluded from Japanese teaching opportunities in the Textbook Scandal of December 1902. Many educators all over Japan, including prefectural superintendents and principals of normal schools, were accused of bribery in giving favorable treatment to certain textbook publishers. Others also went to China for better payment than Japan.[15] Some were regarded as having personality defects. The wife of Unokichi Hattori, Shigeko, who accompanied her husband and contributed greatly herself to the development of women's education in Beijing, made the following comments on some Japanese teachers in China:

> I have an unpleasant memory of ill-behaved Japanese teachers and frequent fights between them when we were in Beijing. At that time, there were at least five, and sometimes as many as ten, Japanese teachers at each school. It was really a serious problem that those teachers frequently fought in front of Chinese, and therefore, some Japanese supervisors suffered from nervous breakdowns due to these occurences.[16]

Chinese Students in Japan

The significance of sending students to Japan was emphasized in China after their defeat in the Sino-Japanese War. This trend can be clearly seen in the enthusiastic support of some reformists, such as Liang Qichao and Zhang Zhidong, for the translation of Japanese books into Chinese and for sending students to Japan. Zhang suggested the project of sending students to Japan for the following reasons, as explicated in *Quanxuepian*: (1) the geographical closeness enables them to send more students with the same budget; (2) the similarity between China and Japan in customs and habits enables students to get used to the study environment easily; (3) Chinese characters used both in Japanese and Chinese enable students to master the Japanese language easily; (4) the essential parts of Western books have already been chosen and translated into Japanese, and therefore, it is easier to get Western knowledge through Japanese translations.[17] This was the typical viewpoint shared by liberal government officials and intellectuals.

First, 13 Qing government-sponsored students were sent to Japan in 1896. On the request of the Qing government, Jigoro Kano, President of Tokyo Higher Normal School, accepted them and opened an institution for their education, which later developed into the *Kobun Gakuin*, the leading institution for education of Chinese students in the late Meiji period.

During the period of the Hundred Days Reform of 1898, the Qing government had made a plan to send students to Japan, but it was cancelled due to the coup d'état. By that time, however, there were some provincial viceroys and governors that sent students to Japan as their own projects. In order to accept those students, the *Seijo Gakko* for the prepartory education of army students, and the *Nikka Gakudo* for other students were established in Tokyo.

It was during the period of reform under the Empress Dowager after the Boxer Uprising that the Qing government really started the project of sending students to Japan. They regarded this project as an urgent task, parallel to the introduction of a modern school system and the reform of the Civil Service Examination System, in order to secure personnel prior to other reforms. Especially on the promulgation of the School Regulations of 1904, they were to establish modern schools of various levels all over the country. For that purpose, they had to develop not only long-term programs to train educational personnel but more intensive programs to meet the urgent need for modern educators. The reeducation of traditional intellectuals by sending them to Japan as inspectors or students and the invitation of Japanese teachers and advisors were two such programs.

For this purpose, the Qing government ordered viceroys and governors of all the provinces in 1901 to encourage studying abroad sponsored by both public and private funds. The government itself enacted Regulations for Encouragement of Studying Abroad in 1904 and regarded those returnees as *juren, jinshi,* and *hanlin*, titles equivalent to those given to candidates who passed the traditional Civil Service Examination, based on the degrees they received abroad. In addition, they started a special examination in 1905 to recruit government officials from students returned from their studies in foreign countries. In the same year, the Civil Service Examination System was finally abolished, and thus the modern school system was given official recognition as the source of candidates to be trained and recruited as officials by the government. At that time, due to the inadequacy of modern schools in China, studying abroad was expected to provide a substitute. Especially the number of students who went to Japan to study dramatically increased, exceeding by far those going to other nations.

As the the exact number of Chinese students in Japan at that time, different figures are given. According to H. E. King, the number was as great as 591 in 1903, doubled in 1904, reached 2,406 in early 1905, 8,621 in November of that year, 13,000 in the autumn of 1906, and 15,000-17,000 in Tokyo alone in 1907.[18]

Table 4.6
Chinese Students in Japan in the Early Twentieth Century (1906-1919)

Fiscal Year	Number of Students
1906	7,283
1907	6,797
1908	5,216
1909	5,266
1910	3,979
1911	3,328
1912	1,437
1913	
1914	3,796
1915	3,111
1916	2,790
1917	2,891
1918	3,724
1919	3,455

Note: Figures as of the end of May of each year.
Source: Japan, Diplomatic Records, "Zai-honpo Shina-ryugakusei-kankei Zakken: Rikugun-gakusei Kaigun-gakusei-gai no bu" (Concerning Chinese Students in Japan Except for Army/Navy Students), "Zai-honpo Shinkoku-ryugakusei-kankei Zassan: Nikka Gakkai" (Concerning Chinese Students in Japan: Nikka Gakkai).

According to Keishu Saneto, at its peak, the number reached 20,000.[19]

We have to admit, however, that there is no solid evidence for these figures. Fortunately, the writer and his associates had an opportunity to examine the Diplomatic Records of Japan several years ago. On that occasion, we discovered some survey results on Chinese students in Japan, conducted by the Ministry of Foreign Affairs of those days. Judging from the survey results, as shown in Table 4.6, it seems safe to say that even at its peak in 1905-06, the number was between 7,000 and 8,000.

Now we turn to examine the details of Chinese students who studied in Japan in the late Qing period. Tables 4.7 and 4.8 represent the situation in detail in 1907. Approximately 6,797 Chinese students were enrolled in various educational institutions in 1907. Among them, only 363 students (5.3% of all) studied at government schools such as Tokyo Imperial University, and around 6,434 (close to 95%) were enrolled at private schools, especially those in Tokyo including Hosei University and *Kobun Gakuin*. 5,818 students (almost 80%) were enrolled in the 20 major private schools.

The largest and best known school for Chinese students at that time was *Kobun Gakuin* established by Jigoro Kano in 1902. The predecesor *Kobun Gakuin* was the educational institution which Kano started when he first accepted Chinese students, and later it was called *Ekiraku Shoin*, and then in 1902 it was reorganized as a more official school. For the purpose of giving Japanese language training and general education to Chinese students, a major three-year training course was established. However, in response to China's strong request for intensive training, one-year-and-a-half, one-year, eight-month, and six-month courses for intensive teacher training, intensive police training, intensive science/chemistry education, intensive music education, etc., were organized and students were grouped by the provinces of their origin. According to a survey at the end of October of 1906, 1,959 students had already graduated and 1,615 were enrolled at the time. The total number of graduates, by the time the school was closed in 1909, reached 3,810. Among them, the greatest number of graduates were from the intensive teacher training program.[20]

In interesting contrast was an institution which never tried intensive education but stuck to the long-term education of Chinese students, the Chinese Students' Division of Waseda University. Their program consisted of three years in total — one year of preparatory education, and two years of specialized education. According to their original plan, in the first year preparatory course, they were to teach Japanese language and general subjects, and in the following two years, they planned to divide students into three major sections: politics/economics, teacher training and commerce. In reality, however, they only established the teacher training course. The total number of graduates by 1910, when the Chinese students' division was closed, was 1,119.[21]

Jissen Girls' School, where Utako Shimoda worked hard to educate Chinese female students, is also worth mentioning. They opened the Chinese Students' Division in 1903. Although the original program was a two-year course, many students took the one-year intensive teacher training course. Besides they also had the six-month sewing and embroidering course. By 1910 when this division was practically closed, about 200 Chinese students had enrolled in total, and 92 of them graduated with diplomas.[22]

Besides these schools for general students, there were also schools for preparatory education for those who wanted to enter a Military Academy, such as *Seijo Gakko, Shinbu Gakko,* and *Tohin Gakudo.*

As we have observed, the sending of Chinese students to Japan contributed greatly to meeting personnel needs for the modernization of nation and society in face of insufficient modern school places in the early twentieth century in China. However, there were a number of problems associated with it.

First, the quality of education Chinese students received was relatively poor. The kind of education that they received at Japanese institutions was mainly general education of the middle level instead of higher education. In order to promote studying abroad, the Qing government did not require any specific qualifications at the early stage for candidates who intended to study abroad.

In addition, the majority of those students concentrated on intensive training courses. It is a reflection of the expectation of the Qing government which desperately needed qualified people in various fields as quickly as possible.

Table 4.7
Chinese Students Enrolled in Government Schools (1907)

Name of Schools	Number of Students
Tokyo Imperial University	35
Kyoto Imperial University	10
Sapporo University of Agriculture	19
Tokyo Higher Normal School	44
Hiroshima Higher Normal School	2
No. 1 Higher School	31
No. 2 Higher School	5
No. 3 Higher School	13
No. 5 Higher School	3
No. 7 Higher School	6
Morioka Higher Sch. of Agriculture/Forestry	9
Tokyo Higher School of Engineering	73
Kyoto Technical School	2
Osaka Higher School of Engineering	23
Tokyo Higher School of Commerce	41
Tokyo Foreign Language School	15
Tokyo Fine Art School	4
Tokyo Music School	9
Chiba Medical School	18
Nagasaki Medical School	1
Total	363

Therefore, the government hoped that students would take short-term intensive courses of one year or so instead of regular courses. Students also found that studying in Japan might be a good substitute for Civil Service Examinations which would enable them to secure a better job in the government, and it is evident that they did not hesitate to take the chance. Most Japanese educators also thought that intensive education was the most efficient way to teach Chinese at that time. Thus the majority of Chinese students were enrolled in intensive courses and general courses. Classes were conducted with the assistance of interpreters. While this short-term intensive type of education met urgent manpower needs in China at this time, it was far from what might usually be expected from study abroad.

Second, among those private schools which accepted many Chinese students, there were a considerable number of profit-oriented institutions. On accepting Chinese students, the Ministry of Education made "Special Regulations for Foreigners Entering Schools under the Direct Control of the Ministry of Education" in 1900 and 1901. According to these regulations, government schools admitted only those who were recommended by ambassadors, consuls, or other officials. However, it is evident that those schools could not accomodate the surging crowds of Chinese students, and so they let local and private schools share

Table 4.8
Chinese Students Enrolled in Major Private Schools in Tokyo (1907)

Name of School	Number of Students
Hosei University	1,125
Kobun Gakuin	911
Waseda University	820
Keii Gakudo	542
Meiji University	454
Tohin Gakudo	321
Shinbu Gakudo	286
Tokyo Police School	213
Toa Railroad School	165
Iwakura Railroad School	153
Tokyo Dobun Shoin	145
Seijo School	110
Nippon University	109
Chuo University	104
Kensu Gakkan	89
Nippon Physical Ed. Ass., School of Gymnastics	80
Tokyo Railroad School	64
Jissen Women's School	47
Tokyo School of Physics	45
Dojin Medical/Pharmaceutical School	35
Total	5,818

Source: "Zai-honpo Shinkoku-ryugakusei-kankei Zakken" (Concerning Chinese students in Japan except Army/Navy students).

this responsibility. This is the way in which a great number of private schools for this purpose were established in Tokyo.

The educational facilities at these private schools were poor. The period of study was as short as six months, or even three months. There were a number of phony profit-oriented schools, selling an extremely intensive education, and they were criticized by students as *xuedian* or *xueshang* (school businesses). It was for the purpose of extending control over these profit-oriented private schools, and thus improving the Chinese students' education, that the Ministry of Education enacted "Regulations on Public and Private Schools Accepting Chinese Students" in November 1905. These regulations, however, also had an another purpose, responding to the request by the Qing government, to control those students in terms of political movements against the Qing government. Therefore, Chinese students opposed these regulations as "Chinese students' control regulations." Their resistance took the form of school strikes and a mass exodus, which caused a serious international social problem.

The trouble caused by the regulations was settled in 1906. From the Japanese side this problem triggered a concern about the intensive style of education for Chinese students. Some even suggested that this problem was originally caused by intensive education. In addition, they also started to worry about the quality of Chinese students' education in Japan when they realized that the test results of returnees from Japan in the government officials employment examination, which started in 1905 especially for students returned from abroad, were much poorer than those of returnees from Western nations.

On the other hand, the Chinese, backed by the improved educational conditions in China, started to criticize the quality of intensive education in Japan, and many suggested that the government should strictly control the qualifications of candidates planning to go abroad to study. Responding to these criticisms, in August 1906 the Chinese Ministry of Education stopped sending students to intensive courses, and allowed only those who had finished at least a middle school education to study abroad. After this point, the required qualification to take the government officials employment examination was also raised.

Thanks to the changes both in China and Japan, Chinese students' education in Japan was gradually improved. Along with the Student Division of the Chinese Embassy in Japan, 19 schools including Waseda University and *Kobun Gakuin* organized an "Educational Council for Chinese Students Studying in Japan," and agreed to improve the level of Chinese students' education by abolishing intensive courses and extending the period of studies for the general course and teacher training course to three years. In August 1907, the Ministry of Education of Japan and the Chinese government concluded an "Agreement Regarding Special Arrangement with Five Government Schools," in which they decided to accept 165 Chinese-government-sponsored students every year at five government higher/specialized schools including No. 1 Higher School in the following fifteen years. This agreement was put in force immediately, and in the three years up to 1910, 460 Chinese students were admitted by those five schools.[23]

Probably due to those policies for improving the quality of education for Chinese students in Japan, such as eliminating students of intensive courses and restricting the qualifications to study abroad, the number of Chinese students studying in Japan continued declining after the peak of 1906, as shown in Table 4.6. It never recovered the level of its peak period even under Republican China after 1911.

Summary and Conclusion

It is often said that Japanese education was a model for China in their process of educational modernization in the period of the Reform Movement toward the end of the nineteenth century. In practice, however, it was in the beginning of the twentieth century, especially after the promulgation of the School Regulations of 1904, that nation-wide educational reform on the Japanese model was launched. At that time, Chinese leaders believed that wide-spread modern education in Japan since 1872 had been the basis of the rapid modernization of the country. Thus they came to see the necessity of taking Japan's example and spreading modern education. This belief may have been reinforced by Japan's victory over Russia in the Russo-Japanese War in 1905.

For several years after this, they energetically worked for educational reform on the Japanese model in all aspects such as the system, purpose, contents, and methods of education. In this process, the major sources of information probably were *Jiaoyu shijie* by Luo Zhenyu and *Dongyou conglu* by Wu Rulun.

In the educational reform in the early twentieth century, the leading figures were progressive government officials such as Zhang Zhidong and Yuan Shikai. Japan, on the other hand, contributed to it by assisting them through sending Japanese teachers to China and accepting Chinese students to Japan.

At its peak in 1905 to 1906, the number of Japanese teachers working at Chinese schools surpassed the level of 600. Most of them were either teachers or vice presidents, but there were a considerable number of those who became administrative advisors for whole provinces. Saishi Nakashima, Unokichi Hattori, Ryusei Watanabe, Kenjiro Kikuchi, and Michie Tono were all leading educators in this period.

At the same time, education in Japan was regarded as an alternative to their own education which had not sufficiently been modernized, and in the period around 1905 to 1907, as many as 10,000 Chinese students were studying at various schools and universities, such as *Kobun Gakuin,* Hosei University, *Keii Gakudo,* and the Chinese students' section of Waseda University.

It is evident that the educational developments of the late Qing period were greatly assisted by the projects of sending Japanese teachers to Japan and of sending Chinese students to Japan. However, it is also true that those projects were not carried out as well as they might have been. Some Japanese teachers sent to China were not necessarily academically qualified, and some were those who had been expelled after the Textbook Scandal. On the other hand, there were some entirely profit-oriented private schools in Japan which focused on short-term intensive education of foreign students, and therefore, the quality of education at those institutions was not satisfactory. As a result, once the modern educational system was established in China, Japan's role in Chinese education was destined to diminish quickly. The political and social confusion following the revolution of 1911 brought an end to the era of Japan's contribution to Chinese education.

5

Technical Education as a Key to Cultural Cooperation: The Sino-German Experience

by Françoise Kreissler

Introduction

The German presence in China was relatively late in comparison with other western powers. This fact made a permanent mark on Germany's relations with those foreign nations which were regarded as competitors seeking to limit the influence of this late-comer to the Chinese scene. In face of this situation, Germany had to make her presence felt, and one way of presenting herself as a cultured nation both to China and to the other western powers was through model cultural institutions. In contrast to other western nations, from the beginning Germany imposed limits on her cultural activities in China.

However, the German cultural influence in China was not limited to educational establishments. From the second half of the nineteenth century, both German missions and certain Chinese institutions published Chinese translations of German historical, philosophical and technical writings. These publications made possible some understanding of German culture, as well as German science and technology, but gained attention only from the Chinese literati, students and political figures. The German influence in China depended also on other cultural enterprises, which for the most part turned out to be less promising than had been hoped by their promoters. The creation of a succession of Sino-German cultural associations in the first half of the twentieth century, the travelling exhibitions of German books and educational materials, the exchanges of books with Chinese university libraries, the launching of a German journal in the Chinese language were all initiatives taken to channel German culture to China. However, the political and economic motivation behind them meant that they were greeted with indifference by the Chinese. It was only German educational establishments which succeeded in reaching a wide public and thereby becoming an essential factor in German cultural influence on China.

Unlike the British, the Americans and above all the French, Germany could not leave it up to missionaries to take responsibility for educational work in China, since German missionaries did not arrive in China until the mid-nineteenth century. It is true that there were early missionaries from various German states, Jesuits such as Adam Schall von Bell and Protestants such as Karl Friederich Gützlaff, who went to China to spread the Christian faith, but they did not adopt the role of propagating German culture. In the second half of the nineteenth century, some German missionary societies, mainly Protestant, became established in Guangdong province, but they faced great difficulties and made few converts.[1] As for Catholic missions, they came even later and chose to establish their work in Shandong province at the beginning of the 1880s.[2] After the occupation of Jiaozhou in 1897, the Protestant Missions also set up work next to the Catholic missions in Shandong.[3]

For the most part, German missionaries were devoted to their Church rather than the German nation or culture. They were of course representatives of their home country in China, yet their principal task was not to spread the German language and culture. This role was left to German authorities and the institutions established in cooperation with private individuals and associations not attached to missions. In this study, it is the different factors which determined German cultural and educational activity in China that I propose to analyze. The secondary role of the missions, also the tardy development of a unified German nation and its evolution into an imperialist power, together with the slow building up of an infrastructure which made possible a coherent cultural policy, were all determining factors in the German achievements which are discussed in this chapter.

The educational ideas which the Germans sought to transfer to China were largely drawn from pedagogical models which had proven their value in Germany and gained some prestige in the modern West: the *Realschule,* the *Ingenieurschule* and the *Technische Hochschule.* The ideas behind these institutions might be termed in contemporary sociological language "proven values."

Tongji University in Shanghai should be regarded as the principal center for the diffusion of German pedagogical ideas in China. After several decades of isolation, Tongji's German educational tradition has been revived in the post-Cultural Revolution era, giving evidence of the strength of its German roots in spite of the internal crises which it suffered through its development. There is now no doubt that Tongji remains the model of Sino-German cooperation. It is equally true that a just estimation of the value of this exemplary cultural enterprise must take into account the fact that it was only one of the pillars of German cultural activity in China, though it may have been an essential one. The fact that most educational establishments created before the First World War did not survive the war was due largely to the political situation in Germany and China.

After a brief discussion of the Sino-German secondary schools and the higher technical schools, it will be useful to look in greater detail at the evolution of Tongji University as a German educational model. This evolution is strongly linked to Sino-German relations. In a situation after 1918 where Germany was excluded from political and cultural dialogue in the West, it was invited by China to take up once again its activity at Tongji. Germany could thus enjoy the satisfaction of being treated as a partner rather than a conquered nation. Above all, it was the only opportunity afforded to her to escape the intellectual isolation imposed by her western victors.

Sino-German Relations in the Late Nineteenth Century

It is scarcely possible to speak of Sino-German relations before the mid-nineteenth century. Up to that time, in Chinese eyes, the German states were nothing more than an appendage of the all powerful Great Britain. Likewise in China, the Germans, who were very few in number, had an insignificant political influence linked to a German economic presence. Apart from that, in this period the Germans regarded themselves as representatives of such German states as Prussia, Bavaria, Saxony, etc., rather than as German citizens.[4]

In 1861, Prussia, the most powerful of the German states and their leader, signed the Treaty of Tianjin with China, which gave it the political privileges which the other western nations had exacted from China in 1842-44. On the part of the Chinese Empire, this was a first step towards the political recognition of the German state. Only after the Prussian victories over Austria in 1866 and France in 1870-71 did China move from *de jure* to *de facto* recognition of Germany as a political, economic and, above all, a military power, one that was resolved to conquer and to affirm its position among the great powers.

From the creation of the German Reich in 1871, German merchants and missionaries became more numerous in China. Of course the Treaty of Tianjin had not been the beginning of Sino-German economic relations, since there had been regular economic interaction since the eighteenth century. Likewise missionaries from the German states had labored in China before the mid-nineteenth century. Yet from 1861, merchants and missionaries gained the protection of Prussian consular representatives and so a position of strength similar to that of citizens of other western nations. After 1871, Prussia's reputation as a great power, gained through its military success in Europe, opened China to a German penetration that embraced culture, politics, finance and the military.

As a result of the Prussian victory over France, modern German weaponry aroused admiration and a growing interest in China, so much so that in 1871 China acquired her first Krupp canons.[5] Germany was also admitted among the great powers in China's cultural policy. The Peking Languages School (*Tongwenguan*) added the teaching of German to its other foreign languages in 1871.[6] On the other side, it was 1887 before the Institute of Oriental Languages was established in Berlin and the Chinese language was taught to Germans. In 1872, the German Asiatic Bank opened its first branch in Shanghai, and the Administration of Chinese customs, which was under foreign control, appointed some German employees.[7] Throughout the 1870s, the Chinese army called upon German instructors and in 1876 the first Chinese officers went to Germany to complete their military education there.[8] By the end of the nineteenth century, this military influence revealed itself through the recruitment of German teachers to work in certain Chinese military schools. Much as these activities confirmed the prestige of the Prussian army, they remained limited in scope and could not be interpreted as a German hold over military education in China. In the 1870s and 1880s, the German Reich intensified its political and economic relations with the Middle Kingdom and further underlined its status as a great power. But only in the 1890s, several decades after the other western powers, did Germany indulge in political expansionism. This was after the Emperor Wilhelm II had dismissed Bismarck, who had long been reticent to initiate aggressive policies in the Far East. After its official recognition by China the German Reich made considerable and successful efforts to make up for its late arrival in both diplomatic and commercial areas. Its purpose was not to get left behind in the escalation of imperialist aggression which was to be unleashed in the final years of the nineteenth century.[9]

At the end of the Sino-Japanese War (1894-1895), Germany gained concessions in Hankou and Tianjin in exchange for its intervention on the side of France and Russia. Up to this time Germany had had no concessions or leased territories in China. The western powers finally gained agreement from Japan that she would remain with the Liaodong peninsula at this time. Two years later, in 1897, the German Reich annexed Qingdao and the surrounding region by a direct act of aggression, taking as a pretext for the intervention the murder of German missionaries in Shandong. From that time on, Germany had a foothold in China alongside of the other western powers.[10]

The Establishment of a German Cultural Infrastructure

Even though Germany was now one of the great powers of the western world, external cultural policy was not an immediate concern of the German nation, a situation directly linked to the interior administrative structure of the government. The German Constitution of 1871 did not give the central government any power over cultural policy, and education, science and the arts were under the jurisdiction of the individual states making up the Reich. This absence of central political authority over the educational system made it nearly impossible to develop a structured policy of external cultural relations. Aware of this problem, certain leading figures succeeded in getting the state to create an educational fund (*Reichsschulfonds*) controlled by the Ministry of Foreign Affairs and intended to give financial support to the many schools founded outside of Germany as a result of the ground swell of nationalism which had swept over German communities abroad after 1871. Up to the end of the nineteenth century, this was the only support given by the German government to German cultural activity abroad.[11] In addition, it must be remembered that these educational institutions were exclusively for German children in these overseas communities. As for other German scientific and cultural institutions then existing abroad, these were initiated by individual German states, by private organizations and by mission societies. The most influential of the private associations was the Association for Germanness Abroad (*Verein für das Deutschtum im Ausland*).[12]

Only at the turn of the century did the question of an external cultural policy become a matter for parliamentary discussion and debate. By this time German leaders realized that the dissemination of German culture could not be entrusted solely to individual Germans abroad who were given very little government financial assistance. In 1906, the *Schulreferat* was established, a bureau attached to the Justice Department (*Rechtsabteilung*) of the Ministry of Foreign Affairs and responsible for educational matters. This was the first step towards an external cultural policy.[13] From that time the creation of schools and other establishments intended for the local population (*Propagandaschulen*)[14] became more common. Since these schools exercised a cultural influence on the future elite of the country, they gained financial support from German industry which in its turn stood to gain material profit for their efforts.[15] In the case of China, this task was relatively easy since the Chinese government had begun, in this very period, to carry out reforms of the educational system. Early reform efforts were expressed in legislation of 1902 and 1903, but the central control of education was only effectively established in 1905 with the creation of the Ministry of Education (*Xue bu*). The abolition of the imperial examination system in the same year aroused a growing interest in modern schooling among the Chinese, which in effect meant foreign schools and western methods of teaching.[16]

The new regulations gradually introduced by the Ministry of Education concerning the length of schooling at each level and the curriculum were generally followed by the Sino-German schools. With this conformity to Chinese law, the schools and their diplomas were thus given official recognition by the Chinese government, a situation which greatly increased their popularity with the Chinese population.[17]

After the establishment of the Republic in 1911, a modern Ministry of Education (*Jiaoyu bu*) was set up, headed by Cai Yuanpei, a Chinese scholar who had spent some years studying in Germany.[18] He undertook the reorganization of the education system in accordance with republican principles, including the revision of textbooks, the suppression of classical Chinese teaching and the introduction of manual labor into the educative process. These reforms were also implemented in the Sino-German secondary schools.

On the eve of World War I, German cultural policy abroad was the subject of more and more frequent debates in the Reichstag. On the demand of certain deputies, a committee was set up to take stock of the educational institutions abroad and write a memorandum which would guide future lines of foreign cultural policy.[19] However the war brought an end to all governmental projects and the conclusions of the study, in which the authors strongly advocated an expansionist cultural policy, were not made public for several decades.

Only after World War I did the German government set up the institutions necessary to guide a structured cultural policy abroad. With the establishment of the Weimar Republic, the Ministry of Foreign Affairs was reorganized to include a department of culture (*Kulturabteilung*) charged with the task of elaborating and developing German cultural policy abroad.[20] But the government was faced with difficulties as much financial as economic and political. The devaluation of German currency and the payment of reparations further delayed the resumption of foreign cultural activities until the late twenties.

Just as before 1914, part of the cultural activity continued to be carried out by private organizations which were more free of bureaucratic restrictions in their movement than the central government and also less suspect of having a political motivation in the eyes of other nations.[21]

Following this over-view of Sino-German relations and their institutional patterns, I now turn to the development of German technical education in the nineteenth century, then to the educational institutions set up in China through which the Germans proposed to transfer to China the educational experience they had acquired.

Technical Education: A German Pedagogic Model

At the end of the nineteenth century when Germany sought to strengthen her presence in China as one of the great powers, Britain, the United States and France were several decades ahead of her in both political and cultural domains. Aware that she was not in a position to catch up entirely, Germany did not seek to exert cultural influence on the whole of China. Rather she aimed to set up a few schools which should be highly effective. For her cultural program in China, she relied on institutions which would provide technical education, an area where long experience in Germany had been crowned with success. In fact at the end of the nineteenth century Germany was considered the fatherland of technical education in the West. Early in the century Paris had been regarded as the centre of the exact sciences, most notably after the creation of the Ecole Polytechnique in 1794. It was thus in the French capital that the first German scientists had congregated seeking to familiarize themselves with modern scientific ideas. For example, Alexander von Humboldt lived in France for nearly twenty years. Higher level technical education, modern technological thought and the close linking of technical knowledge with the natural sciences and mathematics which were promoted by the Ecole Polytechnique all served as a model for Germany. Between 1827 and 1830 almost all the German states established higher technical institutions called *Polytechnische Schulen*.[22]

Over that period, the polytechnical schools had rather diverse aims; some were to serve commercial trades, others to focus on the technological sciences, and still others remained true to the technical-military aims of the Ecole Polytechnique in Paris. Over the years the curricula of the polytechnical schools were strengthened little by little through the addition of mathematics and natural sciences, with the result that they evolved towards a new type of higher institution, the *Technische Hochschulen*. These succeeded in raising their status to that of the classical universities when, on the centenary of the Berlin Technical School in 1899, the Emperor Wilhelm II gave the right to confer on the students the degree of *doctor-ingenieur*. The efforts made by the *Technische Hochschulen* to acquire the status of universities received the unconditional support of the Association of German Engineers (*Verein der deutschen Ingenieure*), which had been set up in 1856 and saw these schools as a means of gaining greater prestige for the profession of engineering in the public eye.

At the end of the century, when Germany was caught up in the process of mechanization and industrialization and had a great need for qualified engineers, many new *Technische Hochschulen* were founded. German industry, acting in its own interest, contributed substantially to the financing of these institutions. Parallel to them at a lower level were the engineering schools (*Ingenieurschulen*) which had replaced the old polytechnical schools. Thanks to these higher technical institutions and engineering schools, Germany had a system of technical and engineering education which became a model among western countries in the early twentieth century. The success of German industry was widely attributed to these schools.

It is true that the *Technische Hochschulen* were an essential component in Germany's rapid industrialization but the support of the Association for German Engineers and the financial aid given by industry to the schools were equally important in the modernization of the country. There was one further element, the setting up of *Technische Hochschulen* in strategic economic regions. Here their role was not merely to train engineers and technicians but to encourage teachers and students to devote themselves to research oriented towards the industrial needs of the region. This action greatly accelerated the industrialization of the whole country.

Modern technical education aroused the interest of countries not yet well developed technically such as Turkey and China which envisaged setting up similar institutions for the sake of stimulating the modernization of the country. As for the Germans, they saw technical schools as exportable products, all the more valuable, as, sooner or later, their success was to benefit the German economy. It was this rationale that inspired the important financial aid which German industry was prepared to give to technical schools established abroad.

In China there were two main types of German educational institution: Sino-German secondary schools and higher technical schools for university-level training.

Sino-German Secondary Schools

Between 1907 and 1910, a whole series of Sino-German secondary schools were set up, in Hankou and Tianjin in 1907, in Canton and Chengdu in 1909 and in Jinan in 1910. The internal Chinese situation was highly favorable to this development. These schools were conceived as institutions for the teaching of ordinary level subjects in the German language and were exclusively for Chinese pupils. Entrance requirements were either a certificate of graduation from a Chinese primary school or success in passing the school's own entrance examinations. The program covered four to five years of study, providing both a curriculum similar to that of the *Realschule,* where the focus was on modern languages, mathematics and physical sciences, and a Chinese curriculum taught by Chinese teachers and conforming as closely as possible to that of a standard Chinese secondary school (*zhongxuetang, zhongxuexiao*).

The first Sino-German schools did not have their own German teachers but generally had to appeal for assistance to interpreters and officials of the local German consulates. However before long these were replaced by colleagues from Germany with teaching qualifications from a university or normal college. These teachers, who were selected by the Ministry of Foreign Affairs in Berlin, had to do preliminary studies in the Chinese language at the Oriental Institute of the University of Berlin. They thus had the advantage of possessing some basic linguistic knowledge which would help them adapt to the Chinese environment. Nevertheless, the new conditions of work and life required a period of adjustment differing in length for each person. For German teaching methods could not be purely and simply transferred to Chinese schools, without at least partial adaptation to local customs and the local young people. All in all, however, the German teacher succeeded in overcoming the difficulties caused by age disparities, and the differences in family background and educational level of their Chinese pupils.

At the end of their secondary education, most of the pupils face the choice of either seeking work or following further studies. The teaching program was planned to prepare pupils for commercial and industrial occupations. However, above all, these schools were preparatory institutions for the two Sino-German higher schools existing before the war at Qingdao and Shanghai. Only a very few Chinese young people proceeded from these secondary schools to higher study in universities or *Technische Hochschulen* in Germany itself.

The brief existence of the Sino-German secondary schools — less than a decade — and the very rare and terse Chinese comments on them make it difficult to evaluate their significance with any certainty. However, it is possible to give precise figures on the number of Chinese pupils who attended these schools. These are presented in Table 5.1. Though the numbers remained small, they do indicate a growing interest with a considerable increase even in the war years.

The parallel curriculum in German and Chinese offered real advantages to Chinese parents. On the one hand, this double program held definite promise for the professional future of their children, since China was progressively turning towards modernization. In addition, the certificates issued by these schools were officially recognized for the purpose of entrance to Chinese higher institutions. Furthermore the pupils continued to benefit from a Chinese cultural formation. There was no threat of de-culturation, particularly since these were secular schools which excluded all religious teaching. In this matter, the schools conformed to German government regulations which were drafted to avoid all the problems which the religious question had aroused between Chinese and foreign authorities in the past. In order to emphasize their secular character, some of the schools put into their statutes a ban on all religious propagation within the school precincts. By the eve of China's declaration of war on Germany in 1917 all the Sino-German secondary schools had been officially recognized as equivalent

Table 5.1
Number of Pupils at Sino-German Schools, 1910-1917

Year	1910	1914	1917	
Canton	40	80	140	
Chengdu	20	50	70	
Hankou	30	50	60	
Jinan	20	60	70	
Tianjin	70	100	190	
Total	180	340	540	

Source: Schmidt, "Ziele deutscher Schularbeit in China," *China-Archiv,* 3[11], 24 Nov. 1918, p. 466.

to Chinese schools. Although the two countries were officially at war from that time on, the schools did not close down until 1919-1920, when the Germans were forcibly repatriated.

Higher Technical Schools

At the beginning of the century, the German Reich envisaged the creation of three Sino-German higher institutions, in Hankou, Qingdao and Shanghai respectively. I will give only a brief account of the higher technical school of Hankou (*Hankou Zhongde gongxiao*). Its construction was completed in 1917, yet it never opened its doors to Chinese students, not even after the war was over. Although the Hankou school never got beyond the stage of a project, it nevertheless merits some consideration since its conception conformed perfectly to the cultural and economic objectives of Germany in that period. Educational institutions such as the one at Hankou were intended in the long-term to allow German technique to make its mark on an industrialized and modern China.

The Hankou school had as its objectives the formation of Chinese engineers for the steel works of Hanyang (Hubei province), and it was to become a center for technical education for the whole mining region of Daye, Hubei province, one of the main industrializing regions of China. However only in 1933 was the Association for the Far East (*Verein für den Fernen Osten*) able to take possession of its property which had lost most of its value in the meantime. The political conditions of the period, both Chinese and German, were not conducive to the implementation of such a project, and so the Association hastened to sell the property.[23]

The other two higher education projects conceived by the Germans in this period were both realized. The idea of creating a higher institution in Qingdao (*Qingdao tebie gaodeng zhuanmen xuetang*) was that of the German plenipotentiary minister of the period, the Count Rex, who saw in it a means of intensifying German cultural activity in China. As the political and economic capital of the "German colony" in China, Qingdao lent itself very naturally to such a project and might even become "the German cultural center of China."[24] The marine ministry which governed the administered the leased territory of Jiaozhou had entrusted the sinologist Otto Franke with the drawing up of a project which the latter submitted to the German authorities in 1908. Not long after he added to this a memorandum on the foundation of an institution of German education in China. ("Denkschrift betreffend die Einrichtung einer deutschen Lehranstalt für Chinesen in Tsingtao.")[25] In this study Otto Franke underlined the point that such a project could only be envisaged as one of cooperation between China and Germany. In his eyes, it was inconceivable that China should not have a say in administering the institution, especially if one counted on gaining the official recognition of the Chinese Ministry of Education for its graduation certificates. Franke's idea of cooperation with the Chinese evidently aroused the hostility of certain Germans at Qingdao, especially that of Truppel, the governor of Jiaozhou.[26] Yet the irrefutable arguments presented in the memorandum and its general good sense enabled it to carry the day in face of the criticism of those who opposed giving this right of participation to Chinese authorities.

The negotiations between Otto Franke and his Chinese counterpart, Zhang Zhidong, were rapidly completed, as was the signing of a contract between the German representative in Peking and the *Zongli Yamen* (the traditional Chinese ministry of foreign affairs), with the result that the first class started up in the autumn of 1909. The spirit of cooperation between the two sides was very evident in the eighteen articles of the school's statutes which underline, among other things, the joint direction of the school (article 1), a Chinese education parallel to a western formation for all students (article 2) and the nomination by the Chinese government of an inspector to supervise the Chinese teaching (article 14).[27]

Although the institution was called a "higher school," it also included a lower level preparation of six years, corresponding to secondary education. This was followed by preparation for a higher degree in programs that differed in length in accordance with the specialty chosen. These were four higher sections: law and political science (three years); medicine (four years of theoretical study followed by a one-year internship in the German hospital at Qingdao); technological sciences (three to four years) and finally silviculture and agriculture (three years). Higher studies were accessible to students who had not followed the secondary level program at Qingdao on condition that they passed entrance examinations. Although the school only functioned for a brief five years, being closed with the Japanese occupation of Shandong in 1914, it should be considered as a model institution. Its mode of financing, programs of study and whole style of organization are a rare example of cultural cooperation between an imperialist power and China.

Still it is difficult to make any definitive evaluation of this project, due to the brevity of its existence. Only a few students graduated in its five-year history with no medical students able to complete their studies. Yet there was an intellectual dynamism evident in the eagerness to make known the school's activities beyond its doors through public lectures, German language classes for adults and publications, most notable among them several journals.[28] The devotion of the teachers and the enthusiasm of the students give evidence of the undeniable appreciation of this Sino-German educational experience, in spite of the minor personality conflicts which were inevitable.[29]

Tongji University and Sino-German Cooperation

The most important educational institution in Sino-German cultural cooperation was undoubtedly Tongji University in Shanghai. Its evolution over the years is not only proof of the centrality of its role in German cultural activity in China, but also a reflection of the whole history of Sino-German relations.

Its origins go back to the creation of a German hospital for Chinese in Shanghai in 1899 (*Tongji yiyuan*), situated in the international concession [Burkill Road, *Baikelu*].[30] A few years later the Association of German Doctors in Shanghai (*Deutsche Ärztevereinigung*) received a proposal from the Consul General of the time, Knappe, for the creation of a medical school for Chinese students in association with the hospital, a project they embraced with enthusiasm. The organization of the preparatory work and the fund raising were taken in hand by a German committee whose members were people of some stature in German political and intellectual circles (*Ausschuss zur Förderung der deutschen Kulturarbeit in China*).[31] For its part, Tongji hospital promised to set apart some of its premises for the future establishment and made its technical facilities and laboratories available. Finally some German publishers and many specialist firms donated scientific books and medical and surgical instruments to the school.[32]

While preparing the medical school, the committee saw the need also for a German language school (*Dewen zhongxuexiao*) or preparatory school (*yubei xuexiao*) in which students could obtain linguistic training and the elementary scientific knowledge needed for higher specialist study. In this, the objectives and organization of the preparatory school were nearly identical with those of the Sino-German secondary schools, and those of the lower level of the Qingdao school.

The medical school (*Tongji Dewen yixuexiao*), which had two tiers of study, and the language school were opened in 1907, the same year as the secondary schools at Hankou and Tianjin. The two institutions in Shanghai were managed by an administrative council made up of Chinese and German members and each was placed under the leadership of a German director. In the years that followed, Tongji's organization and development was progressively strengthened. In Shanghai, as at Qingdao, these institutions functioned very well and enjoyed an excellent reputation with the local Chinese population. The fact of official Chinese collaboration in their management — a collaboration which went right back to their creation — greatly contributed to this popularity.

German firms and banks wished to profit from this favorable situation. They were aware of the success of the educational institutions and in 1910 they decided to form the Association for the Establishment of German Technical Schools in China (*Vereinigung zur Errichtung deutscher technischer Schulen in China*), an association which set as its objective the establishment of higher technical schools in Shanghai, Hankou, Tianjin and Canton. Due to the good reputation of the medical school among official circles, the press and the German population, the Association succeeded in building up a good financial reserve intended for the various establishments being planned, but in fact used finally for the one in Shanghai. For both practical and financial reasons, as well as organizational ones, the technical school of Shanghai (*Tongji gongke xuexiao*) was linked to the already existing medical school.

From an organizational point of view, each of the establishments kept its autonomy, but they had a language school in common and were managed by the same administrative council. Some engineers who taught in the technical school became members of the council. At the same time the preparatory school was adapted to the needs of the new engineering school which opened in the summer of 1912.[33]

From 1913, with the extension of the French concession, the engineering school, preparatory school and the first level of the medical school, originally all on Chinese territory, now found themselves located within the concession on the rue Lafayette (*Lafeidelu*). The Germans and the French agreed on an arrangement which assured Tongji's autonomy.[34] The outbreak of hostilities in Europe in 1914 did not affect the position of the Sino-German school, except for a brief period of disruption in the summer of 1914 when most of the teachers were called to defend Qingdao against Japanese aggression. A great number of them had to spend the rest of the war period in Japanese prisoner of war camps. This shortage of teachers was compensated in part by the recruitment of members of the German community in Shanghai, and of engineers from German firms who volunteered to replace on short notice the teachers who had gone to Qingdao.[35] Their task was made more difficult by an influx of Chinese students from the higher school of Qingdao, who made their way to the German institutions in Shanghai. But after a period of disturbance, the organization and the teaching returned to normal once again. Work proceeded smoothly until March of 1917 when China declared war on Germany. At this juncture the buildings on rue Lafayette were taken over by the French.

Although China had broken diplomatic relations with Germany, this action on the part of the French caused violent Chinese protests. The Jiangsu Educational Society (*Jiangsu jiaoyuhui*) and certain well known Chinese personalities made the point that China had contributed to the construction of Tongji through Chinese donations, and for this reason it could not be considered solely as German property. German and Chinese teachers as well as students made up their minds to "overcome all difficulties together" (*tongzhou gongji*) and organized the continuation of classes and practical work to this end.[36] Due to the assistance of

Carsun Chang (*Zhang Jiasen*), who intervened with the Chinese authorities, the school obtained the temporary use of two local school buildings.[37]

Sino-German cooperation thus continued at Tongji, although with the two countries at war it was necessary to make some changes in the management of the school. The administrative council was replaced by 1917 by a Tongji committee (*Tongji weiyuanhui*) made up of Chinese members and financed by the Chinese government. From that time on, it was this committee which paid the teachers and bore the current expenses of the institution. On the other hand, it was also the Tongji committee which took charge of all receipts, mainly school fees. The school thus managed to survive financially. Chinese control was reinforced through the appointment of a Chinese director who headed up all three establishments.[38]

Some teachers managed to avoid the forcible repatriation of Germans in 1919 and classes were commenced again in the autumn of that year.[39] Beginning in 1920 the situation improved gradually, with the release of prisoners of war by Japan. Among them were a number of teachers and engineers who took up their places at Tongji once again. For nearly two years the school continued to operate in quarters which it hoped were merely temporary. But the Treaty of Versailles, signed in June of 1919, put an end to these hopes. Article 134 stated that Germany renounced possession of the technical school situated in the French concession which should become the property jointly of the French and the Chinese.[40] The French, who up to then had done no more than occupy the buildings, now decided to set up an educational institution there themselves. In August of 1920 the French doctor, J. J. Matignon, supported the idea in an article appearing in the *Journal de Pékin,* "Why do we delay in using the German medical and technical school in Shanghai?" To illustrate French intentions it is adequate to quote the succinct conclusion of Matignon's article:[41]

> The Treaty of Versailles has given us, quite gratuitously, a splendid instrument, which is entirely relevant to present needs, and has merely been temporarily disrupted.

However article 134 of the Treaty stipulated that the former Tongji property should belong jointly to the French and Chinese governments. The French thus could not take sole jurisdiction over the establishment and exclude the Chinese. This problem was resolved with the creation of a Franco-Chinese Institute of Commerce and Industry under the direction of C. Maybon. This new institution saw itself as a preparatory school for the Université Franco-Chinoise of Lyons. However both the organization of the school and its approach to teaching soon aroused dissatisfaction among Chinese students to the degree that they organized a strike, which the French tried to suppress by using force. The Chinese reaction was to march out of the school en bloc, causing it to close down in 1923.[42]

Although China and Germany were still officially at war, since China had refused to sign the Treaty of Versailles, cultural cooperation continued at Tongji. In order to further strengthen this cooperation, Tongji's director, Ruan Shangjie, who had himself studied at the University of Berlin, travelled to Germany in 1920 in order to renew contact with German industry and solicit material and financial support for the school. This trip proved to be a great success. In March of 1921, still before the May 1921 peace treaty between China and Germany, representatives of the two sides signed an agreement which restored to Germany some right of management over the school and extended to it certain prerogatives, while maintaining Chinese direction over the establishment.[43] The reorganization was carried out in 1922 and 1923.

But soon internal political developments brought further perturbation to the school. The May 30th Incident, with its strong protests against British and Japanese imperialism, led to a temporary cessation of classes, as students participated actively in the demonstrations in Shanghai.[44] But it was the greater internal changes of the year 1927 that affected Tongji most seriously. The coming to power of the Nationalist government meant that Tongji lost the financial support of the provincial government of Jiangsu, which had been so important. This was the most serious crisis since the events of 1917 to 1919. In March of 1927, the Director, Ruan Shangjie, and the Tongji committee gave in their resignation. To this problem was added the question of the financing of the school, a matter which had to await a decision of the new Chinese government. Tongji itself took the initiative in setting up negotiations with the new Minister of Education, Cai Yuanpei. The latter gave his assurance that the school would be maintained with adequate financial support for its work. In August of 1927, Zhang Zhongsu, who had studied in Berlin and Leipzig, was appointed Director by the Nanjing government. From this time, Tongji's financial and administrative difficulties were solved. It was now recognized as a national university (*guoli daxue*) and placed under the direct control of the national Ministry of Education in Nanjing (*Jiaoyu bu*).[45] This was the beginning of a decade in which the university flourished.

In the late twenties, when Tongji became a national university, it already had a good reputation and was highly regarded by Chinese leaders, since its cooperative management with Chinese direction and German participation harmonized with the new ruling that all foreign institutions which wished to be officially recognized must be under Chinese leadership. In the period from 1927 to 1937 Tongji reached its greatest heights. The faculty of technology was particularly successful, and its student body grew constantly. The teaching program emphasized practice as much as theory, in this following the patterns of German engineering schools. This practical emphasis was also expressed in the development of specialist courses for technicians which were very popular with Chinese students. In 1913 a school for apprentices (*Lehrlingsschule, yitu xuexiao*) had been set up and in 1916, one for craftsmen (*Werkmeisterschule, jishu xuexiao*). Another point that gives evidence of the central role Germany played in technical and professional education is the fact that most of the Chinese students who went to Germany chose to study fields for which Tongji was well known (medicine, technological sciences and chemistry).[46]

In the early thirties, the university found itself in a more and more favorable situation, partly due to the good relations between Chiang Kai-shek (Jiang Jieshi) and his German military advisors. The fact that a number of Guomindang leaders sent their children to study at Tongji further enhanced its prestige.[47] Without doubt, the political developments in both countries were favorable to the university in a period of growing national consciousness.

The admiration shown by the Guomindang leaders for Germany's political and economic achievements, while rejecting the racial theses of national socialism, seemed to be based on a certain fascination with German strength in defying the great western powers, also on respect for the disciplined, obedient and hard-working German people. It is these factors which may explain the relatively large number of students who were familiar with Tongji at this period. Table 5.2 shows the growing number of graduates during the 1930s which suggests a considerable increase in students in the late twenties. The total number of students was considerably larger, since quite a number never completed their studies, for one reason or another.

After a decade of prosperity, Tongji faced another political crisis in 1937, which once again brought into question the future of Sino-German cooperation. In 1937, with the outbreak of the Sino-Japanese war, Tongji decided to move to the interior, as did most other Chinese higher institutions. After a long journey through Jiangsu province and Yunnan province, it was finally decided to settle in Li Zhuang, Sichuan province. This series of moves greatly disrupted teaching, but finally in Li Zhuang work and study conditions were arranged which constituted a great improvement.[48] In the course of its travels, Tongji had lost most of its German teachers, although it had been possible to replace some of them through hiring local German teachers for longer or shorter periods, as well as Chinese students who had returned from study in Germany and some of Tongji's own graduates. Even though the university was no longer an institution in which Germany exercised a preponderant influence over teaching content and methods, the Germans living in China, most notably the engineers, insisted on the necessity of keeping their contacts with Tongji. In their view, if the Germans could preserve the good reputation enjoyed by their technical education, they could, over the long term, continue to influence Chinese technical education and thereby Chinese industry, possibly even the whole economy of China.[49]

With the return to Shanghai in 1946, a new phase in Tongji's history began, one in which the German tradition continued, although the Germans themselves were less and less involved. After the establishment of the People's Republic, Tongji gradually "forgot" its German past. Only in the late 1970s did it take up once again the role of a center of Sino-German cultural cooperation in the area of science and technology. In spite of the long intermission, the German side immediately resumed the role it had had so many years earlier, though of course there had been fundamental social and political changes in China since 1949. The engineering and technological sciences remain the most important fields at Tongji. The historical continuity is also reflected in the large number of Chinese choosing to study the applied sciences in West German universities.[50] For its part, the Federal Republic of Germany, whose economy is essentially oriented towards exports, is perfectly aware of the fact that its assistance and contribution to the formation of Chinese technicians and engineers are a further asset in the favorable economic relations it has with China.[51]

Table 5.2
Number of Graduates of Tongji University 1912-1949

Year	Medical School	Engineering School	Total
1912	3		3
1913			
1914	6		6
1915	12		12
1916	16	13	29
1917	6	5	11
1918		11	11
1919	7	29	36
1920	19	16	35
1921	12	18	30
1922	11	15	26
1923	11	29	40
1924	14	13	27
1925	18	20	38
1926	23		23
1927	18	18	36
1928	9		9
1929	8	10	18
1930	15	21	36
1931	20	7	27
1932	34	8	42
1933	31	8	39
1934		14	14
1935	46	1	57
1936	32	15	47
1937	28	34	62
1938	33	27	60
1939	30	73	103
1940	40	53	93
1941	37	53	90
1942	43	77	120
1943	30	92	122
1944	34	105	139
1945	45	106	151
1946	32	56	88
1947	35	119	154
1948	45	142	187
1949	84	146	230
Total	887	1364	2251

Source: Guoli Tongji daxue biye jiniankan (Yearbook of the graduates of National Tongji University) (Shanghai, 1950), pp. 393-400. (Graduates of the School of Languages and the School of Apprenticeship are not included.)

6

Catholics and Socialists: The Paradox of French Educational Interaction with China

Ruth Hayhoe

Introduction

In 1903 a remarkable little book was published under the title of *The Educational Conquest of the Far East*. Quite unblushingly, its author opened with the remarks, "The methods of campaign employed by the West against the East may be briefly described as conquest by arms, by machines, by church and by school. It is with the conquest of ideas, of mind over mind, that we have to do."[1] In this chapter I will analyze the influence of French educational ideas on China, both those that were introduced by Catholic missionaries as part of the battle for the minds and souls of the Chinese, and those that were consciously selected from the secular and socialist currents of French experience by Chinese educators of the early twentieth century.

An analysis of the transfer of educational ideas from one culture to another immediately raises fundamental issues of the nature of social change. The researcher examining the *impact* of the West on China in the nineteenth and twentieth centuries has to face the question of whether this was definitive for China's subsequent development, or whether it was marginal to processes of social change engendered from within a Chinese historical process. While finding a diffusionist view of social change deeply appealing,[2] my own research has led me to regard internal change processes as primary. The task of research then requires sensitivity to these processes as a basis for the analysis of how external ideas, institutional patterns, and political and economic interventions contributed to them.[3] Did they combine with reactionary aspects of Chinese culture or society to inhibit the flow of change, did they sharpen contradictions that hastened the change process, or indeed did they strengthen progressive ideas and movements already afoot?

This affirmation of the primacy of the internal historical process harmonizes with classical Marxist notions of historical progress, and with Mao's robust insistence on the explication of China's weaknesses and problems primarily from within and his challenge to the Chinese people to stand up and take conscious control of their historical destiny. Marxist periodization, however, presents many problems for the historian of modern China. The remarkable series of policy swings in the three post-Liberation decades, all justified by the use of Marxist-Leninist-Mao Zedong Thought in differing ways, gives some evidence of the elusive and slippery connections between Chinese social development and China's official ideology. My own position is that of the agnostic, or at most the neophyte, not yet skilled enough in the doctrine to find it a useful and illuminating tool of analysis.

I prefer to stay with the simpler, less universal and more Chinese view of social change expressed in Sun Yat-sen's *Three Principles of the People,*[4] affirmed at a certain level in Mao's *On New Democracy*[5] and apparently underlying Chinese policies in the post-1978 period, which are more pragmatic and piecemeal than coherently Marxist or Maoist.[6] The three lines of change which Sun identified, without postulating their inter-relations, were economic development, democratization and a consciously fostered spirit of nationalism. The role of education in providing the skills needed for economic development has been recognized in Chinese government educational policy since the late nineteenth century. Democratization in the Chinese context, where traditionally the links between knowledge and power were so strong, has meant as much the access of the people to knowledge, as their access to power. But what kinds of knowledge are the people to gain access to and what sort of role are intellectuals to play in a democratization process? These have been vital questions, dramatized by the red-expert debates in the post-1949 period. Finally, nationalism, the creation of a collective consciousness of modern nationhood, of China as a responsible member of the community of nations, represents a crucial aspect of social change in which education and knowledge have also been of key importance.

Given these three general lines of change, and the way in which education is implicated in each of them, the central questions of this chapter can be sketched out. What, if anything, did French educational ideas and patterns contribute to China's economic development? How far did they facilitate or inhibit the democratization process in the kinds of knowledge they offered access to? To what extent did they support the inculcation of a spirit of nationalism?

Four main chapter sections will be used to address these questions. First, a historical overview of French-Chinese political and diplomatic relations in the nineteenth and twentieth centuries sets the context in which educational transfer took place. Secondly, the two main channels whereby French educational ideas and patterns were introduced to China will be considered. The central paradox of the chapter lies in the contrast between these two channels. While the French missionary movement was dedicated to forms of education that would preserve the Chinese from contact with the atheistic and revolutionary ideas that had infected modern France, French socialists and radicals responded warmly to the initiatives of Chinese progressive educators who were interested precisely in the success of France's secular post-revolution education system.

After this discussion on the channels of educational transfer, I turn to the specific educational ideas and institutional structures that were found attractive by various actors in the transfer process. Finally, the outcomes of transfer are considered. Which of the ideas and patterns have found a place in the modern Chinese education system and to what effect?

It remains in this introduction to say a few words about sources. For the broad lines of argument, the various secondary sources drawn upon offer a general literature review. For more specific and detailed illustration of certain aspects of the argument, I draw upon journal series that give insight into the way in which educational ideas were transferred from France to China. The journal of the Université l'Aurore reveals the views of members of a French Catholic university in China, while the journal of the Université Franco-Chinoise expresses concretely the intellectual cooperation and flow of ideas between French and Chinese thinkers who prided themselves on their socialist orientation. French missionary journals such as *Relations de Chine* and *Missions de Chine* indicate more generally the way in which French missionaries viewed the educational aspects of their mission, while progressive Chinese educational journals such as *Jiaoyu zazhi* and *Xin jiaoyu* give hints of what attracted Chinese educators in the French experience.

Sino-French Political and Diplomatic Relations

The period in which French educational ideas and patterns had their strongest currency and made some contribution to the establishment of a modern Chinese education system lies between the 1911 revolution and the outbreak of the Sino-Japanese War in 1937. Cai Yuanpei, briefly Minister of Education and author of a great deal of educational legislation in 1912, was deeply influenced by French, as well as German, educational ideas. The May Fourth Movement of 1919 opened the door wide for the intellectual exploration of ''modern'' forms of education, and French influence had its share along with dominant American ideas in the educational experimentation of the twenties. With the establishment of the Nationalist government in 1927-28, French educational influences were again felt through French-returned educators and a League of Nations Mission of Educational Experts invited to advise on reform by the Chinese government in 1931. The outbreak of war in 1937 precluded further significant educational innovation, yet the resilience of the Nationalist education system and its contribution under war-time conditions suggest that it may have been one of the more effective of the modern social institutions created under this regime.

In this brief sketch of the political and diplomatic context, however, we must go back in history to look at the roots of the French interest in China, as these had considerable importance for the early introduction of French educational ideas into China. French government support for Catholic missions abroad started in the seventeenth century, when Louis the XIVth gave direct support to the formation of the Société des Missions Etrangères in Paris in 1662,[7] and French missionaries were seen as much as emissaries of French culture as of Catholicism. Louis XIVth was also directly behind the sending of French Jesuits to the court in Peking. The first Christian Church there, built in 1699, gained his support as well as that of the Chinese Emperor.[8]

The eighteenth century saw a growing French cultural and religious influence in such South East Asian regions as Cochin-China, Siam, Cambodia and Tongking, with French government support only briefly diverted by the French Revolution and the anti-religious currents of the time. Napoleon clearly saw the value of religious missions for enhancing French prestige abroad, and was prepared to allocate 25,000 francs to support the sending of French Lazarists to Peking in 1805.[9] Throughout the nineteenth century, periods of conservatism in French politics saw a strong policy of French government support for Catholic missions abroad, which was not reversed under more progressive regimes. While France had no commercial interests of importance to defend in the Far East, the period of 1830 to 1870 saw the negotiation of a whole series of treaties with the Chinese for the protection of not only French but all Catholic missionary activities on Chinese soil. This French protectorate gave France the opportunity to enhance her international prestige, free from the constraints of the vital commercial interests which led the British to give a far more grudging support to their missionaries on Chinese soil.[10]

Only with the Sino-French War of 1884-85 and the French colonization of Tongking did French commercial interests begin to play a role in diplomatic relations with China, and these naturally focused on the southern provinces, particularly Yunnan, where France developed railway interests. The acquisition of the French concession in Shanghai in 1849 by M. Montigny, one of the strongest diplomatic supporters of French missions, later proved of considerable economic and political importance,[11] as did the other advantages the French gained in the treaty ports. However, it was considerations of political prestige rather than economic benefit which dominated France's diplomatic relations with China, and the protection offered to missionaries made possible the penetration of some aspects of French education and culture throughout the Chinese Empire. One measure of French Catholic influence can be seen in the fact that 850 of the 1,500 Catholic priests in China in 1914 were French, although the Protectorate had formally ended with the French Separation Act of 1905.[12] The First World War was to greatly weaken the French missionary presence, however, and a papal edict of 1922 led to the reorganization of the Society for the Propagation of the Faith that moved its center from Paris to Rome and reduced French influence. Up till that time, however, Catholic education in China had been a major channel for certain patterns of the French educational tradition. The next section of this chapter will examine its extent and influence.

Other aspects of French-Chinese diplomatic relations that should be kept in mind are the French involvement in the imposition of the Boxer Indemnity on the Chinese in 1900, and some covert French support for Sun Yat-sen's revolutionary activities in Canton, which was clearly linked to French interests in the region.[13] The French victory in World War I enabled France to hold on to most of her privileges in China, while the defeated European nations had relinquished theirs, as had post-revolution Russia. Along with the British, the French insisted that the abolition of extra-territoriality and the unequal treaties must be preceded by the Nationalist government's success in establishing a modern legal system. In fact it was not until 1943 that these privileges were fully relinquished.[14]

French Missionaries and China's Modernization

The four major missionary societies responsible for transmitting French culture to China were the Jesuits, the Lazarists, the Société des Missions Etrangères de Paris, and, to a lesser degree, the Franciscans. The celebrated presence of Jesuits at the Imperial Court from the late sixteenth century became a channel for French influence in the late seventeenth and early eighteenth centuries, when French dominance in Europe was reflected by a considerable strengthening of the number of French participants in the mission.[15] The importance of education, however, was far outshone by the mathematical and scientific studies of these Jesuits. With the dissolution of the Society of Jesus in 1733, the era in which Catholic missionary efforts in China were marked by outstanding works of scholarship passed, never to return with the same lustre even after the restoration of the Jesuits in the nineteenth century.

A decade after the Jesuits were forced to vacate China, the Peking Mission was committed to the French Lazarists, a congregation of secular priests whose primary commitment to the service of the neglected poor marked them as an order with a very different orientation from that of the Jesuits. The first Lazarist priest had come to China in 1692 and, by the end of the eighteenth century, Lazarist missionaries were active in the provinces of Henan, Jiangxi, Jiangsu, Anhui, Zhejiang and Mongolia. With this new responsibility for Zhili (now Hebei province) and the capital, their efforts were somewhat diluted, but in the 1840s and 1850s the recruitment of 52 French and Chinese priests added to their strength. By the end of the nineteenth century, there were a total of 122 Lazarist priests, 41 of them Chinese, working in six *vicariates apostoliques*.[16]

The Société des Missions Etrangères dated back to the year 1653, when a group of young men at the University of Paris joined in a concern for foreign missions and by 1663 had gained ecclesiastical permission for the formation of a seminary dedicated to the purpose of converting infidels in foreign states. The Society was officially established in 1700 as a society of secular clergy more suited to parochial mission work than the great dominating orders of the day. In 1699 one of their number, Leblanc, was made *vicar apostolique* of Yunnan, and in the eighteenth and nineteenth centuries the Society gradually gained exclusive responsibility for the provinces of Yunnan, Sichuan, Guizhou and Tibet, Guangxi, Guangdong and Hainan Island. By 1900 there were around 190 French priests and 98 Chinese priests working in these areas under the society.[17]

The fourth mission society, the Franciscans, drew its members not only from France but also from Italy, Spain, Holland, Belgium and Germany. Over the nineteenth century, the Franciscans took responsibility for the provinces of Shandong, Shanxi, Shaanxi, Hubei and Hunan.[18]

Table 6.1 indicates the extent of the educational influence of these four societies in terms of the schools and students under their care. The figures for the first three are drawn from Piolet's great study, fittingly titled *La France en dehors*, and represent the situation approximately in the year 1900. Figures for Franciscan educational efforts, drawn from Chardin, reflect the status quo in 1914.

What was the nature of these missionary schools and what contribution did they make to social change in nineteenth century China? I first consider broad aspects of this educational activity, then more specifically the Jesuit Mission and its leadership in initiating new roles for Catholic education in the early twentieth century.

By far the majority of French Catholic schools were primary schools, separately organized for boys and girls, catering mainly to the children of Chinese Catholics. Their purpose was to teach the children to read and write so that they could understand the catechism and receive a solid religious education. A certain amount of material from the Chinese classics was also used in the curriculum, and prob-

Table 6.1
French Missionary Schools and Students in China c.1900

| Society | Provinces | Schools (Students) | | College | Seminary | Date |
		Primary	Normal/ Prof.			
Lazarists	Zhili, Zhejiang, Jiangxi	502(9,818)	8(149)	12(483)	13(284)	1900
Jesuits	Jiangsu, Anhui, Zhili	940(23,563)	?	?	?(42)	1900
Missions Etrangères	Sichuan, Guizhou, Yunnan, Guangdong Guangxi	922(12,755)	11(191)	4(233)	12(366)	1900
Franciscans	Shandong, Shanxi, Shaanxi, Hubei, Hunan	772(21,411)	?	4(69)	?(399)	1914
Total		3,136 (67,547)	19(340)	20(785)	25(1,091)	

ably simple mathematics. But no foreign language was taught and there is little evidence of any effort to introduce "modern" knowledge. Most of the higher schools had specific purposes related to the needs of the church for a submissive and dedicated membership. Separate male and female normal schools prepared teachers to teach in the primary schools, while lower and higher seminaries formed catechists and Chinese priests for work in the church.

The only institutions which related directly to the economic needs of Chinese society were the professional schools, teaching vocational subjects related to agriculture and simple industry. Of these there were very few, but they were supplemented by workshops which provided some informal education. Other institutions which had a social vision beyond local church needs and which taught the French language were the colleges. They were patterned after the French *lycée* and offered a simplified form of the classical curriculum found in France. While they were clearly the vehicles of foreign knowledge, it is questionable whether this could be called "modern" knowledge.[19]

There was some disagreement among the missionaries over the utility of teaching French even at the college level, and the small number of colleges developed by the Paris Society was explained by the fact that this knowledge was largely useless in the broad expanses of south and southwest China, where French was little spoken. While they admitted the work might be premature, missionaries nevertheless justified the need for a few colleges "pour la religion et la patrie." "La langue est le canal des idées, le francais facilitera l'étude du Catholicisme, ceux qui l'apprendront resteront nos amis et, bon gré mal gré, se rapprochement de la vraie foi."[20] In the higher seminaries for the training of priests, French was also used along with Latin and Greek for a full theological and philosophical education. Again it was an education that related more to European scholasticism than to "modern" currents of French thought.

French missionary education thus contributed more to the forces of reaction and the preservation of the imperial order than to the currents of change already in evidence in the nineteenth century. In startling contrast to the work of such Protestant missionaries as Timothy Richard, John Fryer and W. A. P. Martin,[21] there was little concern for exposing the Chinese to an understanding of western science, or of western political and social thought. Such research as was done under the Jesuits was intended for the use of an elite, and not disseminated through educational work. The knowledge which was made widely available supported the hierarchical patterns of imperial society and reaffirmed the subservience of those Chinese people who had been touched by the Catholic faith. Catholic missionaries were proud of the fact that they, unlike the Protestants, had never had the slightest sympathy for the Taipings,[22] and through the French protectorate they contrived to hold positions of power and authority parallel to those of the Chinese bureaucracy. They dressed like the mandarins, and created a sense of imperial authority and splendor in the style and location of their buildings,[23] thus sustaining in China an ecclesiastical power structure already seriously eroded in France. A Chinese imperial rescript of 1899, designed to annul the French protectorate and strengthen the authority of provincial officials in face of Catholic power, laid down rules which actually confirmed the parallel nature of the French *imperium in imperio*, already specified in the treaties of 1858 and 1860. Bishops were to relate to Chinese viceroys and governors, provincials to provincial treasurers, *taotais* or judges, all priests to prefects and district magistrates.[24]

Naturally French missionaries did not want to see the dissolution of a system which served them so well. The backing of the French government enabled them to ensure maximum benefit for the Church from the Chinese imperial system. The way in which Chinese Catholics were encouraged to a submissive reliance on two forms of imperialism, internal and external, comes across in the following passage: "La France protège des sujets de l'Empereur de Chine, qui tous connaissent le nom des Francais et savent l'existence, de l'autre côté de leur terre, d'un grand peuple qui leur a conquis par les armes la liberté religieuse, qui veille sur eux de loin. . . ."[25]

The early twentieth century saw some changes in emphasis in French missionary education which represented a modest adjustment to the now explosive currents of change in Chinese society. The need for a strong Catholic contribution to secondary and higher education was felt, and the hierarchical style in which its development was envisaged in 1914 illustrates the continuing dominance of the French influence. In that year "a program was outlined which contemplated the establishment of a primary school in each head station, a higher school in each mission district, a secondary and normal school in each *vicariate* and the formation of a Catholic university for the entire country."[26] The fact that there was some discussion over what European language should predominate and whether there should be several universities using different European language mediums indicates the already reduced status of France within the Catholic missionary movement, which the First World War was to erode even further. When Furen University was finally opened in 1925, under a Papal Charter, English was the main language of instruction and American Benedictines were responsible for its work, reflecting both the impact of American wealth and the currency of American educational ideas in China of the twenties.[27]

However, it may be of interest at this point to look more closely at developments within French Jesuit education in the provinces of Jiangsu and Zhili (Hebei), which represented certain forward trends in French missionary influence. More by good luck than by their own vision or foresight, the Jesuits opened one of the earliest modern universities in 1903, l'Université l'Aurore, which they described alternately as a French or a Catholic university in China. This stimulated the development of secondary colleges emphasizing the teaching of French which acted as feeder schools to Aurore. In 1923 they opened a second higher institution, the Ecole des Hautes Etudes Commerciales et Industrielles in Tianjin, an institution patterned after the French *grande école* and consciously designed to serve the modernization of Chinese industry and commerce.[28] In addition to the continuing Catholic orientation of this educational influence, certain features of the French higher education tradition can be traced in these efforts: the excellence of modern French professional education on the one hand, and the institutionalized separation of teaching and research on the other.

L'Aurore and Its Influence

When the Jesuits returned to China in 1837, at the invitation of Chinese Catholics in the Kiangnan region (Jiangsu and Anhui provinces),[29] a part of their mission was once again works of scholarship, including natural history, centering in the Musée Heude,[30] astronomy and meterology. They also developed a magnificent library. Yet this commitment to scholarly research was not combined with a vision of higher education beyond that provided in the secondary colleges such as Le Collège St Ignace, founded in 1852, and the seminaries which offered a very high level of intellectual training for priests. The vision of a "new style university that would keep pace with western universities" had come not from the French Jesuits but from a Chinese ex-Jesuit, Ma Xiangbo.[31] In his travels abroad in service of the Chinese modernizers of the late nineteenth century he had visited Oxbridge, the University of Paris and certain distinguished American universities. He had concluded that these institutions were responsible for the prosperity of the West. With the vision of a modern institution which would teach "European sciences" in mind, he had provided the endowment for Aurore, giving his considerable family properties to the Jesuits in 1900.[32]

The Jesuits, for their part, saw this new project as an opportunity for Catholics to compete with the growing number of Protestant and secular higher institutions throughout China.[33] Convinced of the superiority of both Catholic and French educational traditions, they dedicated themselves to creating a French Catholic university on Chinese soil. This would enable them to offer to talented young Chinese the best French education while preserving them from exposure to the atheistic and socialist ideas that had infected modern France.[34]

L'Aurore (Zhendan) opened its doors in 1903, fittingly located in the Jesuit Observatory in Xu Jia Hui (Zi-ka-wei), with its links to the scholarly work of the seventeenth century Jesuits and Ricci's famous convert, Xu Guangqi. Within less than two years, however, irreconcilable differences between Ma Xiangbo's rather progressive, student-oriented approach to higher education and the highly authoritarian Jesuit approach created a "student storm" in which Ma and most of the students walked out. In 1905 they created Fudan University, a revolutionized Aurore, which became one of China's earliest patriotic universities.[35] Still in possession of Ma's large endowment, the French fathers proceeded to develop the original Aurore into a university of some distinction.

The structure and curriculum were modelled very closely on the French with a three year *cours préparatoire* leading to a *baccalauréat* degree, followed by a three year *cours supérieur* in two sections, leading to the *licence-ès-lettres* and the *licence-ès-sciences*. By 1908 about 242 students were following these courses. In 1914 medicine was added as a third section to the *cours supérieur* and *lettres* was expanded to become *lettres-droit*. The latter gradually expanded into a strong law faculty with a *section juridique* and a *section politique et économique*, offering a formation up to the level of the French *doctorat* in these two areas. Letters and philosophy, however, were confined to the *cours préparatoire* and to the provision of "liberal" courses within the professional faculties. Medicine became a highly distinguished faculty and added dentistry in 1933. The faculty of science and engineering was created in 1914 and grew to embrace the four departments of mathematics, civil engineering, electrical and mechanical engineering and chemical engineering.[36]

Student numbers grew from 242 in 1908 to 400 in 1923, 672 in 1936[37] and 1,064 in 1939, 549 at the preparatory level, 381 in the three faculties, 52 in the school of nursing attached to the Guangci Hospital, and 82 in the faculty of letters established for women in 1937.[38] The foreign staff in 1935 included 50 French personnel, 1 English and 1 Swiss, of them 24 being Jesuit priests. There were in addition about 48 Chinese staff members.[39] In accordance with Nationalist regulations, administration was formally under Chinese control with a Chinese rector and a predominant number of Chinese on the Board of Governors. Yet it was an open secret that all real power was in Jesuit hands.[40]

Student numbers make it clear that this was intended as an elite institution, preparing a small number of highly qualified people for positions of leadership in Chinese society. They in turn were selected from an elite group who had found their way into the various feeder secondary schools, either those run by French missionaries in Shanghai, Songjiang, Suzhou, Yangzhou and Nanjing, or the French language secondary schools run by French authorities in the various concessions.[41] Graduates in medicine were assured posts in various Catholic medical institutions throughout the country, while law graduates increasingly found their way into high positions in the Nationalist bureaucracy. Aurore students were used as interpreters by the Nationalist government when they called in high level French consultants in establishing a legal system in the early thirties.[42] By 1936, Aurore staff could boast of 70 graduates in the National government, two of them ministers (the Minister of Education and the Vice-Minister of Justice), and a large number in middle-echelon positions, especially in the Ministry of Foreign Affairs.[43] It was probably the engineering graduates facing the economic crises of the thirties who fared worst, but they often found posts in French dominated construction interests such as railways or civil works in the concessions.

If we reflect on this brief sketch of Aurore's development, it is evident that the university represented a truly French conception of service to modernization. Economic development was to be served by the creation of an elite corps of highly trained engineers and modern administrators such as were produced in the French *grandes écoles*. Democratization or the access of the people to knowledge was to be limited to the few who could benefit from highly sophisticated professional knowledge in key areas, and use this in service of both rulers and the masses.

As for the conception of China as a modern nation, participating in the world community of nations, it was here that the Aurore ethos proved most distasteful to the Chinese. If the explicit elitism and hierarchical assumptions of Aurore's service to economic and political modernization might be seen as Confucian patterns turned to modern uses, and thus attractive to some Chinese leaders, Aurore's evident insensitivity to Chinese nationalist concerns was offensive to almost all actors in China's modernization process. Its role as a mediator of French legal influence on the modern Chinese legal system directly served the French imperialist insistence on an "acceptable" modern Chinese legal system being established before French privileges should be relinquished. Even more offensive was the attitude of French Jesuit priests to student participation in all of the patriotic movements, from the student storm of 1905, through the May Fourth Movement, to student involvement in effective anti-Japanese activities in the twenties and thirties.[44] The fact that Aurore stayed in Shanghai during the War and welcomed such visitors as the French Ambassador, M. Cosme, a Vichyist who kept the French embassy in Peking instead of moving it to Chongqing, and the Japanese puppet ruler Wang Jingwei, must have offended even the most conservative of Chinese patriots.[45]

In China's worsening political and economic conditions, the excellence of French-style professional education, as mediated by the Jesuits, thus meant little. Not only was it restricted to a tiny elite of uncertain loyalty,[46] but inadequate links between research and teaching meant that even this elite did not benefit fully from the research that was going on. Aurore was renowned for its natural history museum and its links with Jesuit meteorological and astronomical work in Xu Jia Hui, yet these fields of knowledge were not closely related to its educational mission.[47] An even greater anomaly existed in the Ecole des Hautes Etudes Commerciales et Industrielles in Tianjin, which also housed a distinguished natural history museum associated with the work of the paleontologist Teilhard de Chardin, yet taught industrial and commercial courses totally unconnected to the research that was going on.[48]

The Jesuits had consciously selected Shanghai as the centre of the mission's efforts since its geographical position gave any work done there a high profile in Chinese mission circles.[49] They saw one of their roles as providing models or exemplars for missionary work throughout China and in some ways they were both ahead of and emulated by other Catholic mission groups. It is not surprising, therefore, to find rather similar attitudes towards the role of education in a modernizing society among other Catholic mission groups in China. A small section entitled "Questions Scolaires" appearing regularly in the journal *Missions de Chine* from 1921 gives indications of similar views to those sketched out above, particularly with relation to student involvement in patriotic and political activism.[50]

Fortunately, however, the Chinese found access to other aspects of French educational thought and practice through a channel they themselves created. A small number of Chinese progressives set up a base in Paris early in the century and established valuable contacts with radical and socialist elements among French republicans. The next three sections deal with this second channel of French educational influence on China.

French Socialists and China's Modernization

In an elegantly argued monograph on the Ecole Normale Supérieure and the Third Republic, Robert Smith traces the development of the school from one of the least prestigious of the post-revolution *grandes écoles* to a center of socialist thought which produced a generation of radical leaders for France's Third Republic.[51] While the concept of the Confucian meritocracy and the fact that the famous *concours* had been inspired by ideas introduced from China in the seventeenth and eighteenth centuries[52] is never mentioned, the ethos of the Ecole as captured in Smith's study must come as close to an enlightened Confucianism in service of modernization as any Chinese could hope to find in the West. Some of the central values of the moderate socialist, exemplified best in Edouard Herriot, were anti-clericalism, the democratization of educational access, and a deep belief in hard work and its just rewards. Smith also dwells on the spirit of independent critical thought which invigorated this group, whom he saw as forming a transition "republic of professors," idealist, democratic and egalitarian, between the republic of notables and dukes of nineteenth century France and that of technocrats and businessmen which was to follow.

If this depiction is an accurate one, it is easy to understand the affinity between Herriot, his fellow radicals and socialists, and the group of Chinese progressives, deeply attracted to anarchism and a gentle socialism, who had come to France in the early twentieth century. They had come to seek an understanding of precisely the aspects of French society that the Jesuits wished to shelter their protégés from: secularism and socialism. Their key and probably most representative figure, Li Shizeng, had had a thorough classical education arranged by his official father but leaning more toward the liberal and open approach of the *shuyuan* than the rigidity of the examination system. Coming to France in 1902, he distinguished himself in his biological research at the Institut Pasteur in Paris, and thus gained access to the circles of some of France's best-known left wing parliamentarians. His scientific interests were immediately turned to practical uses in the establishment of a soyabean factory which provided cheap and wholesome food for French workers and, even more importantly, jobs for working class Chinese who would otherwise have no opportunity to come to France and participate in cultural and educational exchange.[53]

This vision of a socialism that upheld the dignity of manual labor and emphasized extending educational opportunity as widely as possible drew together Li Shizeng, Cai Yuanpei, Wu Zhihui, Zhu Minyi, Wu Yuzhang, to name a few of the Chinese involved, and French socialist leaders such as Edouard Herriot and Marius Moutet in a whole series of joint cultural and educational projects that culminated in the creation of a Sino-French University. A detailed description of the genesis and development of these projects lies beyond the scope of this chapter,[54] but a few highlights can be touched upon which illustrate the contrast between this channel of educational ideas and that created by the French missionaries. The latter confined their work at the secondary and higher levels of education to an elite drawn from areas where French commercial or religious interests were strong, and their intention was to form future "officials" who would be sympathetic to Catholicism and to France. In direct contrast, the "Frugal Study Society", created in 1912 and superseded by the "Diligent Work and Frugal Study Society" in 1915, was established to bring to France young Chinese from such remote areas as Sichuan and Hunan provinces and from class backgrounds that would normally not aspire to a secondary education even in China. Learning was to take place in combination with labor in the French factories, which were in need of workers during the war years. It was soon found necessary to offer preparatory classes before the young people left China, and by 1919 there were over 20 schools across the country.[55] By 1920 about 2,000 Chinese worker-students were in France, and the economic problems of the post-war period were diffusing some of the early idealism of the project. Jobs were simply not available, leaving many close to starvation.[56]

The result was a bifurcation of the movement in two different directions, each having important consequences for China. I will look first at the transformation of these ad hoc work-study schools into formal educational institutions centering on Peking, Shanghai and Canton within China and on Lyons and Charleroi in Europe, and restricting the scope of educational opportunity to less than one tenth of the number of young people originally served. The second direction, exactly opposite to this educational formalization, was the radicalization of Chinese worker-students and their experience of political struggle in face of repressive Chinese and French authorities. This culminated in an enhanced political consciousness and organizational capacity, the forced return of many worker-students to China and the movement of others on to the Soviet Union, where they could continue their political education in more favorable circumstances. Since these young Chinese cannot really be regarded as participating in a process of educational transfer, only brief consideration will be given to them in this chapter. Some of them were to become major architects of social change in China, yet it is doubtful whether French ideas or the educational experiences France provided deserve any credit for their achievements. If anything, France had the dubious honor of exhibiting a form of imperialism that aroused them to constructive rebellion.

L'Université Franco-Chinoise and Its Influence

By 1920, Li Shizheng and his coterie seemed to feel the need for a more specific organizational and geographical focus. Convinced that the modern French education system was a suitable model for China, they set themselves to create formal institutions that could serve more or less as exemplars for China. While the Jesuits had seen Shanghai as an ideal location for "model institutions" of missionary penetration, these Chinese patriots and progressives naturally chose the national capital of Peking for their experiment in creating a Sino-French university.[57]

The raw materials were already present in the informal schools of different types and levels which had sprung up under the auspices of provincial branches of the "Sino-French Education Society" and/or the "Diligent Work and Frugal Study Society." Table 6.2 indicates the number of schools existing in each province in 1919-1920 and the number of students sent to France from each province over those two years. Obviously some students of inland provinces did their preparatory studies in the coastal centers.[58]

Their programs lasted from six months to two years and focused on French, Chinese, mathematics and various applied sciences; some were specifically technical, others stressed teacher education. Study programs usually involved work experience, and great emphasis was put on frugality of life style and a spirit of self-reliance. A strong element of student self-government was common and included student responsibility for cleaning and simple maintenance tasks.[59] In many cases the schools were mixed and female participation in the movement was strongly encouraged.[60] While some schools had their own buildings, others simply rented school space from established institutions. In addition to running these informal schools, provincial branches of the Sino-French Education Society made efforts to strengthen the teaching of French in all schools, and took it as their mission to introduce texts and journals on modern French literature and social philosophy as available.[61] They acted, therefore, as channels for a different set of social ideals emanating from France than those introduced by the missionaries.[62]

Not surprisingly, there was a concentration of these preparatory schools in Peking and the surrounding regions.[63] The Auguste Comte school, established in 1917 and one of the most fully developed in its educational program, was chosen to be part of the new Sino-French university system in 1920.[64] A second school

Table 6.2
Sino-French Preparatory Schools and Students Sent to France by Province 1919-1920

Province	No. of Schools	No. of Students Sent to France
Sichuan	2	378
Hunan	3	346
Guangdong	1	251
Zhili (Hebei)	5	147
Fujian	1	89
Zhejiang	—	86
Jiangsu	5 (in Shanghai)	69
Hubei	—	40
Anhui	1	40
Jiangxi	—	28
Shanxi	—	28
Henan	—	25
Shandong	1	15
Guizhou	—	7
Shaanxi	—	7
Guangxi	—	7
Yunnan	—	6
Fengtian	—	5
Total	19	1,574

in the western hills, along with a Biological Research Institute and Infirmary, founded by Li Shizeng in 1917, were also incorporated. These were the raw beginnings of a teaching and research institution which the Chinese and French governing board[65] envisaged along French lines as embracing every level of education from primary to tertiary. Between 1920 and 1925 several more primary and secondary schools were created, and by 1925 four higher institutes or colleges were in place: Comte College for the social sciences, Voltaire College for the arts, Lamarck College, linked to the Biological Research Institute and providing biological studies related to medicine and agriculture, and Curie College, teaching chemistry and physics. In 1931 and 1932 respectively, institutes for radium research and pharmaceuticals research were set up in association with Curie College. Also a school of pharmacy was opened in Shanghai in 1929, which had close links to the University.[66] The Canton preparatory school became a College of Fine Arts in 1924 and then merged with Zhongshan University which continued to send a large number of students to Lyons.

While most of the informal preparatory schools gradually disbanded in face of the economic problems of the work-study movement, there was now in place a formal set of institutions geographically spread over the whole capital, financed at first largely by Chinese donors, and from 1926 subsidized by French Boxer Indemnity funds.[67] The structure was formal, six years of primary school, three years lower secondary, two years upper secondary and four years university, and the curriculum, a formal academic one, represented a combination of French and Chinese ideas.[68] Student numbers were modest, with a total in all institutions of about 1,300 in 1925, only a small proportion at the tertiary level.[69] By 1933 there were reported to be 200 at the university level[70] and by 1947 a total of 495 in the colleges and institutes.[71]

In spite of the fact that its ideals were much more in tune with the spirit of the time, l'Université Franco-Chinoise never developed into an institution of the level of academic prestige and distinction of Aurore. It did, however, open up significant channels for the introduction of modern French thought to China. Its journal, published monthly from 1926 to 1937, carried a broad range of articles on French social and literary theory, as well as numerous articles exploring scientific and technological ideas. Unlike the bulletin of l'Aurore, which was dominated by Jesuit contributors who screened western knowledge through their own views on what was good for the Chinese, this journal carried articles both on and by distinguished French thinkers of radical or progressive bent, also a growing number of articles by Chinese contributors, including some distinguished Chinese scholars.[72] From a bilingual publication it gradually became a fully Chinese one. It was clearly intended to open up popular access to the intellectual wealth of modern France. How widely it was actually read and what impact these ideas had is difficult to judge.

Another important aspect of the work of the university, which may have provided the most significant channel for the introduction of French ideas to China, was the Institut Franco-Chinois of Lyons[73] and its parallel smaller institute attached to the Université de Travail in Charleroi, Belgium.[74] These were closely associated with the university in Peking, and took a certain number of their graduates for higher studies on a regular basis, as well as recruiting students from Zhongshan University in Canton, and through various provincial government education offices.

The Lyons institute acted as a tutorial college for about 100 students at a time, who followed degree programs in various faculties of the Université of Lyons and certain *grandes écoles* in the region. Between 1926 and 1946, 473 Chinese passed through programs there, 138 in applied sciences, including a strong emphasis on medicine, 122 in pure sciences, 122 in arts and 89 in social sciences and law. Of the total, only 51 were women. The provincial origins of the group were much more strongly representative of the East Coast provinces than the earlier work study movement.[75]

By 1930, 84 scholars had returned to China. Of them 45 were employed in higher teaching, 4 were directors or administrators of hospitals, and 35 held posts in the Chinese bureaucracy or in international organizations.[76] Clearly a considerable number were in positions from which they could apply both the knowledge and the values they had imbibed in France to reform activity in China. Later sections will look at the French educational ideas which appealed to them and other Chinese thinkers of their time, and the outcomes of these ideas when implemented in the Chinese context.

However, the university itself remained underfunded and marginal within the Chinese higher education system. It was patriotic, and unlike Aurore, its members could justly boast of relations with French socialists that were untainted by imperialism. Yet the original vision of a higher institution open to the working classes and offering a practical service to China's development was never fulfilled. Ironically, just as Catholic educational work had made certain concessions to modernity in face of rapid economic and political change, the Sino-French educational movement was forced by economic and political exigency to scale down the original ambitious idea of a socialist education movement that would open up educational opportunity to a large number of working class young people and to women. The university in Peking served a small elite and the Institute at Lyons used the academic prerogatives of the French university system to exclude the majority of the worker-students who had looked to its establishment in 1921 as an answer to their increasing desperation in France.[77] In this way they missed the opportunity of providing a higher education for some of China's most distinguished future leaders within the Communist Movement.

France and the Communist Movement

Communist historians see 1921 as a turning point for the Communist Movement in France. It was a year marked by three revolutionary movements, the last one involving the storming of the Institut Franco-Chinois in Lyons. It was also a year in which, for the Communists at least, the reality of French imperialism and the futility of even the best of socialist intentions became evident. In the first movement of February 28, 1921, Chinese worker-students demonstrated in front of the Chinese Embassy demanding that a telegram be sent to China calling for support for their study, also that the new institutions in Lyons and Charleroi be opened up to them. While Chinese leaders begged off responsibility for the plight of the students, the French formed a committee which provided 150 francs a month support for them. When, however, the students got wind of a 300-500 million franc loan being negotiated from France by China, they organized a protest against this expression of imperialism in August, and as a result their support money was cut off by the French committee in September. In that same month the first group of new students selected by examination in China for study in Lyons was arriving at the Institut Franco-Chinois, and this sparked off the *Lida Yundong* (Lyons University Demonstration). On September 20, 125 worker-students travelled to Lyons and staged a sit-in to take over the new institute. The police were called in and the majority were arrested and eventually sent back to China. Zhou Enlai, one of the leaders of the movement, managed to escape arrest, but other distinguished figures such as Chen Yi, Li Lisan and Cai Hesen were ignominiously repatriated by the French authorities.[78]

The young Communists left in France were now ordered by the Comintern and the Chinese Communist Party to proceed to the Soviet Union, where they could study the principles of a scientific socialism already in the making. The growth of the Chinese Communist Party, its victory in 1949 and its choice of a Soviet development model in the early fifties, was to assure the ultimate predominance of Soviet educational patterns in modern China. While these embodied much that was new in Marxist-Leninist thought, they also carried remnants of the European, particularly French, tradition which had affected Russia in the eighteenth and nineteenth centuries. For this reason the French patterns, introduced both by missionaries and by Chinese progressives, continued to influence Chinese development long after the channels themselves had been destroyed.

The next section offers some reflections on the appeal of French educational ideas and patterns to Chinese thinkers in the twenties. The final section considers the place they found in the Nationalist education system and their outcomes in the Chinese context.

French Educational Ideas and Their Appeal for China

Durkheim's *Evolution of Educational Thought* beautifully illuminates certain key ideas of French education, locating them in the medieval tradition on the one hand and in the Jesuit modifications to it which so deeply influenced Napoleon on the other. If the age of scholasticism had been characterized by a passion for clarity of thought and expression central to the *formation* of medieval youth, the age of humanism, which the Jesuits successfully dominated in the French context, added to this a spirit of competition, a stress on written as well as oral expression and a sense of hierarchy, order and discipline which was almost military.

Durkheim saw the revolution as a new phase in which history and science, engaging the outer world, gained greater emphasis in relation to the literary studies which had been designed to form the inner world of the mind into an instrument of perfect clarity and precision.[79]

The two dominant educational ideas of the revolution, in Durkheim's view, were the encyclopedic viewpoint and the belief that the totality of human knowledge should be made accessible to all. The first idea stresses the unity of knowledge, the notion that all of its parts, relating to inner and outer worlds, the pure disciplines and their practical applications, are interdependent and inseparable. The curriculum should therefore be organized in such a way as to create awareness of this unity. The second idea, universal accessibility to knowledge, lay behind the central schools of the revolutionary period, and the first Ecole Normale Supérieure, which recruited 1,400 prospective teachers in 1794, in remarkable contrast to its later principle of rigorous selectivity and recruits of only 30-40 students per year.[80]

When Napoleon created the modern French university in 1808, these revolutionary ideas were made subservient to earlier patterns, which were essential for the legitimation of his rule. In a situation where he had neither the conservative justification of heredity nor the liberal one of democratic election, he needed a mechanism to assure both the fidelity of his civil servants and the loyalty of his citizens. The new French university, encompassing the whole education system, with each *académie* under the jurisdiction of its university, was actually inspired by the Jesuit system, with its sense of hierarchy, order and discipline. Through rigorous competitive examinations it articulated the movement of a few from primary to secondary school, and a tiny elite to master new professions in the *grandes écoles* suited to civil service needs. University trained scholars in the traditional professions and disciplines of arts, medicine and law, who now exercised supervision over all levels of education, could be counted on to hold in place a system that ensured their own privileges and that derived legitimacy from the very structure of the academic disciplines they were committed to. Meanwhile, some of the new ideas of republicanism and modern citizenship could be gradually introduced through the *grandes écoles*, including the Ecole Normale Supérieure which led the teaching profession. Centrally organized curricula articulating the stages of access to human knowledge were to be used all the way up through the secondary school before the specialization of higher studies.

In his study of French education from 1800 to 1967, Antoine Prost identifies the Napoleonic university as the main obstacle to educational evolution over the modern period.[81] It embraced and rationally ordered every level and type of education, giving to university scholars an absolute monopoly over educational decision-making by the end of the nineteenth century. If the *universitaires* were not remarkable for their advocacy of progressive educational ideas, they did at least afford the developing education system some protection from the more reactionary views of ecclesiastical authorities. The popularization of primary education and the formation of *instituteurs* to teach at the primary level was accepted as state responsibility by Napoleon, yet depended in fact on local initiative and the growing economic resources that became available for education through the nineteenth century. However, Catholic attacks on the primary system and its teachers for spreading socialist ideas and fomenting social disorder in the mid-nineteenth century threw into relief the importance of the protection provided by the university corporation.[82]

A system thus emerged in the nineteenth century which provided a secular education for teachers at two levels, who were to give their students both an education in republicanism and an initiation into the encyclopedic knowledge tradition. At the higher level a specialist *formation* in the disciplines and professions was provided for an elite. The greatest strength of the system may have been in the excellence of its modern professional education in the engineering and administrative sciences.[83] One of its weakest features may have been the neglect of technical education at lower levels.[84] As for the university, it held a mediating position between ecclesiastical forces of reaction and the movement towards a technocratic and elitist style of modernization led by the *grandes écoles*. Within it there was the possibility of progressive or radical intellectuals gaining leadership and so liberalizing the education system, an example being the reforms initiated by Herriot in the twenties and thirties.[85]

What was it in French educational experience that appealed to Chinese thinkers of the early twentieth century? Could it have been the tension between old and new, with the Napoleonic university firmly lodged between? Articles in such progressive educational journals as *Xin jiaoyu* and *Jiaoyu zazhi* indicate a widely felt fascination with the French conception of the university. The human desire to reap the benefits of modernization without paying the costs must be a universal one yet it is particularly evident in China's hesitating moves towards modernity. Could it therefore have been that the French model of the university seemed to offer an approach to modernization that could proceed within the Confucian spirit, and provide a Confucian role for intellectuals in the process?

Clear and accurate information on all apsects of French education was available in China in the early twenties. A lengthy article covering the history, the administrative structure, the school system at all levels and curricular details including the timetabling of each subject nationally appeared in *Jiaoyu zazhi* in April of 1923.[86] Numerous other articles published in the early twenties reveal aspects of the system which were of particular interest to Chinese thinkers: a lengthy history of the University of Paris in a serial of two instalments,[87] a detailed discussion of education for citizenship in France,[88] a careful consideration of reform in the primary curriculum that was being implemented in 1923,[89] an account of the higher levels of teacher education,[90] and an article on the provision of informal education for young people between the ages of 13 and 18.[91]

It is evident from a perusal of these articles that it was the principles and ideas lying behind three aspects of education that captured attention. The accessibility of knowledge to all is a point constantly remarked on, the fact that any French citizen could attend lectures given in the university or in such institutions as the Collège de France and the Institut Pasteur, whether they were registered as students or not. A second aspect greatly admired was the structure of the university with its rational hierarchy expressed geographically in the 17 académies or university districts through the country and philosophically in its integration of all the disciplines of knowledge, embodying both their fundamental unity and their diversity. There were articles, such as one by Julien Champenois, elaborating on the obstacles created by university scholars to curricular reform and the modification of the degree system to suit changing needs, yet the ideal still held a deep appeal.[92] A third attractive facet of French education was the way in which it fostered young citizens both through the formal teaching of civics within the curriculum and the creation of young citizens clubs in the schools, of which there were a reported 4,000 with a membership of 870,000 in 1914. The Chinese felt that French society had displayed a remarkable cohesion and resilience in the trying years of the World War I, and attributed this to the success of their programs for citizenship education.

More than anyone else, it was Cai Yuanpei who took the core ideas of the French university and applied them to the Chinese situation. He had spent most of the war years in France, was a key figure in the Sino-French education movement, and as Chancellor of Peking University from 1917 to 1927 held a position of great influence in Chinese educational circles.[93] In two articles which appeared in *Xin jiaoyu* in 1922 he expounded on the value of a French-style university organization for Chinese education. In the first, "A View on Educational Autonomy,"[94] he stressed the need for the education system to be free from political control, since politicians tended to focus on the short-term good of society, and from religious control, since missionaries represented forces of reaction as well as foreign interference in his view. He saw the French pattern with the *Ministre d'Instruction Publique,* advised by a council of scholars, presiding over the whole education system and represented at lower levels by the rectors of university districts, as an ideal structure within which China's enlightened intellectuals could shape all aspects of education for the long-term good of the nation. For financing he favored the American system of local taxation for educational needs, and for aspects of the internal organization of the university, including a focus on research and the democratic election of the rector from within, he recommended German patterns. But overall, he saw the French structure as an ideal means of safeguarding the education system from forces of political and religious reaction. His confidence in China's scholars as a progressive force in society is noteworthy.

The second article, entitled "An Introduction and Explanation of the Hunan Self-Study University,"[95] reveals other aspects of the appeal of the French model, particularly its geographical rationalization. Here Cai suggested that ideally each Chinese province should have two or three university districts with a university heading up the education system in each. Recognizing the economic impossibility of such a development in China at the time, he suggested three centers of excellence, one bringing together the eight higher institutions in Peking, a second located in Southeast China and a third in Southwest China. These should be supported by the central government under a university council. In addition scholars in each province should be encouraged to get together and organize a provincial university on the model of the Hunan Self-Study University. In its emphasis on research and on the provision of library and laboratory facilities for all who wished to study without the pressure of exams or rigid timetabling can be seen some of the informality of the Chinese *shuyuan* tradition. In fact the *shuyuan* is explicitly mentioned as a model for developing a scholarship suited to the needs of each province without the expense of formal university institutions.[96]

Outcomes in the Chinese Context

While French educational ideas had some currency in the early twenties, as shown above, it was American progressivism that dominated the scene and influenced the educational legislation passed in 1922 and 1924. However with the success of the Northern Expedition of 1926-27, and the establishment of a new national capital in Nanjing, Cai Yuanpei and such Francophile associates as Li Shizeng, Zhu Minyi and Zhang Jingjiang seized the opportunity of establishing "the University Council of the Chinese Republic" (*Zhonghua minguo daxue yuan*) as an organ independent of the Party political control of the new government and responsible for all educational activity throughout the nation. In the areas already under the control of the new government, Zhejiang and Jiangsu provinces, university districts were organized and headed by French-educated Chinese. The Peiping district was to be placed under Li Shizeng, assisted by Li Shuhua, the rector of the Université Franco-Chinoise.[97]

   This initiative soon came up against strong opposition from several sources, and the university council was dissolved in 1928. Party leaders were unwilling to leave education in the hands of scholars. They saw the universities as professional training institutions which should focus on the application of science to national development rather than on pure research. At lower levels they wanted to see closer links between education and daily life, and they did not consider scholarly control of education to be conducive to this. For their part, many university leaders were opposed to the geographical and organizational rationalization implied by the university district system, as this interfered with the autonomy and the special characteristics of their institutions. Finally lower level educators feared that scholarly control of the education system would result in a large proportion of funds being allocated to higher levels of education at the expense of secondary and primary levels.[98]

   The French university district pattern was thus roundly defeated in a situation where China's intellectuals did not enjoy either sufficient unity among themselves or sufficient political and popular support to be entrusted with the role Cai envisaged for them. However an invitation of a League of Nations Mission of Educational Experts to make recommendations on the reform of the Chinese education system in 1931 resulted in certain French-inspired patterns finding their way into the Nationalist education system quite independently of Cai and the Sino-French Education Movement. The European leaders of the Mission, including the left-wing French scientist, Paul Langevin, were strongly critical of the prevailing

American influence on the Chinese system, the common secondary school which used a credit system to organize curricular knowledge, the formation of teachers who were well versed in educational theory yet had no solid knowledge of academic subjects, the proliferation of colleges, private and public, to meet social demand at the higher level, and the lack of any mechanisms for the setting and maintenance of nation-wide academic standards. These were some of the issues they raised.[99]

In response to suggestions made by the team, measures were taken to strengthen the academic disciplines in general secondary schools and ensure high standards through standardized university entrance examinations along the lines of the *baccalauréat* at the end of secondary school.[100] At the university level, greater emphasis was put on knowledge in the basic disciplines by the imposition of a comprehensive examination and a graduation thesis before graduation.[101] Also national procedures were established to monitor the academic quality of university faculty.[102] Some geographical rationalization was attempted, which reduced the number of universities in favor of higher technical and professional schools focusing on the applied sciences. For these the French *grandes écoles* were regarded as models.[103] At the secondary level, vocational and technical education was developed as a separate stream from academic education.

From the economic point of view, these measures appeared to make good sense, especially those relating to professional and technical education. It was unfortunate that the Chinese economy was not better able to absorb the engineers, applied scientists and technicians trained. Also, unlike the *grandes écoles*, these professional schools remained much lower in prestige than the universities and academic secondary schools. On the other hand, the Nationalist leaders' use of academic measures suggested by the team on educational grounds to exercise firm political control over professors and students in the universities was clearly seen as a kind of servitude by intellectuals, more and more of whom came to sympathize with the Communist cause.[104]

Ironically, with the success of the Communist Revolution in 1949, and the beginning of an economic and political reconstruction that has represented a whole new era for China, the Soviet educational patterns introduced in 1952 served to revive and consolidate aspects of the European-inspired policies tried out by the Nationalist government in the 1930s: the encyclopedic curriculum, the use of examinations based on academic disciplines as a selection mechanism, the geographical rationalization of higher education, and the strengthening of the applied sciences needed for national construction tasks.[105] In a sense the university gave way to a system not unlike that of the *grandes écoles*, creating an elite with the political and scientific qualifcations to fill assured places within the new socialist bureaucracy. Unlike France, it was a bureaucracy subservient to the final authority of the Communist party. Intellectuals found a role, but it was not the role which Cai Yuanpei had envisaged for them within the university.

There can be little doubt about the liberation of productive forces in the fifties with the success of China's industrialization. Yet on the issue of democratization, and the access of the people to knowledge, not all saw the Soviet model, with its European residues and its open acceptance of two distinct tracks, as liberating. In the Cultural Revolution, such concepts as academic disciplines, competitive examinations and the creation of a technocratic elite, all key features of the French pattern, were viewed as a yoke of political servitude that must be smashed. In the post-1978 period, they are back in place, and regarded once again as an essential element of a modernization strategy that emphasizes attaining economic prosperity over principles of egalitarianism.

Ultimately, the paradox may lie less in the contrast between French Catholics and French socialists, who introduced to China essentially the same patterns with modest modifications, than in the contrasting Chinese views of these patterns in different periods of modern Chinese history. At times they have been seen as emblems of political servitude, at others as essential mechanisms for the liberation of economic forces of production.

7

American Progressivism in Chinese Education: The Case of Tao Xingzhi

Hubert O. Brown

Introduction: From the Bird's Eye

Straight Roads and Historical Quagmires

The career of American-bred Progressive Education[1] as a distinct movement in Republican China has been well described, most notably by Barry Keenan,[2] to the point that the story and its interpretation have become standardized in the literature of the period. From a distance, the channel of its course in clear, the lines of development sharp and distinct. As we move closer in, however, things are not so well defined — the shoreline tends to dissolve into bogs and marshes, the direction of flow becomes more uncertain, the source of the current more obscure. This is particularly true if we turn from Keenan's interpretation of Progressivism as a quasi-political movement, trying through education to shape the political development of the fledgling Chinese republic, and examine instead Progressivism as an educational movement, more diffuse in its effects and yet more persistent.

In this paper I shall examine some of these finer details of Progressivism's history in China by examining a more limited terrain, i.e., the biography of one of its chief exponents, Tao Xingzhi, during his early career when he was most associated with the movement. The upshot is not a negation of the accepted history, which I am persuaded is essentially correct, but rather some doubts regarding its certainty in every detail, an awareness of the actual complexity involved in the apparent transfer of educational ideas from culture to culture, and thus an appreciation of the qualifications that must considerably modify any general interpretation such as the one commonly accepted by Western historians.

The Rise and Fall of Progressive Education in Politics

With Yuan Shikai's ruthless quashing of Sun Yat-sen's "second revolution" in 1913, some Chinese reformers turned from direct attempts to implement democratic political and social changes, to indirect efforts at the same goal via the prior transformation of Chinese culture. Intellectuals ranging in orientation from the post-Confucian Liang Qichao to the proto-Marxist Li Dazhao argued that cultural change, in particular the abandonment of traditional Chinese modes of thinking and behaving, was essential to the building of a strong, modern, and democratic state. Traditional Confucian culture should be replaced, they thought, by selected Western values, i.e., by a world view based on very broad interpretations of "science" and "democracy." For many the key institution to effect this cultural change was education.

American Progressivism was by no means the only intellectual influence in the movement for cultural transvaluation, what Hu Shi would ineptly call the "Chinese Renaissance,"[3] yet many leading reformers such as Hu Shi, Jiang Menglin, Guo Bingwen, Zhu Jingnong, and Tao Xingzhi, studied at the center of Progressive thought in the United States, Columbia University, and counted themselves at some point in their careers as followers of its acknowledged master, John Dewey. Dewey's influence spread even further when he himself paid an extended visit to China in 1919-1921. He lectured at China's principal universities to halls crowded with admirers, invariably drawing an enthusiastic response, though more from educators than from professional philosophers.[4]

With the growth of the movement, national organizations espousing the ideals of Progressive Education, such as the Society for the Promotion of New Education and the National Federation of Education Associations, became major forces in attempts to restructure and reform Chinese education along Progressive lines. The influence of Progressivism peaked with the issuance in Peking of the School Reform decree of 1922, which combined a reorganization of schooling along American lines with an attack upon traditional educational aims and an assertion of the fundamental significance of individualism, "life activities" in the curriculum, and the need to adapt schooling to "the needs of social change." [5]

Yet in spite of its auspicious beginnings, only a few years after the 1922 School Reform Decree, American Progressivism, as represented by a distinct educational movement in China, would be finished. By 1926, the Society for the Promotion of New Education and the National Federation of Education were both disbanded, and the key journal of the movement, *New Education (Xin jiaoyu)*, had ceased publication.[6] What had happened?

Clearly, a new, virulent, and militantly anti-imperialist nationalism, fueled in 1925 by the May Thirtieth incident in which Britieh-led police in Shanghai fired on and killed Chinese demonstrators, had gripped the country and many of its educators. [7] At the same time, a widespread conservative reaction undercut the assumption that China could only be saved by the "New Culture" advocated by the Progressives. This led to educational experiments, such as those proposed by Liang Shuming, predicated upon the renovation of traditional Chinese philosophies rather than their wholesale replacement.[8] At the other end of the political scale Marxism, with its radical critique of liberal reform, the essential social philosophy of Progressive Education, was also rapidly gaining new adherents.[9]

Yet Progressive Education was not merely overtaken by the inevitable march of events and the swings of the ideological pendulum to which education seems so prone, whatever the time or country. Progressivism had within it the seeds of its own destruction, given the chaotic social and political soil of warlord China in which it was planted and expected to flower. Ironically, the central paradox that paralyzed Progressivism was best summarized by Dewey himself in his reflections on China appearing in *The New Republic.*

> The difficulties in the way of a practical extension and regeneration of Chinese education are all but insuperable. Discussion often ends in an impasse: no political reform of China without education; but no development of schools as long as military men and corrupt officials divert funds and oppose schools from motives of self-interest. Here are the materials of a tragedy of the first magnitude.[10]

It was, as Keenan points out, a classic "chicken and egg" problem. Chinese intellectuals influenced by Progressivism believed there could be no democratic political reforms without fundamental cultural renewal through education, yet there could be no cultural renewal through education without the stable social and political climate that would permit such a renewing education to develop and thrive. It was precisely this climate that was lacking in the warlord dominated China of the early 1920s. As Schwartz notes, it was not that warlords were incapable of promoting educational reform — in fact, some did just that. Education, however, was of little relative importance to them:

> In the brutal and desperately insecure political environment of this period in China...holders of power and privilege were not easily to be diverted from their narrow obsessions with political survival.[11]

At the same time it was part of the ideology of the Progressives, in the name of "science," to distance education from the toils of politics, to deliberately keep education removed from the dangers of entanglement and compromise in the struggles of various factions for political power. This policy, however, did nothing to preserve either the political purity of the movement, or its very existence. What it did do was turn educators away from the evident, though perhaps insuperable, need to either create or appropriate a strong national constituency. As a result, Progressive educators in China found themselves with neither mass popular support nor the backing of an effective government willing and able to implement the ideals of the Decree of 1922. Under these conditions, the movement disintegrated, superseded by despair, as in the case of Jiang Menglin, by new passions, as in the case of Tao Xingzhi, or, for most of the others, by resignation. Schwartz's conclusion could be extended to the whole of the movement and not just to its leading proponent: "The fatal weakness of Hu Shih and the ultimate strength of his opponents was his notion that one could proceed to the solution of socio-educational problems without confronting the tragic problems of political power."[12]

Yet while Progressive Education may have perished politically in 1925, its educational influence continued long after. The mission schools that had been so instrumental in introducing a highly disproportinate share of prominent Chinese (including, as we shall see, Tao Xingzhi) in the Republican period to Progressivism continued to operate. Educationists continued to imbibe Progressivism's doctrines in American schools of education up until 1950, including many who studied with Dewey, Kilpatrick, and other Progressives of various stripes at Teachers College. The six year primary, three year lower secondary, and three year upper secondary organizational format of the schools, as determined by the Reform Decree of 1922, has remained more or less in effect up to this very day. Further, the leaders of the Progressive Education movement in China did not perish with it, and neither did their influence. To take one example of their continuing effect, the textbooks Columbia graduate Zhu Jingnong wrote to implement the Reform Decree of 1922 are credited with having had "a great influence on the thought and training of an entire generation of young Chinese."[13] To take another, there was the case of Tao Xingzhi.

Tao Xingzhi: From Confucianism to Progressivism to Marxism

Tao Xingzhi was one of that band of intellectuals born near the end of the nineteenth century whose career began in studying for the imperial examinations and ended either in exile under the Guomindang or in acceptance of the fledgling People's Republic. Tao lived through one of the most turbulent yet creative and exciting periods of China's long history, participating in each phase, each new wave of trends and ideas, with enormous energy and enthusiasm. Whether it was the introduction of Progressive Education to China, the May Fourth Movement, mass literacy, rural reconstruction, wartime education, or workers' universities, Tao was at the forefront, tirelessly organizing schools, running education societies, editing journals, and writing enough inspirational prose, poems, songs, and public letters to fill the six large volumes of his recently published (and notably incomplete) collected works.[14] He began as a child memorizing Confucian couplets from the doorpost of a private village school, and ended at his untimely death as a likely candidate to become the first Minister of Education in the People's Republic.

Early Education and Enthusiasms

Tao was born in 1891 in the small, isolated village of Huang Tan Yuan, She County, in Anhui Province.[14] The third of four children, Tao was given the courtesy name of Wenjun (he signed himself Wen Tsing Tao), which he was to change later to Zhixing, and then again to Xingzhi.[16] Tao's father ran a small condiment shop, but gave up his failing business to become a farmer when he inherited some land. His mother, to whom Tao was exceptionally close, was illiterate, but his father was sufficiently schooled to give Tao his initial instruction in Chinese characters. According to communist hagiography, Tao's family were poor peasants. They were well enough off, however, to educate their surviving children, including Tao's younger sister, Wenmei, through college, and to provide much of the initial financial support Tao needed to travel to and study in the United States — which, as Y. C. Wang has shown, places them above poor peasant status.[17] There is in fact some suggestion that Tao's paternal grandfather belonged to the petty gentry of his village. Both his parents were Christians.

At the age of five Tao entered the local Confucian school, where he stayed, off and on, until the abolition in 1905 of both the Imperial examinations and the rationale for the Classics that formed the school's curriculum. He then joined his mother, who was working at a nearby China Inland Mission station, and there entered the mission school. In 1908 the mission teacher, G. W. Gibb, was due to return to England, which required the closing of the school and the graduation of its students, including Tao. Ascribing the deaths of his older brother and sister to Chinese medicinal cures, and having already expressed a strong desire to make a significant contribution to the rebirth of China, Tao borrowed enough from parents, friends, and Gibb, to travel to Hangzhou to study medicine. He passed the matriculation examinations to enter Chung Chi (Guangji) Medical College, but found that since he was not a Christian he would neither be allowed to study medicine nor be entitled to have his tuition forgiven. After only three days, Tao withdrew his registration and returned home to study English.[18]

In the fall of 1909 Tao entered Huiwen College in Nanjing to study literature, and from there transferred early in 1910 to Jinling University (later Nanjing University) to study literature and philosophy. This three years at Jinling had a profound effect upon Tao's intellectual development. It was there that he first was converted to the philosophy of the Ming Confucian idealist Wang Yang-ming, with its emphasis upon the authority of immediate intuition rather than tradition, and the unity of thought and action rather than mere scholarly reflection; both doctrines were suited to Tao's activist disposition. Tao was so impressed with Wang's philosophy that he changed his name to Zhixing, signifying the unity of thought and action, the first necessarily, or ideally — it is not clear which — leading to the second.

Tao's conversion to Lu-Wang idealism (an enthusiasm shared, incidentally, by many of China's reformers in this period, including Sun Yat-sen and Chiang Kai-shek) undoubtedly inclined him towards a favorable response to Dewey's experimentalism. Both Dewey and Wang infused thought with moral purpose by linking it necessarily to social action. For both, thought without action is meaningless, i.e. lacking purpose and consequences. Both had something of an instrumentalist view of knowledge, a view Tao would wholeheartedly, if crudely, adopt. However, on the critical question of the function of immediate intuition, an issue which completely divides Dewey from Wang, Tao, with his Robinson Crusoe ideal of problem solving in a cultural vacuum, clearly opted for Wang, and not Dewey.

A second major influence on Tao while he was a student at Jinling was the overthrow of the Qing dynasty in the revolution of 1911. Tao took leave from his studies to return to his village, where he immediately became involved in politics as secretary to the newly elected assembly. When he returned to Jinling, Tao continued his political involvement, founding a number of patriotic societies, and a journal, the *Jinling Light,* which as editor he used to air his views on China's future, false intellectuals, medical ethics, physical culture, and literature. He still managed to graduate first in his class, and in three rather than the normal four years of study.

In 1913, in his final year at Jinling, Tao became a convert to Christianity through the guidance of the mission staff running the university, and the reading of *The Political and Social Significance of the Life and Teachings of Jesus* by Jeremiah W. Jenks.[19] Christian doctrines and theology seem to have made no impression on Tao — indeed, he showed little interest throughout his career in any theorizing that did not have immediate, direct connection with action. This must have been one of Tao's first written introductions to something approximating Progressivism, albeit in the guise of the "social gospel," with its emphasis upon gradual social and political progress, inevitable in the evolution of God's kingdom on earth but still demanding active commitment and participation of the individual. Conversion to such a gospel could only strengthen Tao's commitment to Wang Yangming's philosophy, and his predisposition to Dewey's social philosophy.

Upon graduation, Jinling's principal, a Dr. Bowen, recommended Tao to study in the United States, and offered to help finance his way there. Tao first married a classmate of his younger sister, and then, with the help of Bowen, family and friends, left China to study government at the University of Illinois. He intended to continue his career somewhere in government office, the proper sphere for the educated in China since before the founding Qin dynasty. Though he also wrote a poem while on voyage celebrating the limitless potential benefits of science, he showed as yet no inclination towards a career in education.

Tao studied at the University of Illinois from the fall of 1914 through the summer term of the following year. While completing the coursework necessary for his master's degree, he had a change of heart about his future career, moving from government to education. The catalyst for this change was probably a Professor Lotus Delta Coffman, Ph.D. Columbia and a convinced Progressive. Tao took Coffman's course in educational administration in his first semester at Illinois, and thus was introduced to Progressive Education and Teachers College.[20] In his final, summer, term, Tao took nothing but courses in education. That same summer he determined at a YMCA summer conference to devote his career to educational administration.[21]

Tao entered Teachers College in the fall of 1915, and continued his studies there for two years. According to the hagiography, Tao worked to support his studies. In fact, while Tao did work, he was mostly supported by Chinese government scholarships and, thanks to Paul Monroe, scholarships administered by the University. His coursework was heavily biased towards educational administration, and social and historical foundations of education. He took only two introductory courses in educational philosophy. At the end of his two years of coursework, with the support of his thesis supervisor, George Sayers, and the intercession on his behalf of Paul Monroe with the University authorities, Tao was permitted to be examined on his thesis before submitting it. This was intended to allow him to return to China to gather data, without having to go back to the United States to defend his completed dissertation. Coincidentally, Tao was recruited by Guo Bingwen, the President of Nanjing Higher Normal College (renamed Southeastern University in 1921) and the first Chinese Ph.D. from Columbia, to join the education department there. Tao never finished his dissertation, although he was later awarded an honorary doctorate by St. John's University of Shanghai.

Judging from his transcripts, Tao's formal brush with Dewey's philosophy was minimal. He took only two courses in educational philosophy while studying in the United States, and neither these, nor any others, were taught by Dewey.[22] Tao's thesis advisor, George Sayers, was a professor in educational administration, and a person of broad, eclectic, academic tastes. If Tao had any mentor at all while at Columbia, it would have been Paul Monroe, who seems to have befriended Tao, as well as taught him a course in the history of education each semester of his stay there. Monroe's influence on Tao is evident in the historical allusions to Western education in Tao's writings after his return to China, and in Tao's first book, a collection of Monroe's observations on education in China stemming from his visit there in 1921. Monroe was friendly to the humane reforms of Progressivism, yet far more skeptical and pluralistic in his writings than his philosophical colleagues in their early days. While little of these attitudes is evident in Tao's writings — he was, characteristically, concerned above all with Monroe's organizational recommendations — Tao did not have much opportunity for a thorough grounding in Dewey's philosophy of education.

This may explain the marked paucity of references to Dewey in Tao's writings. In an essay on experimentalism, for example, Tao gives DesCartes, the German neo-Kantian idealist Friedrich Paulson, and Frederick the Great, among many others, more mention than the one line devoted to Dewey.[23] Tao's two page introduction to Dewey's thought written on the occasion of the latter's visit to China is no more than a few biographical details and a short list of some of Dewey's more well-known publications.[24] Indeed, although Tao is frequently cited by friend and foe (as well as historian) alike as being a disciple of Dewey's, there is nowhere in Tao's vast bibliography any sort of systematic discussion of Dewey's educational thought.[25]

What Tao did come away with from his years at Columbia was a handful of specific causes, such as universal kindergarten education. Also, far more important, he acquired a belief in education as the fundamental means of social, cultural, political, and economic renewal for China, a belief that would prove unshakeable in the midst of all the other changes Tao would later go through. Having rejected medicine, and then government, Tao had, in education, discovered the Way. Further, in the reforming zeal of Progressive Education, Tao had discovered the tool by which education itself could be renewed for the task of renewing society. This tool in Tao's hands may have been a vague collection of mottoes, inspirational principles, and adages, bound together loosely with catch-words such as "creativity," "experimentation," "science," "progress," and "democracy," but it gave to Tao a sense of being on the cutting edge of a radically new history for China. It was, perhaps, the very amorphousness of Tao's educational beliefs that allowed for the great scope and variety of his actions.

Tao, 26 years old, his studies incomplete, and with no experience in education of any sort, was nominated by fellow Columbian Guo Bingwen to be Director of Educational Science at Nanjing Higher Normal College. Since his candidacy had to be ratified by department members, Tao lectured his colleagues for two hours on the New Education he had brought back from America, and how he would use it to thoroughly reform the department. Not surprisingly he failed to win them over. The upshot was a wait for Tao of two years before Guo finally made the appointment, and an essay attacking educational conservatives, in which he wrote, "The vast petrification and isolation that characterize life in the teaching profession [in China] result from the fact that the people who are engaged in it stick to familiar paths and cannot revise their direction."[26]

The new paths Tao staked out, however, were defined in only the vaguest of clichés. Teachers should be responsible for leadership, students for studying. Teachers should teach students to learn, rather than teaching only books or students. Teaching students to learn meant not just giving them right answers, but guiding them through the correct processes of coming up efficiently with the right answers.

> For any given problem the teacher should not simply pass on a ready-made method of solution to the student but should sort out how this ready-made method is arrived at and guide the student, making him go through the process, come up with similar reasoning, and deduce the method himself in the shortest possible time.[27]

This parody of Dewey's inquiry method, familiar to both sides of the Pacific, was characteristic of the lack of depth in Tao's understanding of experimentalism.

Dewey's Educational Philosophy, Chinese Style

In part, this superficiality may have been the result of the way in which Progressivism was marketed for foreign consumption. Dr. Frank J. Goodnow, Columbia Professor, first president of the American Political Science Association, and a well known reforming Progressive in New York, was also a political adviser to Yuan Shikai in the latter's bid to destroy parliamentary democracy and establish himself as dictator. In spite of Goodnow's rationalizations, it was clear that his Progressivism in the U. S. was not the same as in China.[28] The same could perhaps be said of Dewey, although in more subtle ways.

In 1919, largely at the instigation of Hu Shi, Dewey and his wife visited China, and stayed on for two years giving courses at major universities as well as numerous public lectures. When Dewey visited Nanjing, Tao acted as his host and translator. This was probably the most extended direct formal contact Tao had with Dewey's teachings, and it is worth closer examination to see just what Dewey said in China. [29]

Dewey's lectures on education, as we have them, read far more like tracts on cultural reform than essays in philosophy.[30] They are replete with advice and inspiration, but short on the sort of theoretical discussion found in his written work. He devotes, for example, only one vague paragraph in the lectures translated by Ou Tsuin-chen to his central principle of habit, a topic that requires five pages in *Experience and Education,* and whole chapters in works such as *Human Nature and Conduct.*[31]

What the lectures lacked in theory, however, they made up for in practice. Many of the concrete innovations Tao tried to introduce to China were explicitly contained in them. Both Dewey and Tao strongly advocated the universal establishment of kindergartens in China, in spite of the widespread lack of any sort of schooling. Tao also adopted the use of theatricals as a teaching device, as suggested at length by Dewey, in the experimental schools associated with his Xiaozhuang rural education project, and in the wartime Yucai school in Chongqing. Even the "little teacher" device of having school children teach literacy to ignorant parents and friends is prefigured in Dewey's suggestion that the teacher "appoint the brighter pupils as his assistant teachers, and arrange for them openly to assist the slower pupils," though, typically, Tao's version of Dewey's proposal applied it outside as well as inside the classroom.[32]

More importantly, there is often a strong coincidence of viewpoint between Tao and the Dewey of *Lectures in China.* Dewey attacked traditional education in ways that Tao continually echoed, both of them castigating its elitism, intellectualism, lack of "organic" connection with the larger society, and consequent irrelevance to modern mass culture. Both appeared to accept what they perceived as the method of science as the means of salvation, not only of education, but, through education, of society itself. "Salvation" is not too strong a word — there is a mystical quality in Dewey's notion of science as a social panacea that went far beyond the tentativeness of his philosophical writings on the subject:

> It is true that the development of science has increased our fund of knowledge about education; but it is much more important that it has been responsible for new methods and a new attitude, that it has made it possible for us to move out from under the cloud of pessimism, passivity, conservatism, dishonesty, and disregard for facts, into the sunlight of hope and new courage and a new dimension of honesty, where men are capable of discovering the truth.....[33]

Tao, like Dewey, adopted both a highly generalized methodology of experimental problem solving — through the two were not identical — and a belief in the fruits of science leading to both material and moral progress.

As corollaries of this romantic view of science, Tao fully shared Dewey's belief in what the latter called "associative living," a fuzzy notion in *Lectures in China* that on the one hand is merely a recognition of a social fact, "that every human being lives in — and can live only in — some sort of association with other human beings," and on the other hand is the attitude of cooperation achieved through incidental learning in "creative dramatics," class projects, and the like.[4] Tao would turn this into an egalitarianism of teachers and students at Xiaozhuang and, after the war, at his workers' universities, an egalitarianism based, in theory, on solving practical problems.[35]

The second corollary Tao and Dewey seemed to share was an anti-intellectualism in the name of the thoroughly pragmatic view of knowledge. This appeared in two ways: first, an attack upon the glorification of the traditional man of letters, the specialist in humanistic studies of little relevance to the actual needs of society. As Dewey was reported to have summed it up, "[W]e must resolutely abandon the traditional regard for the bookworm," i.e., those of "the relatively small class which engages in endeavor that is primarily intellectual," and instead adapt education to "the great majority, who must earn their living by the sweat of their brows . . . to whom intellectual studies are largely irrelevant."[36] When Tao first opened his rural education project, Xiaozhuang, part of the entrance examination was a day's manual labor reclaiming waste land, the advertisement explicitly warning away mere scholars. Over the door of the library was the inscription "The Place Where Bookish Fools Come Early," the auditorium was called "Plow Hall," while inside were couplets encouraging the students to make friends with horses, oxen, sheep, and other farm animals.[37]

This anti-intellectualism was reconciled to the glorification of science through an utterly pragmatic concept of knowledge. For example, Dewey contended that geography and history ought to be the core subjects of school curriculum, but he construed these in a very inspirational sense. History "is the story of man's struggle to subject nature to his ends" as that story is told in time. It is a story of evolution and progress, particularly with the application of science and technology to man's needs and desires. Geography is the same story, only with spacial variations. Eskimaux in arctic climates overcome their environment differently than African bushmen overcome theirs, but the point of the story, the triumph of intelligence through scientific and technological control of the environment, is essentially the same.[38]

Tao was, if anything, even more pragmatic. "Books," he held, "are just tools, just like a hoe. They are all just for doing something."[39] Tao spelled out what he meant in an extraordinary double list of needs or problems, and the book one ought to read to meet the need or solve the problem. If you want to know how to play basketball, the book to use is "How to play basketball," if how to prevent colds, read "How to prevent colds," if how to encourage the circulation of fresh air, read "How to encourage the circulation of fresh air." If you want to know how to write poetry, read "How to write poetry," if how to love then read "How to love," and if you want to build a prosperous society, read "How to build a prosperous society." In all, Tao suggested seventy "life forces" and the corresponding instructions for achieving them.[40]

At a still more general level, Tao and Dewey appeared to share some basic assumptions about educators and education. Dewey, in spite of his belief in economic factors as the fundamental determinants of the structure of society, nevertheless argued that "Social progress is dependent upon educational progress" as if it were possible to move directly from education to social reform.[41] Tao, as has been noted, shared the latter belief, though not the former.

Both Tao and Dewey also believed it the proper role of the educator to assume the vanguard in effecting social change. Dewey saw this as the task of the educational expert, the educational technologist applying the method and findings of the science of education to problems of teaching, learning, curriculum, and management. Dewey's faith in the power of scientific education to affect social events was remarkable: he at one point argued that it was even the way for Chinese to avoid strikes:

> Effective and widespread education in science would, I am sure, obviate a great deal of labor unrest and thus improve the situation; for workers are much more likely to be interested in their work if they understand and see meaning in what they do. I foresee wide application in China of the method we are advocating.[42]

Both in method and content, educators were to be the leaders in this scientific approach to reform.

Perhaps because of his awareness of the urgent poverty of China's masses, Tao's view of the value of science tended to emphasize its promise of increased production and material goods, rather than philosophies of life. Yet he was no less an apostle of scientism, and was if anything a far more messianic educationalist than Dewey, particularly with regard to his own calling.[43] Tao's sense of personal mission, and his eulogies of science, however, pre-date his contact with Dewey and Teachers College by a matter of years. His American experience may have reinforced and given directon to these predilections, but it did not create them.

What Tao did not share, judging from his writings, was Dewey''s glorification of the West, and in particular the United States, as the home of true Progressivism, democracy, and scientific enlightenment, and his negative assessment of China by comparison. This went considerably beyond simple cultural ignorance, as in Dewey's suggestion that Chinese children be taught about electricity by beginning with "an electric light, a telegraph key, a telephone, or the battery of a car, all of which are within the daily experience of a child. . . ."[44] Dewey actually held up the West as the living model of progressive values, suitable for imitation by the Chinese.

For example, "The United States affords a good example of the value of public schools."[45] In spite of its size, and hundreds of thousands of recent immigrants, the United States was a highly integrated, unified country thanks to the public schools, which "all children of all people may attend without charge. In these public schools, children from different lands study and play together, and this associated living in school contributes greatly to the ideal of national integration."[46] This was the same John Dewey who had struggled against Polish ethnic identification during the War, and was a co-founder of the National Association for the Advancement of Colored People. Dewey was well aware of the ethnic and especially the racial divisions that rived American society. But what he presented to the Chinese was an ideal of an integrated American culture; an ideal, masquerading as reality, of unity of purpose and belief which, though not yet perfected, thanks to the public schools could well be realized "within a relatively few years."[47] The message to what James Sheridan called a "China in Disintegration"[48] was clear, as was, undoubtedly, the assertion of moral superiority. What most of Dewey's listeners could not have know was how unwarranted the assertion actually was.

Dewey was even more explicit in his invidious comparison of Chinese and Western attitudes to science. "[P]eople of the West understand the real meaning of the development of modern science better than people of the East" because the West has developed not only a high material culture, but corresponding values which direct that culture to "the promotion of human welfare."[49] That is, the West had developed its material civilization

> without paying too high a price for the benefits it brings. Oriental people, on the other hand, do not really grasp the significance of the development of science; they confuse the results of science — the development of technology — with science itself, and consequently fail to develop a scientific attitude.[50]

Again Dewey was perfectly well aware of the cataclysm of World War I, although perhaps he was not yet fully aware of its shattering consequences for Europe. Whatever, he presented the West to China as embodying an ideal of science and progress to which China should aspire, an ideal that appears, in hindsight, bizarre.

Although Tao accepted the importance of science both in what he understood to be its method and in its results, there is no indication in his writings of a belief in the superiority of the West (in contrast, for example, to Hu Shi), and there are repeated warnings against taking the West as a model. Take for example the project that most links Tao to Dewey, Xiaozhuang Experimental Normal School. Tao interpreted his innovative practices at Xiaoxhuang as a reversal of Dewey's views on the relation between education and society, a reversal appropriate to China's vastly diffferent conditions. Dewey, he thought, would approve under the circumstances, although Tao had gone well beyond what Dewey had himself advocated.[51] Tao repeatedly voiced his opposition, especially after 1923, to the mere imitation of Western models. This was not, as in the case of Liang Qichao, from disillusionment with the West as an ideal, but rather from an acute awareness of the uniqueness of China's situation. He was, his colleagues noted, the "most thoroughly Chinese" of the students returned from America.[52]

Tao in the Aftermath of the Progressive Education Movement

The years from 1917 to 1922 were the ones in which Tao most directly identified himself with American Progressivism in China. Aside from his close association with the visits of Dewey and Monroe, Tao was at the center of all the Progressive movements of the period. In 1919, possibly as a result of the impetus of the May Fourth Movement, Tao was appointed Head of Educational Science at Nanjing Higher Normal College, and from that post initiated the Progressive reforms staff had blocked for the preceding two years. For the next two years Tao voiced his support for Progressivism in the pages of its organ, *New Education,* from its opening issue. In 1922, through the sponsorship of fellow Columbian Jiang Menglin, Tao became executive secretary of the newly formed Chinese Association for Educational Advancement *(Zhongguo jiaoyu gaijin she),* and editor, following Jiang, of *New Education.* Tao was closely involved in the formulation and advancement of the measures contained in the School Reform Decree of 1922, and even a signatory to the manifesto that contributed to the formation of the progressive "Good Government" cabinet of 1922.[53]

In 1923, however, the direction of Tao's educational work changed abruptly when he joined the budding mass literacy campaign initiated by James Yen (Yan Yangchu). Yen may have been caught up in the reformist fervor of the period, but he was not strongly connected with the Columbia clique of Progressives. Rather, Yen was educated first at the University of Hong Kong, going on to take his first degree from Yale in 1918, and a Master's degree from Princeton, in history, in 1920.[54]

Yen got into education via his work among the Chinese coolies brought to France during World War I to dig trenches and other earthworks. Part of his duties included writing letters home for the illiterate sappers, his first real contact with ordinary Chinese peasants. Yen was impressed by their wit and intelligence, and by how disabled their native abilities were because of their lack of basic literacy. He determined, upon returning to China in 1921, to develop a mass literacy program. He wrote a basic text of 1000 characters, and with it a corps of volunteer teachers began an extensive literacy campaign that eventually covered much of central China.

One of the principal sponsors of this movement was Zhu Qihu, the wife of China's first republican premier, the industrialist and philanthropist Xiong Xilong. It was Zhu who introduced Tao to Yen in 1923, an event that completely reoriented Tao's education work. Tao returned south to organize the Nanjing People's Education Advancement Association, but shortly thereafter resigned from his posts at Southeastern University, and threw himself totally into the work of spreading mass literacy. At the second annual meeting of the Chinese Association for the Advancement of Education in 1923, Tao, along with James Yen and others, formed the National Association for the Promotion of Popular Education. With Yen as director, this became the umbrella organization for widespread mass literacy education among the urban poor.

At about the same time, either as symptom or cause of this reorientation, Tao reported another conversion to his own peasant roots and his personal identification with peasants and their needs. Symbolically, he exchanged his Western clothes for peasant togs, including grass thongs, in an experience he described ''like the

Yellow River bursting its dikes. I flowed back toward the path of the Chinese common man."[55] In later years, he may have switched back into Western clothing, but Tao's determination to work on behalf of ordinary peasants and workers remained constant, as did his habit of promoting his educational reforms outside regular government channels.

It was perhaps this experience that led Tao to develop his own literacy program, aimed primarily at the countryside. With Zhu Jingnong he wrote his own "thousand character" basic text, and his own set of readers, rather than using the materials already developed by Yen. What is striking about the innovation — and Tao seems to have been aware of it — was how much it was in the tradition of Chinese basic education. Aside from the use of an updated "Thousand Character Classic" as the basic text, the non-formality, dependence upon budding scholars for teachers, flexibility, and practical utility combined with traditional prestige were all characteristic of basic literacy education in China since before the Song dynasty.[56]

Further, the similarity between the traditional private school *(sishu)* and the literacy schools is unmistakable in Borthwick's fine description of early modern Chinese schools:

> In areas where the new schools imposed uniformity, compulsion, and rigidity, however, the *sishu* was arbitrary, fluid, informal, responsive. Those boundaries that define the modern school as being other, different from the outside world, were absent in the *sishu*. A *sishu* never had its own premises in the sense of having a building designed for its occupancy; this would have needed an administrative structure and income beyond the resources of the small community it served. . . . The role of the teacher was no more fixed than that of the room he occupied. . . . Attendance was easily broken off but just as easily resumed. Nor was there a fixed starting age: a beginning reader of ten might be chanting the same lessons as a precocious four-year-old.[57]

This and much more that Borthwick describes in the same chapter could be ascribed, in principle if not in precise detail, to schools of the mass education movement. Not for nothing was it, then, that Tao likened himself to Wu Xun, an illiterate nineteenth century entrepreneur who set up numerous charity schools for the poor, or that Tao fell from favor in the People's Republic during the anti-Wu Xun campaign of the early 1950s.[59]

The Xiaozhuang Experimental Normal School project is an even more remarkable case of the ambiguity of the cultural resources Tao called upon to explain and justify his innovations. Tao originated Xiaozhuang in the rural suburbs of Nanjing in 1927. His intent was to found a school for the preparation of rural teachers, but one that would address and prepare teachers for the whole range of problems that plagued China's impoverished, backward countryside. Xiaozhuang became a center not for traditional book learning, but for village management, defense against bandits, agricultural research, cultural renewal, economic planning, and so on. It was, in Tao's view, expanding education to emcompass all life, to make education equivalent to life.

Xiaozhuang could be understood as an outgrowth of Tao's contacts with Dewey, as an elaboration or adaptation of Dewey's philosophy to China. Tao himself described the rationale of Xiaozhuang in similar fashion in the 1929 article "Life Is Education" cited earlier. Tao claimed to have taken Dewey's formula of "Education Is Life," meaning that the classroom should be the larger society in miniature, and to have turned it around, investing the new slogan "Life Is Education" with the meaning that all of life, particularly all of human social existence, was the proper arena of education.

However, there are problems with taking Tao's analysis at face value, as if it were sufficient. To begin with, Tao's reference to Dewey is difficult to pinpoint. Dewey did argue for closer continuity between the classroom and the larger society, but in the sense of exploiting the surrounding culture for realistic, purposeful, and socially relevant educational problems and materials. He also recognized that, like it or not, the classroom had a definite social structure. But he did not suggest that the classroom ought to be a microcosm of the larger society, as he made clear in *Democracy and Education,* which Tao had edited in Chinese translation. Further, while Dewey suggested no metaphysical relationships between education and life, he did propose, both by precept and example, the use of schools as centers of social activities and reforms in ways strongly reminiscent of Xiaozhuang: "[T]he school must be made into a social center capable of participating in the daily, life of the community," as Curti summarized Dewey's views.[60] Dewey simply did not fit the paradigm Tao was suggesting.

It is difficult not to conclude that Tao's cloudy references to Dewey were an ad hoc rationalization, made two years after the founding of Xiaozhuang, and upon the occasion of the visit of Dewey's colleague, J. H. Kilpatrick. This of course is not to propose that Progressivism had no place in Tao's thinking regarding Xiaozhuang, only to open up the possibility that that role was relatively minor by comparison with other, more immediate factors.

Where else, then, could the idea of Xiaozhuang have originated? There is no doubt but that the spirit or aura of Progressivism, particularly its emphasis upon the social origins and practical social responsibility of education, may have urged Tao on or confirmed him in the rightness and zeal of his experiments at Xiaozhuang. But the idea of linking education to rural renewal was something that was already in the air in China, and had been for decades; according to Ye Shengtao's portrayal of educational reformers, it was familiar to returned students from Japan from before the 1911 revolution.[61] In 1923 Rabindranath Tagore had lectured in China on his experiments in using education to effect rural reform at Shantiniketan, begun in 1901.[62] But what must have had at least some influence upon Tao was the experiment in rural reconstruction begun by James Yen in Ding Xian, Shandong Province, in 1926, one year before the founding of Xiaozhuang.

Xiaozhuang and Ding Xian were sufficiently similar to suppose that there had been some cross-fertilization. But there was a distinct and important difference in attitude between Tao and Yen towards peasants, and towards peasant education, that accounts in part at least for their separate histories. Yen believed in the basic intelligence and wisdom of the peasants, a wisdom and intelligence that only needed enabling through education to effectively transform the quality of rural life. He approached rural reconstruction as a problem of enabling and selective reform of a people and tradition, and not its wholesale recreation. Yen's position was intrinsically conservative — Pearl Buck reports him thus (the italics are hers):

> We respect the traditions of the people, and one of the things we must always bear in mind is that *while we aim to create a new society, we must not forget we are doing it with an old society.*[63]

Tao, on the other hand, had no such "illusions." "The brains of China's peasants and women have been vacuum tubes for several thousand years," he wrote, and they still were empty, and would continue that way without a sage teacher.[64] The function of the rural teacher was to "transform the village into a Buddhist paradise and its people into joyful living spirits" by showing peasants how to farm, govern their villages, manage their transport, defend themselves, and so on.[65] The object was not to learn from the peasants, except how to save them. Tao was in no way an early apologist for Maoist rustication programs. Indeed, for Tao, the Chinese peasant, with his stolid conservatism, superstition, and ignorance, was the problem; hardly its solution.

A perspicacious visitor to Xiaozhuang observed to Tao that the life the students led there was "simply rudimentary; it is not a peasant's life."[66] Tao agreed. It was necessary to get back to an utterly primitive existence, before peasant life ever came to be. The peasants had lived for millennia without an iota of questioning, so that their life was "very unprogressive." "Although rural education is intended to make peasants prosperous, it is very doubtful that this can be achieved if we begin from the realities of farmers' lives *(nongmin shenghuo).*" Tao believed he was introducing a whole new order of things, an order based upon science and experimentation to which the extant peasant culture would only be an impediment.

Tao's belief in the role of the educator as a savior of the people was not inconsistent with the Progressive view of the educational expert, above and outside politics, using science as both the method and content of education to transform man's social and economic life. Dewey himself was by no means opposed to radical change. With his extraordinary belief in the possibility and power of utterly rational planning, he argued that every aspect of traditional culture should be tested to determine experimentally what should be retained, and what jettisoned.[67] Where Tao and Dewey differed — and it was a fundamental difference — was in the method of transvaluation. Dewey maintained that it was the nature of scientific inquiry to deal with only one, well-defined, problem at a time, while holding all else as given. In Tao's vision of Xiaozhuang, however, all cultural presuppositions were to be swept away, and a new start made, freed of the suffocating wraps of millennia of Chinese tradition.

Thus even before Tao's drift to Marxism in the 1930s and 1940s he embraced a view far more open to revolutionary solutions to China's ills than did Dewey or James Yen. The astonishing thing is that for Tao this view had roots that were deep not only in the modern myths of science and progress, but in the Confucian legends as well. The ancients, like primitive man, had no tradition to impede them, and therefore had to rely on their own experience. This, according to Tao, is what accounts for the remarkable creativity and intellectual ferment of China's classical philosophers, and the generally moribund state of Confucianism since them.[68] Tao even suggested a three-stage development of history (as did the reformers Kang Youwei and Liang Qichao), one that "progresses" to an ancient golden age. In the first stage, education is education and life is life, and the two do not mix. In the second stage education is life, and the school is transformed by society. In the third stage, however, life is education, and education transforms life — just it did in ancient times.

> In this period it is like driving a car in reverse, so that it is driven back to ancient times. This is because in ancient times society was school, there was no telling the difference. It was in those times that education advanced to its highest plane.[69]

It is tempting at this point to invoke Levenson's famous distinction between "history" and "value," and argue that Tao used the rhetoric of traditional Chinese metaphors to promote Progressive measures as a means of preserving both his commitments to Chinese culture and to Chinese nationhood. [70] This interpretive principle works better, however, when applied to those who actually felt confronted by the West, were aware of the chasm between the two, and required some mode of intellectual reconciliation between them, persons such as Kang Youwei, Liang Qichao, and perhaps Hu Shi. Tao gives no evidence in his writings of fundamentally divided loyalties. His works are peppered with references to Chinese history, literature, and philosophy, but to understand, explain, and justify his actions through references to things Chinese was for Tao not to deny Western values. As Chinese from before Zhang Zhidong to after Mao Zedong have also imagined, Tao believed he could use Western ideas without becoming Westernized, that methodologically Progressivism was merely a kind of Western variant on the finest flower of Chinese culture thousands of years before.

Retrospective

Xiaozhuang was closed by Guomindang authorities in 1930, three years after it opened. The occasion was the participation of Xiaozhuang students and staff in anti-Japanese demonstrations, demonstrations that embarrassed the government. There had been communist cells at Xiaozhuang, but there had also been Guomindang cells and a variety of other cliques as well. Tao claimed to follow Cai Yuanpei's ideal of keeping the school out of factional politics, though he and his students were frequently involved in nationalistic movements, including the final demonstration against the Japanese closing of Yangtze River ports.

Tao is also credited with not having shown particular deference to Chiang Kai-shek on two of the latter's visits to Xiaozhuang, to the point of discourtesy if modern chroniclers are to be believed.[71] Whatever, there is considerable evidence of a close association between Xiaozhuang and the "Christian warlord"

Feng Yuxiang, Feng not only supplied Tao's anti-bandit militia with decrepit weapons, but even detached some of his officers to train them. He was a frequent visitor to Xiaozhuang, and unlike Chiang Kai-shek, who was left standing, had his own private chair reserved for his visits. Although Feng's relations with Chiang were, to say the least ambiguous, this was a period when both were joined in a drive to unite the country and to eliminate Communism. Feng's close association with Xiaozhuang contradicts recent claims that Xiaozhuang was little more than an early educational arm of the Communist Party, and that it was this that led to its closure.[72] In the end, it was probably as much the desire of the government of the Republic of China to control education, and in particular teacher education, as it was political activism that led to Xiaozhuang's demise.

Although Tao's career in education continued with many new twists, Xiaozhuang remained its apogee for historians, and for Tao himself.[73] The establishment of part-time urban schools for waifs in the 1930s, and the technique of using children themselves as teachers, were both understood by Tao as urban extensions of the Xiaozhuang idea. Many of the staff in these schools were also former students at Xiaozhuang. According to recent reports, Tao had wanted to build a new Xiaozhuang outside Chongqing during the Japanese war, but was discouraged by his colleagues from doing so on the grounds that the government would not allow private teacher training institutions. Tao then proposed an agricultural institute, but again he was blocked. What emerged was Yucai, a school for gifted orphans, which success as it was, was far from Tao's intentions.[74] The crest of reform had in fact passed Tao by. It was no longer possible, as in earlier, more freewheeling days, to launch major educational projects near the center of government power without being a part of the national educational system. In the 1920s Tao's innovations led the way in Chinese education. After 1930 they were merely peripheral.

It is, then, perhaps the right moment to assess Tao's relationship to Progressivism. How do we know when philosophies of thought and action, in the sense of general orientations to life such as Progressivism, pass from one culture to another? What sort of evidence should we seek and accept to argue for, say, transmission rather than parallel development, for genuine movement rather than the adoption of a certain rhetoric that masks the actuality of traditional concerns and behaviors? To what extent is Progressivism (for example) a relatively insignificant wavelet riding on a far more fundamental trend itself? Tao's example, and the evidence for it, merely heightens the ambiguity.

First, there must be exposure to and adoption of the culture to be transmitted. Tao wholeheartedly embraced Progressivism, but was what he embraced any more than an adjunct to Neo-Confucianism, already well in place in China and in Tao as the basic philosophy of social reform, that predisposed him to it in the first place? The second sort of evidence might be some reasonably exact correspondence between what is being transmitted and the expression of its transmission, i.e., between Tao's thought and action and those of American Progressives such as Dewey. Here there certainly was some agreement at a superficial level — both advocated kindergartens and theatricals. At any deeper level, it was only in his participation in the events that led to the Education Reform Decree of 1922 that Tao's affiliation with Progressivism was unambiguous. In both the mass education movement of the mid-1920s and in the Xiaozhuang Experimental Normal School Tao's reliance upon Progressivism is far less clear than his debt to James Yen, to the opportunity for individually led educational experimentation in an otherwise chaotic China (as portrayed for example by Ye Shengtao), and to the thorough-going intellectual ferment and competition that allowed for a "fresh start" without, yet, the stifling need to conform to political orthodoxy, communist or republican.

The third sort of evidence, and perhaps the most convincing, would be the self-identification of the transmitter with the culture being transmitted. Did Tao think of himself as somehow at one with Progressivism? There is little doubt that he thought of himself as identified with Columbia, and with Dewey and Kilpatrick as educational leaders in their country, as he was in his. It is also true that upon the visit of Kilpatrick to Xiaozhuang he interpreted his experiment there as a kind of going beyond Dewey. Tao may have thought of himself as at one with other Progressives, but there is no doubt that he also understood himself and his actions in Chinese terms as well, particularly after 1923. He did not seem to be aware of the need for an intellectual, versus moral, choice (if there was one), and this lack of choice, this syncretistic affirmation of both at once, makes any precise assignment of intellectual origins most precarious.

Looking more closely at Tao's identification with the Progressive movement in China leads to the conclusion that exactly what in his thought or actions can be unambiguously ascribed to the influence of progressivism is problematic. It is clear from his writings that Tao used the rhetoric of Progressivism. Yet the reality of his debt seems, on closer examination of any particular instance, partial at best, and sometimes doubtful altogether. Such was the case with many Chinese progressives, but especially Tao Xingzhi.[75] He may have adopted the visions and energy of Progressivism, and in some cases the specific practices advocated by Dewey. Nevertheless the source, thrust, and telos of his ideas and behavior were most clearly rooted in Tao's personality, the ambiguities of his enculturation to China and acculturation to the West, and the evolving historical situation of Republican China. Tao was influenced by Progressivism, there is no doubt, but somewhat in the way the gravity of the sun deflects starlight that grazes it, starlight whose source and destination is elsewhere.

8

The Multiplication of Ourselves: Canadian Medical Missionaries in West China

Karen Minden

Introduction

Overwhelmed by the futility of providing medical care to a population of sixty million, the first Canadian medical missionary in Sichuan Province decided to train several Chinese assistants. It was 1907, and Dr. Omar Kilborn soon realized that the "one-man medical school" was a hopeless endeavor; a handful of missionary doctors could not solve China's need for health care. By this time, Protestant missionaries in China had become convinced that appealing to the poor and illiterate masses would never be as effective as evangelizing an influential, educated elite. It was this conjunction of ideas, that the missionaries were too few to serve the needs of China's population, and that focusing on the elite would be a more efficient way of influencing the acceptance of new ideas, that lay behind the West China Union University's (WCUU) decision to establish a medical college in Chengdu in 1914. The Canadian Methodist Church was one of the founding missions of the university in 1910, and Canadian medical missionaries formed the majority of the Medical & Dental faculty throughout the College's history.[1]

The Canadian medical missionaries of the West China Mission in Sichuan set out to establish a foundation on which the Chinese could build a modern medical system. They sought to establish an educational institution that would train physicians imbued with Christian ethics and a commitment to modern scientific medicine.

Their ultimate goal was "the Multiplication of Ourselves": to create a corps of Chinese doctors who would eventually develop a modern health care system for China. For these missionaries, the "Good News" was not so much the Christian Gospel as Scientific Medicine. Their institution was dedicated to establishing a center of excellence for medical education, but their ultimate goal was to transform China into a modern nation through the adoption of Christian values. The medical missionaries were confounded by the juxtaposition of these two goals: the establishment of an educational institution which could be devolved to their Chinese students, and the transformation of China's ethical climate to one that reflected both Christian values and the ideas of modern science.

Rather than devolve the responsibility of the Medical College to Chinese colleagues, the goals of the institution began to serve the expansion of the College itself. The Medical and Dental schools did not come under Chinese jurisdiction until the missionaries were forcibly evicted by the Chinese Communists in 1950.

In October 1985, Sichuan Medical College reverted to its former name of West China University of Medical Sciences and celebrated its seventy-fifth anniversary. This acknowledgement of its missionary origins in 1910 signified the clear demarcation between the xenophobic educational policies of the Maoist regime, and the so-called "open door" policies of Deng Xiaoping's government. It is in this context of China's willingness to consider transfer of technology and ideas from the West that there has been renewed interest in the historical experience of China's educational relations with the industrialized world.

This chapter evaluates the role of the Canadian medical missionaries in the development of medical education in Sichuan province. It examines the model for medical care and education which was established at the West China Union University, and the extent to which it influenced the emerging modernization of medicine in West China. An important focus of the analysis is the context in which the medical mission was developed, including the social and political milieu of United Church Mission policy, and the particular characteristics of one of China's most remote interior provinces, Sichuan.

Sino-Canadian Relations before 1949

Unlike the experience of other western nations, Canadian educational activities in China were not an integral part of a broader political and economic relationship between the two countries. Until 1943, when the Canadian government established its first Legation office in Chongqing (Chungking), Canadian diplomatic links with China were through the British Government. Even after the upgrading of the Legation to Embassy status in 1944, Canada's presence in China's wartime capital was relatively insignificant. The Embassy's facilities were meagre compared to those of Britain, the United States, and even Australia, and the Canadian ambassador lamented the vagueness of Canada's policy in China.[2] He did however report that Canada was perceived as a friendly, non-threatening "middle power."[3]

In the area of trade, activities were confined to a few commercial agents in Shanghai and Tianjin. Bilateral trade was negligible for both countries, and was limited by Canadian protective tariffs.

In contrast to the low profile of political and economic links, Canadian missionaries had a substantial presence in China. It is noteworthy that when the first Canadian diplomats arrived in Chongqing, they were housed at the United Church of Canada's Mission Hospital compound. Ambassador Victor Odlum's guide and interpreter in China was Dr. Leslie Kilborn, a medical missionary who served as Dean of the West China Union University College of Medicine. The Canadian presence in China before 1949 was largely characterized by missionary efforts to evangelize, educate and provide medical care.

In the century before 1949 there were four major Canadian Protestant missions in China: the West China Mission (WCM) in Sichuan, the North China Mission in Henan, the Anglican Diocese in Henan, and the South China Mission in Guangdong. The West China Mission was the largest, both in the number of missionaries assigned there (including sixty-one medical missionaries between 1892 and 1949), and in the scope of its institutions, which included a university with a medical and dental college, and ten station hospitals. The Canadian presence in medical missionary work in Sichuan province exceeded that of any other nationality.

The United Church of Canada and West China

By the end of the nineteenth century, most of the coastal areas of China had been occupied by missionary groups who had established their schools, churches and hospitals in the accessible treaty ports. Canada came late to this venture, and found a vast area for potential influence in West China, beyond the unnavigable Yangzi gorges. Reverend Virgil C. Hart surveyed the territory in 1888, and found "an empire in itself, with its teeming millions."[4] The missionaries' goal was to bring the benefits of their religion and civilization to the masses of Sichuan. Far from the established missions in China's treaty ports, West China was almost virgin territory, to be conquered by a pioneering mission. Hart was enthusiastic about the possibilities for a Canadian missionary enterprise: "Only think of the opportunity God has given me to establish another mission — and for Canada!"[5] Later missionary statements echoed Hart's excitement about the opportunity to establish Canadian Christian influence, and the importance of Sichuan as a strategic centre for the development of their mission. Described as "China's largest, most populous, wealthiest, most strategic province,"[6] it was destined to exert a "great influence upon neighboring provinces of China and upon the spread of Christianity in Thibet and other parts of Central Asia."[7] It was believed that the impact of Western civilization in Sichuan would reach beyond its borders: "As goes Szechwan, so goes China."[8]

Missionaries at the West China Conference in 1898 at Chongqing had decided to divide the province into spheres in order to avoid rivalry and duplication of efforts. The then Methodist Mission of the Canadian Methodist Church[9] was given an area of 20,000 square miles. Between 1892 and 1913, the West China Mission established ten central stations and eighty-one outstations. The Methodist Board's policy of concentration[10] was reflected in the strategically located central stations, each with access to hundreds of surrounding market towns, and each equipped with a "foreign style hospital, or at least dispensaries."[11] By 1910, the mission had "accepted the responsibility for the evangelization of 10,000,000 in West China . . . equal to twice the Protestant population of the Dominion of

Canada. . . ."[12] Its territory included "26 walled cities, over 1000 market towns, and tens of thousands of small country villages."[13]

Omar Kilborn, an ordained Methodist minister and physician from rural Ontario, requested the inclusion of medical work in the mission, and offered his services in 1891.[14] To ensure the health and indeed survival of missionaries in the field, and to help open the doors for Christian influence in the Chinese community, it was agreed that medical missionaries were necessary to establish a successful West China Mission, and Kilborn joined the first group of eight Canadian missionaries to Sichuan province in 1892.

In the early years from 1892 to 1925, when the West China Mission was a Canadian Methodist institution, all medical missionaries were fully trained as Ministers, professionals in both evangelical and medical work. If evangelical duties were pressing however, medical work was subordinated. The establishment of medical missions was not yet a *sine qua non* of foreign missions. Kilborn had to convince the Canadian Board of Foreign Missions that the added expense of appointing medical missionaries was worthwhile. It was a controversial issue both theologically and politically. The detractors of medical mission expansion argued that medical work was too expensive and time consuming and would deplete evangelical work. They reasoned that the saving of souls was of more consequence than the saving of bodies, and that there was no place for lay people in foreign missions. The champions of medical missions, represented in Canada by Omar Kilborn, presented the counter argument that the "Ministry of Healing" emulated the life of Christ; furthermore, it was the most effective means of introducing the Christian way of life — personal cleanliness, public santitation, institutionalized care of the sick, and public and governmental responsibility for medical care — to the "constituency of over one hundred millions of people . . . in the Chinese Empire, and destined to wield an enormous influence upon the future civilization of Central Asia."[15] As the debate progressed, it became clear that Christian medical missionaries saw their mission to improve the quality of life as well as saving souls. They sought to respond to the emergent Chinese "spirit of inquiry as to Western science and religion,"[16] by introducing modern Western medicine with its technology, concepts of science and public health, and institutions for the care of the sick.

This "modernist" belief in the Social Gospel rejected the fundamentalist emphasis on individual salvation. The Social Gospel was concerned with the social and political implications of Christianity, with the redemption of social injustices and national politics. The fact that medical missions developed at all was based on the growing conviction in the United Church that evangelization could be better achieved through the improvement of the quality of life by the contributions of modern education and medical care. This notion reflected the "modernist" precept that individual conversion and physical welfare were allied, and that a new spiritual life could be better built on a strong material foundation.

It soon became apparent that in medical work at least, travelling among rural communities was counter-productive. While Virgil Hart's intention in 1888 had been to use the station hospitals as the nucleus for itinerant medical missionaries, it was decided by 1910 that the medical center could give better services and more beneficial results than itinerating could.[17] There, the medical missionary had access to colleagues, supplies, instruments, adequate care facilities for the sick, and an institution in which patients could be observed more carefully and encouraged to comply with the doctor's instructions. This attitude to medical care, that the hospital, rather than the home, is the better place for recovery, reflected the growing centralization of medical care in Canada.[18]

The ten central stations, strategically located in county towns which were political, social, economic and cultural centers, were each to have "an experienced physician and sufficient funds to start both dispensary and hospital."[19] Virgil Hart, the first representative of Canadian Methodist missionaries to reach West China, recognized the value of medical missions in "softening the hearts of the masses,"[20] but he warned in 1888, just prior to the founding of the West China Mission, that large institutions were anathema to the cause of initiating a native church. "Christian charities were not for the purpose of founding large institutions to be controlled by foreign boards," he wrote in his recommendations; rather the germ of a new institution should be introduced, to be "developed by the people themselves."[21]

In spite of Hart's earlier admonition, the United Church, influenced by the growing emphasis on public institutions in Canada, and the achievement-orientation of its financial elite membership, concentrated on "the development of great institutions."[22] The 1910 projections for the development of the "Mission plant" called for "a considerable missionary force and a thoroughly organized and equipped mission."[23] In medical work, it was acknowledged that although dispensary work could be valuable,

> They can multiply their helpfulness many times through properly equipped hospitals, and without these hospitals they are denied the opportunity of the continuous oversight which is so important for the best physical and spiritual results.[24]

The increasing secularization and bureaucratization of the mission enterprise was evidenced by the inclusion of laymen with specialized skills to offer to mission work. The first medical missionaries were ordained men whose professional skills were merely an adjunct to their evangelical work. By 1920, however, a recruitment patterns reflected the shift of emphasis: the West China Mission had on its staff doctors, nurses, dentists, a pharmacist, builder, architect, accountant, business agent, teacher, printers, as well as evangelists.[25] The rationale for this division of labor was the increased efficiency both in missionary work and financing. The burgeoning physical plant of the institution had to be supported by greater differentiation of labor, and this development in West China mirrored the increasing organizational complexity of the Church in Canada.

The emphasis on excellence and high professional standards, reflected in the appointment of not only medical specialists, but dentists and pharmacists as well, was indicative of the secular nature of Church policy, based on a broad interpretation of the "cause of Christianity." The three tasks the Foreign Mission

Board undertook, evangelism, educational work and medical work, were considered inseparable and mutually complementary. The ambition of the messengers of the Social Gospel was "to embed ultimate human goals in the social, economic, and political order,"[26] by creating a Christian civilization in China.

The Medical Missionaries: Background

Canadian medical missionaries were not only part of a Social Gospel movement in Canada, but also of a North American Student Christian Movement. The belief that all of society had to be Christianized, not just individual souls, and that it was the responsibility of a just nation to carry out this task, influenced the students in the North American Student Volunteer Movement, and later Student Christian Movement. Student study groups emphasized the need for social and economic reform as well as religious reform. The approach to these reforms, the study of social needs and the planning of social action, was based on the newly developed methods of social science: survey research, principles of professional social work, and behavior theory.[27] As such, this professionalized approach was most prominent among university students, represented by the Student Christian Movement (SCM).

"SCMers" were characterized as idealists who were open-minded to the validity of non-Christian religious beliefs, committed to world brotherhood and world peace, and to the Social Gospel as an impetus to political change.[28] Their theological beliefs were strongly influenced by H. B. Sharman's *Jesus In the Records*, an historical study of Jesus, aimed at presenting the ultimate values of Christianity without the dogma of the organized church.[29] The SCM was action-oriented, devoted to "the reconstruction of society" through social welfare agencies.[30]

The humanitarian focus of Social Gospel theology influenced Church, and particularly mission policy. As Canada emerged as an actor in the international sphere after the First World War, the trends towards secularization and institutionalization in the United Church were accompanied by its increasing perception of itself as a distinctly Canadian institution. The Canadian nation experienced a surge of growth in population and economy, attended by a parallel surge of national pride. Canadian missionaries and Mission Board members perceived that a stronger Canada could exert greater influence in the non-Christian world. Their commitment to mission expansion was ambitious and enthusiastic. The Methodist Mission Statement of 1910 indicated that the Church had accepted responsibility for ten million souls in West China, "equal to twice the Protestant population of the Dominion of Canada."[31] The challenge to go "Forward with China" appealed to the citizens of an emerging nation. The Canadian church saw its "share of Szechuan . . . China's wealthiest, most populous and most strategic province"[32] as an unparalleled opportunity to bring Sichuan's millions into the modern era. An appeal for missionary support in 1928 expressed this challenge to its Canadian constituents:

It is indeed difficult to realize its stupendous significance. It means that in Szechuan alone . . . we of the United Church of Canada hold missionary mandate for a population approximately one and a half times as numerous as all the peoples scattered far and wide over the vast expanse of Canada's many provinces . . . for weal or for woe, to us and to us alone in the order of Providence is committed this great opportunity.[33]

Indicative of the Canadian missionaries' new sense of national strength and significance in the world of nations, a wooden gavel presented by overseas missionaries at the Church Union ceremony on June 10, 1925, was constructed as follows:

The hammer was made of wood obtained from the eleven areas in Asia, Africa and Trinidad where they were at work and the handle was made of Canadian maple.[34]

Clearly, the United Church of Canada Missionary enterprise considered itself a force to be reckoned with in the non-Christian world, and the medical missionaries regarded themselves as an integral part of that force.

The Chinese Context: Sichuan Province

The Canadian Methodist Church in 1892 chose to establish its West China Mission in the central part of Sichuan. This densely populated area known as the Chengdu Plain is the most arable land in an otherwise mountainous province. Traversed by the Min River, the Yangzi and its major tributaries, it has an extensive riverine transportation system for its many and varied natural products. Besides the two main cities of Chengdu and Chongqing, the former a political and cultural centre and the latter commercial, the population was rather diffuse, with ninety percent living in rural areas. In spite of its excellent river transportation, the numerous market towns were connected by poor and frequently hazardous roads, and railways were all but non-existent. During the half century in which the West China Mission occupied this region, the rural area flourished commercially but, as one scholar describes it, it never achieved significant economic modernization.[35]

With its great wealth in agriculture, salt, textiles, and opium, and its population in the 1920s of sixty million, Sichuan was frequently a battlefield for political and economic control. The missionaries also recognized the challenge of winning Sichuan. They saw its potential for growth and visualized it as a "field in which to test the heroic spirit of modern Christianity." When Virgil Hart surveyed the area in 1888, he wrote:

. . . to the prophetic mind it possesses latent possibilities which enlarge its consequence and make it a peculiarly interesting section of the empire. . . . The past year has seen it introduced to North, East, and South by means of the electric wire, thus giving it politically all the privileges enjoyed by other provinces. Steam will tame the wild rapids of its mighty river, and bring an unimagined commercial prosperity to its wealthy centers . . . it will become a highway of nations.[36]

Although twentieth century Sichuan was more in touch with events in the rest of China than it had been in 1888, it was not until the Japanese occupation forced the Nationalist Government to retreat to that province in 1937 that it became the hub of Chinese national development. The enthusiasm of the missionaries during the period when Chongqing was the capital of unoccupied China echoed Hart's a half century before, as they envisioned the profound influence they could exercise on China's future from their strategic base in Sichuan province.

In spite of the province's great wealth and commercial activity, it suffered a long period of political instability. This situation is perhaps best described by the parenthetical remarks of a missionary in the early 1920s: "Politically, the province of Sichuan is divided into five circuits (that is, when the province is sufficiently at peace to be considered politically) . . ."[37] The Revolution of 1911 which ended dynastic rule in China left a power vacuum in Sichuan, as it did in much of China. The abolition of the civil service exams in 1905 had already seriously undermined the bureaucratic structure of the Imperial government, and confusion compounded disintegration as the avenues to political authority became unclear. The new political career pattern which emerged was military as opposed to the civil-bureaucratic system which had existed in Imperial China, and a new generation of provincially oriented militarists emerged to grasp control of whatever regions they could. Sichuan was controlled by five major warlords who were described as "dim figures," poorly educated, oppressive, ruthless, cruel and incompetent.[38] After 1927 the warlords had carved the province into five locally autonomous regions known as garrison areas (*fang qu*).[39] Each warlord had his own elaborate bureaucracy with numerous petty officials. The bureaucracy was essentially powerless to carry out any of its functions except for tax collection. In some areas taxes had been collected twenty years in advance, and yet this corrupt system never had funds to provide services to its population.

Although a Department of Health was formed in 1928 under the National Ministry of the Interior, no provincial counterpart was formed in Sichuan until the National Government moved to Chongqing in 1938. Detailed plans for a modern Public Health Administration existed by 1925,[40] but lack of funding, personnel, and effective political control of the provinces confined the public health administration to the Nationalist Government's capital at Nanjing, and a few experimental stations.[41]

Subsequent to the Nationalist Government's consolidation of political control in Sichuan in 1938, a Provincial Health Administration was formed under the leadership of Dr. C. C. Ch'en, a native of Chengdu, and graduate of the prestigious Peking Union Medical College. This administration, in spite of its well-laid plans and rational priorities, was severely hampered by the lack of funds and effective administrative infrastructure which might have allowed it to develop a health care delivery system for the province. The condition of local government was one of a rather elaborate structure characterized by inefficiency and powerlessness. Provision for public welfare was essentially non-existent. It was in this context of political instability and the absence of health care services that the medical missionaries developed their approach to modernizing medical care in Sichuan.

The Missionary Model

The medical missionaries in Sichuan attempted to provide medical education through their College of Medicine and Dentistry, and primary health care through their station hospitals. Their priorities were informed by their model for medical modernization: the most effective strategy to disseminate modern medicine would be to train a corps of native physicians who would in turn be the future teachers in Chinese medical schools. Their influence would multiply from the first seeds sown by a few foreign medical missionaries. The model for medical modernization was to create a highly trained professional elite, and to build the physical and administrative infrastructure to deliver curative health care from urban centres. This concentration of modern medical facilities would gradually expand and filter down to serve the rural community. The missionaries' strategy for gaining the acceptance and support of modern medicine by the Chinese was to eventually devolve authority and responsibility for medical education and care to the Chinese themselves.

The model for medical and dental education adopted by the missionaries reflected their goals, and their own educational and professional backgrounds. The first call to the medical missionary to teach in a Christian medical college was put forth by Omar Kilborn as "the duty . . . to multiply himself by making medical missionaries among the Chinese."[42] The Medical College was organized to train leaders so that "the multitudes of suffering men and women living in Sichuan and adjoining areas should receive the benefits of modern medicine."[43] The missionary doctor was of value only to the extent that he could change the conditions of China's suffering on a large scale, and to do this "he must be able to reproduce himself among China's young men."[44] Thus the medical missionary, with his high level of scientific medical training, professional code of ethics, and Christian spirit of service and self sacrifice, was the model for the development of a modern Chinese medical profession. Dr. Ashley Lindsay, Dean of the College of Dentistry, was more specific about the aims of his faculty, and their vision for China's future development. Their goal was to educate scientists rather than technicians, individuals who would be imbued with a model for dental education which would equip them to be "dental administrators and teachers for the dental colleges which are about to be organized throughout China."[45]

E. N. Meuser, the pharmacist on the Medical Faculty, stated his purpose to train Chinese students in the "science of modern pharmacy" and at the same time to "develop systematic research in Chinese crude drugs."[46] In addition to applied research and professionalization of the Chinese pharmacist, Meuser envisioned his department as a model for pharmacy education in China. William Band of the British Council visited the department in 1944 and reported:

> On the classroom walls is a large map of the United States and Canada, showing the location of pharmaceutical educational centers in North America. Every student is encouraged to dream of a similar map for China.[47]

The rationale for providing professional medical education was its contribution to China's future development by serving as a "strategic basis" for the solution of China's health problems.[48] The justification for providing a university environment for medical education was given in the 1936 *Report on Policy:*

> The wider background and greater detachment from the deadening effect of the immediate environment permit the medical missionary to supply a steady stream of vital Christian enthusiasm and scientific spirit . . . Furthermore, the very great opportunity embodied in our Medical educational institutions for establishing the healing professions of whole nations upon Christian foundations is so challenging that the need for missionary medical educationalists is greater than ever before.[49]

The College of Medicine and Dentistry was the largest faculty at the University, and commanded the majority of personnel and funding of the Canadian medical missionary enterprise.[50] Dr. Leslie Kilborn, Omar Kilborn's son and his successor as Dean of the College, pointed out that most of the staff were Canadians, and two wings of the Medical-Dental building were built with Canadian funds: "Our Mission has always regarded this college as its very special sphere in this University."[51] A report in 1939 explained the "'unbalance' where medicine and dentistry have grown out of proportion to the other departments and faculties" as a result of "the self-evident need of medicine."[52] As early as 1926 the University's medical budget was ten times greater than that for the Department of Religion.[53] The support for medical education at the University was the most extensive commitment made by the United Church in this field. In their African missions, medical missionaries trained "low-grade assistants"; in India, "relatively little has been done towards medical education under mission auspices"; in North China, paramedical assistants were trained; and in Korea, North and South China, the United Church co-operated in supporting university medical schools.[54] In West China they not only co-operated in the support of the University and its Medical college but provided three of the four hospitals used for clinical teaching, the majority of the dental faculty, and specialists in pharmacy and hospital technology.[55]

While the medical missionaries were preoccupied with their professional goals, they were cognizant of their role as Christian missionaries in a non-Christian land. Many of them chose to integrate their Christian ethics and ideals with their professional behavior rather than preach their faith outright. Dr. Bruce Collier's goal as professor of biochemistry was "to relate Science to life as a whole, thus demonstrating its spiritual value."[56] However, rigors of teaching in Chinese as well as administering a department and updating its technology made it difficult for teachers to spend time conveying their spiritual values. In addition, the conflict between science and the superstitious aspects of Christian religious belief were not lost on the students. A handwritten note inside a 1916 publication of the mission read:

> One of the greatest difficulties that seems perennial in my scientific work with the students seems to be the virgin birth of J. C. (sic).[57]

Most medical missionaries were so preoccupied with their teaching and clinical work that they had neither time nor inclination to evangelize, and as illustrated above, the Christian message was not always consistent with the teaching of science. Many missionaries relied on personal contacts outside their teaching and clinical duties to transmit their Christian ethics if not their religious beliefs.[58]

Curriculum and Students

The organization of the University and the curriculum of the professional schools reflected the professionalization of medical and dental education in the West, and the predominantly University of Toronto background of the medical missionary group.[59] "The Oxford Plan" used at University of Toronto was adopted by WCUU, whereby denominational, autonomous colleges were responsible for "all matters pertaining to the life of the students, except instruction."[60] This organization reinforced the separation of evangelical and secular education at the University.

The curriculum for the College of Medicine reflected the North American emphasis on basic sciences and hospital-oriented clinical training.[61] The United Board for Christian Colleges in China, a co-ordinating body of the thirteen Protestant Universities, reported that the curriculum of the College of Medicine "followed the general pattern of Grade A schools in the United States and Canada as laid down by the Association of American Medical Colleges."[62] The medical course was seven years, the first two being devoted to basic sciences and English.[63] Like the University of Toronto program, the last year of study included a "clinical clerkship" in the hospital, followed by a one year rotating internship.[64] Following the University of Toronto's example, specialization was not allowed prior to attaining a general knowledge of medical practice during the internship year.[65] In 1932, Kilborn required senior students to write a thesis.[66] By 1937 the College also offered a postgraduate Diploma in Opthalmology and Otolaryngology, and a Certificate in Hospital Technology,[67] indicative of the increasing scope and differentiation of the institution.

The dental curriculum was unique in that it shared the first two years of basic science training with the Faculty of Medicine, and was also a seven year course with a clinical internship in the University Dental Hospital.[68] Like medicine, it adhered to the standards of "Grade A" dental schools in Canada. An observer from the Peking Union Medical College remarked that the quality of teaching and curriculum exceeded those of medicine.[69] The WCUU integration of medicine and dentistry in the preclinical years was an innovation, designed to train scientific dentists rather than technicians.[70] This followed the trend in Canada towards the professionalization of dentistry, but was a departure from standard dental education in North America,[71] and more appropriate to the training of potential university professors of dentistry.

The pharmacy curriculum was four years in length, and also stressed basic sciences.[72] In addition, it promoted technical skills and applied research into Chinese materia medica.

Since students were encouraged to pursue postgraduate study abroad, and to return to China as leaders in their profession, English language proficiency was stressed during their training. To facilitate premedical studies, Chinese was the language of instruction in the first two years and English was gradually introduced.

In spite of the urgent need for physicians, dentists and pharmacists in China, the University opted for an elitist model of medical education. The medical missionaries believed that their greatest contribution to China's development would be the training of men and women who could staff future medical colleges and thus maximize their influence. They rejected the alternative model, to train paramedics or lower grade doctors to provide the immediate need. There were no self-conscious arguments given for this decision; the alternative model had in fact been the original means of training mission hospital assistants and was rejected as inadequate. Omar Kilborn's remarks in 1910 are indicative of the spirit of great institutions which inspired the College of Medicine and Dentistry: "There is a general realization that the day of small things is over, and that larger and more thorough-going and more advanced work must be undertaken."[73]

In spite of the emphasis on academic achievement, social action by the students was encouraged. In 1929 a group of medical students produced a "Public Health Sheet" for the two Chengdu newspapers, and presented public health lectures and demonstrations in the rural district near Chengdu.[74] Leslie Kilborn was faculty advisor to the campus Student Christian Movement, which had seventy or more students involved in social projects, including a night school for workmen and servants, a neighborhood kindergarten, and public health work among peasants.[75] Inspired by the Rural Reconstruction Movement of the Nationalist government after 1935, medical interns staffed a rural clinic during their summer vacation.[76]

The first students to enter the Medical College were mostly from poor families, and were subsidized by the missionaries.[77] In devising the plans for the College in 1908, it was suggested that dormitories for Chinese students should be simple so as not to give students "the habit of a style of living beyond what they would be able to command after leaving college."[78] However, the student body changed over time, with more "sons and daughters of many of the best families in West China" enrolling in medicine and dentistry, presumably inspired by the successful careers of earlier graduates.[79]

The students were generally characterized as pragmatic and conservative. One graduate reported that most students were disinterested in politics and professed no political affiliation.[80] Only twenty-five per cent were Christians in 1945,[81] so it can be assumed that their primary motive in attending the University was to secure professional training. Most came from middle class families who could afford the tuition at a private institution and few were political or social .revolutionaries.

The total number of graduates by 1948 was 398 in medicine, and an estimated 130 in dentistry.[82] Dr. L. G. Kilborn observed in 1931 that "we could easily place many times the number of medical and dental graduates we are able to turn out."[83] By 1934 government entrance exams attempted to restrict university enrollment to prevent a surplus of university graduates who would not be able to find employment.[84] However fifty percent of the Union University's students in 1934 were enrolled in medicine or dentistry, "professions greatly in demand in this country."[85]

Devolution vs. Institutional Growth

The pattern of placement of graduates indicates that the original objective of the missionaries to devolve medical education to Chinese graduates was not achieved, at least before 1949. Until 1938, when the Nationalist and Provincial Governments had established their Health Administrations in Chongqing, most medical graduates were used to staff the mission hospitals. Of ten graduates in 1931, seven worked in mission hospitals.[86] As of 1938, forty-five per cent of the total one hundred and fourteen medical graduates and forty-seven per cent of the dental graduates were employed in mission hospitals.[87] The rest were divided between private practice and government service. Only nine per cent pursued post-graduate courses.[88] In 1934 Jiang Jieshi (Chiang Kai-shek) personally appealed to the graduating class, urging them to "work for their country."[89] Between 1938 and 1943, a significant increase in government employment of physicians occurred, with thirty-six per cent of medical graduates placed in administration or government hospitals. This shift in recruitment was due to the introduction of "compulsory national service for new graduates," whereby a graduate from a private university had to give one year of "national service" to the National Health Administration.[90] In 1944, medical graduates were conscripted by the government.[91]

The development of the National and Provincial Health Administration, and the military crisis from 1937 to 1949, introduced radical changes into the context in which the medical missionaries first conceived of medical education for China. Underlying the missionary model was the assumption that Chinese medical schools would be the first stage in the development of an indigenous system of modern medicine. The missionaries projected that their graduates would be needed to staff these schools and administer hospitals as they developed in China. The speech to the graduation class of the College of Medicine in 1944 illustrates how far those original expectations were from actual developments.[92] Dr. Hu Dingan urged the graduates not to specialize, but to meet the urgent need of their country for basic medical care:

> Our country needs, at the present time, well-trained general practitioners . . .
> You are an elite. You are over-educated. Don't feel badly about not specializing; the present situation needs standard doctors more . . .[93]

A further critique of the University's policy of elitist medical education was its failure to develop public health as an important sphere of medicine.[94] Dr. Li Dingan contributed an article to the student medical journal indicating that although the Soviet system of health care would not be adopted in China, their model of health care delivery, which gave equal weight to curative and preventive medicine, was appropriate for China.[95] This model formed the NHA's plan for the organization of "medical benefits to all classes of society."[96] When the missionaries introduced scientific medicine in Sichuan, there were no government plans for the administration of health care; medical care was not even remotely a concern of government. Now that the Chinese government controlled medical service and education, it had different priorities for these Western-trained medical graduates. Chiang Kai-shek's plan for the post-war reconstruction of China emphasized the role of public health, and the rapid increase in medical personnel.[97] Until China's basic health needs could be met however, the Guomindang government was content to let foreigners teach in foreign-subsidized institutions, while their Chinese graduates administered medical services.

The evacuation of the Central Government and universities to Sichuan in 1938 was a turning point in the development of the WCUU. The University campus served as host to four refugee universities: Ginling, Nanjing, Cheeloo (Shandong Christian University), Yenching,[98] and the Peking Union Medical College (PUMC) School of Nursing. The influx raised the number of students from four hundred to a thousand in a six month period.[99] These were heady times for the previously isolated "backwoods" campus, and it envisioned its role in providing "leaders destined to create and shape a new China."[100]

The increasing importance of Chengdu as a centre of modern medicine was accomplished by the development of Sichuan's Provincial Health Administration (PHA), and the location of the National Health Administration (NHA) in the province. The sophisticated Chinese medical institutions and personnel from "downriver" (the Coastal regions and industrial cities) stimulated the medical missionaries to meet the challenge by either competing or co-operating. Both responses were apparent. Kilborn suggested to the Mission Board that "with government education constantly improving . . . with the necessity of maintaining higher and therefore costlier standards," it might be advisable to amalgamate the two major Christian medical schools, Cheeloo and Chengdu, to improve their efficiency and standards.[101] It was generally agreed however, that mission policy should concentrate on the medical schools as the cornerstone of medical missionary endeavor.[102]

Paradoxically the expansion of the Medical College led to its decline. The University Hospital as a modern teaching institution was far more costly to maintain than the mission hospitals.[103] In 1945, eleven members of the medical faculty left Chengdu, with no replacements forthcoming, and the teaching hospitals were operating on a serious deficit.[104] The medical school had relied on teaching staff from the refugee universities, and with their departure in 1946, its staff would be inadequate to carry on.[105]

The missionaries who remained were exhausted by the war, and felt abandoned by the home Board which was not sending replacements to maintain an adequate staff.[106] Postwar inflation in China, combined with the reduction in staff, contributed to the further deterioration of the Medical-Dental College. Kilborn however maintained his optimism and proposed that the United Church take full responsibility for the University staff, arguing that it was already a Canadian institution: "without the Canadian personnel this would become a non-missionary institution . . . It would be taken over by the government within a few years."[107] This was both the irony and the core of the medical missionaries' dilemma: at what point did they devolve the medical work to the Chinese? What combination of professional competence, Christian values, and Christian commitment determined the achievement of their goal?

Within the University, it was generally agreed that devolution was a distant goal. Bruce Collier, the professor of biochemistry, indicated that Sichuan's backwardness, compared to the "downriver universities," clouded the prospects for "building up a permanent Chinese staff."[108] Ashley Lindsay also remarked on the low level of pre-university education in Sichuan, the lack of second generation Christians compared to East China, and therefore the scarcity of suitable candidates for faculty appointments.[109]

In spite of China's growing autonomy in the planning and delivery of medical care and education, the missionaries were reluctant to relinquish control of the institution. Furthermore, the University was responsible to the Mission as a whole, and graduates were appointed to staff station hospitals, thus restricting their opportunities for post-graduate training and a future university position. Dr. Claude Forkner of PUMC relayed the assessment of other missionary groups that "the Chengtu missionaries are twenty years behind the times."[110] Forkner wrote that he thought "the attitude of some of the missionaries was definitely wrong," and that eventually the government would nationalize educational institutions and eliminate foreign administration.[111]

By the time Chinese physicians were given leadership positions in the University, it was embarassingly late. By 1947, Dr. Clifford Tsao was appointed Dean of Medicine, Dr. Y. T. Beh was Superintendent of the University Hospital and Dr. T. H. Lan was head of biochemistry.[112] In 1950 Dr. Gladys Cunningham gave up the chair in obstetrics and gynecology to her student, Dr. Helen Yoh.[113] On January 1, 1951, the University was taken over by the Chinese Communists,[114] and devolution was no longer an issue, except as part of the campaign to discredit Christian influence as imperialist cultural aggression.[115]

In assessing the extent to which the medical missionaries at the University devolved authority to the Chinese, it is argued that their apparent failure in this respect did not signify their failure to achieve their goals. As a result of the vested interests of senior professors in their individual departments, of the ever-expanding scope of the institution, and the consequent confusion of institutional goals with mission goals, the medical missionaries were reluctant to divest themselves of the authority to administer what they perceived as "their" institution. Furthermore, there were no circumscribed standards to indicate at what point they had achieved their objectives. Had a medical missionary in 1920 been told that by 1955 Sichuan would have its own Provincial Health Administration, municipal hospitals, *xian* health stations, and a government medical school with Western-trained faculty, he might have said that the medical missionaries have outlived their usefulness, and it was time to go home. However a medical missionary in 1940 would measure China's medical modernization by different standards. True, the government had an elaborate health administration, and medical schools, but they could not possibly achieve their goals of providing health care for China's vast population without external assistance. Moreover, China's medical profession was not predominantly Christian, nor was her population, and there was still the opportunity to exert Christian influence.

The gauge for "the best of modern medicine" had changed dramatically since 1888, and continued to change as medical science and technology advanced. And the measure of "Christian values" was at best ephemeral. What the missionaries did accomplish, however, was the establishment in Sichuan of an institute for modern medical education, the mobilization of social and political elites to participate in the development of health care and medical education, and the formation of a professional technological elite upon which to build an indigenous health care system.

In the process of providing medical education and care, the medical missionaries also served as a valuable resource to the administrators who were developing China's health services. They attempted to widen their influence to include the government sphere by encouraging the Chinese to accept financial responsibility for medical education and care facilities. In addition, they served as advisors and teachers, and as the provincial and national health departments developed, as subordinates to the Chinese administrators.

As early as 1925, when Sichuan's government was as much characterized by its absence as by its unreliability, Joseph Beech, the University's president, encouraged Governor General Yang Sen (who controlled Chengdu at the time) to participate with the University in the development of medical education and services for the province.[116] Recognizing that the Government did not have the revenue to contribute to such a project, he requested a grant on Yang Sen's behalf from the American Boxer Indemnity Fund.[117] This effort was designed in part to secure for the medical work funds not readily available to a Christian institution, but more importantly, to integrate the University's work in health care development with local political forces.

A further move to involve government with the University, at least by way of recognition, was the immediate compliance with the National Government mandate for the registration of private schools and hospitals, issued in August of 1927. The missionaries, in spite of the obvious political instability of China, submitted their application for registration as a gesture of faith in the local government and in order to protect the institution in case of future regulations.[118] The Nationalist Government had acknowledged, in theory at least, that provision of health care was a function of government, and that missionary institutions were a valuable resource which could lend credibility to the government's health program.

In 1933 the WCUU registered with the Nationalist Government at Nanjing[119] and in 1934 the first "practical recognition of the work being done by the University was shown by a grant of twenty thousand dollars in silver by the Nanking Government."[120] Generalissimo and Madame Chiang Kai-Shek were particularly interested in the University, whose agricultural department supplied them with dairy products and fresh produce.[121] The Government gave funds for a chair in the College of Dentistry in 1935,[122] and it was said that Dr. J. J. Mullett, who provided Chiang Kai-shek with dentures, "put the teeth into the Japanese resistance."[123]

In the absence of their own infrastructure for the administration of health care services, the National Health Administration's Epidemic Prevention Bureau distributed vaccines and serums through the Pathology Department of the College of Medicine.[124] In addition, T. H. Williams' laboratory provided a diagnostic service for the hospitals in West China.[125]

The Dental College in particular was recognized by the National Health Administration (NHA) for its leadership. Lindsay served as an advisor on the NHA's dental committee, to create "a national program for dental teaching, the nucleus for which is our Dental College."[126] In 1949, Lindsay's former students, the National Dental Board of Health, and the West China Dental Association honored him as "the founder of scientific dentistry in China."[127] The Chinese Ambassador to Canada, Liu Jie, communicated to the Canadian Department of External Affairs that Lindsay would be awarded the Order of the Auspicious Star of the Republic of China[128] for his pioneering contribution in "the promotion of dental studies in China and . . . in raising the standard of dental health throughout the country."[129] Dr. W. Crawford, professor of public health at the University, was also offered this official recognition, for his contributions "to the field of medicine . . . and especially in view of his medical services in China during World War II."[130]

The medical missionaries played a distinctive role in the development of Sichuan's Provincial Health Administration (PHA). In May 1939, Dr. C. C. Chen was appointed Director of the first Sichuan Provincial Health Administration.[131] He stressed "close cooperation with the mission hospitals" as a "means of helping the people," and entered into cooperation with the University's department of pharmacology to manufacture drugs and medical supplies.[132] The WCUU participated in the Sichuan Public Health Training Institute, which provided personnel for the Administration's health centres.[133] The United Hospital of the Canadian Mission supplied laboratory facilities for the training of laboratory technologists for the government's Institute of Infectious Diseases.[134] Although Dr. Chen remarked that the WCUU Medical College was inadequate and out of touch with the actual needs of the health system in China,[135] the evidence suggests it made a significant contribution to the development of government resources for medical modernization, albeit within the framework of government plans for health care development.

The development of national capabilities for health care delivery resulted in a shift in the relationship between government and medical missionaries. Whereas previously the government had been dependent on missionary facilities and resources, after 1941 it began to consciously view mission medical work as instrumental to national needs. In 1941 the Mission was alarmed that the PHA was setting up *xian* health centers and competing with the mission for medical personnel.[136] Government policy was to choose strategic locations for their health service centers, disregarding the existence of Mission hospitals, and thus competing with them for patients.[137] Chen's perspective was that the standards of missionary hospitals were not high, and they stressed curative rather than preventive medicine.[138] The missionaries were gradually being replaced by an indigenous force for medical care, and they reacted cautiously to this threat to their sovereignty.

In 1944, the National Health Administration requested cooperation from Christian hospitals in their plan for China's postwar rehabilitation, but emphasized the subordinate role of Christian medical work. This would place the University under the authority of both the Minister of Health and the Minister of Education, to whose regulations it would have to conform.[139]

By 1949 the Nationalist Government, although it did not have the resources to carry out its full program for public health, was in full control of the administration of health services. When the Communist government took over the mission institutions in 1950 it requested that three of the Canadian medical missionaries continue teaching at the nationalized West China University. However, most missionaries would not accept the tightening controls of religious and academic freedom, and one medical missionary in Chongqing was imprisoned by the Communists on a charge of refusing to turn over mission drug supplies to the authorities.[140] On January 4th, 1951, the United Church Mission Board closed the West China Mission and instructed the missionaries to return to Canada.[141]

Summary and Conclusion

The West China Union University College of Medicine and Dentistry was established to train leaders of China's medical modernization. Faced with the overwhelming need for medical service, the medical faculty decided it could make its most effective contribution by concentrating its limited resources on medical education. Although the institution did not achieve a national reputation for excellence in scientific teaching, it did serve as a valuable resource for the development of China's, and particularly Sichuan's health care system.

The College labored under the constraints of inadequate funding and personnel, and further suffered from the isolation of Sichuan from the rest of China and from Western intellectual influence. In spite of its policy of concentration on educational goals, the College was faced with the demand for staffing its affiliated mission hospitals. Divided between its functions as a service institution and a teaching institution, its staff and budget were stressed to the limit. There was no time or money provided for research, and thus the College did not develop as a scientific institution. Unlike PUMC, which was the model for an elite educational center in the medical field, WCUU did not attract accomplished researchers, and had limited funds to provide post-graduate fellowships abroad for its students.[142] The College did not have an administrative staff, and its professors were burdened with excessive paper work in addition to their teaching and clinical responsibilities.

Despite these disadvantages, the medical work expanded, and its growth surpassed that of the Chinese church and evangelical missions. Its goals became autonomous from those of the Mission, and as the institution became increasingly differentiated, its objectives were increasingly secularized. What was initially an evangelical mission to the Chinese, became a source of advisory, material and technical assistance to the Chinese government's efforts towards the development of a modern health care system.

The medical missionaries failed to devolve the administration of their institution to their Chinese colleagues. This is attributed to both the institutionalization of the goals of the College, and the resulting conflict with Mission goals for Christianization of the medical profession as a means of evangelizing the nation. The confusion of these goals was one of the factors which inhibited the missionaries from relinquishing control of the institution.

The greatest obstacle to devolution however was the cost of maintaining a modern medical institution. The teaching hospital which also provided subsidized medical services was not a source of remuneration, but an excessive financial burden to medical school and mission. The lengthy curriculum, designed to train teachers, was costly and extravagant in the face of the desperate need for medical services in China, and the financial constraints of the Mission. Had there been no concurrent development of China's medical system, with its own priorities for personnel and institutional development, the College of Medicine might have been viewed more favorably as establishing the foundation for medical care. However the policy of the University did not adapt to changing conditions. It could not maintain the scope it had established prior to 1927, and rather than retrench, the Mission attempted to spread its meagre resources to cover both medical education and medical service. The institution thus deteriorated to a minimum of staff and equipment with which to carry on medical education.

When the missionaries left China in 1951, however, they left the Medical School in the charge of doctors whom they had trained and financed for postgraduate study in Canada. The Medical College, renamed Sichuan Medical College by the Chinese Communists after 1950, reverted to its original name in 1985, and many of the alumni are in leading positions on its staff.[143] In terms of contributing to China a corps of medical professionals, the missionaries succeeded in "The Multiplication of Ourselves."

9

Convergence or Copying: China and the Soviet Union

Ronald F. Price

Introduction: the Problem

Soviet influences on Chinese education are of special interest because of the relationship between the Soviet and Chinese Communist Parties and the enormous influence this has had on the history of modern China. It is from the Soviet Communist Party that China learnt its Marxism-Leninism, a key aspect of which is the theory of the Party as the guiding force in society. Comparison is specially interesting because of the significance which both state Confucianism and Communist Party doctrine attaches to the educative process, to the moral-political education of a ruling group and of the general population. While many have seen the relationship between these two Parties as one of wholesale borrowing, in recent years it has become clearer that this oversimplifies a subtle and complex process.

Soviet influences, involving the concepts of socialism and communism adopted by the Chinese Communist Party, go far beyond the questions of schooling which all too frequently form the horizons for our discussions of education. They involve much wider social structures and the learning processes which occur when teaching and even conscious and intentional learning is absent. They involve the learning of moral-political behavior which occurs in the political and economic spheres and they also involve learning through the informational, artistic, scientific-technical, and entertainment structures of society. Soviet influences are intimately connected with the shaping of knowledge within society and with the selection and grading of educational knowledge for the different publics among which it has been hierarchized.

The question of influence, whether Soviet or any other, is far from a simple one. It may be direct, through the copying of some institutional form, the transfer of some cultural object (a book, or a school syllabus), or it may be indirect. It may be no more than encouragement to do something in the knowledge that it has supposedly been done successfully elsewhere. Or it may be something forced upon the "borrower" by some means, often nowadays described as "aid." Statements by officials alleging borrowing cannot always be taken as sufficient evidence of direct transfer. Officials may be motivated by quite other considerations, or simply by misunderstanding of the process concerned. The latter is the more likely, the more general the nature of the object said to have been borrowed. Spare-time adult worker education, a case in point, has since its inception assumed similar forms in many different countries. To allege borrowing is easy. But it is more likely that the particular form is a result of various determinations difficult to disentangle.

In this chapter I shall begin by setting out the context within which borrowing was possible and the agencies through which it may have occurred. I shall then examine a number of areas of education for similarities and differences between the two countries and evidence that direct borrowing occurred. Finally I shall describe some of the most recent ways in which Soviet education impinges on education in China. Throughout I will question the degree of similarity with the USSR and ask to what extent this is due to direct borrowing, indirect influence or parallel development from an initial common basis. Others elsewhere may wish to pursue such questions as whether the borrowed forms and practices were suited to the conditions and needs of China, and the important questions embodied in such phrases as "cultural imperialism."

The Context

While this chapter concentrates on the period after Liberation in 1949, it must not be forgotten that Soviet influences began very soon after the revolution of 1917. Li Dazhao published three articles on the revolution in 1918, two of them in the magazine *Youth*. In 1920 the second congress of the Third (Communist) International turned its attention to "the colonial and backward countries" and Soviet personnel, both government and Comintern agents, arrived in China. Relations embraced both the Guomindang (KMT) and the Chinese Communist Party (CCP).

A number of Chinese from both the KMT and CCP studied in the USSR in the twenties and thirties. Some attended the Sun Yat-sen University of Toilers of China which, according to one account, was designed to train "'staff officers' of the Chinese revolution."[1] Pavel Mif, later to be one of the Cominform agents in China, was one-time director of this University, and Wang Ming and the other "Twenty-eight Bolsheviks" were students there.[2] Other Chinese may have attended the Communist University of Toilers of the East, an institution founded in 1921 and closing, like other similar institutions, in the late thirties.[3] Qu Qiubai worked in 1922 as a teaching assistant and interpreter in the Chinese section of this University. His brief appearance as commissar of education in the Jiangxi Soviet government in 1934 did less than his translations and writings on Soviet literature to transmit Soviet cultural influences.[4]

While Soviet influences operated from the twenties through to the forties and the decisive model of the Communist Party was laid down in that period, it was in the fifties after the establishment of the People's Republic of China (PRC) that the opportunity was there for major influence in the sphere of schooling. The new government was committed to a policy, as Mao Zedong declared in the opening address to the Chinese People's Political Consultative Conference in September, 1949, of "people's democratic dictatorship and unit(y) with our foreign friends," that is, "first of all with the Soviet Union."[5] In part the choice of "friends" was forced on China by the policy of the USA. But it was also dictated by the belief that the Soviet Union would have digested the experience of the technically advanced countries of the world and made it suitable for adoption in the service of socialism.[6] Here was an echo of attitudes to learning from Japan which have been described by Hiroshi Abe in chapter 4.

Soviet influences on education operated in a context of widespread borrowing of structural patterns in the area of the economy and the state. Soviet style economic planning agencies were introduced in 1952 and in 1953 industry nationally was reorganized on a vertical, ministerial pattern earlier adopted in the North-East under Gao Gang.[7] A Soviet-style legal system was instituted in 1954, but modified to allow the Party more extra-legal control after 1957.[8] Before considering the influences on education in detail let us look at the possible agencies of transfer.

Agencies of Transfer

The degree to which the major leaders of the CCP were involved in the making of educational policy and particularly with adopting Soviet models is uncertain. Mao Zedong does not appear to have concerned himself with the details of school reform in the early fifties. When he addressed the Presidium of the New Democratic Youth League in 1953 it was health and conditions of study on which he concentrated. Speaking about Stalin at the Chengdu Conference in 1958 he referred to copying methods of schooling from the Soviet Union as "pretty bad" and bemoaned failure to "study our own experience of education in the Liberated Areas."[9] While Mao certainly went along with much of the borrowing from the Soviet Union which occurred, it seems likely any influence he may have exerted in education would have been directed at contrary styles. Liu Shaoqi, on the other hand, appears to have been accurately portrayed in the "Two-road Struggle" document. A somewhat conservative "organization man," Liu was concerned for the training of officials and technical personnel and appears to have valued Soviet experience in this connection. One should not, however, take completely at face value the diplomatic enthusiasm he expressed as Chairman of the Sino-Soviet Friendship Association, a post he held from 1949 to 1954, or on such occasions as the opening of the Chinese People's University.[10] At the same time Liu was prepared to encourage part-work schooling for elementary work training, perhaps seeing this differently from Mao, as a necessary, temporary measure similar to those adopted during World War Two by the USSR.[11]

The part played by leading education officials in advocating a Soviet model is equally unclear. Ma Xulun, appointed Minister of Education in October, 1949, and Minister of Higher Education when that Ministry was formed in 1952, was a former philosophy professor and education minister in the twenties and thirties. He appears to have had democratic and patriotic motives and to lack experience of or special interest in things Soviet. Vice-Minister Qian Junrui, Secretary of the Party Group within the Ministry of Education and head of its Higher Education Office, had long specialized in Sino-Soviet relations. However, visiting the Soviet Union briefly on delegations after 1949 seems inadequate to provide an informed view of its education system. Zhang Xiruo, who succeeded Ma as Minister of Education in 1952 was educated in the USA and Britain and a respected non-CCP intellectual. Yang Xiufeng, who took over the Ministry of Higher Education in September, 1954, was educated at the University of Paris and appears to have had no connection with the USSR. The only high officials with personal experience of the USSR were Chen Boda and Lu Dingyi. Both were appointed to the Cultural Education Committee (*Wenhua jiaoyu weiyuanhui*) under Guo Moruo in October 1949. Chen was briefly at the Sun Yat-sen university in Moscow in the late twenties. Lu attended the 6th National CCP Congress there at the same time, staying on for a short time afterwards.[12] Speaking to a research group of the Academy of Sciences in 1953, Chen Boda echoed the sentiments of earlier Chinese who had looked to Japan for guidance. he remarked:

> . . . when we advise studying the Soviet science, we do not mean to say that the works of British and American scientists may not be used as reference. They may and should be. However, generally speaking, the good things in British and American science have already been absorbed by the Soviet scientists; hence, the quickest and best way is to learn from the Soviet Union.[13]

Whoever on the Chinese side may have been in favour of borrowing from the USSR, there were plenty of Soviet educators and officials on hand to give advice. In 1950 five Soviet specialists were invited to work at the Ministry of Education in Beijing. In addition, two worked jointly with the Ministry and the Beijing Teachers University, one in general education and the other in early childhood education. These specialists were expected to attend conferences and meetings, to brief people about Soviet conditions, and to give opinions and answer questions.[14] By June 1952 there were reported to be some 80 Soviet specialists working in tertiary schools.[15] In late 1953 a further six specialists were invited by the two Education Ministries. After touring major cities they attended a meeting of teachers in Beijing to discuss secondary technical education.[16] In July, 1960, it was reported that a total of 861 Soviet specialists had visited China since 1949 on the invitation of education institutions.[17] According to Zheng Zhuyuan (Cheng Chu-yuan), using Soviet figures, 700, or six percent of a total which included scientists working in industry, were in the field of education.[18] The single most important visitor was E. A. Kairov, President of the Academy of Pedagogical Sciences of the RSFSR, and between 1949 and 1956 Minister of Education of the RSFSR. Visiting China a number of times, his articles appeared in *Renmin jiaoyu*, and his textbook for teacher training institutions, *Pedagogy*, was translated into Chinese.[19]

At the same time as Soviet specialists were visiting China there was traffic in the opposite direction. The *Jiaoyu dashi ji* records a delegation organized by the

Ministry of Education visiting Eastern Europe in September 1952, but does not mention the USSR or any other country specifically.[20] Its first mention of a visit to the USSR is the delegation of primary and secondary teachers led by the Vice-Minister of Education, Cheng Cenggu, in October-November, 1955. This concentrated on polytechnical education, teaching work (*jiaoxue gongzuo*) and teacher education.[21] In 1955 representatives of Beijing, Qinghua and People's University attended the 200th anniversary of Moscow University.[22] Other groups or individuals visited the USSR in 1956, 1957, 1958, 1959, 1963 and 1964.[23] In 1960 the head of the Education Ministry General Office (*Bangong ting*) attended a discussion meeting on polytechnical education and in 1961 the Vice-Minister of Education, Liu Aifeng, attended a national higher education conference in the USSR.[24] From 1964 on no education or cultural delegation is mentioned as visiting the USSR. According to Zheng Zhuyuan, 7,500 Chinese students were sent to the USSR to study between 1950 and 1962. Until 1957, when a decision was taken to send only graduate students, the majority of these were undergraduates. Some 1,200 are recorded as being "instructors," presumably staff members of Chinese tertiary institutions. Zheng only cites Wu Shuqin, professor of chemistry at Nankai University, but in a later table lists two tertiary presidents or vice-presidents, two chairmen of departments, four professors and two faculty members out of a sample of 381 tertiary personnel who had studied in various countries abroad.[25] It would be interesting to have evidence of what has happened in the years since 1962. It was recently reported that Chinese were again studying in the universities of Moscow, Leningrad and Kiev. Numbers were very small: 10 in 1983-84 and 70 in 1984-85. Nor did the report list the subjects being studied. Also in 1983-5 an equal number of Soviet students studied in China.[26] Superficial observations suggest a current predominance of American and other non-Soviet influences, but one should not neglect the rise to positions of power of those trained in the USSR during the fifties. This may affect official thinking in the years to come.[27]

Information about education in the USSR was spread by meetings and through specialized periodical and monograph publishing. In the fifties Soviet specialists attended many meetings and when delegations from China visited the Soviet Union there were special report-back meetings arranged on their return. Also in the fifties the pages of such periodicals as *Renmin jiaoyu* (People's Education) and its provincial counterparts were well filled with articles both by Soviet specialists and by Chinese commenting on aspects of Soviet education.[28] During the Cultural Revolution there were articles denouncing Kairov and his textbook, but little one could regard as serious comment. In the freer period following the death of Mao Zedong occasional items appeared in the *Renmin jiaoyu* while an enormous amount of both translation, description and comment appeared in more specialist periodicals.[29] Two names which stand out in these materials are L. V. Zankov and V. Sukhomlinsky. Monographs by these educators have also been translated and published in China during the 1980s.

In addition to information about school systems, teaching methods — the form and content of the teaching-learning process — one should consider the other ways in which the USSR contributed to Chinese learning. In the fifties the USSR became a major source of content in the major disciplines. At the school level this consisted in the provision of textbooks and other teaching materials. One report spoke of 1,393 textbook titles being translated from Russian into Chinese between 1952 and 1956. Another spoke of 629 "teaching materials" being compiled by Soviet specialists, 108 of which were translated.[30] At the factory level there was the provision of huge numbers of blueprints and other technical documents.[31] Then there was the flow of materials through the library system and through gifts by the Soviet Academy of Science. Zheng notes that the latter sent 5,376 backdated copies of 67 different periodicals to the Chinese Academy of Science in 1954. In 1953 it gave 9,648 books to visiting delegations.[32] The National Library in Beijing operated a book exchange in the fifties with 98 libraries and other institutions in the USSR and received 200,000 volumes between 1949 and 1958. In 1958 alone it received 42,000 Russian books.[33]

The role of Soviet specialists as teachers is an interesting one yet extremely difficult to estimate as there is little documentation. One of the few accounts is that of Michail Klochko, a chemist who worked in Chinese universities in 1958 and 1960 and later sought asylum in Canada.[34] From his account it would appear that relations between Chinese and foreigner were kept sufficiently distant for very little useful learning to occur, something which those of us from other countries who worked in China in the sixties had experience of. It would be interesting to know more of the impact of the 700 specialists said to have taught in Chinese tertiary schools, or the 36 Soviet specialists who trained 2,775 Chinese teachers in special classes.[35]

What Was Transferred?

At the outset one must ask to what degree the overall conception of education in China, especially within the leading ranks of the CCP, has been shaped by Soviet Communist Party thinking. I would argue that while the influence has been strong it has been one of reinforcing existing, Confucian, conceptions of education. Education is seen as essential to the maintenance of correct behavior and as essentially moral-political. Training in techniques, in spite of all the current talk of seeking and training talent, is considered secondary. That leaves another important question: to what extent is this conception different from that held in other parts of the world, and therefore what conflicting influences are working today? Hopefully the chapters of this volume will at least begin to answer that question. Finally, one is left with the even more difficult question: what is the relation between the verbal expression of such a conception of education and the practice of education, what is actually done?

Educational Administration and the School Structure
Underlying all administration in both the USSR and China is the principle of Communist Party leadership. As Stalin laid down in the twenties, the CP must exer-

cize the direction of everything. All other organizations are "transmission belts" and "not a single important political or organizational question is described by our Soviet or other mass organizations without guiding directions from the Party."[36] These principles, repeated in various editions of the Constitution of the CCP, are not significantly altered by the doctrine of "the mass line" enunciated by Mao Zedong.[37] In form this leadership involves parallel Party and state structures, the organization of Party members into organizations within the state structures, including the schools, and the control of state structures through Party members holding executive posts in non-Party organizations.

A detailed comparison of education in the two countries would have to consider the federal structure of the USSR with its division between All-Union and Union Republic Ministries and the changes which took place in this structure during the forties to the sixties. By contrast China had a simpler structure of national and provincial bodies. Already in 1906 China had established a Ministry of Education with six departments at the national level and local bureaus. The Ministry assumed very much its modern form in the reform of 1912. Its division in 1952, through the setting up of a Chinese Ministry of Higher Education (*Gaodeng jiaoyubu*), brought it close in form to the Soviet pattern. But, as can be seen from the details, there were many differences. The Chinese Ministry of Higher Education in 1952 was divided into a

1. General office (*Bangong ting*);
2. Comprehensive University Education Department (*Zonghe daxue jiaoyu si*);
3. Industrial Education, No. 1 Department and No. 2 Department (*Gongye Jiaoyu diyi[er] si*);
4. Agricultural, Forestry and Health Education Department (*Nong lin weisheng jiaoyu si*);
5. Secondary Technical Education Department (*Zhongdeng jishu jiaoyu si*);
6. Department for the Management of Oversea Study (*Liuxuesheng guanli si*);
7. Educational Guidance Department (*Jiaoxue zhidao si*);
8. Planning and Finance Department (*Jihua caiwu si*);
9. School Personnel Department (*Xuexiao renshi si*);
10. Political Education Division (*Zhengzhi jiaoyu chu*);
11. Industrial and Agricultural Accelerated Secondary School Education Division (*Gong nong sucheng zhongxue jiaoyu chu*);
12. Basic Construction Division (*Jiben jianshe chu*);
13. Translation Office (*Fanyi shi*);
14. Student Practice Guidance Committee (*Xuesheng shixi zhidao weiyuanhui*); and the
15. Russian Language Teaching Guidance Committee (*Ewen jiaoxue zhidao weiyuanhui*).[38]

The Soviet All-Union Ministry of Higher Education, established in 1946 on the basis of the All-Union Committee on the Higher School, had the following structure:[39]

A. Twelve departments corresponding to the various types of schools under its control:

1. Universities;
2. Pedagogical;
3. Heavy Industry;
4. Defence Industry;
5. Military;
6. Light Industry and Food Industry;
7. Transport and Communications;
8. Agricultural;
9. Medical
10. Economics & the Law;
11. The Arts;
12. Foreign Language and the Teaching of Foreign Languages in Higher Schools;

B. Sixteen functional departments:

13. Military Training and Schools of Physical Culture;
14. Textbooks;
15. Teaching Marxism-Leninism;
16. Budgetary-Planning;
17. Cadres;
18. Distribution (assignment to jobs) of young specialists (i.e. graduates);
19. Material and living conditions of students;
20. Special Department (*Spetsotdel*) in charge of internal political surveillance and of personal dossiers;
21. Control and Inspection;
22. Administrative;
23. Legal;
24. Secretariat;
25. Central Accounting;
26. Academic Institutions of the Ministry (department in charge of schools directly and completely operated by the Ministry);
27. Scientific Research Work at the Institutions of Higher Learning;
28. Housing;

C. Specialized operational units, among them the following five:

29. Lecture Bureau;
30. Committee's Press (*Sovietskaya Nauka*);
31. Library;
32. All-Union Officie of industrial-technical supply for instructional purposes (*Uchpromtekhsnab*);
33. VAK, Higher Attestation Commission (for academic degrees and titles).

It would be interesting to be able to account for the differences which these two outlines reveal. Was the simpler Chinese structure a function of the smaller number of tertiary and specialized secondary school students?[40] Why were the tertiary teacher training establishments administered by the Ministry of Education and not Higher Education, as in the USSR? The questions are numerous but up to now no one has come up with the answers. To our general question one must answer, influence — yes; copying — no.

Another similarity between the administration of education in the USSR and China is the way in which tertiary schools have been jointly administered through the Ministry of Higher Education and some other Ministry. According to DeWitt overall direction and planning has been the preserve of the Ministry of Higher Education while the day-to-day running of many of the institutions was "subordinated to various other ministries."[42] It is not clear just what the division of power in China has been.[43] In both countries the pattern has changed as the number of institutions has changed, and the subject is greatly under-explored. There are other possible European models and borrowing from the USSR remains unproven.[44]

Turning from administration to the structure of the school systems, a sharp distinction can be made between the tertiary school level and that of the secondary and primary schools. As Orleans describes, the tertiary schools were dismembered and remade in the Soviet pattern in China during 1950-51. This was a conscious copying, intended to facilitate rapid industrialization. The pattern of secondary and primary schools, on the contrary, continued to be that consolidated in the reforms of 1922 when an American pattern of six years of primary school followed by six year of secondary school, the latter divided into three years of lower and three years of upper secondary school, was established.[45] However, in the years following the 1958 school reform there was considerable experimentation with different patterns in an attempt to reduce the length of schooling. In different provinces secondary schools tried various combinations: four or five year continuous systems, or divisions into junior two and senior three years. Experiments continued in places until 1965 and the eve of the Cultural Revolution, and several conferences discussed the results.[46] The motive for these experiments was certainly Mao's and others' dissatisfaction with the long period of schooling and its perceived low achievements. The variety of pattern tried speaks against copying from the USSR. But no doubt the Soviet ten-year system acted again as a support for those wishing to reduce the length.

The schools often referred to as "informal" or "irregular" are among the more interesting developments of Chinese education. Parallel primary, secondary and tertiary schools were set up in the fifties to train adults previously denied schooling. These resembled those of the Soviet Union in the twenties and thirties, but it would be far-fetched to suggest borrowing. Then in the late fifties the concept of part-work schooling was developed far beyond its Yan'an expression. Here the major thrust would seem to have been contrary to the formal, expert-orientated bias of Soviet education thinking and practice. At the same time there are also interesting echoes of the ideas of Chen Qingzhi (writing in 1934-35) in the attempts to combine schooling with productive labor.[47]

School Curricula

As was mentioned above, the early fifties saw the transfer to China of enormous numbers of curriculum outlines and teaching materials for various levels of schooling. Here a little detail will be added to fill out the picture.

In the fifties Chinese primary schools had a program similar to that of primary schools everywhere. The bulk of the time was allotted to language and arithmetic, with one or two hours per week each for manual labor, physical education, singing and drawing. With the omission of manual labor this is identical with the curriculum given for the first three grades of the Soviet seven-year school by Medynsky.[48] In the Chinese school two hours per week each of history, geography and natural science and one hour of agricultural knowledge were added in the fifth and sixth grades. In the Soviet seven-year school natural science and geography were added in the fourth grade; combined algebra and geometry, and physics in the sixth and seventh grades, chemistry in the seventh grade, and a foreign language in the fifth, sixth and seventh.

The curriculum of the Chinese secondary school, which overlapped with that of the Soviet seven-year school, consisted of Chinese language in the lower secondary years, and literature throughout the six years. Mathematics was taken as separate courses of arithmetic, algebra, geometry and trigonometry, the first only for grade one and the last only for grades 11 and 12. History was likewise divided into separate courses of history of China, world history and recent (world) history. Geography was divided into physical, world and Chinese geography, taken consecutively in the lower secondary years only, with the economic geography of China in grade 11. Biology was divided into courses of botany, zoology and human anatomy and physiology. Physics began in grade eight, chemistry in grade nine. A foreign language was introduced in grade seven, and then taken up again for the last three grades. Singing and drawing were taken only one hour per week in lower secondary school. Politics and physical education ran throughout the school.

This curriculum would have to be compared with the Soviet one for grades seven to ten. Whatever divisions were made in the classroom, no division appeared for mathematics (other than arithmetic not being listed from grade seven on), history or geography. Biology was dropped in the final grade. Physics and chemistry went through all secondary grades. For a time psychology and logic were introduced into some schools in the early fifties. Astronomy was listed separately for the last two years. Foreign language and physical education also went through all grades, as did draughtsmanship. Interestingly, the only separate moral-political education course, that in Constitution of the USSR, was taken only for two hours per week in the seventh grade. This was later to change with the introduction of a social studies course in the eighth grade, and then in grades eight and ten.

Another way of comparing these curricula is to look at the total hours allotted to the different subjects, though one should be hesitant to draw any conclusions from such crude data.

It would be good to be able to compare this Chinese curriculum with that of schools before Liberation. But at present information is difficult to find, and in addition, paper plans and practice tended to be somewhat different.[49] Chen Qingzhi gives details for 1928 plans.[50] Primary school subjects were: language, arithmetic, civics, social studies, hygiene, nature studies, physical education, labor, art and music. For the academic secondary schools subjects were: language and literature, English, mathematics, natural sciences (botany, zoology, chemistry and physics), history, geography, civics, hygiene, physical education, technical drawing, music and labor. Courses were different for the teacher training and vocational tracks of the senior high level. The League delegation noted that at the senior high level 7.8% of time was devoted to principles of the Nationalist Party and civics and 3.9% to military training.

Superficially at least the fifties' curriculum does not appear very different from that of the pre-Liberation period. Serious comparison would require comparison of textbook context, important because in both periods lessons appear to have closely followed this. One striking difference of content was the emphasis given in China to teaching the Russian language in the fifties. With the importance attached to contacts between the two countries this was not surprising. Special

Table 9.1
Curricular Hours by Subject in Soviet and Chinese Schools

Subject	Soviet 10-yr. School (hrs.)	Chinese 12-yr. School (hrs.)
Language	2,508	2,448
Literature	544	1,010
Arithmetic	1,155	1,411
Other Mathematics	990	978
History	705	589
Geography	528	323
Biology	545	578
Physics	478	485
Chemistry	346	317
Astronomy	33	0
Foreign Language	726	510
Politics	66	336
Physical Education	594	812
Drawing	198	306
Singing	132	306
Draughtsmanship	132	0
Total	9,680	10,409

Russian language vocational schools (*Ewen zhuanke xuexiao*) were established, and their work was laid down in the March 1952 "Decision on National Russian Language Vocational Schools" published by the Zhengwuyuan and People's Revolutionary Military Committee.[52] The emphasis on Russian continued through the fifties, though in 1956 the Ministry of Education attempted to establish a balance between Russian and English.[53] By 1959 the proposal was for Russian to be taught in only one third of high schools.[54] One consequence of the emphasis on Russian may have been the delaying of modern foreign language teaching methods by more than a decade as Russian teaching methods became widespread.[55]

Along with the content of the curriculum Chinese schools adopted many aspects of Soviet teaching methods, methods which the Chinese associated with the Soviet educators, Kairov and his textbook. While the long tradition of written examinations was not substantially changed, the oral method of examining pupils in class and recording their results on the five-point marking system was adopted. This was accompanied by a division of time between examining pupils, introducing the new material and setting the homework which, at least in some cases, became very inflexible.[56]

Teachers and Teacher Training
The form of teacher training in the fifties, its continuing of a system of secondary teacher training schools in addition to schools at the tertiary level must have been as much a measure of the then level of schooling in the country as a result of any influences from the Soviet Union. For Soviet influences one must look elsewhere. T. H. Chen lists the following in his section on the topic: "classroom procedures, methods of asking questions and presenting new materials in class, organization of subject matter, the five-point grading system, collective effort of teachers in preparing their lessons, pedagogical seminars, library indexing system, correspondence courses for teachers, high priority to the development of higher normal education, (and) emphasis on all-round development."[57] But he offers as evidence mainly statements by various Chinese officials about how Soviet experience was being studied. One might as well rely on other statements to the effect that Soviet experience must be studied critically and linked with Chinese realities.[58] As I have suggested above, this is insufficient when not backed by a detailed comparison of both rhetoric and practice. For example, the five-point grading system for oral examinations is very different from paper tests marked out of a hundred, but not from the widely-used grading A-D. Classroom procedures also tell us nothing unless much further specified. Even the datum that 120 out of 153 courses at Zhejiang Teachers College were using Soviet materials tells us all too little since we do not know how different the subject matter and treatment was from other alternatives.[59] What we really need to know, and data are at present unavailable, is in exactly what ways Chinese practice was modified by Soviet experience and Soviet advisors and what was specifically Soviet about it. How different, for example, was joint planning of lessons by teachers of the same grade from what was done previously, and from attempts in other countries to keep classes of the same grade in step? How much was this intended to be,

or indeed was it, a lockstep preventing individual teacher initiative? How was this connected with more general theories about pupil abilities? Lockstep behaviour is in any case in part a question of the general authoritarian nature of the system and the role of the CCP in society, a facet of my main point that the borrowing of Soviet theory of the Party is the fundamental borrowing affecting all others.

The influence of Chinese conditions rather than mechanical copying of Soviet forms can be seen in the training school pattern. Chinese Teacher Training Schools in the fifties were at lower and upper secondary school level. The first admitted graduates of the upper primary school for three-to-four year courses which trained teachers for the first four grades of the primary school. The second admitted graduates of lower secondary school for a three-year course which trained teachers for the upper grades of the primary school. At the tertiary level there were teachers universities (*shifan daxue*), teachers colleges (*shifan xueyuan*) and teachers vocational colleges (*shifan zhuanke xuexiao*). The first two had four-year courses and appear to have differed only in their recruitment area and the area to which graduates were later assigned. Teachers colleges were provincial in this respect. Both trained teachers for secondary level. Teachers vocational colleges trained lower secondary school teachers in two-year courses.

In the USSR from 1954 kindergarten and primary school teachers were trained in pedagogical schools (*pedagogicheskiye uchilishcha*). Previously training the graduates of the seven-year school for four years, from 1954 they trained the graduates of the ten-year school for only two years. Teachers for the first three grades of secondary school (five, six, and seven of the seven-year school) were trained in teachers institutes (*uchitel 'skiye instituty*) and those for the final three years in pedagogical institutes (*pedagogicheskiye instituty*), each training graduates of the ten-year school for four years. Thus there is no exact parallel with Chinese training institutions, only the rough kind which applied to teacher training in Europe and North America at an earlier period.

The curriculum of the Chinese upper secondary teacher training school (1957) offering a three-year course was very similar to that of their ordinary counterpart, with the addition of courses in education and educational psychology. Education was taken for two and then three hours per week in the second and third years. Psychology was taken for two and then one hour per week for each of the semesters of the second year. Methods classes appear to have been offered only for language & literature and for mathematics. These occupied two and two and three hours respectively for the two semesters of the third year. Other subjects were language and literature, mathematics, physics, chemistry, human anatomy and physiology, geography, history, politics, physical activities, music and drawing.[60]

In the equivalent four-year Soviet teachers school (1952) there were courses in education, educational psychology and the history of education occupying about 20% of total time. Brief courses on methods of teaching the various primary school subjects were given, but the emphasis was on the subject matter of the various courses: language, literature, mathematics, physics, chemistry, biology, geography, and history. In addition there were courses in logic, school hygiene, calligraphy, singing, physical education and applied work in workshops and agriculture. A foreign language was also offered as an elective. Politics was represented by a course on the History of the CPSU.[61] Calculation of percentage of total time given to different subjects of the course reveals the picture given in Table 9.2. [62]

In any attempt at comparison one must remember that in the fifties the Soviet Union was already looking to the next decade when they expected teacher training to follow on a full secondary schooling, whereas in China this was clearly a thing for the more distant future. Chinese educators were, when realistic, looking at ways of rapid and irregular training. For rural schools they were to develop the *minban* system, a system which relied on on-the-job training of lower secondary school graduates, and one for which proffered Soviet experience had little to offer.

Labor and Education

One of the major principles of both Soviet and Chinese education is the combination of education with productive labor, following Marx. The similarity of much of what has been said on the subject in the two countries and what has

Table 9.2
Curricular Percentage by Subject in Chinese and Soviet Teacher Training Schools

Subject	Chinese T. Training School		Soviet T.Tr. Vocational School
	1957	1935	1952
Language	7.5	11.1*	7.4
Literature	14.3		10.4
Mathematics	13.1	6.9	13.7
Physics	7.8	3.8	5.4
Chemistry	3.9	3.7	2.3
Biology	2.6	4.2	6.2
Geography	5.2	2.8	5.7
History	10.0	3.7	8.4
Politics	7.5	3.7	2.7
Psychology	2.0	2.8	1.2
Education	6.1	3.2	4.0
History of Education	0.0	0.0	1.4
Physical Education	7.5	5.6	5.9
Music	6.2	4.6	4.5
Drawing	6.2	3.7	5.2
Total time (hours)	2,685	n.a.	4,722

* = Language & Literature

been done would immediately suggest borrowing by the Chinese. But the matter is not that simple. As Pinkevich long ago pointed out, the concept of labor in education is not confined to followers of Karl Marx, though in the twenties Russian followers were nearly alone in wanting to "permeate the entire school curriculum with the idea of labor."[63] There are numerous other possible sources for many of the rather obvious things which have been done. This is not to argue that there was no influence, but rather to question what it was. It was not simply a case of taking over what was said and done in the USSR. As I shall try and show, the emphases in the two countries have been different, influenced by quite different traditions and different economic conditions and possibilities.

In the twenties in the USSR there was a clash between those directly responsible for the economy, anxious for skilled labor, and those in education concerned with providing what they saw as a worthy upbringing for the young in the new society. Krupskaya, with her eloquent defense of polytechnical education (*obrazovaniye*) and anxiety to postpone vocational training until a foundation had been laid for informed choice is a good representative of the latter.[64] For her, polytechnical education was to be a mind-broadening exploration of human social production, the basis for understanding and practical skills. It was also infused with the same strong Enlightenment-inspired vision of freedom which inspired Marx before her, and with a similar vision of workers in control. This was in contrast to advocates of early vocational training who spoke of the need for discipline, or, misunderstanding Marx, of a "love of labor."

In China there would appear to have been no such debate. It may be that this reflects Soviet influences from a later period which excluded the writings of the twenties, or fitted them into a vocational training mode which effectively defused them. More likely it was the pressing economic situation. This would certainly account for the treatment of education in Yan'an. Schooling was conceived as part of the general military-economic effort. Those few articles which have been published from that period which refer to "combining education with productive labor" (*jiaoyu yu shengchan laodong jiehe*) are certainly down to earth.[65] Various forms of what were later to be called "irregular" schools are described, permitting pupils to take part in the labor of their families. There is also the strong message that "to participate in labor is extremely heroic," a message backed up by study of labor heroes.[66] In spite of slogans like that of Kangda, "On the one hand study, on the other hand production," and declarations that to separate education from production is a form of dogmatism,[67] present evidence is unconvincing that there was a meaningful cognitive relation between educational content and production. Teachers and pupils may have opened up new ground for tilling or made straw sandals for the troops,[68] but many regular schools persisted with "reactionary" principles and the schools which "served the people" were spare-time.[69]

Soviet influence on these developments in Yan'an would seem the more unlikely because of the rather different approach taken in the USSR in the thirties. The emphasis there in the schools was on systematically organized, theoretical content in traditional school subjects, especially the three major natural sciences, and polytechnical education became another largely theoretical study. This was spelt out in the September, 1931, statement on primary and secondary schools by the CC CPSU(B) which laid down that

> All attempts to separate the polytechnization of schools from a systematic and firm mastering of science . . . is the greatest distortion to the idea of the polytechnical school.[70]

By 1936 Krupskaya could complain:

> . . . it has now turned out to be a school *isolated from life* which makes the organization of *socially useful work* difficult. Now useful labor, productive labor, is reduced to mere production of *useful objects for school studies.*[71]

Such practice would seem to be the opposite of what the Chinese tried to develop in Yan'an in the late forties, and Soviet wartime practice does not alter the argument.

In the period following the 19th CPSU Congress of 1952 polytechnical education again became a central theme for Soviet writings on education, and was introduced into China in numerous translations and other ways. In the USSR polytechnic became a magic word used to embrace the normal practical work associated with study of the natural sciences and engineering, the kind of labor training on farms or in factories which Soviet school pupils had long performed, and moral-political education in history, geography or in special subject classes to inform pupils of the bases of Soviet institutional theory. The moral-political aim was put clearly by the then Minister of Higher Education in the RSFSR, I.A. Kairov when he said:

> The most responsible and important questions for us are the moral nurture of children, their upbringing in labor and their training for labor activities.

He went on to make clear the new situation facing the schools:

> Now, when a considerable portion of those finishing school will go directly into life, our task is to nurture young people right from the beginning in the habits of work, in the love of work, and in respect for laboring people.[72]

That the merging of polytechnical education and ordinary science teaching is a persistent trend can be seen from the state-of-the-art paper by Skatkin[73] and by the following definition from another paper in the same collection. Here Atitov speaks of polytechnical knowledge being the regular and necessary relations between the laws of the different sciences embodied in productive processes.[74]

There is no doubt that something of this will have been passed into the Chinese schools, especially at tertiary and secondary level, with the borrowing of syllabi, textbooks and other teaching materials which occurred during the early and middle fifties. The vocational slant of Soviet schooling may have partially fulfilled the aims set by the Common Program of the People's Political Consultative Committee of 1950. Setting as its aim "prosperity and strength" the Program envisaged education as "scientific," "training personnel for national construction work," aims clearly embodied in the long tradition of Chinese modernization and probably owing little if anything to Soviet industrialization.[75]

Both similarities and differences emerge with reforms in education which occurred in both countries in 1958. Two statements by Party Secretary Khrushchev prefaced the reforms, the first to the 13th Komsomol Congress in April, 1958, and the second published in *Pravda*, 21 September, 1958. The laws altering the school system followed in December of that year.[76] Khrushchev had argued for the replacement of full-time secondary schooling by a system of part-time work and study, and for a compulsory work break for all between general and tertiary schooling. In the event both these proposals were modified in the December laws.[77] Following an eight-year compulsory general school, which replaced the former seven-year school, a three-year secondary school combining tertiary academic preparation with production training was to extend the total schooling from ten to eleven years. Preference for admission of students to tertiary colleges was, according to article 28 of the basic law, to be given to those who followed secondary school with work experience, and work places, the Party, Komsomol or other such bodies were to provide character references.[78] While the Act stressed the importance of specialized secondary schooling for the training of middle level technicians,[79] the Statute on the Secondary General-Education Labor Polytechnical School with Vocational Training, as it pleased the authorities to call the ordinary secondary school, allowed for pupils completing their vocational training to "be given a trade rating, with a corresponding wage rate or class."[80]

In China the reform was announced by a Directive of the CC CCP and State Council of 19 September, 1958.[81] According to this document a major task was the training of a red and expert working class intelligentsia (*you hong you zhuan de gongren jieji zhishifenzi*). Declaring that "education must serve the proletariat politically" the Directive added that it must also "be united with productive labor." For this purpose productive labor was to be "listed as a separate course" in the curriculum, and "schools should set up factories and farms, and factories and agricultural cooperatives should set up schools."

This Directive brought together a variety of slogans and could have been used to justify different policies. Throughout the clear message was that stated categorically in the *Renmin ribao* summary: education work must be led by the Party. Otherwise, education was to train all-round developed new human beings; to abolish illiteracy; universalize primary schooling; to provide ample tertiary schooling within fifteen years; and to do all this through a mixture of state and enterprise-run schools of a full-time, part-work and spare-time type, a policy known as walking on two legs. The tone of the Directive is more reminiscent of very early Soviet writings, such as the famous *ABC of Communism* than it is of the contemporary Soviet "Law on the Strengthening of the Ties of the School with Life and on the Further Development of the Public Education System of the USSR."[82]

The practice of the next few years further brought out the differences between the two countries and suggests, despite certain Chinese claims to the contrary, "convergent evolution" rather than direct borrowing. In China the labor which was performed both in and outside the schools in response to this Directive was labor for the sake of production rather than formal skill training, though, of course, some element of training was necessarily involved. This was again to be the case when the policy of "schools setting up factories and farms" and vice versa was once again stressed in the Cultural Revolution in the late sixties and early seventies. The educational limitations of such production were described in the latter period in an article from Wuhan University,[83] the only document I know to make such an evaluation.

The concept of part-work schooling (*bangong bandu*) goes back to Yan'an days. While this is a most abused term, used to cover a variety of quite different things,[84] the agricultural high schools developed in the Great Leap Forward period (1958-60) and the part-work secondary technical schools associated particularly with Liu Shaoqi are an innovation arguably different from schools in the USSR. In spite of what was foreshadowed in the aftermath of the 1958 reforms, Soviet education has persisted with essentially spare-time schooling and the promise of "sandwich courses" described in DeWitt have not, it would seem, materialized.[85] Instead the system of evening or shift schools, together with correspondence courses to be taken in addition to a full-time working day, appears to have remained the rule. In addition in certain jobs workers are given time off to attend periods of full-time study.[86] That the Chinese should choose to try to develop part-work schooling is interesting. Could it be because the Chinese working class particularly lacks schooling,[87] or, as DeWitt[88] suggested for the Soviet Union, for moral-political reasons? An economic argument for worker schooling would suggest the Soviet solution, when a full day's work could be extracted from each student to offset the costs of his or her education.

It is interesting to compare the two countries in recent years when few would argue for Soviet influence in China. The Khrushchev reforms of 1958 soon terminated. The attempt to give all secondary school students a trade certificate in addition to a matriculation were abandoned and the emphasis returned to labor as an aid to theoretical understanding.[89] But old slogans of combining education with productive and socially useful labor, and of polytechnic education are retained to justify the ever-pressing demand for technical excellence and labor discipline. In China, following the death of Mao Zedong, there was an initial reaction in the same direction. The emphasis placed on labor during the Cultural Revolution was condemned and school workshops and agricultural plots were largely abandoned. But conditions quickly dictated a renewed concern for ways of educating interest and training skills. On 19 October 1982 the Ministry of Education issued a circular "Concerning the suggested training of labor and technical education classes in the general secondary schools."[90] This was followed by detailed regulations for school "factories" in February, 1983.[91]

While there is no need to try and explain current Chinese attention to "combining education with productive labor" by Soviet influence it may be that the quite new interest in the concept of polytechnic education is so inspired. Up until the last half decade polytechnic education (*zonghe jishu jiaoyu*) was a term used only in Chinese translation of and comments on either Marx-Engels or Soviet writings on the subject. I have never seen it used with a specifically Chinese connotation. But in recent years this has changed and a number of writers have begun to use the term in ways that suggest it may become part of the Chinese repertoire of educational slogans.[92] In addition, the combination of labor and education in its various forms, not least the training of specialists for the economy,[93] forms a high proportion of the current flow materials being translated from Russian and published in Chinese education periodicals.

Moral-Political Education

Both the content and form of moral-political education in China strongly resembles that in the USSR and in large part has been derived from it. But at the same time there is continuity with the short- and long-term past. The Guomindang, itself influenced by the USSR, promoted education in the Three Principles of the People in formal courses (*gongmin*) in the schools and in 1934 started the New Life Movement to promote traditional values of propriety, righteousness, integrity and self-respect.[94] The moral-political nature of education and its pervasiveness in imperial times need no reminder, though the degree of continuity is probably not sufficiently recognized.[95] Perhaps the most significant feature of this continuity is the moralizing tone in which political discourse is couched. Action is discussed in terms of high abstraction; right is opposed to wrong, good with evil, and the social is to be solved by individual unselfishness. It is in this context that the persisting belief in the efficacy of education lies. Then there is continuity in the stress on order and hierarchy, on loyalty and obedience — then to Emperor and officials, now to the Party. Wisdom still resides in the highest level and even the "mass line" is a policy of listening to "the masses," not one which empowers them. But to say all this is still to remain at too high a level of abstraction! Here we must return to comparison with the USSR.

The key organizations for moral-political education have all been consciously modelled on their counterparts in the USSR. The Communist Party with its Propaganda Department and system of Party schools is the most important. But the Communist Youth League (*Zhongguo Gongchanzhuyi Qingnian Tuan*) and the Young Pioneers (*Zhongguo Xiaonian Xianfengdui*) aim to play a significant role in propagating, but not initiating ideas and policies among young people. Formed after Liberation (1949), the two youth organizations have roots in the Yan'an period. Their structures and symbols and the kinds of activities they engage in are closely similar to those of the Soviet youth organizations, though one must remember that activities of analogous organizations everywhere have similarities. To repeat a warning, similarity is no proof of influence or borrowing.

In addition to the two youth organizations many other "transmission belts" between the Party and "the masses" exist. They include the All-China Federation of Trade Unions and the All China Federation of Women. All of these, as part of their functions, conduct some form of moral-political education. In the schools the form in which moral-political education is conducted depends on the level. While it suffuses all activities there are also special periods set aside for special moral-political courses. Similarities of form with the USSR are close here, but the content of the courses is different.[96] Especially at the tertiary level time is spent in both countries on current affairs and Party policies, in addition to a more systematic study of Marxist-Leninist theory. The first interventions by the Party after Liberation in the schools already displayed the degree to which Chinese Marxism-Leninism had become modified, sinified, to suit the peculiar conditions of the Chinese revolution and the desire of the CCP leadership to be independent. In October 1950, following a meeting of representatives of tertiary schools in Beijing in July-August of that year, the Ministry of Education put forward as a basis for teaching anti-imperialism, land reform and five-loves.[97] At that time the emphasis was on studying the Common Program and Mao's essay on "New Democracy."[98] In the years that followed various courses in Party history, "A history of the development of society," "Political economy," "Dialectical and historical materialism," etc. have been evolved.[99] So far there do not appear to have been any analyses by foreigners of these courses. Rather, studies have been of the content of the primary school readers.[100] That is an insufficient basis both for comparisons between China and the USSR, and of the educative possibilities moral-political education allows.

Analysis of the primary readers from the early sixties in China reveals the following common themes: loyalty to such institutions as the CCP, the People's Liberation Army (PLA), and the Young Pioneers; respect for benevolent, but paternalistic leaders, especially Mao Zedong; oppression in pre-Liberation China by the Guomindang and by Japanese invaders; advocacy of "love" of labor, laboring people, and school and study; advocacy of such traditional values as modesty, thrift and diligence; admiration for heroic deeds of a self-sacrificing nature and of cooperation and care for the public good before that of the private. While socialism and communism were mentioned these were never described in such a way as to give real substance to them.[101] It is interesting to compare these with the teachings in the (in)famous teacher training institute textbook by Kairov, *Pedagogy*. These occur in a short section on the formation of character traits in school pupils and a long chapter on moral upbringing (*nravstvennoye vospitaniye*).

The first section stresses the importance of learning from example, especially from people around one, and advocates the use of heroes in teaching. The traits of optimism, patriotism and comradeship are advocated. The approach to moral education is shown by the definition with which the chapter on that subject begins:

> Moral education — this is the influence on children in the process of organizing their various activities with the purpose of forming in them moral behavior, moral concepts, convictions and character traits.[102]

Communist morals are said to be of a new and higher type. Forming an independent aspect of communist education (*vospitaniye*), they are at the same time firmly connected with all aspects of education: mental, physical, and aesthetic, and with polytechnical and labor education. Kairov lists as particularly important a feeling of patriotism, of friendship and brotherly solidarity with other peoples, of duty and honor, of responsibility for entrusted duties, respect for elders, and sensitiveness and sympathy.[103] Patriotism, linked with internationalism, recurs in a long section in which the use of the example of famous people is advocated.[104] The other major themes are the value of socially useful work, the value of a scientific-atheistic upbringing, and the importance of conscious discipline.[105]

It is interesting that while in October 1950 the Chinese Ministry of Education was warning against hurting religious feelings in schools, already by June 1951 it was prohibiting religious advocacy in the schools and urging school leaders to strengthen political and science education.[106] As so frequently in the USSR, religion was either attacked as "superstition" or condemned for its association with imperialism. It seems clear that while religions have been attacked in China's past, Soviet Marxism-Leninism has provided fresh impetus for such actions. The way they have been carried out has differed slightly from similar actions in the USSR because of the different role religion has played in China.

The attempt to use literature and the fine arts as moral-political educators is another story where Soviet influences appear to have been direct and close. Mao's Yan'an speech on literature and art had a precedent in Lenin's writings on propaganda and Party writers. But there are also precedents in Chinese imperial history of censorship and control of writers. At another level there is the use of the press, and particularly the attempt to use worker-correspondents.[107]

Other topics could be explored. There is the re-education of political and other prisoners, and the schools for delinquent youth. At least in the last it would seem that Makarenko has been influential.[108] Something also should be said about worker education and publishing.

Worker education is in part the responsibility of the trade unions. Under article nine of the Trade Union Law of June, 1950, trade unions are required to "educate and organize workers and staff members to uphold the laws and decrees of the People's Government" and to educate them "to adopt a new attitude towards labor."[109] In accordance with this law various forms of schooling have been organized, some of which include as much as 12% of the time spent on moral-political education.[110] In addition to such formal schooling, and more importantly, factories and offices have organized their workers in small groups for weekly study sessions. While probably the majority of the time has been spent on current affairs and Party policy statements, some of the time has been spent on Marxist-Leninist theory. Even such works as Engels' *Anti-Dühring* or writings by Marx, Engels, Lenin and Stalin on the Paris Commune have been set reading for such sessions. All this is remiscent of practice in the USSR and may in part owe inspiration to it. But the intensity of Chinese practice appears to be much greater. More people for more time have been involved, even if only in body, than would appear to have been the case in the USSR. In addition, the Chinese evolved their special form of group therapy known as the struggle meeting which appears to be qualitatively different from self-criticism practices in the USSR.[111]

A considerable volume of moral-political material is published in both countries with the aim of attracting the individual reader outside the framework of the organized study groups. Some obvious parallels exist, like the periodicals *China Reconstructs, China Pictorial* and *Chinese Literature*, each based on their Soviet predecessor. Then there is a vast range of direct translation, among them that notorious *Short History of the CPSU(B)*, which I last saw published in Chinese in 1975, presumably not as a negative example. There are huge printings of pamphlets on current political and economic policies, on education in the family, and a hundred other topics. There are also editions of the speeches and writings of political leaders which may have been inspired by similar collections in the USSR, but which are not unknown elsewhere.

To sum all this up, one can say that both in form and in much of the content there is obvious Soviet influence. But in spite of considerable attention it would seem to be rather poorly theorized. Above all, what is needed are studies of what is learnt from all this, but except at the most superficial level this is impossible for the foreigner, and even from within it has formidable methodological difficulties.

The Eighties — a Renewed Interest?

With the opening up to the outside and the increasing access to Chinese publications which this has brought, the attention being paid to education in the USSR, at least since about 1977, has become visible. While the contrast with the vilification during the Cultural Revolution is obvious, a certain caution is required. Depending on how one defines interest and to whom one attributes it, the question of whether it is renewed or simply now again more openly expressed, is an open one. It seems as unlikely that those who have devoted their lives to a study of the USSR would have performed two somersaults in such a short time, as that the whole academic community would have acquired a genuine interest simply because the Party and government advocated learning from their then senior partner. That said, at the present time there seems to be a solid effort to provide information on, to discuss and to evaluate the history and progress of Soviet education. This is now being done in a much better developed comparative context than was possible in the fifties. Here I will attempt only a brief summary of developments.

The comparative context is being supplied a number of research centres, perhaps the most important of which is the Central Institute for Educational Research (CIER), located in Beijing. Founded in 1956, it was disbanded during the Cultural Revolution and did not resume until 1978. It is divided into eleven sections, including one for Comparative Education. Major specialists are Zhang Tian'en, who is a Vice-President of the Institute, and Jin Shibai, who is also Deputy Secretary General of the Comparative Educaiton Society of the Chinese Association of Education. Other writers on the USSR at the Institute include Bai Yueqiao, Wang Zhen (f), and Zhang Jian.

Another major center for the study of Soviet education is the Foreign Education Research Institute of Beijing Teachers University. Gu Mingyuan, who is a Vice-President and currently President of the Comparative Education Society, is a major specialist. With him are Fang Ping (f), Wu Shiying and Zhou Qu.

Other specialists appear to be scattered and it is not clear to what degree they are supported by collaboration or library resources. Du Diankun works in the Institute of Comparative Education at the important East China Teachers University in Shanghai. Lei Xiaochun is at the South China Teachers University where there is a strong Institute of Comparative and Foreign Education specializing in Southeast Asia and Australia.

Information is being supplied to a specialist readership through a number of important periodicals. These are *Waiguo jiaoyu (Foreign Education)*, produced at CIER; *Waiguo jiaoyu dongtai (Foreign Education Trends)*, produced by the Foreign Education Institute of the Beijing Teachers University; and *Waiguo jiaoyu ziliao (Foreign Education Materials)*, produced by the Comparative Education Institute of the East China Teachers University in Shanghai. In contrast to the fifties when the pages of *Renmin jiaoyu* were filled with such materials, now only popular articles appear there occasionally.

Choice of materials for study and translation is, I am told, made one criteria of usefulness to China's educational needs. Unfortunately it is not clear just how this is judged and by whom. But even a superficial comparison of published topics with current Chinese government policies in education show close similarities. In *Waiguo jiaoyu* between 1980 and 1985 the following topics from the Soviet Union were covered: (number of articles in parenthesis): Zankov (6); Sukhomlinsky (3); Krupskaya (1); tertiary schooling (7); vocational training (3); cadre training (1); general schooling problems (3); selection and training of talent (1); child psychology (3); specialist training (1); moral-political education (3); labor education (4); pre-schooling (1); curriculum and teaching methods (8); and teachers (1). Of these articles, four were translations from Russian authors.

In *Waiguo jiaoyu ziliao*, 1980-82, the range of topics was slightly wider, and, as suggested by the title of the periodical, the number of original Russian articles in translation was much higher, 27 in all. The topics (and number of articles thereon) were: Zankov (12); Sukhomlinsky (12); Kairov (6); Vigotsky (1); tertiary schooling (5); vocational training (1); general schooling problems (3); child psychology (2); moral-political education (6); labor and education (1); pre-schooling (3); curriculum & teaching methods (11); teachers (1); the economics of education (1); and education and the family (3).

In addition to this periodical material there is a substantial publication of monographs. The following is the sample which has come to my notice during regular visits since 1975 to bookshops in several Chinese cities and inspection of one specialist library:

> Two volumes of *Education Laws and Decrees: Soviet Higher and Secondary Education*, published in 1978 and 1983 respectively by the Foreign Education Institute of Beijing Teachers University, under *neibu* classification (internal circulation).

> A translation of F. G. Papagin's *The Administration of Education (Ypravlyeniye Prosveshsheniyem)1 (1977)*, published by the Culture and Education Press in 10,000 copies in 1982-3.

> A translation of E. S. Bieliejilangke (I am unable to find the original of this Chinese transcription), *Soviet School Management*, published by the Education Science Press in 1982 in a run of 14,000.

Gu Mingyuan (trans.), *Comparative Education* (by M. A. Sokolova, E. N. Kuzmina and M. L. Rodionov, Moskva, Prosveshcheniie, 1978) (1982, 19,000).

Zhang Tian'en translated *Problems of Contemporary Educational Theory* by M. N. Skatkin (1982, 20,500).

A number of Sukhomlinsky's works have been translated: *The Spiritual World of the Pupil* (trans. Wu Chunyin and Lin Cheng, 1981, 45,000 copies); *Trust in Human Beings* (trans. as *Trust in Children*, by Wang Jiaju, 1981, 50,000 copies); *A Letter To My Son* (trans. Zhang Tian'en, 1981, 98,500 copies in 3 printings); *Suggestions for Teachers* (trans. Du Diankun, 1984, 60,000 copies).

Zankov is the other favourite author for translation. Du Diankun translated *Pedagogy and Life* (with Yu Xianghui, 1984, 20,000 copies); Du was also one of a group of translators (the others were Zhang Shichen, Yu Xianghui, Zhang Weicheng, Ding Youcheng, and Ye Yuhua) who produced *Education and Development* in 1980 in an edition of 20,000 copies; another collection of Zankov's essays, together with commentaries, appeared under the title *A Discussion of Zankov's New Educational System* (Ed. Yu Xianghui, 1984, 10,000 copies).

One of the most interesting papers to be published during this time was that by Zhang Tian'en and Jin Shibai entitled "A Few Opinions of the Soviet Education System."[112] Presented at the Third National Conference on Foreign Education in May, 1981, the paper discussed the history of Soviet education since the October Revolution and summarized what the authors considered its successes and failures. They noted as strong points of Soviet education: (1) More than 97% of youth now have 10-year schooling and more than 30% of these go on to tertiary schools. (2) The development of quantity has led to the promotion of quality. As examples the authors cite mathematics and the sciences. (3) Emphasis on the unity of education and labor: from grade one on which teaches labor habits and skills. (4) Soviet schools pay attention to scientific research and the training of teachers. (5) There is a close connection between educational and social planning. (6) The importance paid to in-service and spare-time study.

Against these strong points the authors list a number of shortcomings which reflect concerns in China at the present time: (1) The highly centralized system of administration and management often relies on administrative methods and "commandism." (2) The Soviet education tradition is to stress collectivism and balanced development. In tertiary school students are forced to take unified courses with no choice to suit different individual interests. (3) All is state run; there are no private-run schools (*si ren banxue*). Although allowing certain factories, mines and enterprises to assist schools Soviet education has failed to take advantage of the activity of the masses. (4) There is bureaucratic inefficiency and often wasteful duplication of effort. (5) Theory departs from practice, leading to big nation chauvenism and Great Russian Egoism which is widespread in the schools. (6) Early specialization in tertiary school leads to neglect of basic subjects and imbalances between supply and demand for particular skills.

Mention must also be made of a special conference on the work of Kairov and Zankov held in May 1982, the papers from which appeared *Waiguo jiaoyu ziliao* in that year.[113] Du Diankun of the East China Teachers University gives the most thorough account of Zankov's work. Opinions varied on the relationship between Kairov and Zankov. Wang Yuxiong at one point says that without doubt, Kairov's and Zankov's teaching theories are utterly different, though he seems to modify this when he cites Zankov as conceding that his theories should not been seen as replacing traditional ideas. Zhen Deshan also sees them as very different. Kairov's stress on the teacher and teaching leaves the learner passive and a reactant, while Zankov stresses learning and the learner as active subject. Wang Yinxiong sees Kairov as bogged down in formalism while Zankov successfully solves. the connection of teaching and development and discovers the objective laws of this process. Against these views others see Kairov and Zankov in close agreement. Zhang Dingzhang claims that Zankov did not criticize Kairov in person; that Kairov praised Zankov (Zankov became one of the editors of the famous *Pedagogy* textbook); and that on the question of developmental teaching they were in "complete agreement." Chen Xixian also argues that to see them as opposed is wrong. Du Diankun adopts a dialectical formulation in which he sees Zankov as both building on Kairov's work and making a radical break with it. He remarks that without criticizing the old there can be no new and that without Kairov there would have been no Zankov! He reminds us that Zankov had himself said that one cannot completely negate the past in the primary school.

A feature of all the papers cited is that they remain at a high level of abstraction. There is little sense of the classroom or the observations and measurements which were used to test Zankov's ideas. Du Diankun comes nearest to the world of practice in two lengthy sections on "the inspiration of Zankov's teaching theory" and "an exploration of the limitations of Zankov's theory." But even here we get not a discussion of evidence but the demand that Chinese investigate for themselves the controversial question of mental testing, a question Du thinks has confronted Zankov with difficulties.

This discussion raised the important question of how to relate to foreign scholarship. Zhen Deshan thinks that Zankov's ideas could help Chinese educators cast off traditional points of view and deepen and enrich their own teaching theory. But he warns that they must recognize where Zankov is inadequate. Wang Yinxiong begins with an affirmation of the potential value for China of a comparative study of what he sees as two different stages in Soviet teaching theory. Du Diankun reminds his readers of indiscriminate copying in the past, contrasting "learning from Kairov" in the fifties with "using Zankov for reference" today. He uses a nice metaphor when he says: "foreign things need to go through digestive assimilation before they can act as nourishment for us."

Conclusions

It is thus clear that education in China was influenced in both form and content by Soviet precedents, especially in the formative years of the People's Republic in the fifties. Influences on the form of education mainly affected the tertiary system, as is more fully described in this volume by Leo Orleans. The major influence on the content of education was on the peculiar form of Marxism-Leninism adopted and widely taught within and without the schools, both to CCP members and cadres and to the wider public. This latter, especially the theory of the Party and democratic centralism, must be seen as reinforcing the ideas of State Confucianism on hierarchy and authority, and on the importance of moral-political teachings of an overt kind as a major state activity.

It should also be clear that the process of borrowing has been less uncritical and wholesale than has often been asserted both inside and outside China. In judging claims one should remember that alleged borrowing may simply be a justification for doing what on other grounds someone wanted to do anyway. Even more important, the same form can hide a variety of contents. Or, to put it differently, an institution modelled on Soviet lines, staffed by Chinese, may function rather differently.

Looking closely at both China and the USSR one observes a variety of education forms and practices over time and at the same time. Administrative structures at Ministry and provincial level appear to have maintained indigenous traditions. Cadre education and the informal schooling network appears to have "learnt from Yan'an," though there are intriguing similarities to the USSR in the twenties. Looking at Chinese studies of Soviet education today one must ask how representative of educational developments in the USSR they are? To what extent and how are they filtered and selected and what are the judgements made by Chinese observers? To say that they reflect current Chinese government policy is true, but insufficient.

Thus we must still ask, where borrowing did occur, just who, for what reasons, advocated borrowing what. Working out in more detail the interests involved in "learning from the Soviet Union" would bring us to a much better understanding of the social divisions within China and its leadership, and the workings of the local society, than we have at present. But this will require access to archives, biographical and memorial accounts which are conspicuously lacking in current Chinese studies. Even then we shall be left with an "account from above," an account which, while explaining the architecture, will leave out many of the people who inhabit the buildings.

10

Soviet Influence on China's Higher Education

Leo A. Orleans

Introduction

The twentieth century brought to China a new breed of leaders and intellectuals determined to modernize the country and return it to its earlier role as a destined world power. They also knew that if China hoped to replace scholars of ancient classical texts and Confucian ethics with builders and thinkers, she must first create a new educational system. In the search for the most effective educational model which would be suitable to the newly identified national needs, international imperatives prompted the new leaders to turn to Japan, and later to Europe and the United States. The result was a multiplicity of shifting foreign influences and disparate regional development patterns throughout the country. Thus, as China was undergoing an almost continuous political and social revolution in the first half of this century, she was handicapped by an educational system which was also in a constant state of flux.

All indecision about the educational system disappeared after 1949. With the victory of the Communist forces, there was never a doubt in the minds of the new leadership about either the need to scrap the inherited educational system borrowed from Western imperialists, or where to turn for a new model. The Soviet Union, after all, was not only the prime supporter of Mao's revolution, but with a common Marxist-Leninist ideology the two countries were in full agreement that the basic role of education in a socialist country was to train individuals who will serve the defined objectives of the State. It is not surprising then, that just as Soviet economic and technological assistance to China was unmatched in history,[1] Soviet assistance to Chinese education was of a similar magnitude and perhaps had an even more lasting influence — especially on higher education. What may appear striking, however, is that the Soviet model — albeit somewhat tarnished and bruised — managed to survive the break between the two countries and the cataclysmic upheavals resulting from the Great Leap Forward and the Cultural Revolution. The explanation is simple. First, the Soviet model was attractive because it was socialist; second, because its methods and approaches had an affinity with the Chinese imperial tradition and its age-old examination system;

and third, in practice, Chinese schools were so intimately tied to Soviet curricula, texts, and methods that extensive deviation would have been a monumental undertaking. It was not until the late 1970s that the political climate and the needs of the "four modernizations" combined to initiate gradual changes away from the Soviet and toward an American system of higher education.

Although the role the Soviet Union played in the 1950s in the development of China's higher education is well known, in this chapter I have attempted to emphasize Moscow's perspective of its involvement, to contrast when possible the views of the two friends-turned-adversaries, and finally to identify those aspects of the Soviet system which the Chinese are especially anxious to change in pursuing their current educational reforms.

The Soviet Role in Reforming Higher Education

Probably one of the reasons many people found it difficult to take seriously the discord in 1961 between the Soviet Union and China was the contrast between the sudden raucous name-calling and the ostensible harmony that had been projected during the preceding decade. It is not an exaggeration to say that in the 1950s it was difficult to distinguish between Soviet and Chinese writings on issues dealing with Chinese problems and the measures needed to be taken for their resolution. Since then, of course, we have learned that relations were not always as cordial as they seemed even in those early days. We now know that normal frictions which stemmed from close contact in the first half of the decade gradually evolved into much more serious differences of policy and ideology, but that discussion of the mounting antagonism was carefully avoided in both the Soviet and Chinese media. Even after the withdrawal of Soviet personnel from China in the early 1960s the acrimonious attacks hurled back and forth by each side were limited to ideological, political, and territorial concerns, while no mention was made of the differences which surfaced regarding the practical issues of developmental policies. With the everlasting hope that China would eventually "return to the fold," the Soviets would attack Mao Zedong and his "perverse ideas," but stress that his grievous mistakes had nothing to do with the enduring friendship between the Russian and Chinese people. As for the Chinese, since they would never admit the extent of Soviet assistance — a perpetual thorn in the psyche of the Soviet leadership — they were reluctant to complain about the problems that inevitably developed in connection with the thousands of Soviet specialists and consultants in China.

Given the concurrence between Soviet and Chinese writings in the 1950s, a general review of each side's comments on the process of reorganization, consolidation, and expansion of China's educational system after the creation of the People's Republic of China would reveal almost identical pictures. And, in fact, Russian and Chinese sources often cited each other's writings to stress such accord. However, Soviet sources published since the late 1970s reveal that the earlier Soviet approval of China's educational policies soon began to erode and that by

1956 Soviet educators in China were experiencing considerable differences with their Chinese colleagues. Soviet sources also tend to provide much detail not found in Chinese writings about the role Russian advisers played in reforming Chinese education.

Both the Soviets and the Chinese perceived the same problems in China's higher education. In 1949, of the over 200 institutions of higher education in China, almost a third were private or missionary colleges. The quality of these institutions was highly uneven and the absence of coordination and planning resulted in an excess of students in economics, humanities, and social sciences, while there was a shortage of students in science and engineering and other new fields of knowledge for which the national economy was in great need. Furthermore, one quarter to one third of the courses were electives which had no relation to the profession selected by the students. Russian educators believed that the inclusion of such courses as the Chinese novel, poetic form, family questions, and sociology of the village only reduced the time that could be spent on technical and scientific subjects.[2]

As early as 1950, in addressing the First National Conference on Higher Education in Beijing, a leading Soviet educator criticized Chiang Kai-shek's Nationalist educational system for its unhealthy atmosphere of semicolonialism. He stressed the benefits that would accrue if China would follow the Russian experience in reorganizing her educational system.[3] Thus, the Soviets maintain that, thanks to their advisers, Chinese pedagogues realized the failures of the theories of John Dewey and other Americans — theories so widespread in China prior to the 1949 revolution — and began studying the Soviet educational experience in order to create a single authority that would regulate the training of specialists needed for the social and economic development of the country. There was no disagreement from the Chinese: "Soviet teaching materials have proven their superiority through practice. What reason is there for us to depart from Soviet (educational) blueprints?"[4]

In the first three years of the new regime, and despite predictable chaos and confusion, China's system of higher education underwent some fundamental changes. Obviously, institutions of higher education supported by foreigners, and especially those run by foreign missionaries, had to be eliminated. At the same time, the Chinese attempted to duplicate the Soviet system by eliminating most of the comprehensive universities (*daxue*) and leaving the thirteen or fourteen which remained only with departments of natural sciences, social sciences, and humanities. Departments such as engineering, medicine, agriculture and teacher training were split off, sometimes combined with similar departments from other universities, and transformed into specialized colleges or technical institutes (*xueyuan*). Thus, in addition to the comprehensive universities that remained, by June 1953 there were 39 polytechnical colleges, 31 teachers colleges, 29 agricultural colleges, 29 medical colleges, four in law and government, six in finance and economics, eight language institutes, 15 fine arts institutes, five colleges of physical education, and two national minority colleges. The intent was to strengthen specialized education in important fields by concentrating the most competent faculty and the best equipment and research facilities and, by narrowing specializations, to speed up the process of training technical personnel for industrial development. Regional redistribution was also intended to correct some of the geographic imbalance (coastal superiority) that existed in higher education.

What happened, of course, was that by assigning colleges the goal of "training cadres for very specific jobs in the highly complex fabric of economic construction," there became an incredible proliferation of "majors" (*zhuanye*) numbering in the hundreds.[5] One Chinese pedagogue offered yet another rationale for the change to numerous specializations: "The whole educational procedure reverses the pre-liberation process, which, by trying to turn out jacks-of-all-trades, aimed at lessening the chances of their being unemployed if their own particular 'speciality' was already overstaffed."[6] No doubt it was this narrowing of curricula that made it possible to shorten the educational cycle. Although the remaining comprehensive universities and a number of the specialized institutes continued to offer four to five-year courses of study, some normal and technical colleges reduced their courses to two or three years, resulting in a more rapid turnover but, of course, at the expense of quality. It is interesting to note that ever since the creation of the People's Republic, the proportion of students enrolled in short-term professional curricular has fluctuated to reflect the effects of politics on education — the proportion increasing whenever the "politics in command" theme was dominant.[7]

Another fundamental change borrowed from the Soviet system was the placing of primary authority for tertiary education under the Ministry of Higher Education, created in December of 1952 to introduce uniform curricula in all the institutions of higher education and to consolidate and unify the teaching plans. The new Ministry survived until the Great Leap in 1958, when its authority and powers were returned to the Ministry of Education.

The participation of Soviet specialists in all these reforms was both extensive and intensive. In 1950-52, 126 Soviet consultants were sent to China to assist in all phases of the higher education reform. They helped develop new specializations in line with the specific needs of industry, agriculture, and culture, they assisted in the establishment of new curricula, and they developed new teaching plans. By the time the First Five-Year Plan (1953-57) was announced, the number of Soviet education specialists and academics increased further. Soviet advisors were attached to the Ministry of Higher Education where they assisted on matters of theory and policy, while much larger numbers were assigned to specific universities, where they played a key role in implementing the reforms and in teaching (mostly technical subjects). They took part in the development of basic plans and programs for all the departments, acted as consultants on all aspects of the educational system, and helped admininister courses, graduate programs, and even production practices.

Soviet involvement in the reforms was also considered an imperative from a political perspective. According to the memoirs of one Soviet diplomat and academic who spent almost three years in China (1955-57), only about a fifth of the Chinese instructors in institutions of higher education were Communist

Party members, while "the majority were followers of Arnold Toynbee and Hans Morgenthau." Furthermore, Chinese universities had virtually no personnel with a Marxist-Leninist background.[8]

In order to maximize the value of Soviet scholars, their lectures were attended by faculties from other universities in the city as well as by specialists from industry, who were periodically rotated to the university. In order to make sure that research done in the universities would have practical value, Soviet consultants and/or professors assisted in establishing contacts between the technical institutes and related industrial enterprises. Lectures by Soviet instructors were also summarized and shared with educational institutions in other localities. A comment by Mikhail Klochko, a Soviet chemist who spent a number of years in China and defected to Canada in 1961, is undoubtedly applicable to other fields as well: the Chinese expected every Soviet specialist "to be a sort of magician, capable of giving them the one current answer to all sorts of complex problems in pure and applied science in a few minutes."[9] And, incidentally, such grand expectations of foreign specialists have not changed to this day.

How many of the 8,000 to 10,000 Soviet specialists who were sent to China between 1950 and 1960 — most of whom were involved with problems of economic development — came to teach or help with the reorganization of the educational system? There are actually two figures that show up in Soviet texts: 615 and 1,269. When used singly, as they often are, the distinction between the two totals can be elusive and is likely to raise questions. Fortunately, some authors resolve the confusion by using both figures in the same context. Apparently, the lower figure refers to Soviet professors and instructors who were sent to China to teach, while the larger figure also includes pedagogues and other specialists who worked in the Ministry of Higher Education and other administrative organs within the educational system.[10] In addition to the professional teachers, many of the Soviets who came to China under agreements with ministries and industrial enterprises also lectured to Chinese students and professionals.

In addition to sending specialists to China, the Soviet Union undertook an extensive education and training program for selected Chinese in the USSR. Agreements between the two governments, as well as between ministries, institutions, and enterprises, resulted in a steady flow of Soviet specialists to China and Chinese scholars, students, and technicians to the USSR. Perhaps because of the numerous categories and varying lengths of stay there are inconsistencies in numbers, but the Soviets regularly report that "more than 11,000" Chinese students and scholars were sent to the Soviet Union to study, most of them enrolled in undergraduate courses, and 7,324 finished their studies with proper qualifications."[12] In the context of Soviet influence on Chinese education, it is especially interesting to note the Soviet claim that between 1949 and 1960 Soviet experts helped train 19,000 Chinese instructors (17,000 in China and about 1,700 in the Soviet Union), constituting "about a quarter of the teaching personnel at Chinese colleges."[13] The Soviet Union spent large sums of money on sending scholars and specialists to China and educating Chinese in the Soviet Union — amounts which greatly exceeded the rate of compensation by the Chinese side.[14]

Such a basic reorganization of higher education naturally required an extraordinary effort to provide students with new textbooks and other materials. The old texts which dated back to the 1930s and 1940s were deemed qualitatively poor and ideologically inappropriate. Thus, in the first half of the 1950s the effort undertaken to provide Chinese universities with new educational materials was probably unsurpassed in history. Chinese academics were put to work revising old texts and writing new ones. According to the Soviets, the prescribed procedure was for these authors to study Soviet materials, prepare prospectuses of the new titles, thoroughly discuss them with Soviet advisers, and only then proceed to write and publish them.[15]

Once again statistics vary on the extent of the overall efforts to supply the Chinese with Russian textbooks and other educational materials, but a few figures should adequately communicate its magnitude. By 1951 China had received 32,000 copies of books and journals published by Soviet scientific academies and educational institutions. By the end of 1952, 3,114 Soviet book titles were printed in China and some three million copies of Soviet books, already translated into Chinese, were imported from the Soviet Union. In 1956 the library of the Soviet Academy of Sciences sent 70,000 volumes of various scientific writings to China.[16] Between 1949 and 1955 over 20 million copies of 3,000 Soviet books on science and technology were published in China.[17]

The importation of vast quantities of books from the Soviet Union was supplemented by an extensive translation program in China. The Chinese report that in 1954, 2,700 university faculty members were capable of translating from Russian and that more than 3,000 volumes of Soviet titles were collected and assigned to them for translation.[18] Not all the translations were of a technical nature and between 1950 and 1958, 13,000 titles of Soviet literature were translated and published in China in 230 million copies. The Soviets take considerable satisfaction from quoting a 1957 statement by the Union of Chinese Writers: ''Chinese people are constant readers of Soviet books, which for them represent a textbook for life and struggle. . . . Chinese authors always have used and continue to use Soviet literature as an example and seriously study the rich experience of the Soviet authors.''[19]

The flood of Soviet specialists, books, and knowhow naturally made the study of the Russian language a must for anyone who wished to advance in the new society. The enthusiasm which the Chinese tried to generate for the study of Russian can be gleaned from the following lavish description in the 1958 edition of the Guide to Entrance into Institutions of Higher Education:

> The Russian language is the instrument for learning the advanced experiences of the Soviet Union. It is the language by which the noblest thought and the most advanced achievements in culture, science and technology are spread. By mastering this language, we will have the key to open the door that leads to a new world in which we will find an inexhaustible source of cultural, scientific, and technological treasures, as well as fruits of the wisdom of the greatest Russian revolutionaries, scholars, and writers.[20]

It is not surprising, therefore, that Russian became the most popular language not only in the institutions of higher education but in the urban secondary schools as well. Curiously, however, at the time of the shortage of competent Russian teachers, the New China News Agency was warning that "there will be some difficulty in finding work assignments for 3,000 Russian-language graduates" completing their studies in 1957.[21]

Russian was considered to be especially important for professionals in fields of science and technology. As a matter of fact, it was considered to be a short-cut to the acquisition of world science. In a 1952 speech to the Chinese Academy of Sciences, Chen Boda, a member of the Central Committee of the Communist Party, suggested that the works of British and American scientists could be used as reference, but "generally speaking, the good British and American science has already been absorbed by the Soviet scientists; hence, the quickest and best way is to learn from the Soviet Union."[22]

There is no doubt at all about the vital role played by the Soviet Union in China's impressive economic growth during the First Five-Year Plan (1953-57); the multi-faceted help in creating a new educational system was just as important. In fact, both economic and educational assistance must be viewed as an integral part of the overall, wide-ranging, and selfishly generous support for an emerging socialist neighbor. Both seemed to work and both seemed right for the time. As we shall see, however, since the 1950s it has been difficult to get an unbiased assessment of Soviet contribution to China either from Moscow or Beijing.

Changing Attitudes and Increasing Tensions

It is obvious from the earlier discussion that China welcomed Soviet support and considered adoption of the Soviet system to be the quickest way to reorganize her existing educational institutions so they could best serve the new national goals of developing a socialist economy and society. Certainly in the first half of the 1950s there was no shortage of glowing statements about the gratitude of the Chinese people toward their Soviet brethren for their generosity. By 1956, however, the uncritical attitude toward the Sovietization of education began to change and a number of articles and speeches began to appear which, after the prescribed bow to Soviet assistance, started to ask questions and express reservations.

For example, Lu Dingyi who was then Chief of the Propaganda Department of the Central Committee of the Chinese Communist (CCP), proclaimed that "Learn from the Soviet Union" is a correct slogan, but also warned that "...our method of learning must not be doctrinaire, mechanical adoption but must be adapted to the actual situation of our country."[23] Many other Chinese observers also pointed out that the superimposition of pedagogical principles from the Soviet Union is not "linked adequately with the realities of China."[24] Yet others have complained that Chinese students were not adequately prepared to follow the curricula imported from the Soviet Union and that many of the established requirements were too demanding for them.

These complaints were mild, however, compared with the outspoken statements that were made during the brief "blooming and contending" period in the spring of 1957. It became obvious that professional educators, many of whom were either foreign-trained or educated in Chinese universities which followed the American or European systems, deeply resented the forced Sovietization of education, including the requirement to study the Russian language. They also felt left out of the decision-making process. For example, in his broad criticisms of the two Ministries of Education, Pan Shu, a professor of psychology at Nanjing University and a member of the Chinese Academy of Sciences, included the following charges:

> The Ministry of Higher Education and the Ministry of Education have forsaken all the experts of China to rely entirely on the experiences of Soviet Russia. What is suitable for the Soviets may not necessarily be suitable for China. The personnel in both Ministries never discuss any problems with Chinese professional experts. Their unreasonable attitudes are sometimes unbearable. This situation must not be allowed to continue.

and,

> The copying from Russia in the Ministry of Higher Education has been going on mechanically and blindly. Some of the experiences of the Russians are more traditional rather than scientific, yet the Ministry of Higher Education has time and again discarded the more logical Chinese methods for some outmoded and outdated Russian system.[25]

Unfortunately for Professor Pan Shu and others who criticized the system, the hundred flowers movement was quickly followed by the anti-rightist campaign, focused mainly on exposing "the reactionary and bankrupt points of view" of writers, dramatists and other intellectuals. The struggle that ensued in the institutions of higher education to distinguish between "poisonous weeds" and "fragrant flowers" was a bitter one — much of it centering on the role of the Party in academic work. This rectification campaign was the precursor of Mao's "Great Leap Forward." In economic development, the Great Leap was a drive to substitute the muscle and enthusiasm of China's vast labor resources for scarce capital; in education, the plan was to rapidly increase enrollment at all levels, increase the number of students with worker and peasant backgrounds, emphasize local initiative, and integrate education with production. It was, of course, a drastic departure from the (Stalinist) Soviet model of development and, for a variety of other reasons, it turned out to be a failure on all counts.

But although we then suspected and now know that the Great Leap was anathema to the development of China as perceived by the Soviet Union and its advisers in China, both Moscow and Beijing continued to project an image of harmony to the outside world, and from what was published in the late 1950s, it was difficult to detect any serious problems between these "devoted socialist brothers." As late as 1960 the *People's Daily* published a speech by the Director of the Technical Science Department of the Chinese Academy of Sciences, celebrating the tenth anniversary of the Sino-Soviet Treaty of Friendship, Alliance, and Mutual Assistance, in which he exalted the role of the Soviet Union in the rapid development of science and technology in China and called on the Chinese people "Not only to study Soviet science and technology but also learn from the Soviet people's excellent qualities."[26]

Although the Soviet authors had a more difficult time of shedding a positive light on the policies of the Great Leap, they tried. They were still writing positively about the new Chinese directions in education, explaining that the introduction of political and ideological training into institutions of higher education was "in the style of a Marxist-Leninist world outlook." One author even attempted to justify some of the educational policies of the Great Leap and the attacks against university professors by pointing out that for intellectuals, the transition from capitalism to socialism was just as difficult in the Soviet Union as in China and that "sometimes drastic policies are necessary to conquer painful doubts and go over to the side of socialism."[27] Upon his return, one Soviet visitor to China offered the following excuse for China's excesses:

> There is much in the work of Chinese pedagogues which has not been decid-
> ed, many difficulties. They are studying the experience of Soviet schools and
> hope to use imagination in adapting it to Chinese conditions. At the same
> time they courageously, in their own way, decide individual questions of labor
> education and preparation of students for practical work. [28]

In fact, the Soviets did not accept with equanimity China's departure in 1956 from the Soviet educational model. What were some of the specific issues in education that upset them?

The Soviets saw the 1956 decentralization of higher education as the first open rejection by the Chinese of Soviet experience and also as a harbinger of the more drastic changes which indeed did materialize during the Great Leap in 1958. Although Soviet specialists working at the Ministry of Education were still not openly criticized, by ignoring their recommendations and adopting certain organizational measures, Chinese authorities "secretly" but clearly limited the influence of Soviet advisers. The Soviets were also deeply hurt when the Chinese started to blame all the problems in higher education on the Soviet model and became extremely resentful when they learned that in Chinese inter-Party documents, the word "dogmatism" represented a code word for "Soviet experience."[29]

Curiously, but typically of Soviet observers, Franchuk was especially critical of the influence of the Chinese Communist Party in higher education and the whole relationship between the party and the faculty.[30] He took the Chinese to task for diminishing the role of professionals in administering the institutions of higher education, while putting Party functionaries ("of low cultural level") in their place, and cited the example presented by one Chinese professor who complained that at the People's University in 1957 there was actually more administrative than teaching personnel. Soviet instructors in Xi'an reported that the institution to which they were assigned was run by two small groups rather than by a university director. The poorly qualified members of these groups completely isolated the faculty from any decisions made about the education of students, and the whole administrative system was set up "only to send instruction down," while criticisms and suggestions from the faculty could never move up through the official channels. In general, the changes in higher education were blamed on Mao's faulty rationale and inaccurate facts. For example, his contention that 80 percent of the students in Beijing University were children of bourgeois capitalists was termed as a gross exaggeration of statistics that included under this category worker intellectuals, clerks, handicraftsmen and minor tradesmen. To quote Franchuk once again: "Since the control of the administration of the Party and State apparatus slipped from Mao, he constantly searched for non-formal, non-institutional ways of pressuring his foes and for this purpose fully utilized the difficulties of higher education."[31]

There were yet other criticisms of China and, valid though they may be, the Soviets pretended to be totally unaware that the same problems exist in the Soviet Union. There were complaints about the lack of creative thinking, about the strict controls over libraries which could delay access to legitimate research materials by a year or more, about accusations of "individuality" against anyone who did not conform in thought, actions, outlook, dress, etc. And, although social science was not exactly a priority field in the Soviet Union, they attributed the breakup of the social sciences and humanities in China to the "Maoization of higher education," which substituted the thoughts of Mao for all the courses under these specialties.[32]

After 1956 and especially during the Great Leap Forward, Chinese higher education did indeed take a sharp turn away from the Soviet model or, for that matter, away from any known educational model.[33] By placing it under the direction and control of the Communist Party, revising the course work "to serve the political interests of the proletariat," and combining it with large doses of physical labor, enrollment in higher education increased rapidly but at the expense of quality. Great Leap policies were, of course, disastrous, and in education it became clear that China had to abandon Mao's notion of creating an "all-round man" and revert to a system which would shift the balance away from "redness" back toward "expertness." To do this the Chinese pedagogues had few options but to return to the framework and curricula put in place in the early 1950s with Soviet help. Although it is true that by the mid-1960s the "socialist education movement" again incorporated more and more political activities and manual labor into the university students' academic year, the more formal, state-supported sector managed to graduate reasonably well-qualified professionals prior to the Cultural Revolution. It seems surprising, therefore, that the Soviets refer to the period *after* the Great Leap as one in which "a complete break with Soviet education" occurred[34] — a statement which can only be explained by the total cessation of contacts between the pedagogues of the two countries, which did not occur until the early 1960s. The Soviets themselves quote Lu Ping, the president of Beijing University, when he "courageously" announced in 1962 that "Education in the Soviet Union has great advantages over capitalist education. That is why we cannot reject it just because we are fighting against revisionism. . . . It is necessary to utilize that which is good, what we imitated and adapted in the past. . . ."[35] In other words, despite lengthy disruptions and serious perversions of the Soviet model for higher education, whenever the trend was to reinstate academic values ("move to the right"), it was a move toward the Soviet system. And, unspoken though it was, there were many basic similarities between the Soviet and the traditional Chinese systems which made such a shift palatable. By way of historical perspective, however, it should be remembered that rote learning, memorization, blind respect for authority, which characterized traditional education and which grew out of the examination system, were not without critics. Some Chinese educational theorists harshly condemned these aspects of traditional education and some institutions, which managed to remain free of examinations (usually around some prominent masters), also managed to discard such methods of controlling knowledge.

Current Educational Reforms: The Final Break

Major reforms in higher education were not initiated until the late 1970s: after Mao's death, after the purge of the Gang of Four, and after the introduction of the Four Modernizations policy and the convening of the 1978 National Science Conference. The ambitious goals identified at the Science Conference made it especially clear to the new leadership in Beijing that sweeping changes were imperative. To achieve the established objectives, large numbers of highly trained scientists, engineers, and other professionals would be required, and at the same time, the poorly educated cadres would have to be replaced by competent managers. While it is simplistic to suggest the current reforms in higher education are being accomplished by replacing the Soviet model with that of the United States, the facts are that it is specifically the legacy of Soviet education which is being retired and, in the process, the influence of American education is unmistakable.[36]

A discussion of the progression and scope of educational reforms over the past seven to eight years would take us far afield. However, by considering the criticisms leveled at the educational system in recent years and the reforms being implemented in higher education, it is easy to identify some of the more important aspects of the Soviet model which are being changed.

One of the most frequent criticisms of higher education in China is overspecialization, also recognized as a drawback of higher education in the USSR. Huang Shiqi, Director of the Information and Documentation Unit of the Ministry of Education (recently changed to the State Education Commission), discusses the Soviet roots of overspecialization of China. In both countries the central planning authorities are responsible for the overall planning of that nation's manpower needs. Planners make up comprehensive lists of existing industrial products and processes and send them to the Ministry of Education, which draws up lists of specialties to meet the specific needs. Mechanical engineering provides an excellent example of the consequences of such a practice:

. . . specialties have been organized along products or process lines, such as internal combustion engines, steam turbines, cranes, and other material-handling machines. Specialties concerned with internal combustion engines are further subdivided into those used in the automotive industry, the agricultural machine-building industry, the aviation industry, and the ship-building industry.[37]

The obvious result are graduates who are narrowly trained, with extremely limited flexibility in job assignment, and without any capacity for critical analysis, research, or creativity. Even the left-leaning *Red Flag* proclaimed that "Engineers and scientific workers cannot just have a single discipline — they must have the knowledge of many disciplines."[38] The reforms in higher education tackle the problem of overspecialization through changes in the curricula — especially by integrating more theory into the coursework and by including more electives. And even though Beijing will continue to produce the unwieldy state plans for college enrollment based on tenuous long-range estimates of the country's man-power needs, some changes are occurring here too. Not only will the new broader-based graduates be equipped for more professional flexibility when it comes to job assignment, but individual enterprises that previously had to gamble on ob-taining the required specialists can now contract with institutions of higher educa-tion to train the professionals they need by paying for their education.

Another major departure from the earlier Soviet system in higher education is the introduction of research activities into the universities. There are several closely interrelated reasons why research in Chinese universities has been limited. First, serious research was precluded by the just discussed narrow specialization and inadequate theoretical background offered the students. Second, there are minimal research funds and facilities at the institutions of higher education — reflecting both budgetary constraints and the limited qualifications of students. Third, until recently there was no formal graduate education in China. Fourth, and perhaps most important, basic research has been the prerogative of the Chinese Academy of Sciences — a responsibility jealously guarded by the Academy's research institutes. In the past few decades university research in the Soviet Union has been on the increase; in China, however, this has not been the case. Only in the last few years, and especially since the establishment of formal graduate degrees in 1981, has research become part of academic curricula. Much of it is applied research and development under contractual agreements with factories and other productions units, but some of the more prestigious universities now are being allocated funds for key research laboratories which will perform basic research.[39]

There are changes being introduced in the methods of teaching as well. One of the frequently heard complaints about the current system is its "failure to train students to live and think independently."[40] For 30 years the rote character of classroom instruction suited the Chinese very well. First of all, it was not a sharp departure from the highly disciplined traditional approach to education, which required endless memorization (starting with the characters) and total submissive respect for the teachers. And secondly, the educational approach in which the professor was expected faithfully to present the prescribed material without any response or questioning by the students also seemed appropriate to a regime that prized conformity and single answers to all questions. Most pedagogues and politicians now understand that this type of education is not conducive either to innovation or to the development of new interpretations, and is therefore inappropriate for a nation bent on modernization. The transition to a give and take academic environment — a strange and foreign concept to both teacher and student — will be a slow one. Addressing the national education conference in May 1985, Vice Premier Wan Li lamented this fact: "To varying degrees, we still use the force feeding method. The students are required to listen to their teachers in class and memorize what they are taught. They have to rely on mechanical memorization to pass examinations." He went on to say that "it is more important to strengthen students' ability to think independently and solve new problems with the knowledge they have learned. . . . Students should not be force fed: instead, they should be guided to an understanding of the 'hows' and 'whys' of what they learn." Wan expressed a goal for higher education which (especially for China) is a bit utopian, calling for the creation of "the kind of vigorous and lively political situation in which there are both centralism and democracy, both discipline and freedom, and both unity of will and personal ease of mind."[41]

As part of this new atmosphere the Chinese are attempting to institute in higher education, academics are urged to increase interdisciplinary communication, which was virtually eliminated after most of the comprehensive universities were broken up. Universities are now urged to "obliterate the dividing lines between academic departments and teaching and research sections, and establish an organization that cuts across departmental and disciplinary lines."[42] All these suggested changes are, of course, sharp departures from both the Soviet model and the traditional Chinese approaches to education.

Finally, the new reforms in higher education are intended to limit the excessive control by the center and to expand the power of decision-making of the institutions of higher education. By adopting the Soviet system in curriculum, teaching methods, and organizational framework, universities became "overmanaged." In the 1950s "uniform curricula and syllabi were regarded as inviolable legal documents to be enforced with the utmost care. Later on we came to know that the leading institutions in the Soviet Union enjoy far greater freedom in curriculum matters and in initiating reforms. Our own folly in sticking to uniform curricula and syllabi was largely due to our own ignorance."[43] In other words, the Chinese took the Soviet educational system and made it even more inflexible, dogmatic and traditionally Chinese — in the feudal sense.

The new directives clearly spell out the powers of the institutions of higher education — provided they implement the policies, decrees, and plans of the state. These include the power to enroll students; to readjust the objectives of various disciplines, formulate teaching plans and programs, and compile and select teaching material; to accept projects and cooperative agreements with production units and social establishments; to dispose of capital construction investment and of funds allocated by the state; and to develop international educational and academic exchanges by using their own funds.[44] These powers go well beyond the responsibilities of Soviet institutions of higher learning.

The one Soviet characteristic of higher education which the Chinese still retain — but certainly not to emulate the Russians — is its elitist nature. As one American student put it after spending two years in Soviet universities: "Higher education in the Soviet Union is a coveted privilege granted only to a relatively small minority of the nation's youth."[45] Although this is precisely what Mao was trying to change in his periodic forages against Chinese education policy and the elitism it bred, the current drive to raise the quality of higher education effectively excludes the overwhelming proportion of Chinese youth who live in the countryside. In fact, the chances of entering a full-time, key university increase enormously if one happens to be born a male, in a large city, to parents who are professionals within the Chinese bureaucracy. By now instances of fraud associated with college entrance examinations have been cleaned up and the "back door" is no longer a viable access to higher education, but influence can still be useful in making sure that a child will enter a key primary and a key middle school, which are virtually prerequisite to getting high grades on the college entrance examinations.[46]

To a certain degree, the current elitism in higher education can be justified by the need to overcome the shortages in qualified professionals created by the Cultural Revolution. A country in a hurry cannot afford the luxury of egalitarianism in education. Although the leadership obviously has been uncomfortable with this aspect of higher education, new policies to counteract elitism have been stimulated more by practical considerations than by the discomfort. Unable to induce college graduates to settle in the countryside in any large numbers (or to select majors that are likely to take them away from the city), Beijing has instituted a policy which has lowered college admission standards for rural youth who agree to study medicine, agronomy, and other specialties needed in the countryside and to return to their village upon graduation. For the time being this seems like a reasonable compromise and one the Soviets might do well to consider.

Postscript: The Renewal of Sino-Soviet Contacts

Since 1982 there has been a gradual but steady growth in a variety of contacts between China and the Soviet Union. The countries resumed hosting delegations of specialists; more professionals are now attending conferences in each other's countries; Soviet and Chinese friendship societies have become active once again; and there have even been some exchanges of students and lecturers from institutions of higher education. In December 1984, the Soviet Union and China signed an agreement on economic and technical cooperation, a separate agreement on scientific and technological cooperation, and still another agreement to establish a Soviet-Chinese commission on economic, trade, scientific and technological cooperation. The significant increase in trade and other contacts is having immediate economic benefits and is also serving some important political and strategic considerations of the two countries. But will the resumption of contacts have any significant effect on the direction of Chinese higher education in the years to come?

Although predicting China's future has sometimes proved to be a precarious venture, in this instance the risk does not appear to be excessive. In the early 1950s it was not just an absence of a viable option which induced Beijing to follow the Soviet educational model. Many of the authoritarian characteristics of Soviet education were perceived to be appropriate: they were somewhat compatible with China's traditional values and, to a large extent, the new leadership felt they met the special needs of a country emerging from revolution and chaos. In the same sense, the present approach to higher education, which has introduced reforms patterned after Western (especially American) educational systems, is most suitable to China's current needs and goals. It is not unreasonable to suggest that even if China backtracks from some of Deng Xiaoping's more drastic reforms, neither the drive for modernization nor the open door to the outside world are likely to be subverted. Whatever happens, however, one prediction can be made with certainty: the lesson China learned during the Cultural Revolution was much too painful for her ever again to sacrifice education on the altar of political exigency.

11

Maoism in Recent French Educational Thought and Practice

Roland Depierre

Introduction

After two centuries of eclipse, European admiration for the Chinese political and social system was to reappear in the 1960s. However, it was no longer the sinophilia which Isabelle Llasera described in chapter 2, cnetering on China's ancient culture and unchanging moral principles. It was a fascination with the new rebellious China of the Cultural Revolution period.

This was a time in which the West was experiencing industrial expansion, economic growth and rapid urbanization. Its cultural models, in the forms of music, cinema and television, were dominating the globe. Its universities proliferated and were transformed. The social demand for education had never seemed more pressing. In contrast China was isolated after its rupture with the Soviet Union, surrounded by difficulties in its relations with India and Japan, and disturbed by the escalating American military presence in Vietnam. In the periphery of all the international exchange currents of the period, China's troubled economic situation and violent internal policy disputes made it impossible for her to assert an international policy of any prestige or influence. Her cultural heritage was under threat, her artistic spirit was stifled and her universities were either closed or in turmoil.

Yet precisely at this time, western campuses found themselves plastered with pictures of Mao Zedong. The New Wave cinema popularized the revolt of intellectual youth, linking it to China and to quotations from Mao's Little Red Book.[1] Western Maoism sprang into being. Its sudden appearance, followed by its equally rapid demise,[2] constitutes a kind of historical enigma which might be explained in two opposite ways.

On the one hand, Maoism could be regarded as an imported ideology. In spite of effective forms of propaganda and a favorable environment, this transplant was rejected because of its foreign origins. Western democracy was able to resist what was essentially an enterprise of disinformation, even subversion.[3] In the first section of this chapter, I discuss the network of Chinese organizations in France and their impact.

On the other hand, Maoism could be seen as a brief, feverish infatuation of the European intelligentsia, which was more naive and uninformed than ill-intentioned. The Cultural Revolution became a fashion for writers and journalists who were disappointed with the evolution of a world they did not understand. These idealists propagated the myth of a new China, using Chinese terms and colors, yet remaining fundamentally true to the western utopian tradition. The "myth of the educative society," discussed in section two, represented the rebirth of the ancient European vision of an Ideal City under the guise of what I am calling Maolatry.

Maoism was also a cultural phenomenon which provided a new language to the western intellectual elite in a time of ferment when value systems, institutions and behaviors were subject to radical questioning. Its dynamism and ultra-democratic spirit stood out in sharp relief against a Western society perceived as reified and technocratic. Section three of this chapter explores the way in which Maoism affected the new, enlarged cohort of university youth, especially those in the social sciences.

Finally, in the fourth section, I consider the Maoist organizations themselves, their impact on school reform, on pedagogical models, and on the sociology of education. In conclusion, I ask whether there are not some parallels between the Jesuits and the European Maoists in their admiration of a China that is always being rediscovered.

The Chinese in Paris

In establishing diplomatic relations with France, China instituted a variety of cultural exchanges and Chinese students and teachers came to Paris, Rennes and Grenoble. They had been given a detailed preparatory briefing in Peking on the rules of non-interference in the internal matters of a foreign state, they were chaperoned by a vigilant political commissar and they lived in their own sequestered domain, concentrating on their work, refusing to be pressed into taking part in any political or union meetings of their French or foreign comrades. In Rennes, they were only once seen at a turbulent protest against the American war in Vietnam, in 1967. But they were on the sidewalk, mute and paralyzed. It was extremely difficult to recognize in them brothers or sisters of the furies who were at that time rampaging through the streets of Peking in front of the British and Soviet embassies. They were in bed by the time student political and cultural activity came to life in the evening, but it occasionally happened at dawn, when they were on their ways to collective morning exercises on the track of the university campus, that they came across some militant French Maoists returning from a prolonged meeting. Distrustful, even suspicious, they gave only a brief response to the political and trade union groups who accosted them. A prepared stereotypical statement in phrases wooden yet exotic would freeze the atmosphere.

The Chinese students requested to return home in order to participate in the Cultural Revolution and made no political demonstration until the day of their farewell ceremonies. After polite expressions of gratitude, they suddenly launched into virulent attacks on the "bourgeois university" after the showing of the film "The East Is Red." They started several brawls in front of the Soviet embassy in Paris and returned as heros. Their departure from France, as their arrival, created a sensation, but their stay left scarcely any mark except a few volumes of the selected works of Mao which they had presented as gifts. There were not even any broken hearts. How could they have been instruments of subversion?

The Chinese student presence may not have made a significant impact. Yet the Chinese Communist Party (CCP), after the schism with the Communist International in 1962, had sought to reconstitute, along with Albania, the organizations which followed the political line and platform defined in the "25-point letter."[4] By encouraging several old friends to create a publishing house in Lausanne, and to open a bookshop in Paris for the publication and dissemination of bulletins from the New China News Agency, also by bringing back to life an amity association which had been latent, the CCP ended up having secured several definite representatives. Marxist circles joined to form a "movement" which became later a "new" communist party, inspired by the thought of Mao Zedong. The Chinese Central Committee duly gave public recognition to this movement, provided it with free subscriptions to its journals and made possible some meetings with its leaders.

Both the personalities and organizations which appeared to be the open representatives of the international activity of the CCP, and the newspapers and journals which zealously regurgitated slogans and editorials from the Chinese press, were much less manipulated or disinformed than is commonly thought to be the case. The Chinese leadership, which had been burned by its own unfortunate experience with the Soviet father-party, avoided all attitudes of overt paternalism, except possibly in the domain of international politics. So much so, that the behavior of their Maoist brothers and sisters never ceased to intrigue, even scandalize, them.

The objective of wresting the western working class from the influence of modern revisionism was far from being achieved, and no important schism took place in the pro-Soviet communist parties, with the excepton of the tiny Australian party. On the contrary, the Italian, French, Spanish and Portuguese parties saw their influence and their control over trade union movements grow considerably, in spite of the Soviet intervention in Prague in 1968. It must be noted, however, that among the Maoist organizations, many were created to oppose the parties recognized by Peking. One could even add that their ideological influence on university campuses was inversely proportionate to their loyalty to the Chinese line.

Might one say that the CCP tried to counteract the influence of the pro-Soviets by supporting leftist agitation in Europe through the press and other forms of communication? Beginning from 1966, the student unions and political organizations found themselves freely provided with subscriptions to journals of Chinese propaganda far beyond the norm in this type of international relation. However, their stereotyped style and the total ignorance they revealed of the situation in the West ensured that they exerted no direct influence. If the Jesuits sinified themselves in order to approach and convert the Chinese bureaucracy, Chinese propagandists abjured the least accomodation in dogma or the smallest alteration in language.

Many French and other foreign collaborators who worked on the foreign publications of Radio-Beijing International, New China News Agency and other such offices have attested, sometimes in an almost pathetic way, how the institutions they served insisted on remaining ignorant or suspicious of their actual public.[5] Some no doubt feared the accusation of "spritual pollution" but it was mainly a question of an ethnocentric obstinacy about the correct word and the literal translation. For example, *Peking Review* outraged even the most austere of western readers by propagating and justifying the remark of Jiang Qing that modernist art, impressionistic painting, rock and roll and jazz were all the instruments by which the western bourgeoisie corrupted the people.[6] From that point on Chinese discourse was more often an irritating, even comic, monologue which the European Maoists had to give laborious explanations for.[7]

It is worth noting that this proliferation of propaganda coincided with the period in which China was most closed in upon herself and obsessed with her internal disputes. This made her impermeable to external events or debates, particularly in the field of education, even when they echoed her own preoccupations. Take as an example the Chinese debate of autumn 1975 on the dictatorship of the proletariat and the state over science and the serious incidents in the universities and the wider political arena that accompanied it. Can extreme politization sterilize research policy? Does the leaden coat of dialectic principles present obstacles to academic work? This debate had parallels with a discussion among French Marxist philosophers, including some Maoists, concerning "proletarian science" and the role of "dialectical materialism" as the very foundation of scientific theory.[8] Yet the Chinese press totally ignored the Parisian debate. This indifference was reciprocal on the side of French intellectuals.

Such sensational affairs as the report of the student Li Linhua who challenged the academic authority of professors or the "blank examination sheet" of Zhang Tiesheng who denounced the tyranny of examinations, the cult of diplomas and the social selection of the university aroused enormous excitement in the Chinese university community. They also had profound effects on the life of higher educational institutions and the wider political life of China. They ought to have had a certain impact on the French educational milieu which was shaken by matters of analogous or parallel significance, relating to student recruitment policies, the ideology of schooling, student-teacher relations and a selection process which meant failure for many. In the very same period these French concerns triggered strikes and demonstrations.

However, these two movements took place in a situation of total reciprocal ignorance. The local educational press had no echo of these symbolic educational events in China, nor were they taken up by the European Maoist literature, which was struggling hard to demonstrate the gentleness and effectiveness of China's May 7th Cadre Schools and reporting how universities in China recruited students through popular elections. It appears that when the political significance of the Chinese message went against the expectation of the western receiving set, or was too far removed from the Maoist utopia, the information was either over-shadowed or distorted.[9]

Even when all the conditions were favorable, the intelligibility, and even more, the credibility of the Chinese model remained in doubt. The cinema offers the best illustration of the considerable handicap affecting all cultural and ideological messages from China intending to influence a western intellectual audience, even when this audience was kindly disposed towards the message directed at them. In the spring of 1976, the France-China Friendship Society suggested showing the well-known feature film *Chun Miao,* directed by Xie Jin, to an audience of sympathetic students. The script recounts the setbacks of a young country girl from a remote region who wanted to enter the university and had to overcome obstacles of all kinds, bureaucratic, political and linguistic. In principle, the au-dience were supporters of the "revolution in education." They were also cosmopolitan people with an open attitude towards foreign cultural models. Fur-thermore, the film addressed questions of great interest to students in that egalitarian and socially-oriented epoch: equality of educational opportunity, open-ness of the education system to social reality, gap between the language of educa-tion and the language of communication, etc. The director was an internationally renowned master of contemporary Chinese cinema. The production of the film, simple yet effective, raised no problems. Yet in spite of these favorable condi-tions, the French audience received the film with mere polite courtesy, while I saw Chinese students weeping while watching the film for the seventh time!

This wall of incomprehension had nothing to do with the aesthetic standards imposed by Jiang Qing, as the director later claimed, but was linked first and foremost to a form of political argumentation which the western spectator finds extreme, in fact totally manichean. It is also linked to roles which simply didn't make sense to French Maoist students from the suburbs who were taken aback by the virginal purity and the virulent naivety of their distant sister. Behind the analogy in slogans, the Maoist discovered the gap in situations. They could not find the image of *their* revolution in this insipid tale.

Although the Chinese Communists loved to insist that the revolution could not be exported, that Marxism-Leninism must be adapted to each country and that they had been the first to suffer under the Comintern in the twenties and thirties and under the father-party in the fifties, they had striven to reconstitute political groups in western countries who partook of their views. They had put in place a propaganda machine, supported political tourism, and favoured cultural linkages directed towards western intellectual and university circles.

Yet the very tenets of Maoism (self-reliance and autonomy, the primacy of ideological factors, the mass-line, practice as the starting point, principles plac-ing democracy over centralism) made it difficult to control and implement these efforts at external influence. Either an over strict surveillance rendered them ineffective or the resulting effects came back against the initial objectives. The time came when a revolutionary and proselytizing China no longer dared to recognize its spiritual sons and daughters in the Japanese, German and Italian Maoists, whose image and noise were sent back to them by the international media.

Strangely, it was when China was closed upon itself, when it chased away journalists and tourists (that is the very xenophobic period of 1966-68) that its image held greatest fascination for student and intellectual circles. It was nothing new that its attraction grew with the fear and suspicion that it aroused. The Jesuits had already demonstrated their admiraton in the very period of the expulsions and persecutons to which the Qing Emperor subjected them in the eighteenth century. Oriental exoticism was revived by the terror inspired by the Boxers in the late nineteenth century. One of the perverse charms of sinophilia is the attraction of the Forbidden China for the western imagination.[10]

Hegel remarked that it would have been better for the reputation of Confucius if his work had never been translated. "Once his moral system was made known through a German translation, much of his credibility was destroyed with us."[11] Mao Zedong met the same fate as his illustrious rival. The progressive publication of his works (either in spite of or in opposition to Chinese authority) revealed their banalities to his western disciples.[12]

The Myth of the Educative Society

Beyond admiration for the revolution of the Chinese people, the most surprising aspect of Western Maoism was the personality cult of a Super Educator. It is for this reason that I use the term "Maolatry." China was presented as a new Sparta, a model state whose activities and institutions all had an educating function.

Education was the final end of revolutionary power since the ultimate aim of the Maoist revolution was less the transformation of the world than the transformation of human persons. "The enterprise of transforming the inner person would be unthinkable in the West, where the separation of individual morality and the state is part of political tradition. However, it is much more understandable to the Chinese mentality. It was this unprecedented enterprise that the Chinese revolution, true to Mao Thought, constituted for the Chinese people."[13]

Revisionism and economism had under-estimated the importance of ideology for Communism. Certainly, it consisted of an economic change, a new mode of production, but first of all it was a change in social relations. From this perspective, China was far ahead since it was "the anti-model of industrial over-development," claimed Maria Antonietta Macciocchi.[14] Mao had understood that the revolution consisted in modifying the content of human motivation, in bringing about a change in the "human spirit" through a constant and demanding socialist education in the countryside and in rectification movements. "Religious systems had already attempted this sort of conversion, but without giving it the profound character of a science, as did Mao Zedong, in order to undertake the psychological remodelling of human persons."[15]

All politics consist of education on the levels of objectives. The decisive question of socialist power was in the continuation of the revolution and the problem of successors who would lead it to the end. How were they to be educated, if not in revolutionary practice, through the experience of disorder, violence and upheavals? Government was no longer a question of an unchanging civil order, brought about by harmony between emperor and subject, father and son, man and woman. The Prince was no longer the interpreter of tradition which he learned through disciplined imitative action, but he was the Rebel, who stirred up agitation in the Palace of Heaven, who sharpened the contradictions in order to bring about the collapse of the ancient social order, founded in hierarchy, bureaucracy, filial piety and educational discipline. "It is I who set alight the civil war in education," said Mao.

As for the real effects of the Cultural Revolution, the European Maoists were either discreet or skeptical. With regard to the bloody disorders of the autumn of 1967, Han Suyin admitted "Zhou Enlai later told Edgar Snow that there had been hundreds of millions wounded or killed in the army, since they would not shoot at the people."[16] But she herself gave no details and drew no conclusions. Whatever the violence, there was a theoretical justification for the way in which the Cultural Revolution came about. "A choice must be made between a simple palace putsch which remains unexplained, and the road taken by Mao which was to arouse the people in totality and so enable them to understand the true problems of the revolution through revolutionary practice itself."[17] In the political domain, as in all education, a pedagogical choice had to be made. Does the master transmit a knowledge already constituted (the putsch) or does he allow his disciples to create an experienced knowledge (the revolution)? The latter is a heuristic pedagogy, slow and rather messy, to be sure, but much more effective.

As a result of this approach, the masses, once awakened, have an overwhelming enthusiasm for reconstruction. They find themselves gifted with an unlimited creative power which Maoist pedagogy succeeded in creating and channeling. "One of the essential concepts of Mao is the attention he gives to the spirit of initiative, the courage to dare...this is an essential part of the Maoist educational campaign."[18] Once this "daring" is liberated, the master's involvement can remain unobtrusive. "All is reinvented from the bottom up. The directives are enriched because they come from the masses themselves."[19] This in turn brings about a total change in history. All becomes possible to the working class who "have led the cultural revolution, created the revolutionary committees, combated the rigidity of the party and reconstructed the party organs through organizing congresses to elect them. The working class has re-educated the cadres, educated the youth, made enterprises operate under a new form of management, and reorganized production through a collaboration of workers and technicians. They have restructured the division of labor itself."[20]

Yet the people don't always understand the meaning of history. They hesitate and wait, since "it often happens that the masses have an objective need for this or that transformation, yet subjectively they are unaware of the need and have neither the wish nor desire to fulfil it."[21] Therefore pedagogy has to take this into account. It is not enough that the prince puts into subjective terms what the people know objectively, he must practice the pedagogy of upheaval. By arousing those elements of the people who are most aware, it is necessary to awaken the majority and to shake up those who are less gifted in the dialectic.

In conclusion, one could say that this ideological unity, this fusion of the science of the educator and the intelligence of the educated, was to produce a new type of knowledge, a new way of seeing by the people which the European Maoists considered to be the thought of the future, parallel to the new discourse. "A fundamental change in the socio-economic structure and the way of life, the Revolution is impossible unless it creates a new way of seeing and knowing by the people, not science in the service of the people but the practical application of the science of the people. It presupposes the absolute rejection of a division of labor"[22] between worker and intellectual, educator and educated. This will be the collectivization of knowledge itself.

The possibility of a society governed by a Super Educator or a government ruled by an ideology whose final end was the revolution of thought depended on several theoretical conditions. First of all there was the metaphysical presupposition of "an identity between thought and reality."[23] In China this was expressed in the fact that everything was politics. Then there was the political axiom that the authority and legitimacy of the Prince was linked to his absolute knowledge, the invincibility of his thought. It was this infallibility which gave him his mandate. And finally this was the ethical postulate according to which the virtue of citizens and the quality of their civic loyalty was directly proportionate to their fidelity to the thought of the Master, who was above all, a Master of thought. All of his subjects aspired to be "good pupils of Chairman Mao."

Political action thus reached finality in the triumph of this truth, whose criterion was based on the authority of the Prince. "The slogan which claims that all persons are equal before truth is a bourgeois slogan which denies absolutely the fact that truth has class characteristics. Class enemies use the slogan to oppose the thought of Mao Zedong."[24] All that opposed Mao was by definition false through and through, since Truth and Falsity were absolutely at odds. "There are not any number of ways of conceiving of the world, but only two ways. Whoever refuses one, by definition adopts the other. That is all."[25]

This Maolatry emerged from a double mythology: the historical myth of a prince who is founder, legislator and liberator of the collectivity, inspirer and guide of the enlightened few, who inaugurates a new historical period; and the philosophical myth of a king who is not only a philosopher but a true sage. He does not merely comply with the truth, he creates the truth. He does not merely use language, he creates it. He is the unique interpreter of the unique truth of the people, a truth which the people are so far ignorant of. He is thus their consciousness, their very thought.

In this metaphysical fiction, one finds the Platonic inspiration of the Ideal City ruled by the Philosopher King who alone comprehends the true discourse and brings about the harmony of society. One finds also the Hegelian dialectic and the divinization of the Idea. The prince is the figure of this divinization, history is its painful fulfilment and the state its final end: a state for a new man in a new society where perfect virtue is attained. Contemporary China is the favored place where this stage in the consciousness of the self is reached. "The climate, the very atmosphere that one breathes, is revolutionary. The images here take one back to those we created through our reading and analysis of the Paris Commune and the October Revolution."[26] A trip to China appeared like an ordeal of initiation, a mystical adventure. It was the grand philosophical voyage of the eighteenth century. "One felt like Gulliver, when this infant of the eighteenth century arrived in the country of the giants."[27] This spiritual experience, described by Han Suyin, Maria Antonietta Macciocchi, Michelle Loi and others in such enchanting ways was experienced by many pilgrims of this period. They differed from the Jesuits in that they did not go with the intention of converting, but being converted.

But Maoism was more than this transitory and superficial intellectual fashion in western literacy circles, although its effects on the western educational system are now scarcely visible. Even Maolatry itself was part of a great debate concerning the relation between education and politics which was of central importance during the sixties. All genuine educators have become conscious of the essentially political dimension of human and social reality. Inversely, all genuine political action is infused with awareness concerning the struggle for the transformation of individual social consciousness. All politics is a pedagogy, perhaps even a theology, of liberation.

Maoism was a broader phenomenon than the mythology of New China. It was a social utopia which was to modify in a specific way the problematic of pedagogy and directly affect schools and universities.

Maoization and the University

Maoism became recognized as a political force in France during the presidential campaign of 1965. There was an analogous mistrust of the parliamentary process and a similar revolutionary movement in several other countries, the "provos" in the Netherlands, the celebrated Japanese "Zengakuren," the "Falce-Martello" movement, above all "Il Manifesto"of the Italians. The German "Sozial-Demokratischen Studenten" (SDS, a left-wing faction which broke off from the Social Democratic Party) organized its famous critical university and had the most direct and visible influence in France.

On the intellectual level, this mood marked a clear rupture with the three currents of thought of the post-war period: personalism, existentialism and democratic socialism. As part of their denunciation of totalitarianism and fascism in its Nazi and Stalinist forms, people adhering to these three thought systems shared certain fundamental principles. They embraced non-party political commitment as a modern form of sovereignty, they had a liberating conception of history, they put a high value on individual liberties, all of the ideas commonly included under the term "tragic humanism." Structuralism, however, was now announcing "the end of man"; its positivism predicted the end of ideology. It was in this context that Maoism arose, announcing that the imperialist West had come to a decisive crisis which would bring about its collapse and that a new light of hope was appearing on the Far Eastern horizon.

The West, it seemed, did not know how to make peace. First it was the Cold War, also the drama of colonial wars where one saw armies supposedly committed to defending democratic states, more often putting them in peril. Furthermore, in military campaigns in Indochina and Algeria, psychological techniques and "modern warfare" were used. Western youth regarded this as scandalous, yet their reproofs appeared both vain and naive. Elsewhere, it was the hideous Vietnam War which revealed the power and autonomy of the American military-industrial complex and the cynicism of Pentagon strategies. In response, youth hailed "the heroic people of the rice-fields." In October of 1966 thousands of anti-war militants gathered at Liege in Belgium to hold the first European mass youth movement. Something that was even more new was the fact that one part of this movement rejected the humanist and pacificistic reaction of most democractic organizations which denounced the horrors of chemical warfare and called for peace. In France these radicals were found within the grassroots committees on Vietnam which popularized "the just struggle of the people" and cheered "the magnificent support given by China." They declared that the people would be victorious and denounced American-Soviet collusion. They proclaimed that imperialism was a paper tiger and that popular warfare was invincible. They disseminated the military theories of Mao Zedong and praised the Chinese army which they saw as a counter-model: "an army based on an ethic elaborated by Mao and on democratic rules which existed nowhere else."[28]

The apology for just war and the juvenile militarism provided a challenge to the period. The students involved openly opposed the hippy movement, pop music, and all forms of artistic expression which they associated with a decadent way of life engendered by American imperialism, whose consumer society constituted the final stage of rot. This active minority signified a profound change in the behaviour of certain students. The Maoist students dressed in a virile, even military, style taking the Red Guards as their models. They did not fear physical confrontations with the forces of order. They even organized para-military groups whose responsibility was to organize and control the mass demonstrations which they called "offensives." They participated in commandos against American interests. They were quite ready to disturb university life by brawls, agitation and the disruption of classes.

This attitude contained seeds of the casualness, cynicism and taste for violence which subsequently became evident in the so-called *autonomous* Maoist groups, some of whose members became terrorists: small groups in France such as "les Groupes Armés Révolutionnaires Internationalistes" (GARI), "les Noyaux Armés pour l'autonomie populaire" (NAPAP), and "Action Directe," or veritable networks in Italy (The Red Brigades and others), in Germany (the Red Army fraction) or Japan (a split from Zengakuren) which operated against international imperialism and national militarism.

Yet quite apart from these extreme tendencies, the Maoist movement revealed a significant change of attitude in the university towards the Third World, particularly towards its struggles and wars. The traditional anti-colonialist, anti-racist rhetoric gave way to a lyrical image of the guerrilla brandishing his Kalachnikov on the walls of all the campuses. Above all, a new political form emerged, with the innumerable support committees and meetings to express solidarity with the Third World within university campuses. This movement accompanied the arrival of masses of Third World students who also had great admiration for the Chinese experience. All these factors contributed to critical reflections on the question of a development model and on the issue of unequal exchange. The Maoist economist, Bettelheim, was one of the best known theoreticians of this approach, along with Third World scholars such as Tibor Mende and René Dumont, both of whom upheld the "Chinese way" at least as a point of reference, if not a model. But it was in the *lycées,* which up to that time had been indifferent, that the "anti-imperialist" influence of the Maoists was most remarkable. Militant activities or a sensitization campaign in extra-curricular activities, even interventions during history or geography classes, gave rise to a kind of revolutionary exoticism in the secondary school during the sixties. It was often linked to a sense of guilt about the western past.

During the 1960s university departments of the social sciences, economics and philosophy were swollen with students whose concern was not preparation for professional life but "understanding society and themselves." The development of the new areas of knowledge favored critical thought and discussion on the subject of the social and political system. Dozens of books appeared in the USA and Europe to expose the bureaucratic society[29] or the new industrial state.[30] The state was seen to have become an enormous bureaucratic machine, serving only its own selfish ends and quite out of touch with a society which it administered but gave no political direction to. The American-style electoral campaigns showed that parliamentarianism was nothing more than an alienating mascarade. Party political debates were nothing but a mockery or a propaganda exercise,[31] orchestrated by television and the establishment press, the new powers of darkness. Behind the "showbiz" state was hidden the secret power of the great international banks and multi-national companies whose machinations and ramifications were everywhere discussed. The art of politics had been reduced to a technology for managing the state.[32] Political ideas, whether left or right, socialist or liberal, all added up to the same thing: a policy elaborated by a new race of persons, the technocrats. Citizens might believe they could influence the political orientation of society by their votes but they were actually simply the dupes of the media. This was the "technocratic state." There was also the "'benevolent state" that redistributed most of its revenue to the masses and controlled whole sectors of the economy, yet did not change the social relations of its people but aimed rather to maintain the status quo.

Set against this image of a "reified" society was the vibrant dynamic vision of a China which seemed to be moving towards real popular democracy. The Cultural Revolution got the masses moving, gave them the initiative and instituted authentic direct democracy at the level of a whole continent, something neither utopian nor scientific versions of European socialism had ever succeeded in doing. This was truly the power of the workers. The workers could publicly expose leaders at the very top who were "taking the capitalist road" and bring them down. They succeeded in dismantling a hypertrophied state that had spread its tentacles everywhere, in purging a party that had become both despotic and parasitic, in reconstructing the centers of power from the bottom up, in eliminating professional politicians and bringing together old, middle-aged and young cadres, technicians and workers, men and women, soldiers and civilians, in three-way revolutionary committees.

Many students and teachers in the social sciences participated in cultural, social and political movements, usually youth movements, which were to experience crisis or splits of their radical elements,[33] many of whom formed the backbone of the naissant Maoist movement. They admired China's ethos of manual labor, the concrete humanism of working class solidarity and the respect for rural life. China was not merely the way forward for the Third World, it was a laboratory of ideas where the future of all mankind was under experiment.[34]

Mao's China should be studied because it was the living response to many political and social theories. It was becoming the irreducible reality from which critical discourse could draw its examples, as it had "a whole different quality of life."[35] It would constitute an invincible bulwark which could unmask illusions about the American challenge[36] or the German miracle. It was the anti-model which made it possible to refute theories about Swedish socialism or French economic planning. China was nothing less than the Antithesis!

The Chinese case refuted theories that suggested all systems, capitalist and socialist, tended to converge since they pursued identical ends[37] or because their techno-structures were comparable.[38] The Great Leap had first shown the possibility of another way towards industrialization, and the total revolutionizing of the techno-structure during the Cultural Revolution went even farther. This was a route untravelled so far by humankind. China was the laboratory of real practical work for contemporary social scientists. A billion Chinese were searching for and inventing this new society day by day. Modestly, laboriously, with their small notebooks full of numbers and their hands calloused, sitting in a circle in the corner of a field in Dazhai or perched on a pipeline in Daqing, they were creating a new social science, which linked theory and practice, knowledge and action, which dared to invent the impossible. "Even the experts admit that the Chinese have applied to enterprise utopian principles as far different from a hierarchical structure as possible. They have created an independent administrative echelon at the local level, an egalitarian salary system and social relations totally devoid of all competitiveness among staff within their organization."[39]

Still, debates within the departments of social science and philosophy were not sufficient. It was felt necessary to move from "the China hypothesis" to some real life experimentation. Here and now one had to demonstrate that another way was possible. One had to make social investigation and link up with the masses[40] in order to understand the real proletarian outlook on life. The trade unions should be reconstituted as grassroots committees[41] or committees for the support of popular struggle,[42] which "put themselves at the service of the people" and so let the people themselves invent their own way forward.

Some groups of students broke off their studies in prestigious institutions[43] and left the lecture halls for a life of militant activism. In itself this movement of "linkage with the masses" had little effect on either the structure of the university system or the teaching process, since it only involved a few hundred individuals among the thousands of university students. Nevertheless, beyond the fact that it gave evidence of a fascination with the Chinese model, it was to reflect back on the perception which the whole student body had of their role and their mode of life. The Maoists were usually well-known personalities within student associations on campus and they gained an even greater prestige by the fact that their voluntary departure from the university milieu had nothing to do with academic failure. Furthermore they were to continue directing the various Maoist factions from outside, a fact which changed the perception of the political groupuscules. Finally, this movement, minority as it was, made a breach in the wall which separated the university milieu from that of enterprise, the student world from that of ordinary youth, the world of social research from that of work. Symbolically, an embryo of worker-peasant-student solidarity took shape, along the lines of the great Chinese slogan of May 1968. It was Maoism which made this possible.[44]

However, these social investigations did not produce a new and original view of French society. Most Maoist organizations simply reproduced the classical discourse about the highest stage of capitalism developed by Lenin early in the century.[45] While a concrete analysis of the concrete situation was yet to appear, the anchoring of western political discourse in China gave it an undeniable consistency and authenticity. For the Maoist, China was the opposite of a utopia. The Chinese model functioned as a real experience, of geographical weight and historical profundity, which only naive westerners or persons of ill-will could feign ignorance of.[46]

Chinese Maoism restored to Marxism its political and theoretical credibility among progressive intellectuals, who had been disillusioned in face of the Soviet experience. "All that went wrong in socialist countries was not due to socialism but to the survival of the bourgeoisie within the Party itself, it was not due to the revolution, but to the fact that the revolution had not been completed. In short, the great Chinese helmsman was able to save the idea of revolution from the Soviet shipwreck."[47] For the Maoists, the essential task was to "rebuild a true proletarian party" drawing upon the Maoist experience which had been so successful in destroying its party. This was what was called political Maoism.

In terms of the university, this internal criticism of Marxism with its philosophical, theoretical, political and institutional aspects was to be reintegrated in the renewal of socialist revolutionary thought, of which Maoism was a product. In France this was the Marxist positivism of Althusser which found expression in philosophy, history, science, art, literary criticism and general sociology. It was the rediscovery of Gramsci in Italy and of the Frankfurt school in Germany. After 1968 this movement went beyond academic circles and swept through literature, popular culture and the media with such force that Marxism practically established a cultural hegemony. Every Parisian thinker discovered "social practice," "antagonistic contradictions" and "the production of the concept," just as he had discovered the "parent structure" and the "existential anguish" a decade early. Marxism became pop, just as did music, art and China!

The most visible effect of this development was to strengthen European intellectuals in their traditional critical attitude to the social system and economic life. Yet it is difficult to draw up a global balance sheet of the impact of "intellectual Maoism" on cultural activity and especially on the formation of the student generation of the seventies, even more difficult since contemporary historians generally place this period in a sort of naive and magnanimous parenthesis that is both extreme and sterile. As most of the leading Maoist intellectuals were former communists — Loi, Marchisio, Bettelheim, Sollers, Macciocchi — it is difficult to say if their "Maoist" period was a stage in their development leading up to their definitive split with dialectical materialism or a kind of fruitful yet ultimately abortive step forward from Stalinism.

The Maoists and the School

In the sixties the French university seemed to cope neither with the demographic tidal wave which tripled the number of university students in ten years nor with the structural changes which affected employment patterns and the ladder of professional qualifications, nor finally with the massive influx of young persons from social categories which had up to them been excluded from higher education and whose culture and ambitions did not seem likely to thrive in the cramped hothouses of the "liberal" university.[48] An apocalyptic literature pronounced on the bankruptcy of the institution and predicted its downfall. However a range of initiatives and substantial investments developed campuses, opened up new curricula and changed the patterns of aid given to students. In condemning this new "technocratic" university, the first rare pro-Chinese affirmed that "the new structures are responsible to train, at the lowest possible cost, a mass of mid-level personnel with a narrow and specialist orientation suited to the social and technical division of labour."[49] The comment cut across the habitual claims of student and teacher organizations who, along with the socialist and Communist parties, had been calling for "democratic reform."[50] Yet it turned out to be no more than an intransigent Marxism that held to the diatribes of the extreme left. There were no references to Mao the teacher[51] or to the freshness of China's educational experience, not even to the socialist education campaign of this period.[52]

Confronted with crisis and paralyzed by the deafness of the political authorities, the French union of students became more radical. It demanded an officially recognized student status with salary and conditions of "student power." It proposed the implementation of a counter-reform that would increase both variety and choice in university curricula, a reform linked to the transformation of student-teacher relations. It failed to affect the course of reform and at this point militant groups began to appear who openly made reference to the Chinese Cultural Revolution as the source of critical principles related to the "class-based university." In 1966 the pro-Chinese began to take part in shaping the reform and developed a propaganda which echoed in an unmistakeable way the great debates, meetings and big character posters on Peking campuses.[53] Their style took everyone by storm.

From this date, the student union struggle broke into open revolt, led by groupuscules which denounced all the earlier union reform measures. Similar phenomena were found in Italy, where the reform had been adjourned since 1965, and provoked confrontations and conflicts. From February to April of 1965, Rome, Pisa, Turin, Milan and Venice were overwhelmed by student agitation. In Spain students joined with workers committees to demand freedom of expression. And of course in Germany the SDS of Rudi Dutschke organized the critical university of Berlin whose purpose was to bring the contradictions of the bourgeois university to the point of explosion.

In France the leftist movement found itself at two opposite poles developing fundamentally different doctrines: Maoism and situationism. The situationists denounced the destitution and marginalization of the students. "In a society of abundance, students live in extreme poverty. While originally 80% of them come from strata with an income higher than that of a worker, 90% have an income lower than the most frugal wage packet. This situation did not come about by chance. It was caused by "an economic system that calls for the mass fabrication of students who are uneducated and unable to think."[54]

At quite the opposite pole, the Maoists denounced the special privileges of students, who were to be the "future executives of society," in other words agents in the service of the dominant class, guard dogs of capitalism. Students should protest against this expectation and "put themselves at the service of the people."[55] In order to do this, it was necessary to transform their way of thinking and ally themselves with the struggle of the masses. While the situationists shut themselves up in a mocking bitterness, the Maoists launched into an exuberant activism based on revolutionary optimism. Armed with "the invincible thought of Mao Zedong" these "Communists of a new type" promised a radical future. In face of a workers strike, at a rural demonstration, they fanned the spark which was to set alight the whole plain.

At first the Maoists were taken off guard by the student explosion of May 1968, but they soon joined the current of events. They sought to anchor the student revolt in the "proletarian revolution" which they thought could be identified with the general strike of May 14, 1968. Galvanized by official cheers from Peking which saluted "the worthy sons of the heroes of the Paris Commune who are launching a fresh attack against heaven,"[56] they denounced student debates over educational reform as sterile, since the only thing that counted for them was the revolutionary association among workers, peasants and students in the struggle. Most were social science students from arts faculties, mainly coming from popular strata (rural areas, clerical or primary school teacher families). They adopted populist modes of behaviour which did not displease those whom they represented in the working world, in spite of the reservations of the unions and traditional parties. References to a China where the workers were in charge, where the intellectuals allowed themselves to be re-educated, where the cadres had to return to production, in short all the anti-hierarchical and anti-intellectual clichés of the Chinese Cultural Revolution, served as passwords.

European youth proved less attracted to the orthodoxy of the Marxism-Leninism in Mao Thought than to the contagious image of Chinese youth in upheaval and of the enthusiasm of a revolution which appeared, through the televised image of the gatherings at the Great Square of the People, to be smashing the yoke of a hierarchical bureaucracy with impunity. The "debate within the Communist International" had resulted in nothing more than a few small sects, but the enigmatic gesticulation of the Red Guards caused the ranks of the pro-Chinese to swell. Maoism appeared less as a "New Communism" than as a ferment of social corrosion and institutional collapse. Mao was quite right in saying that the essence of Marxism was summed up in one formula: "It is right to rebel."

How should one interpret this mimicry of China? French youth repeated the slogans of revolutionary Chinese rebels, they copied their words of abuse and even the graphics of their silk-screen posters, but the imitation was more an exotic parody than a real political influence, let alone a matter of cultural transfer. One brandished the "Little Red Book" to denounce the "cult of books." One pretended to link up with the masses even though it was not easy to drag up one or two credulous sympathizers within an enterprise. One made "social investigation" while unloading a poorly digested propaganda cyclostyled in Peking. "One did not forget the class struggle" yet this was in order to plunge into petty quarrels among rival groups.

It was in relation to "establishment" that the misunderstanding was most evident. On the one side, millions of educated youth in China were invited to go and settle down in the countryside or in mountainous regions to be re-educated by the peasants. Amid great fanfare, these urban youth were torn from their anguished families to go to the farms and frontier areas, a veritable exile or deportation.[57] On the other side, were highly politicized western intellectuals who infiltrated suburban enterprises[58] in order to do ideological work within the unions. They took on the task of awakening the workers who had been put to sleep by revisionist droning or seduced by the sugar coated bullets of the consumer society. Similarity between the slogans masked the enormous gap in the two situations.

But it was in the course of the "movement of May" that the contours of the Chinese education model began to be outlined. The Maoists launched the slogan "for a people's university" which aimed at disassociating themselves from the reformist tendencies of other students. They proposed the plan for a revolutionary university which would be at the service of the people. No longer an instrument of the bourgeoisie, it would accept workers and give them political education rather than turning out parasitic, incompetent and pretentious cadres. It would lead the research into capitalist exploitation, diabolical production rates, and worker health rather than teaching an economics of profit, capitalist management techniques and medicine for the privileged classes.

Yet the composition of the ideal Chinese school did not draw upon any of the available information about the real education system in China. Sinologues were regarded as incapable of explaining the true meaning of a revolutionary practice of the masses which eluded their skeptical intellectual frameworks. Witnesses were suspected of either malevolence or a colonialist spirit.[59] So the "model" was constructed from the texts of Mao, which had been written before the liberation of 1949, particularly the Yan'an Forum on Art and Literature, or accounts published in the same period by such journalists as Edgar Snow, Agnes Smedley or Anna Louise Strong.[60] One could even believe that the Chinese university of the sixties was modelled on the Anti-Japanese university of the war-time period. In fact, the university had closed its doors, it students were in the fields, its professors were engaged in re-education and it offered nothing but a shadow of itself.

From 1968, a new law in France gave autonomy to the university, recognized its research mission, modernized its administrative structures and made possible conditions of entrance to those without the baccalaureat. It favoured pluralism in the transmission and regulation of knowledge and instituted student participation in university decision-making. The inner cultural life of the *lycée* was profoundly changed. Yet the suspicion and rancor built up through the "reverse of 1968" did not dissipate illusion. The "reformette" was received with skepticism and even aggression by the majority of activist students.

As the direct descendant of the pro-Chinese, the Marxist-Leninists benefited from this systematic protest. They saw their ranks swell. Through their organization and discipline they even gained a hegemony within the student movement, which they tirelessly counselled to "set aside your illusions and prepare for struggle." But all of their activity was subordinated to one over-riding purpose: to establish a party which would replace the French Communist Party. The titles of their journals, their modes of organization, the historical references that they made marked them as authentic successors of the French Communists of the Stalinist era. This "anti-revisionist and anti-social-fascist practice" was general among all the Maoist families in Europe: Italy, Germany, Belgium, Spain and Portugal. Therefore they avoided all behaviour which might appear as chinoiserie in order to affirm their national roots. They operated in secret and avoided action that would draw attention to themselves. Anti-reformist, they voluntarily let go of the student struggles to devote themselves exclusively to the organization of the working class. They displayed a penchant for worker power and an anti-intellectualism that was remarkably virulent, given that most of them were teachers, students or persons employed in cultural institutions. They rapidly cut themselves off from the university world, which could not understand their melodramatic disputes, their Stalinist methods of organization and their theoretical bolshevism. For them, as for most leftists, all efforts to democratize the education system were vain and even dangerous. Vain, because without a socialist revolution and the dictatorship of the proletariat one could not have an authentic democratic school. Even in socialist countries, working class control in the universities was not easy to instigate, as evident in the Chinese experience of teams of propaganda worker who entered the universities and were to manage them thereafter but never really had control of them. They were dangerous because the reforms tended to encourage illusions and to patch up a system that was cracking beyond repair.

In the doctrinaire Marxist tradition, they denounced the school on two counts. First, schools cooled out the children of the people. To prove this, they took up the well-known theory of the French School of Sociology on cultural reproduction which before 1968 had served as the Bible of the student movement. Bourdieu and Passeron had analyzed educational institutions and pedagogical practices as mechanisms of social reproduction and set themselves to demonstrate in a detailed way the differential attitudes and performance of classes and social strata in face of school culture.[61] They particularly denounced the republican tradition in which the secular public school had been regarded as the school of the people, since it was precisely this notion of equality which made possible effective operation and masked the real process of social selection. ''The school takes on, legitimates and aggravates the cultural inequalities of children at entrance point by its very refusal to admit what causes these inequalities in face of its own criteria.''[62]

Mao's two philosophical theses on the fundamental law of contradiction (one divides into two) and the two types of contradiction (antagonistic and nonantagonistic) led them to reorient this analysis and to show that the school was not merely the reproducer of the social division of labor but actually the cause of this division. According to Mao, while the economic base had generally been regarded as the principal aspect in the contradiction between base and superstructure, the reality was opposite. Ideology actually played the dominant role in constituting social relations that were of course linked to economic factors. These new methodological principles were used by Baudelot and Establet in the book *The Capitalist School* which was to become a model and a classic on the method of doing social investigation.[63]

By an irrefutable statistical proof they showed first that the school is two-fold (one divides into two) and second that it is divisive (a critique on the thesis of the unifying school). Revisionist theses and the reformist ideologies that they spawned concerning the democratization of the school ''ignored the basis on which the school functions. This basis is the division of society into two antagonistic classes'' and ''the domination of the bourgeoisie over the proletariat.''[64] The authors rediscovered the main axiom of Maoism according to which, in a class society, the principal contradiction consists in the opposition between two classes, two ideologies and two lines. Everything divides into two.

The unity of the school was a bourgeois illusion. It was the perspective of those who entered the school ''in order to acquire the culture dispensed in the higher learning process. It was they who drew up the laws, set the discourse and wrote the books. It was because of and for them that the primary and secondary school classes came to appear as stages in a ladder, because they had not been eliminated along the way."[65] This point of view must be abandoned for the perspective of the people, whose children largely gave up the competition after primary and vocational education. For them, there were two distinct schools, two styles of education, practically without any interaction between them.

The school transmitted two types of historical knowledge, two language systems, two types of literature, according to whether one studied in the bourgeois system (regular secondary and tertiary education) or the popular system (primary and vocational education). Using textbooks and curricular materials, the authors showed that one group learned to be leaders, the other to be led. In one, a pure, discipline-oriented and theoretical institutional culture was developed, in the other, pupils acquired practical skills and engaged in manual and technical activities. All which worked towards legitimating and reinforcing these mechanisms of division was essentially reactionary. This was particularly the case with psychometric testing since it "only seemed to give scientific validity to the class division reproduced in schools."[66] The Marxist-Leninists also denounced all institutions which legitimated or recognized this "social division" under the mask of psychiatry. They criticized remedial institutes which identified educational handicaps and all mechanisms of cultural compensation or specialist establishments set up to deal with psychological difficulties or "social problems." These were merely instruments for the social denigration, cultural exclusion, political domination and economic alienation of working class children.

These Marxist-Leninist analyses, which were quite original and were violently disputed by other Marxists, went against the lively currents of educational reform and innovation in the period. They attacked the proliferation of new "specialist" institutes of education. They were to have a destructive and destabilizing effect on the centers of teacher training, the organizations of academic remediation and the popular education movements such as the movement of the Ecole Freinet and the new pedagogy. The Marxist-Leninists were not content with running down these efforts and research activities as populist illusions, they went so far as to attack them as provocations against the working class. These negative strictures were to have profound repercussions in a milieu which often has to come to terms with the failure of its initiatives and the futility of its efforts.

Paradoxically, the Maoist movement, which had expressed aspirations for change in the education system, was to become a force which assured the maintenance of the status quo and blocked all the progressive efforts which had been launched.

Essentially there are two types of Maoists: the Marxist-Leninists, centralizers obsessed with the task of creating structures for the party, and the "Maos spontex," who were committed to a broader popular democracy and a life among the masses "like jellyfish in the ocean." The Maos had come from among the student youth, often the elites, and they quickly became known for their iconoclastic verve, their taste for risk taking and their showmanship. They were often considered as representatives of the "sixty-eighters," even though they had great difficulty in gaining acceptance for their anti-intellectual invective ("book learning is hollow'') and their "social autonomy" which consisted in a denunciation of all parties or trade unions. Deeply anti-authoritarian and anti-hierarchical, this movement was one of the laboratories of the period. Their banned journals became famous because Sarte agreed to direct *La Cause du Peuple* and Simone de Beauvoir *L'Idiot International*. By highly symbolic dramatic events, they brought to the surface social problems which had been buried up till then. As defenders of social justice, the Maos organized "people's tribunals" which denounced class justice, exposed accidents in the work place and unmasked the hidden linkages between the justice system and money. For the first time, conditions of life in prison were made a public issue and efforts were made to rehabilitate delinquent youths "who were simply taking what had been stolen from them." The conservatism and moralism of the French press was denounced in the French libertarian tradition. The Maos were one of the forces which helped to popularize forms of illegal action against anti-abortion laws and they upheld the liberty of homosexuals.

Apparently unstructured, but divided into small mobile groups of activists and protesters, they could meet up at hot situations, following the Maoist tactic of "the fingers of the hand." At the height of their prestige, they got together for a funeral demonstration of two hundred thousand persons in Paris, for a young Maoist worker killed by a foreman in one of the Renault factories. But this was not the kind of publicity they were looking for. "When we found the 'Proletariat Left'[68] in September of 1968, we had two ideas: proletarianization and militarization." These double perspectives led them to forms of exemplary action, often marginal, aimed at drawing the workers away from the traditional union mentality which represented a kind of integration within the capitalist system. "We have struggled for the autonomy of the working class, against the trade union mentality which divides the people and represents capitulation to the enemy, and respect for bureaucracy and legality. We have popularized the most effective forms of struggle, those that educate the masses and prepare them for revolution."[69] These were punch-ups for petty bosses, the impoundment of bosses and the sacking of the offices of enterprise.

But these actions rapidly distanced them from China and the Thought of Mao. At the beginning Maoism represented a "new thing" for them, which rose above the economism of Marx and the Leninist conception of the party, but they were soon disappointed by the dissolution of Chinese rebel organizations, the liquidation of the Red Guards and the reconstruction of the Chinese Communist Party at the Ninth Congress of 1969. This was the reason they gave up all reference to China and Mao in order to launch into spontaneous and almost apolitical forms of agitation. "That led the militants to a mentality of outlaw or leftist marauder and resulted in the arrival of low elements and even a number of individuals from the lumpenproletariat."[70] This train of events gave the Maoists the following alternatives: either return to a centralized form of political organization of the Marxist-Leninist type or continue to slide towards "autonomy" and to the systematic violence of marginal youth on the verge of banditry. The French leaders, understanding this danger, decided to dissolve the movement and block all moves towards the reconstruction of the organization. This was what foreign organizations did not do, though they had evolved in a similar way.

How can one explain this difference? Perhaps the French leaders recognized that they had never been true Marxists and their connection with the intellectual left (Sartre and Foucault) enabled them to avoid this rupture into terrorism. Inversely, elsewhere there was a greater isolation from the traditional working class organizations, the presence of American bases on national territory which hardened and expanded the anti-imperialist movement (West Germany, Japan, Italy), a harmonious mix between the marginalized strata of the working class and the proletarianized fraction of student youth (Italy, Spain), national repression by the state which brought with it a sensational heroism (Spain, Portugal). Other national factors favoured the creation of a clandestine groups of terrorists more or less derivative of the "Mao spontex" and made possible a network of sympathizers who protected their existence. In France, the same tendencies were present (GARI, NAPAP, Action Directe) but the strata of sympathizers was too thin for a lasting resistance to the pressure and infiltration of the police.

The vast majority of ex-Maos joined up with or started anti-nuclear, pacifistic and ecological groups from 1975. Some founded cooperatives or communes, set up alternative schools or rediscovered cultural and musical clubs, some even set up commercial or craft enterprises. They were to succumb to the very activities they had denounced as petit-bourgeois illusions of decadent imperialism.

What was their view of the school? As proponents of worker power, anarchy and populism, they denounced a school which oppressed the people and transmitted knowledge that was sterile or deceptive. They thought the school either ignored or rejected true understanding and, like the children of Barbiana,[71] that the working class always knew how to write better than the bourgeoisie. Several Mao teachers were to have conflicts with the established hierarchy, since they did not wish to impose a knowledge already constituted on their working class or immigrant pupils who "understood life" better than they and had good reason for revolting. Their teaching, like the mass line, took popular culture as a departure point, the practical and fundamentally correct knowledge which bourgeois culture had denied legitimacy to, then went on to systematization and theoretical reflection. "In order to become people's teachers, we must become students of the masses."[72] They thus supported the "disinherited" of the school, those who left or denounced it.[73] In this respect they linked up with the most active elements of the Movement Freinet or the Pédagogie Institutionelle, and became associated with the anarcho-syndicalist tradition of l'Ecole Emancipée[74] or with the populist fractions of the SGEN,[75] which had been influenced by Ivan Illich.

China provided them with a utopian model. Children were not bullied or infantilized, but regarded as full citizens. Children from red classes were affirmed, if not favored. The sexes were equal. Children's productive labor (in the small gardens or enterprises of the school) was truly productive, as well as being socially useful and politically instructive. Children composed their own curricula and exercised friendly yet serious self-discipline. The family was a new type of collectivity, in which children re-educated their grandparents, corrected their parents and brought about order within the house and harmony in the cities.[76]

Above all they were fascinated by the Communist utopia of a school which had abolished the division of labor. "In ten or fifteen years, the Cultural Revolution in the schools will have provided a new generation of technicians for industry who have been shaped in a new ideology. For them, political work and manual labor have been part of the educative process from the beginning of their school life. For them there is no qualitative difference between technicians and workers."[77] Their sympathy for China determined their selection of personnages to symbolize this unity between mental and manual labor: Chen Yonggui, the poor peasant who had become a government minister; Hao Ran, the worker-writer who put his pen to the service of the proletariat; the peasant painters of Huxian; and above all, the proletarian rebel of the Shanghai Commune, Wang Hongwen. (After all, Mao was rather too much of a peasant!)

European Maoists approved of the treatment which the Chinese working class gave to political and technical cadres, these mandarins whose science they mistrusted, whose pride they detested and whose power they denounced. Their principal activity under the name of the "Nouvelle Résistance" consisted precisely of denouncing all authorities and shattering the power of the petty bosses.

The protest against academic education and the challenge to university knowledge were to be taken up by some intellectuals, especially in the field of philosophy. Thus Michel Foucault denounced the "system of power of the intellectuals which obstructs, invalidates and bans" the science of the people, taking away their voice. Yet, according to Foucault, some among them had had their eyes opened. "What the intellectuals have discovered since the recent thrust is that the masses have no need of their knowledge; they understand perfectly, clearly and much better than the intellectuals, and they can express their knowledge very well." Intellectuals were simply to struggle against forms of power in the realm of knowledge and discourse. Their principal task was exposing themselves and making a scientific denunciation of their power of ideological oppression.[78]

In the seventies, the Maoist-inspired critique of mandarin knowledge from outside the university was combined with an internal crisis over methodological and epistemological questions and a pedagogical crisis over forms and conditions of control. It was in this sense that Maoism played a catalytic role in reflections about the content of education, even though it had no direct influence on any of the reforms in educational practice. Take as a example the history taught in the university. New journals such as *Le Peuple Francais* made an inventory of the Jacqueries, the insurrections, the revolts and mutinies of French history in an approach similar to the Maoist campaign to criticize Confucius and Lin Biao.[79] But for a long time there had been a converging internal evolution in the discipline, as exemplified by the Ecole des Annales. Numerous historians had taken up the perspective of the rebels long before 1968. This was why some, like J. Chesneaux, considered this to be inadequate. "It is not enough to work on the struggles of peasants and workers, one must work with the workers" so that, as in China, "the record of the past produces a revolutionary ferment."[80] For example, Mao's report on the peasant investigation in Hunan in 1927 was both a historic document and a piece of historical work. Thus "from now on we must reflect on the conditions in which history ceased to be the privileged domain of professionals and became fully possessed by the masses."[81] Is this still possible nowadays? China offered the model in which the people's past became an instrument in popular struggle.[82]

This influence which brought into question the whole basis of the discourse of the teacher, went so far as to undermine the tradition of neutrality which had been an almost sacred tradition of the secular public school in France. Since the teacher's language was not neutral, since all grammar and vocabulary had an ideological dimension, "one could not have a strictly neutral. . . . relation to language without imposing value judgements." Each teacher must understand and take account of this fact. "It may not be a question of an official and unifying state ideology so much as multiple class-based ideologies in society. But it must be a question of ideological struggle. . . ."[83]

Finally, the Maos themselves were not very active in the educational movement or in the educational system, as their exclusive concern was with the working class. Yet, though they had almost no institutional presence, they had substantial influence through the domain of sinophilia, which they drew on, as did the Marxist-Leninists. It was the press, specially the daily *Liberation* which brought together all the currents of the protesting intelligentsia and which became the instrument of Chinese influence. Through it the European Maoists became one of the sources of the anti-intellectual, anti-hierarchical movements which gave rise to the educational developments of the seventies.

Consider, for example, the way in which the well established journal *Les Cahiers Pédagogiques* presented its special issue on the school in China under the title "The School and the Transformation of Social Relations." "News about schools in China is of no interest to a public exclusively preoccupied with educational procedures. Chinese schools are not showplaces of audiovisual equipment or state of the art teaching technology. . . . On the other hand, for someone interested in the function of the school in a given society, an understanding of the Chinese education system makes possible a clear grasp of the connections between the social system and the school. Is the purpose of the school to select a small technocratic elite who are then given the power to shape society's future direction? Or is it, in contrast, to develop as fully as possible the physical, intellectual and creative potential of each person in order to build up a society which serves the whole working class? Is the school the place which produces the division of labor between an elite leadership and the masses whom they lead through distinctions made between "good" and "bad" pupils? Or is the school a vehicle of an ideal of service to the collective and does it prevent social reproduction by creating close links between practical and theoretical learning and explicitly designating workers and peasants as social models? In our developed French society, the education system has reached an impasse since it has met up with an insurmountable contradiction" which sets popular education against the elitist function of the system. "It is for this reason," continued the pedagogue, "that the revolutionary Chinese experience helps us to understand that to change the role of the school we must at the same time transform the social, economic and ideological norms which regulate social relations. We must assign to the school a direct role in this transformation, by changing both its content and its functions."[84] This transformative function of education was a fundamental illusion which nourished the myth of a revolutionary China just as effectively as the social utopia of libertarian Maoism or the paradigm of the "Chinese experience." It was certainly one of the guiding ideas of the sixties.

Yet had not the first pro-Chinese among the students been those who denounced the illusion that transformation or reforms could ever modify the social system in a profound way? Had it not been they who affirmed that a violent social revolution must precede any transformation of the educational system? Was there not here some misunderstanding? The Cultural Revolution had been unleashed in order to prevent the embourgeoisement of Chinese students, many of whom were the children of important families or of high cadres of the regime. But the western Maoist revolt expressed the anguish of a part of the university population facing proletarianization and social marginalization.[85] Were western youth in danger of becoming a gilt-edged social group at the very time when the universities were bursting with the demographic thrust of the children of the petit-bourgeoisie? Here again there seemed to be a contradiction.

"The 1789 Revolution had been a legal revolution, that of 1917 an economic one. One may ask if a third revolution is not now in process, a cultural revolution," suggested a contemporary philosopher. "This time it is no longer the issue of a class that has been alienated on the material level but on the spiritual level, bruised in the deepest part of themselves by a civilization which, in its concern to meet people's material needs, has become progressively imprisoned in production and neglected the vital needs of the spirit."[86] Let's concede that a revolution was necessary for spiritual enrichment. Still, had not the Chinese Cultural Revolution expressed first and foremost the impatience of a population that had come through many years of famine, economic reversal and failure in a political apparatus that could not fulfil its promise of rapid material well-being and accelerated modernization? Is not this then, the most profound point of misunderstanding?

Conclusion

"Utopia comes after nostalgia, the affirmation of an order to which one can be loyal, an order which is nowhere to be found."[87] Was Maoist China then in no sense a real country? It's true that it was at the Antipodes, since it was the Opposite and it belonged to the discourse of Chinese propaganda or the discourse of western educational aspiration or of a western political utopia. Once before it had also been the object of a discourse, the justifying discourse of the Jesuit Apology or the illustrative discourse of the Enlightenment philosophers. But are there any pedagogics or politics which function without discourse and without utopias?

The problem it seems was not one utopia or another, but the fact that China was a real coutnry, where this "utopia" was supposedly realized. Further, it was not simply a question of offering an image of order, but the organization of a disorder, to which we could not be loyal because the discourse kept changing in its real meaning, even though the same words were repeated. The problem was also that the Maoists visited this land of utopia and they experienced it without really understanding it.

From another perspective, the fascination exerted by the Chinese model in the sixties seemed to be profoundly different from that exercised by the Middle Kingdom on the Jesuits. They discovered a heavenly order based on legitimate authority. They observed the regulating principles of a hierarchy based on reason which guided an impeccable bureaucratic apparatus recruited on the basis of merit, unified by a shared set of beliefs, animated by a rivalry for virtue. In contrast, what the Maoists appreciated in the New China was the inexhaustible disorder which shattered all bureaucracy and nearly brought down the state itself. In the Cultural Revolution they revered the motive principles of anarchy since all power was to repudiate itself, all authority could only stimulate revolt and all bureaucracy was by definition corrupt and corrupting.

The Jesuits had admired the examination system which could discern virtue from a servile mentality, and distinguish imagination from rhetoric. They praised the examinations which they saw as a kind of liturgy offered to the Sacred Books, a hymn to equal opportunity, a technique for detecting the talented. The Maoists enthused over a school which refused all distinction based on merit or dignity, which considered the class origin behind all educational effort and all acquired competence, which sometimes burned books and flogged scholars. One group placed an immemorial culture on a pedestal, the other put politics in command. One drew on science, the other emphasized action.

Chinese culture has always offered this paradoxical, even antagonistic, alternative in the realm of philosophy and politics between Daoists and Confucians, Legalists and Moralists. But the two forms of western sinophilia, that of the Enlightenment and of the "Phantom Students"[88] of the sixties, did not know how to bring about the synthesis and maintain the unity of these opposites.

In conclusion, one must note the irony of history. No one denies the fact that the accounts of the Jesuits, much as they were a defense of order, actually contributed to a case against the privileged nobility and thus opened the way that led towards the "Nuit du Quatre-Août" in 1789. Inversely, many contemporary historians consider the Maoist phenomenon, and more generally the so-called "sixty-eighters" movement has actually helped to entrench the social model of mass consumption and contributed to the emergence of a whole new type of student. "In considering what became of the generation of 1968, a hypothesis could take shape to suggest that the supposed breach (the revolt of the sixties) has turned out to be a powerful force for social integration. One is tempted to ask oneself if, unbeknownst to the actors, the movement of May has not served ends which none of the participants could have envisaged?"[89]

Ex-Maoists are today much better integrated professionally and even socially in France than their young successors who are unemployed or in marginal positions. They play a strong reformist and integrating role, with the exception of a tiny minority who have shut themselves up in violent action. Most have become persuasive instigators of new reforms based on "republican elitism." Once again they find Chinese inspiration. Only this time it is the inspiration that, through the literature of the Jesuits, once enriched the pedagogical thought of Condorcet and the Ideologues, ancestors of the French secular school.

12

Contemporary Educational Relations with the Industrialized World: A Chinese View

Huang Shiqi

Introduction: The Evolution of China's Policy on Educational Exchange

Ever since the founding of the People's Republic of China, an integral part of national policy has been the development of international exchanges with foreign countries in education, science and culture. The intention has been to further mutual understanding with different nations and promote the interests of socialist construction. However, the path of this development has had its zigzags, influenced to a large extent by China's internal politics as well as relations with the West and the East. Broadly speaking, we may divide the past 36 years into three stages: (1) 1949-1966; (2) June 1966-1976; (3) 1977 up to the present.

During the first stage China's educational relations were largely limited to socialist countries, especially the USSR, with very little interaction with western countries, almost none with the United States. During this period China sent 8,424 students, mostly undergraduates, to the Soviet Union, and 1,109 students to Eastern European socialist countries. About 7,324 students finished their studies in the Soviet Union, and 776 students returned from East European socialist countries.[1] In sharp contrast to fairly extensive exchanges with socialist countries, China only sent 184 students to France (1964-1965), 93 to the United Kingdom (1962-65), 26 to Switzerland (1959-65), 20 to Denmark (1959-65), 14 to Sweden (1958-65), 12 to Italy (1959-65), 11 to Norway (1959-64), 11 to Finland (1964-65), 5 to Iceland (1965) and 1 to Belgium (1958). No students at all were sent to West Germany, Canada, Japan and the United States.

During the same period, the Soviet Union sent 198 students to China, and Eastern European countries sent altogether 426 students to China, with Albania leading in the list (194), followed by the German Democratic Republic (65), Poland (48), Czechoslovakia (38), Romania (31), Hungary (23), Bulgaria (20) and Yugoslavia (7). In contrast China only received 31 students from Japan (1962-65), 8 students from the United States (1956-63), and 1 student from Canada (1959).

However, there were 87 students from Western European countries, with France leading in the list (44, in 1964-65), followed by Sweden (8, 1959-65), Finland (6, 1953-60), Italy (6, 1957-64), Spain (6, 1957-59), Greece (4, 1960), Norway (3, 1958-60), Belgium (2, 1960-65), Denmark (2, 1958-60), Switzerland (2, 1963), the United Kingdom (2, 1959-62), Austria (1, 1956), Iceland (1, 1957); also 2 from Australia (1958).

The deterioration in relations between the PRC and the USSR in 1960 inevitably had adverse effects on educational exchanges between the two countries, also between China and most Eastern European socialist countries. The Chinese government decided on a sharp reduction of the number of students being sent abroad, also a greater emphasis on the quality rather than the quantity of those being sent. Thus from 1961 to 1965 only 206 Chinese students went to the Soviet Union.

In anticipation of ever expanding diplomatic and trade relations with other foreign countries, the Chinese government decided to step up the scale of training people proficient in foreign languages both in domestic and foreign institutions. The Ministry of Education drew up a three-year plan (1964-66) to send 2,000 students abroad for the study of foreign languages.[2] In November of 1964, the Central Committee of the Chinese Communist Party (CCP) and the State Council jointly approved "Guidelines for the Development of Foreign Languages Education in 1964-1970" submitted by five governmental agencies.[3] Consequently there was a real effort to foster and diversify educational relations with various foreign countries, both developed and developing.

From 1952 to 1953 a large scale reorganization of the higher educational system was undertaken, largely influenced by the Soviet model. There were a number of Soviet advisors working in the Ministry of Education and the Ministry of Higher Education, exerting considerable influence on the course of educational reform followed in China. Soviet influence in higher education and specialized secondary education was most pronounced. In the field of education from 1953 to 1962 altogether 761 Soviet specialists were sent to China by the Soviet government, mostly working in Chinese institutions of higher education. This period has been discussed in chapters 9 and 10.

During the decade of the Cultural Revolution (1966-76), the course of development of international exchanges in education was greatly influenced by the internal political situation in China. For nearly five years international exchanges were suspended. Then in January 1971, the UNESCO General Assembly passed a resolution to restore the legitimate place of the People's Republic of China in UNESCO. In the same year, the 26th UN General Assembly passed a resolution to restore the legitimate place of the PRC in the United Nations. In 1972 the Chinese Government sent a delegation headed by Mr. Huang Zhen, then the Chinese ambassador to France, to take part in the 16th Session of the UNESCO General Assembly. This was an important event marking the beginning of the PRC's resumption of cultural contacts with foreign countries, and it had implication for student exchange.

From 1972 to 1976 altogether 1,629 students were sent to forty-nine countries:

241 to the United Kingdom, 143 to France, 78 to Canada, 42 to the Federal Republic of Germany and 29 to Japan. Most were students of languages. From 1973 to 1976 China received 1,667 students from 65 countries and areas, 96 from France, 71 from Japan, 61 from Canada, 54 from West Germany and 47 from the United Kingdom. Altogether 329 (19.74%) came from these five countries.

From 1970 to 1976 China received 73 educational delegations from 37 countries with a total of 372 persons. Among these delegations nine were headed by ministers of education. In the meantime China sent sixteen educational delegations with a total of 102 persons, visiting 14 countries, including the United Kingdom, France, the United States, Canada and Japan.

From 1975 to 1976 a number of short-term language centers were set up in Chinese foreign language institutes with the aid of seventeen linguists from the United Kingdom, Australia, France and the Federal Republic of Germany for upgrading Chinese teachers of foreign languages.

During the first seventeen years of the existence of the People's Republic very few Chinese scholars from educational institutions had been able to go abroad to attend international meetings. This was due to a comparative neglect of this kind of scholarly contact and to the shortage of funds and inadequate development of scientific research in Chinese institutions of higher education.

A radical new departure in the development of China's educational interaction with foreign countries began with the Third Plenum of the 11th Central Committee of the CCP, when a thorough stocktaking of past policies was undertaken. The left deviations of the period during and before the Cultural Revolution were subject to severe criticism. The plenum resolutely criticized the erroneous policy of "two whatsoevers."[4] Also it was decided that the slogan of "grasping class struggle as the key link" would no longer be used, due to a clear understanding that it was entirely unsuitable for a socialist society which had finished the historic tasks of transforming agriculture, private industry and handicraft industry long before. From now on the focus of the Party's work would be shifted to socialist construction and modernization.

The Third Plenum of the 11th Central Committee of the CCP has had important implications for all major policy issues, including educational policy in general and international exchange policy in particular. To adopt a policy of being open to the outside world is an integral part of the new policy. The Plenum was convened in December 1978. However, prior to its convening in March 1978, a National Conference on Science was convened by the Central Committee of the CCP and from April 22 to May 16, 1978, a National Conference on Education was convened by the Ministry of Education. The decisions made at these conferences were all conducive to the promotion of international exchanges in education, science and culture. It should be added here Deng Xiaoping's personal intervention in policy matters concerning education and science in 1977 were of crucial importance in the shaping of later policies.

As early as May 24, 1977, in his discourse on "Respect Knowledge, Respect Trained Personnel," Deng stressed that "The key to achieving modernization is the development of science and technology. And unless we pay attention to education, it will be impossible to develop science and technology. . . . We must recognize our backwardness, because only such recognition offers hope. Now it appears that China is fully 20 years behind the developed countries in science, technology and education."[5]

Later in August Deng dealt with several aspects of China's educational interaction with foreign countries explicitly.[6] In his speech at the National Conference on Science held in May 1978 Deng stressed that being aware of China's backwardness and not complacent with past achievements should "strengthen our resolve to catch up with and surpass the countries that are most advanced in science and technology." "Only in this way. . . can we encourage people to learn from others willingly so that China can speedily master the world's latest science and technology." "Backwardness must be recognized before it can be changed. One must learn from those who are most advanced before one can catch up with and surpass them. Of course, in order to raise China's scientific and technological level we must rely on our own efforts, develop our own creativity and persist in the policy of independence and self-reliance. But independence does not mean shutting the door on the world, nor does self-reliance mean blind opposition to everything foreign. Science and technology are part of the wealth created in common by all mankind. Every people or country should learn from the advanced science and technology of others. It is not just today, when we are scientifically and technologically backward, that we need to learn from others. Even after we catch up with the most advanced countries, we shall still have to learn from them in areas where they are particularly strong."[7]

It was Comrade Deng Xiaoping's initiative to implement on a large scale the policy of sending many students and visiting scholars abroad from 1978 onwards as part of the open-door policy and the drive for four modernizations. In October of 1983, Deng stressed that education should be oriented to modernization, to the world and to the future. While he has never expounded the full meaning and implications of the "three orientations," this terse admonition has given rise to lively discussion in educational circles. Among other possibilities, it seems to me to imply: (1) a recognition of the importance of the furtherance of lively international exchanges in the fields of education, science and culture; (2) the view that educational institutions should nurture globally-minded citizens and help promote international understanding; (3) a call for Chinese scholars and students to learn from foreign countries what is advanced, valuable and relevant for China's modernization efforts; and (4) a commitment for China to make a distinctive contribution to the family of nations in the advancement of education, science and culture and in furthering the cause of peace.

The Main Forms of International Educational Exchange

From what was said above about the evolution of policy in the field of international exchanges during the past three decades, it can be concluded that to actively promote international exchanges in education, science and culture is now a firmly established national policy of the people's Republic of China which will be implemented resolutely in the years to come. There will be no turning back to a policy of self-imposed seclusion or isolation from the world.

The main forms of international exchanges in existence now are as follows:

(1) Sending students and visiting scholars abroad;
(2) Accepting foreign students in China;
(3) The exchange of visiting lecturers;
(4) Cooperative research;
(5) The exchange of delegations or visiting groups;
(6) The establishment of partnership between sister institutions;
(7) Participation in international meetings and the organization of such meetings in China.

In the following sections more detailed information will be given on each of these forms, with emphasis on relations with the seven industrialized countries dealt with historically in this book, but not excluding occasional reference to relations with other countries. There is also a section on the role played by several international agencies.

Sending Students and Visiting Scholars Abroad

This is by far the most important component of international educational exchanges in terms of its sheer scale and the expenditures incurred, as well as its long-term implications for the development of China's education, science and culture, the national economy and foreign diplomacy.

It was decided by the Chinese Government in 1978 to effect a sharp increase in the number of students studying abroad. On August 4, 1978, the Ministry of Education (MOE) issued a circular notice "Concerning the Increase of Students Studying Abroad and Their Selection." It was envisaged that there would be three categories of students studying abroad, namely: 1) undergraduate students; 2) postgraduates; 3) visiting scholars. The majority of them were to study science, engineering, agriculture and medicine.

Undergraduate students would be selected from newly admitted first year college students and first year students already attending various colleges and universities. Postgraduate students would be mainly selected from the domestic pool of postgraduates enrolled in higher education and research institutions in the current year. Visiting scholars — the most mature group — would be selected from in-service college teachers, researchers working in research institutes, as well as other qualified personnel working in the production sector or governmental agencies.

All potential candidates were subject to unified foreign language proficiency tests administered by the MOE or other competent agencies. In 1978 alone, 13,383 persons underwent such tests and 3,348 successful candidates were selected from them, including 2,456 visiting scholars, 367 postgraduate students and 525 undergraduate students. Out of these successful candidates almost all were able to find appropriate receiving institutions and left China for study abroad within two years.[8] Figures provided by the China International Examinations Coordination Bureau of the MOE, which was set up in October of 1981, give the following picture for later years: 1,061 persons taking the tests in 1981, 1,427 in 1982, 2,395 in 1983, 4,449 in 1984 and 16,483 in 1985. It is impossible to tell how many of these actually went abroad. However, national figures for this period can be provided.

From 1978 to mid-1984 over 26,500 Chinese students and visiting scholars were sent to 63 countries and regions by the Chinese Government or individual institutions through various channels. They do not include those whose stay abroad was less than six months. Of this total, 12,022 went to the United States, 3,847 to Japan, 2,489 to the Federal Republic of Germany, 1,833 to the United Kingdom, 1,452 to Canada, 1,299 to France, and 30 to the Soviet Union. The distribution by broad field of study is as follows. Natural sciences: about 7,500; engineering: about 10,000; agriculture and natural resources: about 2,000; medicine and pharmacy: about 3,000; the humanities and social sciences: about 3,600. In the same period about 8,000 self-sponsored students went abroad, mainly to the United States.

It is interesting to take note of the number of government-sponsored students sent by provincial, municipal and autonomous regional authorities, and the figures are given in descending order. Shanghai — 742; Beijing — 573; Tianjin — 272; Shaanxi — 213; Guangxi — 155; Zhejiang — 117; Yunnan — 102; Heilongjiang — 102 Fujian — 95; Jilin — 92; Guizhou — 25; Xinjiang — 21; Ningxia — 15; Jiangxi — 12. On the whole the order corresponds with that of economic and cultural development with some anomalous cases. For example, Guangxi Zhuang Autonomous   Region sent out more students than Zhejiang Province, which is much richer. The only explanation was that Guangxi placed a higher priority on study abroad as a means to training the highly qualified professionals who are greatly needed.

Accepting Foreign Students in China

Formerly, most foreign students in China came from Third World countries, with a small percentage from industrialized countries, but the order has been reversed since 1979. While the first category of foreign students are mostly studying applied sciences, the second category mainly study the Chinese language and/or Chinese history and culture.

The admission of foreign students by Chinese academic institutions was resumed in 1973. From 1973 to 1978, 2,498 foreign students from 80 countries and regions studied in Chinese institutions. Of the total, 562 (22.5%) came from the seven industrialized countries in question. From 1979 to 1984, 4,956 foreign students from 109 countries and regions were admitted by Chinese institutions. Of this total, 2,423 (48.9%) came from the seven countries, indicating a significant increase in students from the industrialized countries. Tables 12.1 and 12.2 show statistics for long-term foreign students in China from 1973 to 1984. In addition to these students there has been an increasing number of students enrolled in short-term courses (4 weeks to 5 months) of various descriptions offered by Chinese institutions. These short-term courses were initiated in 1978, with a total enrollment of 29. They proliferated rapidly in the early 1980s, with an aggregate enrollment of 12,951 during the period 1978-1984. While nearly one fourth of the long-term students are provided with scholarships by the Chinese government, all students enrolled in short-term courses have to be self-supporting.

Since most foreign students have an inadequate mastery of the Chinese language, they have to attend preparatory courses in several language centers. Most of them are placed in the Beijing Language Institute for one year of language study, with a minority dispersed in several institutions located in Tianjin, Shanghai, and Nanjing. A small but increasing number of postgraduate students from industrialized countries with or without adequate language preparation are now coming to China for advanced studies, involving extensive archival research and/or field work.

Table 12.1

Statistics of Foreign Students in China, 1973-1984

Academic year	Total	3rd World	1st & 2nd World	USSR & Eastern Europe	Aggregate number of students in China	Number of graduates
1973	383	261	122		383	
1974	378	265	113		685	54
1975	432	298	134		885	183
1976	465	324	141		1,177	101
1977	408	272	136		1,217	300
1978	432	229	203		1,207	336
1979	440	75	365		1,278	239
1980	576	144	430	2	1,389	408
1981	744	265	479		1,631	456
1982	865	315	547	3	1,759	662
1983	1,038	458	557	23	2,066	661
1984	1,293	608	592	93	2,593	707
Total	7,454	3,514	3,819	121		4,107

Number of Students Received

Notes: 1. From 1973 to 1984 Chinese institutions of higher education received foreign students from 114 countries and regions. These students were scattered in 55 institutions in 16 cities. Altogether 163 specialities were offered to foreign students. Two thousand new enrolments are planned for 1985.
2. Students from Romania and Yugoslavia are counted among Third World students.

Table 12.2
Statistics of Government-Sponsored Foreign Students in PRC for 1973-1985

Country	Total for 73-85	73	74	75	76	77	78	79	80	81	82	83	84	85	No. of students staying in China September 1985
Canada	202	23	10	14	14	15	11	24	22	13	18	15	10	13	26 (3+23)*
France	354	30	15	26	25	28	27	24	32	26	22	32	32	35	63 (2+61)
West Germany	424	10	12	16	16	14	17	26	20	25	50	51	86	81	123 (20+103)
Japan	709	9	28	16	18	18	36	86	163	234	225	261	295	414	642(140+502)
U.K.	489	11	9	12	15	20	29	54	65	40	49	58	68	59	65 (22+43)
U.S.A.	371						18	56	38	52	53	35	63	56	74 (5+69)
U.S.S.R.												10	69	124	132 (132)

Note: The first figure in the parentheses indicates the number of undergraduate students; while the second indicates the number of advanced students.

The Exchange of Visiting Lecturers

In the early fifties the Chinese government began to send a few Chinese college teachers to foreign countries as visiting lecturers working for two or more years in accordance with the provision of bilateral agreements. This was resumed in 1979 and from 1979 to mid-1985, a total of 721 Chinese college teachers were sent abroad, mostly working in the fields of language, literature or history. So far 29 foreign countries have been involved in such programs, including Canada, France, Japan, the FRG, the UK and the U.S. Also an increasing number of Chinese scholars have been going abroad in the capacity of short-term visiting lecturers since 1979, covering diverse fields of scholarly endeavor.

The other side of this process has been the invitation of foreign college teachers to work in China. From 1953 to 1962, a total of 862 foreign experts were invited to China by the Chinese government to work on long-term contracts in Chinese higher educational institutions. Of these, 761 came from the Soviet Union, with the rest provided by other East European and Asian socialist countries and a few Third World and capitalist countries. Soviet experts, mostly of the rank of associate or assistant professors, played a significant role in the development of higher education during the first and second Five-Year Plans. They exerted immense influence on the structure, curricula and other aspects of the academic life of Chinese institutions. In the Ministries of Education and Higher education there were a number of Soviet experts serving as advisors.

The invitation of foreign experts and professors by Chinese institutions of higher learning was resumed in 1978. Within the scope of institutions under the direct jurisdiction of the Ministry of Education (now superseded by the State Education Commission), altogether 721 foreign teachers were invited to Chinese higher educational institutions on a long-term basis between 1978 and mid-1985. In the same period 4,344 came to China as short-term lecturers. The number of sending countries varied from 10 at the beginning to 26 in the academic year 1984-85, including all the seven industrialized countries of this study by 1983-84.

In accordance with the planned figures covering all universities and colleges in the country for the academic year 1985-86, a total of 1,479 foreign teachers were to be invited to Chinese institutions. The breakdown is as follows: 1,289 (87.2%) as language teachers (English: 854, Japanese: 153, French: 75, German: 80; other languages: 127), 82 in scientific and technological fields and 108 in the humanities and social sciences. Of the total 71.9% are to work in institutions under central ministries and agencies, including the State Education Commission (which alone accounts for 416 or 28.1% of the total) and the rest in institutions under provincial or municipal jurisdiction. The real figures fall short of the planned figures by 150-200.

The massive increase of language teachers in China bears witness to the fact that Chinese higher educational institutions are making a great effort to improve the standards of foreign language teaching. It is encouraging to see that non-language and non-scientific disciplines now have their legitimate place in the contingent of foreign teachers in China.

Cooperative Research

There are mainly four channels by which Chinese scholars may conduct joint research projects with their foreign colleagues in academic institutions or non-university research institutes: (1) Intergovernmental agreements of scientific and technical cooperation in which university scientists may take part; (2) agreements signed by the Chinese Ministry of Education or its successor, the State Education Commission, with foreign governmental or non-governmental agencies; (3) partnership agreements signed by representatives of Chinese and foreign institutions of higher learning; (4) research sponsored by private foundations.

Under (1) we may find many joint research programs in which Chinese university scientists take an active part. This form of cooperation finds its fullest expression in the agency-to-agency protocols or understandings under the terms of the Agreement Between the Government of the People's Republic of China and the Government of the United states on Cooperation in Science and Technology. These were first signed in January of 1979 and renewed five years later.[9] These protocols, with the exception of the agreement for exchange of students and scholars, are related to many diverse fields, such as agriculture, space technology, high energy physics, management of science and technology information, metrology and standards, atmospheric science, marine and fishery science, medicine and public health, hydro-electric power and related water services, earthquake studies, earth sciences, environmental protection, basic sciences, building construction and urban planning, science and technology, nuclear safety, surface water hydrology, etc. Wherever Chinese university scientists have fairly strong research capability in a specific field, they are likely to take active part in relevant cooperative research programs. However, the compartmentalization of Chinese science is not conducive to the full participation of university scientists in such programs.

Under (2) China-U.S. cooperation in the basic sciences sponsored by the Chinese Academy of Sciences (CAS), the Chinese Academy of Social Sciences (CASS), and the Chinese Ministry of Education (CMOE), now succeeded by the State Education Commission (SEDC), on the Chinese side and the National Science Foundation on the U.S. side is a good example. An agreement was signed by the parties concerned on December 10, 1980, in Washington. In the following year cooperation in six fields — archeology, linguistics, natural product chemistry, astronomy, material sciences, system analysis — was initiated. In the two succeeding years, more fields were added to the list and in 1984 all fields in the sciences and social sciences were open for cooperation. Joint research projects and joint seminars are the main forms of cooperation. From 1981 to 1985 about 40 joint research projects or seminars were approved by the CMOE and the NSF.[10]

Some of these cooperative projects have yielded important results highly appreciated by the scientific community and the authorities concerned. For example, the joint research project entitled "System Analysis in Different Social Settings: A Case in Comprehensive Planning for Water Pollution Control" and conducted under the guidance of Professor Zheng Weimin of Qinghua University and

Professor Kan Chen of the University of Michigan, with the active cooperation and participation of the Bureau of Environmental Protection of the Shanghai Municipality, has produced important research findings which are deemed of great value to the drawing up and implementation of a comprehensive plan to solve Shanghai's problem of ensuring a hygienic water supply to its 10 million inhabitants.

Under (3) there have been limited but steadily expanding joint research efforts during recent years. For examples, a joint research project on "Computer-aided Data Processing of Chinese Characters" has been conducted by scholars of Fudan University at Shanghai and Cornell University at Ithaca; a joint research project on Chinese emigration has been carried out by scholars from Zhongshan University at Guangzhou and from the University of California at Los Angeles; a joint research program on problems related to highway design in China was conducted by scholars from Tongji University and the Technische Hochschule Darmstadt; a joint research project on the ecology of Lipotes vexllifer (a species of dolphin living in the middle and lower reaches of the Yangtze River) was conducted by scientists from Nanjing Teachers College, Ryukyu University, Tsukuba University and the Aquarium at Toba, Japan.[11]

Under (4) we may find examples of Chinese scholars recently returned from abroad who wish to conduct joint research with their former doctoral work supervisors. Both partners may apply for financial support from a private foundation. Stiftung Volkswagenwerk has awarded several grants to such joint research projects and the same foundation has given support to institutional cooperation in research, such as that mentioned above between Tongji University and the Technische Hochschule Darmstadt.

The Exchange of Delegations or Visiting Groups

The following account will be limited to a description of developments since 1978. Since that year an ever-increasing number of exchanges of visiting groups has been witnessed. Some of these exchanges were sponsored by bilateral agreements between two countries or by partnership agreements signed between sister institutions, while others were arranged by various UN agencies or other bodies. From 1978 to 1984, the Chinese side sent out 413 educational delegations or groups with 2,506 participants, and in the same period 557 foreign educational delegations or groups with an aggregate number of 3,090 individuals visited China. These visits have contributed very much to mutual understanding between educational circles of China and various foreign countries and to the furtherance of cooperation in the broad field of education, science and culture. Some of the official visits of delegations led by ministers or vice-ministers of education were instrumental in laying ground for bilateral cooperation or exchanges in education by signing agreements or protocols, which provide for various exchanges.

Particular mention should be made of the visit to the U.S. of a Chinese delegation led by Dr. Zhou Peiyuan, then Acting President of the Scientific and Technical

Association of the PRC and Vice-President of the Chinese Academy of Sciences, in October 1978. His visit to the United States and the negotiation conducted between Dr. Zhou and Dr. Richard C. Atkinson, then Director of the National Science Foundation, led to the signing of an agreement on the general framework of an educational exchange of students and scholars, preceding the establishment of diplomatic relations between the United States and the People's Republic of China. This agreement was later appended to the umbrella agreement of scientific and technical cooperation between the two countries signed in January of 1979. Similar negotiations conducted by the Chinese government with other Western countries during 1978-79 led to much expanded programs of educational exchange between China and the West. Negotiations between the governments of the PRC and the USSR in 1982 led to the resumption of students exchanges in 1983 and exchanges of higher education delegations in the last few years, after a break of cultural contact between the two socialist countries for over two decades.

It is encouraging to see that with the passage of time the emphasis in educational and scholarly relations is shifting rapidly from the superficial and limited contacts characteristic of earlier interaction towards multi-faceted and in-depth contacts. The efforts of the American Committee on Scholarly Communications with the People's Republic of China (CSCPRC) in promoting in-depth mutual understanding between scholars in various fields of the two countries are especially commendable. CSCPRC's *China Exchange News,* published since 1973, has played an important role in providing timely information on the development of scholarly exchanges between China and other countries, especially the United States, to the scientific community.

The Establishment of Partnerships Between Sister Institutions

During the 1950s partnerships between institutions of higher learning in the PRC and other socialist countries were initiated on a limited scale. However, such connections were interrupted completely during the Cultural Revolution. Even before the onset of the Cultural Revolution, with the deterioration of relations between China and the Soviet Unon and most other socialist countries, these partnerships were virtually inactive.

However, since 1978 this form of cooperation has been growing rapidly. By June of 1982, 115 Chinese institutions of higher education had established partnerships with 250 foreign institutions of higher education in 22 countries.[12] Since then even more partnerships have been formed. This type of international tie has become an important avenue for promoting exchanges. Between July of 1982 and June of 1985, a further 36 universities and colleges under the direct jurisdiction of the Chinese Ministry of Education established partnership relations with 320 foreign institutions.[13]

These partnerships have been effective in promoting the exchange of scholars and students, the exchange of delegations and visiting groups, the conduct of collaborative research, the provision for short-term training courses, and the exchange of publications and information.[14] However, it must be admitted that some still exist only on paper.

Participation in International Meetings and the Organization of Such Meetings in China

In the 1950s and the 1960s only a handful of university staff were able to go abroad to attend international conferences, giving rise to the situation that Chinese scientists and scholars working in universities and colleges were virtually cut off from effective communication with their colleagues in foreign countries, especially those in Western countries. Their main means of following advances in their own professional field was limited to the reading of scientific journals published abroad. Senior scientists working in the institutes under the Chinese Academy of Sciences were comparatively better off.

However, all this changed in recent years. Beginning with 1979 great efforts were made by the CMOE to allocate more funds to support travel abroad so that more academic staff could attend international meetings held in foreign countries. In that year 181 scholars working in CMOE institutions went abroad to attend 96 meetings. By 1985, 975 academics were able to go abroad to attend 490 meetings, with about half of the travelling funds and accomodation expenses provided by the universities themselves.

From the early 1980s a steadily increasing number of international meetings have been hosted by Chinese universities. In 1985, over 40 such meetings were hosted by CMOE institutions alone with over 600 foreign participants. Their themes ranged over a wide spectrum of scientific disciplines, including the pure and applied sciences, the humanities and social sciences. Some of the meetings had strong international participation. Here are a few examples: The First International Seminar on the Teaching of Chinese held in Beijing in August of 1985; an International Conference on the Properties and Applications of Dielectric Materials hosted by Xi'an Jiaotong University in June of 1985; The International Conference on the Origin and Evolution of Neutron Stars hosted by Nanjing University in April of 1986. There were also two meetings of university presidents, one attended by American and Chinese educators and another attended by Japanese and Chinese educators, providing a forum for the discussion of many vital issues relating to higher education in their countries.

The Role of International Agencies in Promoting Educational Exchanges

A number of international organizations, such as the UNESCO, UNICEF, UNDP, UNFPA, and WHO, have played an important role in promoting educational exchanges. Besides, cooperation with the World Bank has a strong educational component.

Although the legitimate place of the PRC in UNESCO was restored in late 1971, and a Permanent Delegation to UNESCO was set up in Paris by the Chinese Government in 1974, Chinese participation was limited to attendance at its General Assemblies and sessions of the UNESCO Executive Board up to 1977. There was little impact on the development of educational exchanges per se. Since 1978 the situation has changed markedly. The Permanent Delegation in Paris has been strengthened and the Chinese National Commission for UNESCO was formally set up in early 1979, involving the active participation of various governmental and non-governmental agencies and the educational and scientific communities at large in its diverse programs. The Chinese Ministry of Education has regularly sent official delegations to attend the International Conferences on Education held in Geneva (1979, 1981, 1984) and regional meetings at the ministerial level (MINIDASO IV and MINIDAP V held in 1978 and 1985 in Columbo and Bangkok respectively).

The four visits to China made by Mr. Amadou-Mahtar M'Bow, the Director-General of UNESCO in 1975, 1978, 1983, and 1984 were instrumental in expanding Chinese participation in UNESCO sponsored activities. During his visits to China in 1978 and 1983 two memoranda were signed by him and the Chinese Ministers of Education then in office. With the support of UNESCO the PRC has sent quite a number of delegations and visiting groups on study tours abroad. Also many Chinese educators, scientists and administrators have taken part in international meetings sponsored by UNESCO or short-term training courses. Some meetings and training courses have been held in China with a wider participation of domestic educators and scientists. Chinese educational institutions have taken active part in the Asian Program of Educational Innovation for Development (APEID) and become affiliated with APEID. The Central Institute of Educational Research represents China in the International Network of Educational Information (INED), and the Information and documentation Unit of CMOE (now SEDC) has maintained close contact with the International Bureau of Education (IBE), especially its Documentation center since 1983. I myself have been contributing to the Cooperative Educational Abstracting services (CEAS) sponsored by the IBE during recent years by writing abstracts of important educational documents or articles with significant policy implications.

Since 1982 UNICEF has given grants-in-aid to China to support the development of a number of educational programs. The first phase of UNICEF supported programs included the following six projects: (1) Equipping the People's Education Press with a set of photocopying and offset colored printing machinery for children's books; (2) A center for the Development of Teaching Aids in Beijing; (3) Establishment of a special education teachers training school in Nanjing; (4) Setting up a printing shop for Braille texts in Shanghai attached to a school for the blind; (5) A research project on the physical and mental development of children conducted by the Department of Psychology of Hangzhou University; (6) Preschool and primary teacher training in minority areas. UNICEF has provided a total of U.S. $4.8 million matched with 15 million yuan provided by the Chinese side.

Since 1983, three agreements have been signed by CMOE and UNDP for the following projects, each lasting two years:

(1)   Reinforcement of post-secondary technical education among secondary school leavers in the labor force;
(2)   Enhancement of science education in upper secondary schools;
(3)   Reinforcement of vocational and technical education

UNDP provides U.S. $1.6 million matched by 8.26 million yuan provided by the Chinese side for the financing of these projects. These funds provide for sending study groups and trainees abroad, the invitation of foreign experts to China, and the procurement of equipment. In addition, UNDP has provided aid to Nankai University, Xiamen University and others for improving the research and postgraduate training capability in specific scientific and technical areas, also grants to help in the organization of a number of international seminars and workshops in China.

It might be of interest to mention two programs of UNDP in China which take the specific form of an international exchange of personnel. The first is called TOKTEN (Transfer of Knowledge Through Expatriate Nationals). It was initiated in May of 1980 and has operated successfully ever since. Its purpose is to reco-mend Chinese expatriate professionals to serve in China as consultants. About 300 TOKTEN missions have been completed since the progam began, and 150 consultancies are envisaged for 1986. The forms of service provided by these missions are varied and still evolving, from general academic exchanges in the early days to lectures on specific topics, workshops, training courses and even joint research. A new scheme on similar lines called STAR (Senior Technical Advisors Recruitment) was launched by UNDP in 1985 under which the technical expertise of non-Chinese professionals can be called on to serve China's develop-ment. The China International Center for Economic and Technical Exchanges is responsible for operating these programs from the Chinese side. Although they do not directly relate to educatonal institutions, these two programs make an im-portant contribution to the development of human resources in China.[15]

The United Nations Fund for Population Activities (UNFPA) has reached agree-ment with the Chinese Government on providing aid for the following projects for 1980 to 1989 in China:

(1)   Demographic research and training in universities: The first cycle of this project was to support 10 Chinese institutions of higher education in developing research and training in demography, research in population problems and population policies. The UNFPA provided US $3.27 million matched by 2 million yuan furnished by the Chinese side. The second cy-cle of this project started in January of 1985 and will be completed by 1989. UNFPA will provide a sum of US $3.87 million matched by 12.79 million yuan provded by the Chinese side and the program is to be expanded to enlist the efforts of 10 additional higher institutions.
(2)   Population education in secondary schools: The first cycle of the project

began in 1980 and was completed by the end of 1984. Its aim was to dispense formal population education to students of upper secondary schools. UNFPA provided US $800,000 matched with 1.37 million yuan from the Chinese side. Ten institutes of education (*jiaoyu xueyuan*) and ten secondary schools in ten provinces were supported by the project, involving the training of 16,944 teachers and the compilation and supply of instructional materials. The second phase of the project started from 1985 and will be completed by the end of 1989. The number of participating institutions has increased to 59, including 14 provincial institutes of education and 45 secondary schools, in addition to the People's Education Press. Within this phase 1,500 full-time population education teachers will be trained; a center of instructional materials, a centre of teacher training and a centre of curriculum development will be set up, in addition to an expanded program of offering population education to upper secondary students.

(3)   Population education programs in rural schools: A pilot project is to be conducted in Hunan Province with a view to finding an effective way to introduce population education in rural schools.

(4)   A national center for training personnel in the field of demography: The center will be located in the People's University of China in Beijing, the trainees will be recruited form college graduates and the duration of study will last one year. The first class of students were enrolled in September of 1985.

(5)   A training centre for upgrading English and background knowledge in population studies: This is an ancillary project in the service of the project for demographic training and research.

(6)   A book series on Chinese population studies: The project consists of 32 regional volumes, including a comprehensive volume written on the basis of historical data as well as the data collected during the 1982 Census.

The Government of the PRC joined the World Bank in 1980 and since then eight educational projects, including one on agricultural research, have been initiated. These are listed in Table 12.3.

The Chinese Ministry of Education is responsible for the administration of the first and second University Development Projects, the Polytechnic/TV University Project and the Provincial University Development Project, while the Ministry of Agriculture, Fishery and Animal Husbandry and the Ministry of Public Health are responsible for the agricultural and medical education and research projects. Since these projects involve very large inputs of financial, material and human resources, and entail extensive educational exchanges with the industrialized countries, they justify closer examination and more detailed description. In view of the fact that the First University Development Project has been completed and a preliminary evaluation is being done by the Chinese Review Commission[16] and the International Advisory Panel[17] a fuller account will be given of the First University Development Project, followed by a resumé of the other projects.

The First Project was agreed to on November 4, 1981 and became effective on

Table 12.3
World Bank Educational Projects in China

Amounts in US$ Millions

Project Name	Loan/Credit	Total Cost	Years[2]
1. University Development I	200.0	295.0	81/86
2. Agricultural Education & Research I	75.4	201.6	82/88
3. Polytechnic/TV University	85.0	206.2	83/89
4. Agricultural Education II	68.0	175.0	84/89
5. Rural Health & Medical Educ.	85.0[1]	290.5	84/89
6. Agricultural Research II	25.0	59.0	84/89
7. University Development II	145.0	n.a.	85/90
8. Provincial University Development	120.0	n.a.	86/91
Total	803.4		

Notes:
1. Of which $43m is for medical education.
2. In World Bank operations the date of closing is usually one year later than the date of completion. The closing years are shown here.

February 4, 1982. It aimed at helping 28 key universities in science and engineering fields to reach the following goals: (1) increase the enrollment of science and engineering students at both the undergraduate and postgraduate levels; (2) improve the quality of teaching and enhance research capability; (3) strengthen management at both university and ministry level.

The members of the International Advisory Panel (IAP) are expected to help the project universities and CMOE in the following ways: (a) selection of the teaching and research equipment to be procured with the project funds; (b) the updating of undergraduate curricula and postgraduate programs, developing appropriate research programs for selected fields related to the project, and the provision of advice to the management of computer and analytical testing centers set up with the project funds; (c) the development of university faculty in all the designated universities through the selection and placement of fellows for study abroad as specified in the project; (d) the enhancement and improvement of management at the institutional level in five selected universities through improved records keeping and more comprehensive accounting practices; and at the ministerial level through improved educational statistics, including procedures for the collection of statistical data, more rational methods of accounting, and enhanced capability in monitoring and evaluation.

So far 2,411 persons have gone abroad for advanced study, availing themselves of the fellowships provided by the project funds. Table 12.4 gives a breakdown of this group by receiving country and category of the grantees:

Table 12.4
Chinese Scholars Abroad on World Bank Project Scholarships

Name of Country	Number of Graduate Students	Number of Visiting Scholars
U.S.A.	620	840
Canada	124	230
U.K.	84	121
Japan	16	158
West Germany	20	86
France	13	40
Others	29	90
Total	906	1,565

By the end of 1985, 405 foreign specialists had been invited to China to give lectures or other specialist services. Of these, 202 came from the U.S., 67 from the UK, 36 from Japan, 44 from West Germany, 9 from France, 12 from Canada and 35 from other countries. According to a news report carried in the March 6, 1985 issue of *Jingji cankao,* the total enrollment of students in the 28 project universities has increased by 60%, 94% of the laboratory exercises stipulated by the syllabi of basic courses can be carried out now, as against 80% before the implementation of the project, and 91% of the laboratory exercises of special courses as against 79% before. About 500,000 square meters of buildings for housing newly imported equipment and ancillary domestic equipment have been completed. The total number of graduate students and visiting scholars sent abroad, 2,472, is three times the planned figure. Of these 392 have already returned to China. Already 95.5% of the equipment procured abroad has arrived in China with most now in use.

The Polytechnic/Television University Project aims at aiding the establishment of 17 polytechnics and the strengthening of the Central Radio and Television University (CRTVU) and 28 Provincial Television Universities (PTVUs). Polytechnics represent a new departure in post-secondary education in China and are called *duanqi zhiye daxue* (short-cycle vocational universities) in Chinese. They should not be regarded as a replica of the polytechnics in England.

The Second University Development is similar in aim and mode of operation to the First Project, and 36 key universities under central ministries other than CMOE are the beneficiaries. In addition, sector support will be provided to promote programs of exchange and faculty development.

The First Agricultural Education and Research Project aimed to upgrade, expand and equip 11 key agricultural colleges and universities and 6 research institutes and construct and equip a National Rice Research Institute (NRRI). The

Second Agricultural Education Project provided funds to: (1) improve and expand 23 agricultural colleges; (2) establish 8 centers to train extension staff; (3) initiate a pilot program to strengthen 12 agricultural technical schools; and (4) assist 3 central distance learning centers. The Second Agricultural Research Project was conceived to: (1) upgrade facilities, staff and programs of 15 research centers in 9 provinces responsible for priority research in food and cash crops, livestock, aquatic products, forestry, hydrology and meteorology and (2) support a pilot program to strengthen 10 county-level agrotechnical extension stations. These three projects are managed by the Ministry of Agriculture, Animal Husbandry and Fishery.

The Provincial University Development Project will provide funds to help upgrade and expand 60 provincial universities and teachers training colleges. This is the most recent of the eight World Bank educational projects.

During recent years the scope of cooperation between Chinese institutions of medical research, education and hospital care is steadily expanding. With the recommendation of the Chinese Ministry of Public Health, 41 medical units have been designated as collaborative centers affiliated with WHO. These centers are located in Beijing, Shanghai, Guangdong, Shandong, Jiangsu, and Inner Mongolia, etc., and have undertaken research projects and technical services commissioned by WHO in such diverse fields as primary medical care, traditional Chinese medicine, cardio-vascular diseases, control of benign and malignant tumors, neurosciences, mental hygiene, family planning, health care of women and infants and classification or taxonomy of diseases.[18]

The Role of Private Foundations and Individuals

During recent years a number of private foundations, mainly American and German ones, have provided financial support to the development of various educational programs, including the donation of books, support for joint research, the organization of international conferences held in China and support for the exchange of students and faculty. For example the Ford Foundation has given support to the development of a China-U.S. Cooperative Project in Legal Education, which was started in 1983 and will extend over three years, involving the exchange of delegations, exchange of students, the invitation of American senior scholars to China to give lectures on a short-term basis, and the exchange of publications and information.[19] The Hanns Seidel Stiftung has financed several educational projects in China, especially in the field of vocational education and teacher training.

During recent years a number of renowned Chinese businessmen living in Hongkong have donated fairly large sums to support educational programs, including support of scholarships for study abroad. For example, Mr. He Yingdong, President of the General Chamber of Commerce of Chinese Enterprises in Hong Kong, has provided scholarships for 30 students to study in the United Kingdom every year; Mr. Bao Yugang, President of the Hong Kong Global Shipping Consortium, has created a fund bearing his name to be administered by Zhejiang University on his behalf to support study abroad.

Conclusion: Prospects and Trends

In conclusion I'd like to discuss the trends of development and some policy issues related to China's educational and scientific exchanges with industrialized countries.

There is ample evidence to assert that the policy of opening to the outside world and the concomitant policy of promoting educational, scientific and cultural contacts and exchanges with foreign countries have scored success in serving the needs of China's modernization effort and in promoting mutual understanding and cooperation both on a general level and between the Chinese educational and scientific communities and their foreign counterparts.

A recent press report[20] stated that during the Sixth Five-Year Plan (1981-1985), more than 36,500 Chinese government-sponsored students and visiting scholars went abroad for advanced studies and/or research in 63 countries and regions and up to now more than 16,500 or 45.2% of them have returned to China. According to the analysis made by one of the sending agencies, 23.8% of the returned students or scholars scored remarkable or outstanding successes in research or technological innovations or inventions; 53% were regarded as good in academic achievement. The majority of them are working in institutions of higher learning, offering new courses and initiating new directions in research. According to information provided by Zhejiang University, among their 96 returned scholars, five have become supervisiors of doctoral work, 76 have become supervisors of master degree programs, 36 have assumed the responsibility of heads of teaching and research groups or directors or deputy directors of laboratories. According to information provided by Qinghua University, from the end of 1978 to September 1985, 491 faculty members went abroad for advanced studies in 18 countries for at least six months. Of these, 247 of them have returned. If those going abroad for attending international conferences, study tours, visits, giving lectures, serving on foreign aid missions, receiving training in connection with imported equipment are added to the number 491, the total of faculty members and other staff having gone abroad reaches 1,412 (including some multiple counting of those who went abroad more than once). The massive input of these returned students and scholars into Chinese academic institutions cannot but exert significant and long-term influence on the development of Chinese higher education and science.

There is no lack of press coverage on some of the more successful stories. In Zhejiang University alone we may cite the examples of Professors Lu Yongxiang and Lü Yongzai.[21] Both of them have continued the line of research begun abroad upon their return to China and have been able to score significant new successes in a short space of time. Prof. Lu Yongxiang was a visiting scholar in the Technische Hochschule Aachen from 1979 to 1981, studying hydraulic control under Prof. W. Backe and was awarded a Dr. Ing. degree in May 1981. During his stay in Germany he was able to register five patents with the German Patent Office either singly or in collaboration with his German colleagues in the field of fluid control. He has continued research in hydraulic control elements and systems upon his return to China. With the support of the state and the enthusiastic and energetic effort of his colleagues in the Department of Mechanical Engineering, a well equipped laboratory with over 40 researchers and supporting staff has been set up. So far four new inventions have been made, one patented in West Germany, the other three in China. In September of 1985 an International Conference on Fluid Power Transmission and Control was held in Hangzhou. It was chaired by Prof. Lu and drew over 200 participants from 14 foreign countries. Prof. Lu was elected a delegate to the Sixth National People's Congress in 1982, a great honor to a distinguished young scholar. In August of 1985, he became Vice President of Zhejiang University.

Prof. Lü Yongzai is a member on the faculty of the Department of Chemical Engineering and head of the Teaching and Research Group of Automation. He went to the United States in 1980 and did research in Purdue University on a project related to modelling automatic control development and production scheduling for the ingot handling portion of a steel mill. He was able to develop a discrete mathematical model in five months, and his research findings immediately attracted the attention of several major steel companies. Two pilot experiments on industrial scale were carried out by the interested companies with results completely validating Lü's findings. He was honoured as the first man in the world who succeeded in developing a single mathematical model for controlling the operation of ingot heating pit furnace prior to rolling. Since his return to China at the end of 1982 he has continued his research and initiated several industrial experiments in a number of steel plants in China. In June, 1985 an International Conference on Industrial Process Modelling and Control was hosted by Zhejiang University on his initiative, with over 65 foreign participants from 10 countries, including the U.S., Britain, Canada, Japan, East and West Germany. His work was highly commended by the participants, not the least by his supervisor — Professor T. J. Williams of Purdue University. Now he is supervising the work of 7 doctoral and 13 masters candidates. Profesor Lü was recently elected a vice president of the Chinese Association of Automation.[22]

It is encouraging to see that in the social sciences and humanities lively interaction between Chinese scholars and institutions and their foreign counterparts has brought great benefits to both sides. It goes without saying that the field of foreign languages and literature has received the greatest benefit from an ever-expanding program of international exchange. A steady flow of visiting lecturers in languages and literature go not only to the departments of foreign languages in major universities or the Foreign Language Institutes, but also to engineering, agricultural, medical and other colleges, as well as provincial universities.

Several international conferences on certain aspects or dynasties of Chinese history have been held in China. Also foreign scholars doing research on contemporary or historical problems have access to the library holdings of major universities and public libraries as well as archives, though much still remains to be done to facilitate their work. Since May of 1983 a very extensive China-U.S. cooperative project on Legal Education has been in operation, involving the Chinese Ministry of Justice and five Chinese academic institutions on one side, and the U.S.-China Committee on Educational Exchanges in Law and the Ford Foundation on the other side. A similar program in economics has been in existence since June of 1985.[23]

An international seminar on social indicators sponsored by UNESCO and hosted by CASS was held in Beijing from October 30 to November 18 of 1982. Several Western experts and one Soviet expert gave systematic exposition on this subject during the seminar and shared their experiences with Chinese colleagues, including officials and researchers from the State Planning Commission and the State Bureau of Statistics as well as academics. In the near future a China-U.S. joint seminar on science indicators will be hosted by the State Science and Technology Commission (SSTC). Such topics as social and scientific indicators are of vital interest to a wide spectrum of decision-makers in Chinese government agencies. In the field of national accounting, the use of GNP, GDP, etc., is gaining currency among Chinese social scientists as well as government statisticians, with the implication that tertiary industries also contribute to the formation of the national income.

It is of interest to note that even the seemingly purely capitalist concept of venture capital is no longer regarded as incompatible with a socialist economy. China Venturetech Investment Corporation (CVIC) was created in October of 1985, and it is a financial concern run on commercial principles, affiliated with the SSTC and the People's Bank of China and dedicated to assisting the research and development of technological ventures by investment in and managerial support for small and medium-sized companies and new start-ups.[24]

The fate of sociology in China is worthy of note, because it was denounced as a pseudo-science in the earliest years of the People's Republic and not reestablished until 1979. Eminent Chinese scholars such as Fei Xiaotong, Lei Jieqiong and Li Jinghan have contributed to its revival and support has also come from such foreign scholars as Alex Inkeles, Peter Blau and Burton Pasternak. These developments are symptomatic of a trend that ideological differences may no longer pose a barrier between social scientists of the PRC and of Western countries and fruitful dialogue can be held between people of different political, ideological or theoretical persuasions. Marxism-Leninism is not a set of dogmas but an ever-evolving world outlook which seeks to enrich itself from all the positive achievements of modern science, including the contributions of Western social scientists.[25]

Informal personal contacts between individual scientists and scholars of different countries are of immense value to the furtherance of science and scholarship and to the cause of promoting international scholarly exchanges. This is all the more significant for most Chinese academics due to many years of seclusion and isolation. Before 1978, the year active international exchanges in various fields were resumed, Chinese scholars had to depend on the information provided by scholarly journals published abroad in following the advancement of science in their field of interest without any benefit of direct contact with their foreign colleagues. When the "left" line held sway, it was not possible for Chinese scholars to maintain personal contacts with their foreign colleagues freely, and the artificial barriers thus set up could not but be extremely harmful to the development of education, science and culture in China.

Not all scholars who had studied abroad could expect to have the favorable conditions provided to the more fortunate ones like Professors Lu and Lü mentioned above. The problems of providing a favorable environment and creating the necessary physical facilities and organizing a viable research group in Chinese institutions of higher education may arise from a number of causes which need different approaches. It might be of some interest to quote a press report[26] on the measures taken by Shanghai Jiaotong University in coping with these problems. Firstly, in case the new expertise acquired abroad cannot be fully utilized in the original unit, the faculty member is reassigned a suitable job in another unit. For instance an associate professor from the department of electronics, who became an expert on computer-communications-networks, has been assigned a job in the computer center of the university where he can continue his research related to the development of such networks. Secondly, effective steps are taken to organize a viable research group with a clearly defined research objective or direction and well-staffed collaborators and supporting technical staff. For example, Professor Zhu Jimao of the department of shipbuilding and ocean engineering has been able to organize a research and development group in deep-diving technology. Thirdly, returned scholars with outstanding achievements abroad are to be promoted to higher academic ranks. This is not easy to do in Chinese society where seniority always carries weight in matters of promotion in academic institutions.

The re-integration of returned students and scholars poses a problem which needs to be tackled in a rational way. Visiting scholars are usually mature people in mid career in a position to choose the right institutions and research theme to work on. On return they are usually in a better position than students to adapt to the home environment. Yet even they need sympathetic consideration from their institutions and colleagues, if they are to avoid frustrations. It is more difficult for graduate students with new doctorates to adapt to the home environment, especially in case the research themes of their choice have little relevance for their institutions and so are not given the necessary support. They may have to shift to other work not of their own choice, and this causes pain. In order to alleviate such difficulties, wherever practicable, young doctoral candidates should be assisted to establish suitable contacts with potential employers and be given guidance by mature scientists. Another solution is to insist on a certain number of years of working experience as a pre-requisite for study abroad. It is likely that the state will impose such a requirement in future for certain disciplines at least.

In connection with providing better opportunities of research for young postdoctorals and with a view to helping them to find the most suitable place to settle down for permanent employment, a number of mobile postdoctoral research stations (MPRS) have been established in major universities and CAS institutes. A complete list of them was published in a recent issue of *Zhongguo jiaoyu bao*.[27] These newly created stations seek to provide congenial conditions for young postdoctorals who have recently earned their degrees at domestic or foreign institutions to conduct research in a good academic environment conducive to creative work and to vigorous interaction between mature and young scientists. The primary purpose of these stations is to do frontier research in various fields of science and technology rather than to create a new stage of formal schooling.

This experiment was officially sanctioned by the State Council on July 5, 1985. Prof. T. D. Lee of Columbia, a Nobel Lareate in Physics, has been appointed as an advisor to the Committee of Management and Coordination of MPRS's. Its office is located in the (SSTC) Bureau of Scientific and Technological Cadres.[28] In accordance with the regulations in force, the postdoctoral fellows conducting research in these MPRS's enjoy the status of faculty without any commitment to employment. This is not unlike the system of postdoctoral fellowships prevailing in the United States and other western countries. Usually a postdoctoral fellow is allowed to do research in two MPRS's of his own choice consecutively for a term of two years each before settling down for formal employment at the end of the second term. In particular cases, a postdoctoral fellow may choose to settle down at the end of the first term of research at a station.

Another significant step taken by major universities and the Chinese Academy of Sciences recently is the designation of a number of well-equipped and productive research laboratories or institutes as ''open'' ones. This means researchers from other domestic or foreign institutions may apply to conduct research in them. These laboratories must satisfy the following conditions: (1) the ''actuality'' or significance of research topics of directions; (2) the availability of highly qualified leading scientists in the specific field and a core of outstanding middle-aged and young investigators; (3) distinction for research output and the training of advanced students; (4) the availability of essential facilities for research; (5) a good academic environment conducive to the management of an open laboratory and the provision of accomodation for visiting researchers. Each open laboratory will have an academic council composed of Chinese and foreign experts distinguished in the related field. Members of the host institutions shall not exceed one third. On this count any Chinese or foreign researcher interested in conducting research in an open laboratory may apply with a proposal, which is subject to a process of peer review. Visiting researchers from domestic institutions are allowed to go there accompanied by their post-graduate students. It is also possible for self-funded researchers to avail themselves of these facilities.

Among the key universities under the direct jurisdiction of the State Education Commission, nearly thirty research laboratories are eligible for being designated as open laboratories. However, a number of them still suffer from an inadequate level of funding, and therefore only seven of them have been approved by SEDC so far. They are: (1) the Laboratory of Solid Microstructure Physics of Nanjing University headed by Professor Feng Duan; (2) the Genetic Engineering Laboratory of Fudan University Headed by Professor Sheng Zujia; (3) Nankai Institute of Mathematics of Nankai University headed by Professor H. S. Chern; (4) the Structural Chemistry Laboratory of Beijing University headed by Professor Tang Youqi; (5) the Laboratory of Structural Engineering and Vibrations of Qinghua University headed by Professor Shen Jümin; (6) the Laboratory of Fluid Transmission and Control of Zhejiang University headed by Professor Lu Yongxiang; (7) the Laboratory of Strength and Vibrations of Xi'an Jiaotong University headed by Professor Tu Mingsheng.

In a similar vein the Chinese Academy of Sciences has designed two research institutes and 17 research laboratories as CAS's first group of open institutes and laboratories.[29] As regards the sources and level of funding, the CAS laboratories are in a much more favourable situation than university laboratories.

In spite of the measures taken and described above it remains a formidable problem to create favorable conditions for returned students and scholars to continue their research along the lines pursued abroad. As it is unrealistic to expect all academic institutions to be able to provide the necessary conditions and facilities for doing frontier research, a significant proportion of returned scholars have to do their research and teaching under unsatisfactory conditions. This problem has its political implications, as a contributing factor to a ''brain drain'' from the People's Republic of China. Evidently, steps have to be taken to keep such a '' brain drain'' to a tolerable level. Undoubtedly the PRC cannot afford to provide everywhere first-rate research facilities for scholars and to pay salaries competitive with Western countries. We have to depend mainly on the loyalty of Chinese scholars sent abroad to their motherland and to the cause of socialist modernization. The main problem here lies with those doing postdoctoral work in the United States.

Another important policy issue is to improve the planning and selection of candidates for study abroad. Mr. Li Peng, Vice Premier and concurrently Chairman of SEDC, recently dealt with this problem in a speech delivered to the Working Conference of the SEDC for 1986 held in March in Beijing.[30] Better planning means that the number of candidates allocated to different fields should better meet the needs of the modernization effort. A more careful selection of candidates means the application of more stringent standards. Although most Chinese students abroad study hard and have high standards of character, it cannot be denied that some have been below standard professionally, morally or physically.

Another related question is how to ensure that the research fields selected by the students or mature scholars studying abroad fit the needs of the country. Some students and visiting scholars are eager to go abroad without giving adequate attention to the question of whether the host institution or the supervisor of post graduate work is well chosen or not. With the current emphasis placed on applied research and developmental work by the Chinese Government, Chinese students and visiting scholars would appreciate very much the opportunities given to them in getting in touch with industrial enterprises or R & D establishments. This kind of arrangement involves the sensitive question of proprietary knowledge and it is not easy to find a satisfactory solution.

From 7-13 May 1986 a National Conference on Study Abroad was convened in Beijing by the State Education Commission, reviewing the work done during the past seven years (1979-1985) and charting the course for the future.[31] According to the decision made at the conference the total number of government-sponsored students studying abroad during the Seventh Five-Year-Plan (1986-1990) will be kept at the current level in terms of the number of students sent abroad per year, while provincial and municipal governments and central ministries are authorized to increase the number of students sent by them, provided that they can find additional financial resources to support these students. Among the more important policy issues dealt with at the conference the following three loom large:

(1)   Better and proper planning: It was stressed that in the process of planning the needs of the state in promoting economic and social development as well as the needs of the sending institutions should be kept in mind. In view of the fact that postgraduate education at the master's level in domestic institutions has expanded significantly during the past few years, dependence on foreign insitutions at this level will be smaller and smaller in the future, and thus more financial resources can be diverted to the support of doctoral candidates studying abroad. It was envisaged that new possibilities or avenues should be explored for training doctoral candidates jointly by Chinese and foreign institutions and supervisors. Applications-oriented fields will continue to be given higher priority in the distribution of awards by disciplines or fields of study, while foreign languages and basic theoretical sciences will be given due attention. A proper balance of the numbers of students sent to different recipient countries will be kept.

(2)   Better selection of candidates: This means the application of more stringent standards. Besides professional capability and attainment, language proficiency and physical health, the moral quality of candidates will be given greater weight. It was suggested that in the future most government-sponsored awards for study abroad might preferably be distributed to grassroots institutions or potential employers, so that the latter may take care to make proper selection of qualified candidates for study abroad by a proper combination of examinations, reviewing process and recommendations.

(3)   Proper placement of returned students: During the Seventh Five-Year Plan period a great number of Chinese students and scholars now studying abroad will finish their studies and return to China. It was deemed imperative to do a good job of placement and to make efforts to provide proper facilities for teaching and/or research and proper living conditions, especially housing, for the returned students.

A number of new agencies and organizations, governmental, semi-official or otherwise, engaged in promoting international exchanges have cropped up in China during the past few years. One of them is the Chinese Education Association for International Exchanges, which was formally founded in September 1984 in Beijing. Mr. Huang Xinbai, member of the SEDC and ex-Vice Minister of MOE, is its President. A number of provinces now have a chapter of CEAIE. They form an increasingly effective network for promoting international exchanges and providing various services to visitors going to China. The lack of adequate accomodation facilities and inconvenient air travel in China are serious handicaps. The SEDC has taken steps to build a number of medium-size conference centers in several cities. Upon their completion Chinese academic institutions may host more international conferences in China.

Another new agency is the China Association for the International Exchange of Personnel (CAIEP). It is a national non-governmental organization. It maintains regular contacts with all the ministries and provinces, finds out their needs, and tries to help them establish cooperation with related institutions, enterprises and individuals in other countries, including partner relationships and the exchange of specialized personnel.

In closing this chapter I would like to quote Premier Zhao's tenth point or principle of China's foreign policy expounded in his report delivered to the Sixth National People's Congress:

> China attaches great importance to contacts among people of different countries. To further mutual understanding and friendship among the people of the world, the Chinese Government encourages mass organizations, non-governmental associations and people from all work of life to have contacts with those of other countries and supports cooperation between them in the economic, cultural, scientific and technological fields and in matters relating to the press, public health and sports.[31]

There is every reason to look forward to fruitful and ever-expanding international exchanges between China and foreign countries in the years to come.

13

Educational Modernization as a Search for Higher Efficiency

Jürgen Henze

Introduction

The intention of this chapter is to place recent education developments, problems and prospects into the broader context of the intended modernization of Chinese society. While much of this book has dealt with specific foreign influences on Chinese education, this chapter analyzes the gradually evolving process of introducing the foreign concept of "efficiency" as a new point of orientation in bureaucratic and administrative behavior. It will be argued that this process took place within the growing relationship between China and the Western world, especially between China and the World Bank. Both the advantages and disadvantages of this westernized concept of "efficiency" in the context of Chinese education will be discussed.

Modernization in the Context of Education, Science and the Economy

The term "modernization" *(xiandaihua)* has always been used as a verbal weapon among competing factions in the People's Republic of China to push forward a program for immediate action, favored by particular groups in the leadership. The term has been used to call attention to Chinese backwardness in comparison with developed nations, that is to say, "modern" societies, predominantly those of the West. The most outstanding advocate of "modernization" within the political elite is certainly Deng Xiaoping. Since the mid-seventies he has strongly emphasized the need for recognizing China's backwardness in certain fields of the economy, education, and science and technology. For Deng as well as for a growing number of high ranking bureaucrats, "modernization" means "to make modern,"[1] that is to make China more like Western industrialized countries, at least in terms of economic output and the social well-being of the majority of the population.[2] (See chapter 1 of this volume for a comprehensive account of historical developments with parallels to the present idea of modernization.)

The well-known development goal set by Mao Zedong in 1965 and picked up by Zhou Enlai in 1975 only stated the necessity to

> accomplish the comprehensive modernization of agriculture, industry, national defense and science and technology before the end of the century.[3]

This was a set of proposals, often rather diffuse in operational terms, aiming at improving "quality" without, however, going into details on how to define and measure "quality." They were published in the Chinese media as a reflection of ongoing internal debates and factional criticism. Without further sociological connotations, this concept meant improvements in a number of major areas of the economic and social accounting system, as well as gradually evolving structural changes. The main improvements envisaged were:

(a) an increase in national income and in the output of industrial/agricultural production as well as freight volume;

(b) an expansion in commodity flow and domestic as well as foreign trade;

(c) an increase in industrial labor productivity and in the average wages of workers and staff;

(d) an overall rise in living standards (including housing and the availability of consumer goods);

(e) an improved (planned) linkage between production and scientific research, and

(f) an increase in output within the higher education system, paralleled with a balanced reduction on the level of secondary general education and a more diversified structure of educational opportunity through the provision of secondary vocational education.[4]

Within this frame of reference for mapping out a detailed concept of "modernization," science and technology became identified as crucial to promoting economic reforms. Science and technology as an institutionalized system of "thinking," "utilized" in research and development activities, was to become the main supplier of pure and applied knowledge to ensure economic growth, product quality, and an overall economic efficiency, what seems to be a managerial efficiency.

Although there was no explicit mention of "education" as a separate component of the "four modernizations," without question it must have been viewed in this way as early as 1974-75 when central documents like the "General Program," "Some Problems in Accelerating Industrial Development" and the "Outline Report on the Work of the Academy of Sciences" were generated by Deng Xiaoping and his supporters and criticized by the Cultural Revolution left.[5] Deng rather quickly became the driving force for an interpretation of education as a productive force and as a necessary prerequisite for developing science and technology. This process of reinterpretation lasted until the midst of 1977, when Deng finally became fully rehabilitated.[6]

Already in May 1977, in a talk to members of the Central Committee, Deng set the tone for future interpretations of modernization with his remarks that the development of science and technology were "the key to achieving modernization," that "it is necessary to improve education at every level . . . to promote scientific and technological work" and that improving education comprised two aspects to "raise the standards of education at the same time as we make it available to more and more people."[7]

Around the same time long-term plans for science and education were mapped out and scheduled for public discussion and promulgation in national conferences on science and education in 1978. The major contribution of Deng and his followers during 1977 must have been initiating change in the overall reform climate. This included the positive re-appraisal of "specialized knowledge" and the rehabilitation of the intellectuals as part of the working class on the basis of the ideological equality of physical and mental work, accompanied by recognition of a corresponding division of labor within society. In school and academic practice, this has led to increased social esteem for those engaged in teaching and research activities and to a general re-evaluation of scientific theory formulation, research and methods. On several occasions Deng improved his previously rather unspecified idea of what we might call "educational modernization" (jiaoyu xiandaihua) — in contrast to "educational revolution" (jiaoyu geming), the central keywords during the Cultural Revolution. Translated into policy options, Deng's "educational modernization" was summarized at the National Conference on Education Work in April 1978 as follows:

> First, we must improve the quality of education and raise the level of teaching in the sciences, social sciences and humanities so as to serve socialist construction better. . . .
>
> Second, our schools must make an effort to strengthen revolutionary order and discipline, bring up a new generation with socialist consciousness and help to revolutionize the moral tone of our society. . . .
>
> Third, education must meet the requirements of our country's economic development.[8]

Retrospectively, these overall reform activities fell under three broad topics. Firstly, Deng's call for an improvement of quality led to reforms in textbooks and curricular structure, bringing a pronounced increase in the number of teaching hours in the mathematics and natural science subjects in comparison to those in politics, and practical work. At the same time, the methodological-didactic aspect of the combination of school learning and practical work, which had been dominant until 1976, decreased in importance. Secondly, methods for classroom instruction were to be based on advanced models used in foreign countries, partially in the Soviet Union, but dominantly in the United States and Western Europe. The same request has been made for developing new criteria for evaluating learning outcomes. Thirdly, a mis-match between the education and employment system was to be avoided in future by establishing more effective methods of macro-planning and an improved coordination between the qualifications required by economic units and those supplied within the formal education system.

It is noteworthy that Deng normally didn't refer to a concept of "efficiency" although his arguments did constitute a framework for claiming higher "efficiency." In relation to the third point noted above, however, he linked education and the economic system in this way: "rapid economic and technological progress demands rapid improvement in the quality and efficiency of education. This includes steady improvement in the methods of combining study with productive labor and of selecting the type of labor appropriate for this purpose."[9]

This very restricted meaning of efficiency suggests a correlation between total numbers of graduates on all levels of the education system who have a defined standard based on academic disciplines of knowledge and an estimated or real demand for qualified manpower within the employment system. A dictionary definition of efficiency as "the ability to achieve desired results with economy of time and effort in relation to the amount of work accomplished"[10] seems to be the most appropriate one in describing the Chinese working concept in 1978.

But the situation was to change very soon. In 1979, following the new economic policy of "readjustment, restructuring, consolidation, and improvement,"[11] the first signs of a growing awareness of the need for higher efficiency appeared in the media, although the discussion was still very much centered on pure economic issues. The new policy guideline envisaged a two phase development program based on the demand "to generate steady and balanced growth by raising economic efficiency"[12] and to increase "the supply of quality inputs such as technical manpower, technology-embodied capital and management techniques.".[13] Because the second of the above mentioned aspects was closely related to the productive function of the education and science system, the discussion quickly changed over to the issues of science and education. Two conditions became most important factors for this development: (1) the growing number of Chinese scholars who stayed in foreign countries on a short-term basis and returned to China with impressions to be transformed into proposals for reforming Chinese education; (2) the economic restrictions in terms of reduced capital investment which caused discussions on measures to achieve definite aims under restricted financial capacity.

The result was a debate which saw a diffusion of economic arguments to educational and scientific circles considering the following issues:

• How to determine the amount of investment to be spent on education;[14]
• how to restructure higher education on the premises of the new emerging discipline of "scientific management";[15]
• the establishment of a new branch of science relating the economy to the science system, so-called "techno-economics" (jishu jingji, jishu jingji yanjiu),[16] and
• a more critical assessment of the keypoint principle which had been introduced as a major principle in restructuring the education system after the Cultural Revolution.[17]

Summarizing these developments we may conclude that as early as the end of 1978 and the beginning of 1979 there was a general concern about more efficiency in education as a necessary prerequisite to developing the Chinese economy, although the conceptualization was heavily in favor of numerical input-output relations. No distinction between output and outcome was visible in the discussion.[18]

A major challenge to this position occured in the fall of 1979 when the term "spiritual civilization" was first introduced to the political language by Ye Jianying during his speech on the thirtieth anniversary of the founding of the PRC.[19] If we describe the first kind of efficiency as a technocratic point of view, then the new element pushed forward in the wake of the "spiritual civilization" campaign may be called a moralist view. As new regulations for elementary and secondary schools revealed in 1980 and 1981, a growing tendency towards stress on political-ideological education became evident as a reaction to changes in domestic policy.[20]

Alarmed by the fact that a growing proportion of Chinese youth had lost confidence in the Communist Party and its modernization policy and thus created a "youth problem," the Central Committee, the State Council and the Ministry of Education adopted a number of decisions to put things right through the school.

Similar developments took place even earlier in higher education institutions.[21] Moreover, by the end of 1979 it became clear that efficiency no longer could be a function of factor-combination only, but had to take the socialization function of schooling more closely into account. Parts of the political leadership seem to have had diverging opinions on the use and abuse of a technocratic interpretation of efficiency which upheld a one-sided view of how to evaluate a school's performance. Although we are not able to separate opinion-groups by systematic analysis of relevant articles, it seems likely that the Ministry of Education had to reduce tensions between obviously competing political factions by releasing new documents on the problem of how to evaluate school performance and how to organize political instruction at primary, secondary and tertiary levels. This would explain the gradual growth of activities in these fields of state control.[22]

How these different opinions were translated into policy guidelines for the national-level educational policy around 1979/80 was disclosed in a policy document of the Ministry of Education in the 1980s:

1. Education must be geared to the needs of socialist construction and modernization, and the proportion of expenditure on and investment in education must be adjusted and raised;

2. education is to be developed effectively and steadily in accordance with the policy of readjusting, restructuring, consolidation and improving the economy;

3. in view of our large population, and poor economic foundation, and the unbalanced development of economy and education, in developing education, there should be priorities, and resources shouldn't be evenly distributed among too many projects.

4. the relationship between popularization and the raising of standards should be handled correctly; to make primary education universal should be taken as a priority, and enough attention should be given to education in areas inhabited by minority nationalities;

5. educational structure must be transformed;

6. a diversified educational system should be adopted so as to achieve greater, faster, better and more economical results in educational development; and

7. efforts should be made to raise the level of teachers and to further strengthen the teaching force.[23]

The discussion about the correct evaluation of keypoint schools and primary as well as secondary schools in general was treated separately in 1982 and should be seen in connection with points one to seven above, thus forming an official outline of the Ministry's policy orientation:

8. primary and secondary education should strive to develop moral, physical and intellectual capacities and should not over-emphasize examination scores. The schools should not concentrate on the graduating class and ignore others; and

9. keypoint schools are necessary for ensuring the quality of education;

however, since primary education should aim at becoming universal, there will be no entrance examinations to the schools. All students to the key-point schools will be admitted from the neighborhood.[24]

As it can be easily seen, the Ministry's document put together all major pieces of the discussion in education since the end of the Cultural Revolution in 1976. The second and third points clearly state the necessity of efficiency without going into detail and the whole document seems to prove our argument that no more than a general concern for efficiency was in existence at the end of the 1970s. There were at least two different lines of interpretation, one more in favor of a technocratic approach, the other one voting for a higher degree of "Marxist moralism."[25] In principle, this situation of two parallel streams of argument has not changed until now. What has changed is the degree of conceptualization of the concept of efficiency. Materials published in and after 1981 emphasize an economically oriented approach, especially in statements published in academic journals.[26] At the same time official statements still take into account the moralist approach, laying stress on the socialization function of schooling, thus enforcing political instruction at school.[27]

Given these conditions we might ask how school administrators actually evaluate schools' success or failure in daily work. The question is difficult to answer, when only scattered information on internal evaluation schemes is available. However, drawing on field research done in 1985 and 1986, I can describe the situation observed in selected geographical areas.[28]

Chinese Indicators for Measuring School Quality

Probably based on the experience of Soviet assistance during the First Five-Year Plan (1953-1957), reinforced by a strong Confucian tradition of grading and ranking the results of intellectual activities, an evaluation system for elementary and secondary schools has come into use that comprises at least ten different indicators to measure school quality. So far as we know the system didn't work during the Cultural Revolution (1966-1976) and was reactivated only in 1977-78, when a number of documents of the 1960s were implemented in a slightly revised form.[29]

These indicators have been put together in Table 13.1. The first seven may be classified as being valid for the micro-level of schooling, whereas the last three serve as means for macro-level evaluation of state controlled education. Most of the indicators seem to be self-evident and in a broader perspective some of them come close to or are identical with measures for wastage, that means for efficiency in schooling, defined by international classification systems of UNESCO and OECD.[30] This is especially the case for the "promotion rate," the "repetition rate" (number of pupils leaving school in grade i during school year t as percentage of pupils in grade i during school year t) although it could easily be calculated on the basis of the "consolidation rate" and the "rate of students who moved during the school year" (actually the number of students who changed location due to various reasons).

Finally, three indicators which are not in use internationally need further explanation: First, the "qualification rate" takes those students into account who pass final examinations in a particular grade or who reach a defined educational standard as measured through continuous assessment (class work and class tests) by the end of a grade.

Second, the rates for "outstanding" and "qualified" students measure the percentage of students by achievement scores. This is based on a scale ranging from more than ninety percent of possible achievement scores in the case of "outstanding" students to less than sixty percent for those who are "unqualified." In total the list of indicators represents a composite index which is more related to measurement of quality than efficiency in schooling and as a rule is enlarged by a more general assessment of "how the schools' leadership put relevant Party documents and guidelines into effect,"[32] whatever that means in reality.

In contrast to these quality-oriented measurements, we find a number of additional indicators in the field of education which are more related to efficiency than to quality and mostly form so-called "utilization rates" (liyong xiaolü). Taking into account what has been said on methodological problems before, we discovered a number of indicators which seem to be in use in virtually all Chinese regions:

(1)   So far as the financial aspect is concerned, as an overall indicator the "utilization rate of educational resources" (jiaoyu ziyuan liyong xiaolü) has been defined as the relationship between "the total result of schooling (or training) in a particular year and the total consumption of educational resources in the relevant period." In this relationship the "result" is measured in terms of students in the school year and the "consumption" in terms of the total amount of monetary expenses, a classical efficiency-oriented measurement.[34]

(2)   So far as the manpower aspect is concerned a utilization rate for measuring the teachers' usage has been defined (total number of teachers needed in relation to the total number of teachers present in the unit) and an overall utilization rate for manpower resources at school, including teachers, staff, and workers. In that case two forms are in existence: either the relationship between the total number of students and the total number of teachers, staff, and workers or between students and full-time teachers only.[34] Normally this kind of indicator is known as the teacher-student ratio and is used for cross-national comparisons.

As a whole the indicators mentioned so far stress the productive function of schooling, mainly the quantitative aspect of the outcome of schooling.[35] More difficult seems to be to estimate the socialization function, the process of generating outlook (orientation) and behavior. Although the "qualification rate" and the rates of "qualified" and "unqualified" students comprise a grading of the effectiveness of political instruction and may take individual behavior at school into account, there is virtually no operational definition for measuring the socialization function of schooling accurately. This is by no means a unique or surprising fact because the situation is common to other socialist and capitalist countries as well.[36] The result is, in both developed and developing countries, that measurement of quality or efficiency is strongly biased in terms of technical input-output indicators as we put them together already. In China this process has been reinforced since 1978 by the growing inflow of research literature from the West, mainly from the United States. This intensified international exchange in education and science has been paralleled by the gradually evolving new discipline of educational economics *(jiaoyu jingji)*. Especially the issue of adequate finance in the field of education was brought to the fore by scholars in the new field. In December of 1979 the first article on educational economics appeared in the leadng journal *Jiaoyu yanjiu* (Educational Research), in September of 1980 the Central Institute of Educational Research in Beijing organized a conference on the state of the art, and in November of 1981 the first national conference on educational economics was held. The publication of books on the new discipline made tremendous progress during these years, covering general introductions, text books, as well as more theoretical works.[37] All these developments were finally strengthened in the wake of relations between the Chinese government and the World Bank within the first university development program. Negotiations between the Chinese government and World Bank staff resulted in a gradual introduction (and internal discussion) of further indicators for efficiency which in future could become accepted by the Chinese because of the existence of the already mentioned general sensitivity to that problem.

The World Bank University Development Project and Implications for Discussions of Efficiency in Education

China was recognized as a developing country by the OECD in 1979 and assumed its membership in the World Bank in May of 1980. Subsequently preparatory meetings for a higher education development project supported by the World Bank took place in the summer and fall of 1980. These culminated in the agreement on the project by the Chinese government on November 4, 1981. The project, called "Chinese University Development Project I" (CUDP), involved a total credit volume of U.S. $200 million, and was expected to support the first phase of the government's program to strengthen higher education by helping to increase the output and quality of education and research in science and engineering.[38]

Three broad objectives were to be achieved by the new project:

> First, . . . to increase the number of graduates and the volume of research at twenty-six universities selected by the government by improving utilization of staff and space, and by developing graduate programs.
>
> Secondly, . . . to raise the quality of graduates and research at the twenty-six universities by strengthening teaching and research programs, improving staff quality, and modernizing laboratory equipment and facilities.
>
> Finally, the project will strengthen the management of universities through

Table 13.1
Measuring School Quality: Indicators Used in the People's Republic of China

	INDICATOR	DEFINITION	
1.	Consolidation Rate *(gonggu lü)*	$\dfrac{\text{number of students at the end of school year}}{\text{number of students at the beginning of school year}}$	X 100
2.	Promotion Rate *(shengxue lü)*	$\dfrac{\text{number of graduates admitted to the next grade}}{\text{number of graduates}}$	X 100
3.	Repetition Rate *(liuji lü)*	$\dfrac{\text{number of repeaters during school year}}{\text{number of students at the end of school year}}$	X 100
4.	Rate of Students' Mobility *(liusheng lü)*	$\dfrac{\text{number of students who moved during school year}}{\text{number of students at the beginning of school year}}$	X 100
5.	Qualification Rate *(hege lü)*	$\dfrac{\text{number of graduates with academic standards in accordance with regulations}}{\text{number of planned graduates}}$	X 100

6.	Rate of Unqualified Students (*chasheng lü*)	$\dfrac{\text{number of unqualified students}}{\text{number of graduates}} \times 100$
7.	Rate of Outstanding Students (*youdengsheng lü*)	$\dfrac{\text{number of outstanding students}}{\text{number of graduates}} \times 100$
8.	Enrollment Rate (*ruxue lü*)	$\dfrac{\text{number of students of school-age admitted to school}}{\text{number of students of school-age}} \times 100$
9.	Universalization Rate (*puji lü*)	$\dfrac{\text{number of students in grade 1 during school year t}}{\text{number of students in respective age-groups}} \times 100$
10.	Rate of Fit to Manpower Needs (*zhuanye duikou lü*)	$\dfrac{\text{number of graduates employed in accordance with training}}{\text{number of graduates}} \times 100$

improved record-keeping and more comprehensive accounting practices. At the Ministry of Education level, it will do the same through developing improved educational statistics, more comprehensive accounting practices, improved monitoring and evaluation capacities, and better preparation for future investments in the education sector.[39]

This long quotation indicates how nicely this program fit into the general level of conceptualization of efficiency in Chinese education around 1980-1981. Table 13.2 reveals in more concrete terms the means intended to achieve the goals mentioned. To operationalize the intended activities the Chinese government was advised to introduce a number of indicators for measuring efficiency which almost certainly were not in use before that time. These indicators were as follows:

(1) "staff utilization";
(2) "space utilization";
(3) "school location planning";
(4) "systematic use of education evaluation" and
(5) "improved collection and utilization of education statistics."

In principle it is not surprising that this list of indicators was introduced by the World Bank to the Chinese government because this is part of the Bank's regular lending policy, part of a so-called "project circle" with the "project" defined as a "discrete package of investments, policies, and institutional and other actions designed to achieve a specific development objective (or set of objectives) within a designated period."[41] So far as the Bank's strategy for development projects in education is concerned, each program to be designed has to take into account the recipient country's economic, social, financial and institutional characteristics. Regardless of what differences exist between developed and developing countries (measured in the World Bank's own terms), the basic assumption underlying the project approach in education is that governments should have five principal objectives

1. "As a first priority, provision of basic education to all children as quickly as resources, both financial and human, permit; and ultimately, development of a comprehensive system of education at all levels and for all age groups.

2. More equitable distribution of educational opportunities and reduction of existing inequalities based on sex, economic status, and geography.

3. Greater internal efficiency of the educational system, through a reduction of the waste of resources caused by students dropping out or repeating grades, and improved quality of education.

4. Greater external efficiency of the educational system, through an increase in the relevance of schooling to the job market, so that students are equipped with the knowledge and skills needed to find employment.

5. Development and maintenance of an institutional capacity to formulate and carry out educational policy and to plan, analyze, manage, and evaluate education and training programs and projects at all levels."[41]

In a more critical way we can turn the argument around and assume that if a country doesn't have these five principle objectives the Bank is likely to make the respective government accept these as a prerequisite to receiving any financial or material assistance in the form of educational projects. Thus, in all cases the government in question will be confronted with a western concept of education and efficiency. China's experience follows the rule.

For analytical reasons, I'll set aside the first, second and fifth points and center the interest on the third and fourth points: internal and external efficiency as it has been viewed by the World Bank. According to the Bank's understanding[43] *internal efficiency* comprises

> the flow of students through the system with a minimum of waste and the quality of learning achieved in the system[43]

while *external efficiency*

> involves relationships between general and vocational education and between schools and work opportunities — what schools and teachers can be expected to do in preparing for future occupations, and what may be expected from a combination of learning in and out of school.[33]

According to this outline *internal efficiency* has two aspects. One is related to a concept of wastage, that is measurement of retention and drop-outs. The second one is related to the quality of learning — the more controversial one. To come up with a certain clarity in defining single issues the Bank suggests distinction among *input, output,* and *outcomes:*

> Input, often the indicator of educational quality, includes factors such as the size of class, qualifications of teachers, material facilities (both software and hardware), and years of schooling.

> Output, in contrast, refers to the learning achieved — knowledge, skills, behavior, and attitudes — whether measured by tests, by diplomas, or in some other way.

> Outcome refers to the external effects of output — that is, the ability of people to be socially and economically productive.[45]

On the other hand *external efficiency* has at least four aspects. First, it is important to satisfy the needs of the economic system for qualified manpower, which is mainly a problem of generating skills (expertise). Second, there is the problem of unemployment and underemployment. Third, there is the problem caused by individuals trying to maximize their stay within the formal education system as long as possible in order to earn the highest degree and find a well paid job in the modern economy. (The problem of the so-called "qualification syndrome" or "diploma disease.") Fourth, there is the problem of moulding work-related behavior or attitudes.[46]

If we put these pieces together, including those ideas of efficiency which are dominating the international scholarly community, we come up with a model of efficiency in education as it is represented in figure 13.1. The model consists of four broad elements, input, the education system as a transforming and interactive societal subsystem, output, and external systems (for example the employment system) which permanently interact with the education system.

Table 13.2
Education in China: Issues, Plans and Programs

Issues		Government Plan (A) Government Program (B)	Comments
I.	Shortage of qualified high-level manpower in industry, agriculture, transportation, construction, administration, research, computer technology, etc.	(A) Expansion and improvement of undergraduate and postgraduate university and college education	The Government's plans/programs would meet an urgent long-term need. Equipment, staff development and improved management are needed. Programs should also include measures to meet short-term needs. Existing spare-time colleges, TV universities, etc. should therefore also be expanded to provide in-service upgrading programs in enterprises and elsewhere.
		(B) 26 universities in a first phase and 43 universities in a second phrase	
II.	Shortage of qualified middle-level technicians in industry, agriculture, transportation, construction, etc.	(A) Significant expansion of vocational/technical secondary/postsecondary education	Execution of the plan would meet urgent needs but should be preceded by a review of vocational/technical education and of the respective roles of the authorities and enterprises. The costs would be very high and programs would probably have to be phased over a longer period than originally anticipated. Serious constraints in staff, equipment and facilities. Both enterprises and formal schools should be used for training.
		(B) Pilot projects. Community Colleges	

III. Quantity and quality of primary and secondary education

(A) Government plan proposes universal primary education and in some respects universal secondary education by 1990. Some qualitative improvement suggested

(B) Projects to improve teacher training (IV), supply secondary schools with laboratories, and expand production of textbooks and education equipment. Pilot projects

It should be fairly easy to reach the quantitative targets in 1990 because of the shape of the population pyramid although the introduction of six years of primary education should be gradual. The Government should take measures to avoid a sharp peak in junior secondary school enrollment in the mid-1980s. Curricula appear outdated and the Government should be advised to review and revise them prior to executing a large program in teacher training, and textbooks and equipment production. The quality of school buildings should be improved.

IV. Teacher quality

(A) The Government proposes programs in preservice and in-service teacher training

(B) Pilot projects, general staff and facility improvements

It is necessary to reduce the high percentage of unqualified teachers in primary and secondary schools. This should primarily be done through in-service programs. Demand for new teachers could be reduced if the Government applied international LDC standards for student/teacher ratios. Teacher training should continue to use TV universities and other "nonformal" programs. Pre-service and in-service teacher training institutions should merge.

(Table 13.2 cont'd.)

V.	Efficiency	No Government plans	The Government should be advised to improve the efficiency and cost effectiveness of education in China through: (a) increased staff utilization; (b) increased space utilization; (c) introduction of school location planning; (d) systematic use of education evaluation; and (e) improved collection and utilization of education statistics.
VI.	Education funding	The Government expects education funding to increase nation-wide during the 1980s (but not necessarily from central government sources)	The Government should be advised that education in China could be expanded and improved without expenditures going beyond the average range for developing countries (measured as a percentage of GNP).

Source: World Bank, *China: Socialist Economic Development*, Vol. III *The Social Sectors. Population, Health, Nutrition, and Education* (Washington, D.C.: The World Bank, 1983), p. 230.

Figure 13.1
A Model of Efficiency in Education

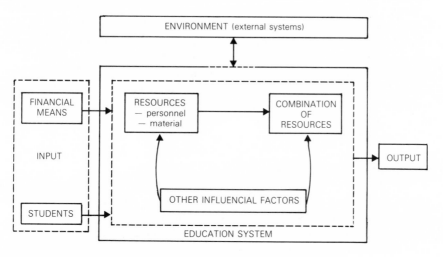

Source: Adapted from Manfred Weiß, Effizienzforschung im Bildungsbereich (Berlin: Duncker and Humblot, 1982), p. 39.

First financial resources and students (pupils) function as input. Second financial resources are transformed into material and personal resources and in combination create certain results, in our case educated (trained) persons at certain costs. In both stages, in supplying material and personnel resources and organizing the combination of both to achieve educational means, there are expenses, capital investment and recurrent expenditure for creating the schooling environment. Both the transformation of financial resources into material and personnel resources, and the combination of resources to achieve educational means may be influenced by a number of "other influencial factors" which may possibly create additional costs. This happens through introducing different modes of instruction, using different sets of textbooks or arranging different class sizes.

The dotted line, embracing "resources," "combination of resources," and "other influencial factors" represents the system of parameters which can be influenced intentionally by state or lower echelon decisions in order to reach a certain amount and quality of output — a number of graduates on all levels of formal and informal education with a defined standard of qualification. The assessment of whether the education system works efficiently or not can then be made on the basis of an evaluation which either takes output in terms of graduates (and their qualification) into account or interprets this outcome as an input to new systems (external non-educational systems) and relates the efficiency of system one to that of another one, say the employment system or the political system.

In the first case the manpower aspect represents the center of interest, in the second it is the aspect of political socialization. (Relationships like these are called outcomes in the World Bank's model.)

Finally, we now know what the Chinese evaluation of quality and efficiency in education looked like at the beginning of the 1980s, and what the World Bank model looks like, which has since influenced the discussion on efficiency in China. The question is, are we able to put a value on both approaches and reach a conclusion as to whether these models are suitable for explaining and measuring efficiency in Chinese education, and reforming the education system towards higher rates of efficiency. In the last section I make a first attempt to deal with this problem, although much research still has to be done.

Conclusion

For a comparison of World Bank indicators of efficiency and those in use in China (see table 13.1) we first have to look closer at those indicators which were proposed to the Chinese government within the first university development program. They are as follows:

1. *Staff utilization:* The general finding of the World Bank's missions to China was that "staff work load, as measured in class contact hours, is low by international standards at all levels of education in China."[47] This finding is in line with genuine Chinese statements in a number of articles and is usually measured in terms of the so-called student-teacher-ratio (relationship), which as an aggregated figure was about four to one in recent years. But it is important to note that this indicator covers several aspects of reality in Chinese higher education institutions. First, it simply describes a numerical relationship between a given number of students and teachers which does not necessarily reflect the actual reality, that the total number of teaching staff is far from being the exact figure for those persons actually doing teaching work. According to various sources, only a part of them have a regular teaching load, between 6 and 12 hours per week, while the rest have been characterized as "members of the faculty who are (a) unqualified to teach (especially the young faculty trained during the Cultural Revolution); (b) unable to teach (usually because they are too old); and (c) unwilling to teach (because they only do research)."[48] Any indicator which is not adjusted to this particular Chinese situation can't be characterized as a valid measure.

2. *Space utilization:* This indicator was clearly in use in China before the World Bank proposed to use it.[49] But the new idea behind the World Bank's expectation is that, especially in higher education institutions, laboratories and classrooms are underutilized (for example because the total number of students is small in relation to the total amount of space or because the time arrangements for using the facilities lag behind what would be possible if a more rational approach to

planning were used). Space standards, differentiated according to natural, engineering and social sciences should be lowered to be in line with internationally comparable values.

3. *School location planning:* So far as we can see this kind of measuring the rate of return for a particular investment in education — dominantly in higher education — in particular regions is a new concept for the Chinese administration. Clearly, the danger underlying this concept is that of giving justification for capital investments into higher education institutions only into those regions where the medium and long-term returns are most likely to have maximum results. This would result in creating disadvantages for underdeveloped regions and advantages for already developed areas in China.

4. *Systematic use of education evaluation:* If any culture, then the Chinese could be classified as the one with the longest tradition of testing and grading learning achievements, in order to relate a definite achievement to a definite social position or chance to receive this position. A more systematic use and discussion of educational evaluation, taking into account western concepts of testing, surely would be one of the greatest results within educational reform. Yet permanent complaints by parents and students over too heavy work loads in preparing for all kinds of examinations on all levels of education are already common in the Chinese media and are part of the examination tradition of China. The World Bank concept of efficiency is almost certain to exacerbate this situation.

5. *Improved collection and utilization of education statistics:* There can be no doubt about the fact that the confrontation of Chinese cadres and scholars with the requirements of the World Bank ''project-circle'' led to activities on the level of information and documentation — first of all at the Ministry of Education and State Education Commission level — which caused a number of changes in contrast to the period of the Cultural Revolution and for the most part, in contrast to the situation before 1966, also:

• The statistical reporting system was improved and in general more data have been published than ever before.[50]

• A more differentiated set of data in education as well as in other areas of society became available (especially comprising more regional data).[52]

Parallel to these developments and parallel to the growing influence of the discipline, the ''economics of education,'' since 1980-82, the Ministry of Education supported research in the field of systems engineering, combining several attempts to rationalize state manpower planning procedures.[54] In the wake of this support new projects were started by a number of prestigious research institutes and universities to come up with long-term forecasting models in the field of manpower requirements.

Based on the assumption common in western countries during the 1960s that manpower forecasting is necessary, that results can be achieved by mathematical operations which describe future constellations correctly, and that measures can be put into effect to link output in the education system and required input in the employment system, a lot of research has been done since 1982. To be critical, however, the amount of research intended to solve the long existing mis-match between education and the employment system is by no means an indicator of progress. The reason for the failure in supplying the right number of graduates qualified for their job in a particular region is not necessarily reflected in the indicators which form the basis for scientific forecasting. Inter-ministerial, inter-regional and inter-university competition for graduates form the most important retarding elements to a more rational job assignment system, and the danger is that reform activities only cover the technical field of forecasting, not the level of structural reforms needed to cope with these inter-administrative imbalances.

Summarizing what we have said so far, the question of how to judge recent developments in measuring quality and efficiency in Chinese education under the influence of China/World Bank relations has no simple answer. There are certainly signs of an awareness that something is wrong in Chinese education, that this can be measured by certain indicators. This does not mean however, that anything will happen in reality to change the situation! An ongoing discussion of methodological aspects could become a means of broadening genuine Chinese horizons in methodology without involving the uncritical acceptance of what is "important" from abroad. However, the acceptance of technical indicators as a way of measuring efficiency in education may prevent the leadership from going into action to reform the traditional structures which cause inefficiency. Rather, new forms of measurement should be used because traditional concepts of quality led to the traditional ranking of educational institutions which benefited more or less developed units in developed areas. For example universities like Beida, Bei Shida or Qinghua receive more money, have more opportunity to organize reform, are more attractive to students and teachers, but are not necessarily efficient. A smaller university in a less developed area may, in reality, be even more efficient, given its disadvantage in terms of material and personnel facilities. Yet it will not attract the bureaucracy because the "quality" is not high enough.

Finally, one important point remains to be made. Efficiency concepts like the one from the World Bank simply become an important argument in the factional competition over how to improve China's education system. At the moment the group close to Deng Xiaoping tends to profit most from the international argument in their activities to reform the system. However, this situation may change in future reform activities.

14

Past and Present
in China's Educational Relations
with the Industrialized World

Ruth Hayhoe

Servitude or Liberation?

The research question which inspired this volume carries with it the implication that educational ideas and patterns borrowed from abroad could be of primary importance in either a "liberation" from perceived bondage, such as the stranglehold of tradition, or a "servitude" to dominant external interests. Retrospectively, almost every chapter has brought out the primary importance of internal social, political and economic developments and the secondary role of borrowed educational ideas and patterns applied within particular internal conditions. Marianne Bastid's opening chapter lays the groundwork for this understanding, in the broad historical demonstration she gives of the way in which the Chinese consciously borrowed particular sets of patterns and ideas from nations whose political and economic involvement in China as often succeeded as preceded these educational inputs. She also suggests cycles relating to internal conditions within Chinese society in the way in which foreign patterns were utilized — for the purpose of unification and mobilization in the case of the Japanese patterns in the last years of the Qing dynasty, and of Soviet patterns in the early years after the Communist Liberation, and in a more eclective and critical way in the adaptation of European and American patterns under the Nationalist government and once again in the post-1978 period. Other chapters have filled out this picture with details of China's educational relations with each of the major industrialized powers.

In this final chapter I'd like to pursue the internal theme first, using some tools of reflection drawn from German sociology. Then I review China's historical experience with foreign educational influences from the evaluative perspective of Habermas' idea of communicative action. Finally I turn to the approaches to educational transfer being taken by OECD nations in the contemporary period. In spite of the dramatic changes — political, economic and social — on both sides, certain cultural continuities remain as a link between historical and contemporary educational interaction. These may offer valuable clues for anticipating the future of educational cooperation between China and the industrialized world.

The Rationalization of the State

In chapter 2, Isabelle Llasera considered the first great period of educational transfer between China and the West, the seventeenth and eighteenth centuries. The Jesuits offered to European thinkers a utopian depiction of a modern state based on reason rather than religion and ruled by moral philosophers who were selected according to merit and suffused with a deep knowledge of classical precepts. As both the greatest of the scholars and the hereditary ruler, the Chinese Emperor commanded from the Jesuits a loyalty equal to that they accorded to the French King. Their need to defend this loyalty to an alien ruler and justify the aspects of Confucian practice which they had integrated within their missionary endeavors led them to offer voluminous descriptions of the Chinese empire in European languages. Their urge to make known the superiority of the Chinese social and educational system was also rooted in the central currents of Enlightenment thought — the search for a reasoned, philosophical basis for the modern state that would replace an arbitrary religious legitimation of imperial authority. To this search for a state based on pure reason and governable through universally recognized principles of justice and morality the Jesuits provided an answer. They had discovered that it actually existed "on the other side of the world." Furthermore, a state education system was an integral part of it.

Clearly their intellectual formation as educators within a Europe that was seeking to "rationalize" state and society shaped their observation of China, both the utopia they depicted and the features they screened out of that picture — the religious complexities of Chinese society, the diversity of Chinese philosophical traditions and the range of educational institutions which provided the real educational opportunities outside of the civil service examinations. How far their persuasively drawn utopia actually contributed to the "rationalization" of European society is difficult to estimate. It was only one current among many. Yet convincing evidence of one aspect of institutional transfer has been amassed: the introduction of competitive written examinations within European higher education and as a means of entrance to the civil service. This measure, intended to ensure a leadership selected on the basis of merit, was adopted in many European nations in the eighteenth and nineteenth centuries.[1]

The process of "rationalization" that started in the European Enlightenment has been identified by Max Weber as a definitive axis of social change in the emergence of modern capitalism. In his broad sweep of historical sociology,[2] Weber traces the gradual victory of *Zweckrationalität* — purposive-instrumental rationality — in every sphere of life, resulting in a definitive separation of the spheres of science, morality and art. Scientific creativity made possible a technology increasingly enhancing the forces of production. The separation of law from morality and the emergence of a non-personal and fully calculable system of rational law provided the social and economic conditions necessary for capitalist development. This was complemented by urbanization and the erosion of the sib-relations that had formed the particularistic ties of traditional society. Parsons' pattern variables of modernity — achievement, neutral affectivity, specificity and universalism — sum up the final results of the rationalization process depicted by Weber.[3] Economic and administrative efficiency, the formalization and universalization of law and a disenchantment with all illusion and self-deception came to be seen by Weber as an "iron cage of modernity," from which there was no escape for modern man. Ironically, the ethos which had been the driving force of this process was the other-worldly and ascetic Protestant spirit, which battled with the forces of nature to subjugate them and accumulate, in a rational and disciplined way, the capital that was the vital moving force of early capitalist development.[4] Once the rationalization process was underway, Weber saw it as likely to be even more all-embracing under state socialism than under state capitalism.

After identifying the Protestant ethic as the catalyst of a historical development which did not emerge spontaneously in any other society, Weber proceeded to a series of comparative studies including China, where the Jesuit literature had pointed to principles of a rational state developed at an earlier stage than in European society. Weber identified three major obstacles to spontaneous capitalist development in China: the persistence of sib-relations, which led Parsons to categorize China as a particularistic-achievement oriented society, the failure to develop a calculable and impersonal legal system separate from morality, and an ethos of "radical world optimism" on the part of Chinese scholar-officials which contrasts strongly with the Puritan's adversarial relation to the natural world. Many of the necessary pre-requisites for capitalism were present in Chinese society, including a sound fiscal system and an enlightened economic policy, yet a lack of the economic mentality of capitalism on the part of the scholar-official class also helped to stifle capitalist development.[5] To a degree, these areas of resistance to full "rationalization" within Weber's occidentally-shaped definition persisted after the 1911 revolution and even after the Communist revolution of 1949. The Communist regime may have finally broken the stranglehold of sib-relations, replacing them with affective norms of Communist comradeship, but it did not fully disengage law from morality. To this day the creation of a legal system that is calculable in economic terms remains problematic. In 1966 China's Cultural Revolution saw a strong revival of moral fervor and a moral-political determination to smash the de-humanized iron cage of a modern system modelled after Soviet state socialism.

The conjunction of the victory of Maoism in post-revolution China and a European awakening to the relentless advance of the rationalization process led to the phenomena which Roland Depierre has depicted in chapter 11. Philosophers of the Frankfurt school drew on Weber to develop a powerful critique of the one dimensional man emerging from the totalization of purposive-instrumental reason which had taken place.[6] Marcuse's view of the dilemma of modernity has been summarized in this way: "Productivity and prosperity in league with a technology in the service of monopolistic politics seem to mesmerize advancing industrial society in its established structure."[7] The solution he expected was the eruption of a psychic rebellion, encouraged by the one sphere which retained some freedom, the sphere of art. Art was to recreate reason along lines of justice, freedom and happiness. The rationalization of the state which had appeared to Enlightenment thinkers as the road to freedom had culminated in the iron cage. This was now to give way before a new definition of reason, one that embodied passion and morality rather than neutral affectivity and impersonal law. Once again, as in the seventeenth century, this utopian vision was discovered to exist " on the other side of the world" in the successful rebellion of Maoist China against the chains of socialist bureaucracy.

The progressive dismantling of the Maoist vision and the revelations that have been made about the cruelty and anarchic destruction of that period of Chinese history have coincided with the taming of western radicalism and its channeling into more pacific, institutionalized forms such as as those of the green movement and the peace movement. Yet the search for an escape from Weber's "iron cage of modernity" has not been abandoned. Probably one of its most serious proponents is the German social philosopher Jürgen Habermas. Nurtured in the school of Critical Theory, Habermas has moved beyond the hopes for an new concept of reason emerging from art and aesthetics to a thorough study of the whole project of modernity.

Habermas rejects Weber's conviction about the inevitability of the gradual victory of purposive-instrumental rationality. He seems to be seeking for a new reconciliation among the kinds of reason informing science, morality and art.[8] While the critical theorists regarded legal-moral rationality as the superstructural expression of the capitalist economic and administrative basis, Habermas sees hope in this sphere for the reassertion of human values in a process he describes as "communicative action." Capitalism may have historically been characterized by the absorption of law into the purposive-instrumental rationality of science, and totalitarianism by its absorption into morality, but Habermas sees hope for a middle way between these two. He identifies a cultural "life-world" which remains a source of moral values reflecting universal aspirations of the human spirit. Unconstrained mutual discussion among human persons seeking truth and justice is the necessary condition for the reproduction of this life world. This process of human sharing is what Habermas seems to mean by "communicative action."

Emancipation, for Habermas, is not the overthrow of the whole superstructure of modern capitalism in favor of the "general will" of the proletariat, but a state of society in which the reproduction of the cultural life-world is brought about by the communicative and interpretative action of individuals. This in turn calls for new social and political institutions which would represent "the normative anchoring of the system in the life-world." These institutions "would protect the communicative structures of the life-world themselves and serve a rational and democratic control of the system by the life-world."[9]

To return to China, it was precisely the lack of social and political institutions which could embody the radical values of egalitarianism and participation during the Cultural Revolution period that led to the anarchic and destructive outcomes which are now being revealed. One of the strongest thrusts of the post-1978 leadership has been towards the strengthening of legal and political institutions which will protect the individual and make possible a measured participation in political life through the press, the election of representatives to Local People's Congresses and the revitalization of the law courts. However, legality remains closely integrated with morality and aspects of the affective and particular in social relations remain strong. The important question now is how the massive inflow of scientific and technical knowledge from the industrialized world will affect this situation.

In chapter 13 Jürgen Henze shows how the concept of "efficiency," emanating from the World Bank, has found its way to the heart of contemporary educational policy-making in China. The calculability of economic inputs and outputs this entails is very different from the sweeping moral-visionary statements that have characterized Chinese policy in the past. For example, neither Nationalists nor Communists hesitated to make the universalization of primary education public policy, but this did not entail the detailed computation of the resources necessary for implementation and the expected economic benefits. It is this calculability that is now appearing for the first time in such policy documents as the recent educational reform document.

Parallel to this strengthening of purposive-instrumental rationality and its pervasive influence through the practices of "scientific management" being introduced at all levels of the economy and society, there has been a series of eruptions against "spiritual pollution" and assertions of the importance of moral-political values which might be seen in Habermas' terms as emanating from a cultural life-world that has remained more interactive in the context of Chinese tradition and Chinese socialism than under western capitalism. This life-world may now be in danger of colonization through the rapid inflow of scientific knowledge in all areas from the industrialized world.

Before examining contemporary forms of knowledge transfer from OECD countries, I turn now to a retrospective look at China's past experience of educational interaction with the industrialized world. Parallels between the past and present may shed light on future possibilities and problems.

Communicative Action: Historical Reflections

A few further points on the theory of communicative action may be helpful as a background for reflection on China's historical experience of educational interaction with industrialized countries. Habermas suggests that the classical distinction between economic base and cultural-political superstructure should be replaced in advanced capitalist societies by the categories of "work" (purposive-instrumental action initiated in the economic system and colonizing the political and social system) and "communicative action" (the forms of interaction which characterize the cultural life-world of human society). "Communicative action" is not merely the superstructural reflection of "work," as Weber and the critical theorists would have it, but is capable of engendering social values that express a human control over "work" and shape its future direction. It is thus a new kind of rationalization, a process of reaching consensus through a discussion free from domination, which offers some hope for the project of modernity.[10]

This perspective on the industrialized world points to a central question of interest in looking back on China's historical experience. How far was the transfer of educational patterns and ideas grounded in the realm of communicative action, making possible the mutuality of an in-depth shared exploration of social and cultural values? Or how far was it characterized by knowledge orientations which may have served the domination of external political-economic interests?

The German case, discussed by Francoise Kreissler in chapter 4, may be an interesting one to start from since here technical education was unequivocally chosen as the most appropriate contribution German official circles could make to Chinese development, a decision strongly supported by German industrial interests. Nevertheless, the involvement of a distinguished German sinologist, Otto Franke, a person who clearly had a deep respect for Chinese culture and Chinese autonomy, ensured that the technical colleges were managed jointly by Chinese and German leaders from their inception, giving them a high level of acceptability with the Chinese public even in the years when China was at war with Germany. They were regarded not merely as channels of advanced German technical expertise but as centers of cultural cooperation with ancillary curricular and extra-curricular activities which promoted a mutuality of cultural understanding. Germany's very political defeat and humiliation may have been a factor in the strong Chinese support given to Tongji. This enabled it to survive all the vicissitudes of war and revolution and re-emerge as a center of cultural and scientific cooperation between China and West Germany in 1978.

The British case, depicted by Delia Davin in chapter 3, could hardly be more different from the German one. The domination of British political and economic activities was already established in the nineteenth century and persisted into the twenties and thirties of this century. Nevertheless, consistent with their colonial policy elsewhere,[11] the British did not seek to impose British educational patterns as a means of consolidating politico-economic domination. Rather they saw strong "native" institutions as more appropriate to their interests. In the context of this lack of official intervention, missionaries found scope for the widespread diffusion of both Christian and general knowledge, especially scientific knowledge. The relations of John Fryer and Timothy Richard with both progressive Chinese intellectuals and Chinese officialdom opened up channels of communication that made possible some Chinese understanding of the roots of British commercial strength and political institutions. The fact that no Oxbridge was ever established on Chinese soil and that Shanxi University, established through British Boxer Indemnity funds, could so quickly become absorbed within the modern Chinese higher education system indicates a certain British affinity for diffusing key ideas in the cultural realm without using them for political or economic purposes. Possibly it was the unchallenged nature of British superiority at this time that made it possible. In any case, apologists for British educational ideas right up to the twenties and thirties seemed genuinely eager to promote communicative action rather than imposing knowledge patterns that would serve the purposes of domination.

The French case provides a significant contrast. The French colonial policy of assimilation is reflected in the Chinese context in the paradox of a self-consciously secular state offering strong support to French Catholic missionaries in their educational efforts in China. Zhendan's law faculty clearly supported the French political demand that the unequal treaties could only be dealt with when China had a "rational" modern legal system in place, while engineering and commercial education at both Zhendan and the Ecole in Tianjin favored French economic interests in China. The authoritarian administrative control of the Jesuits over these institutions left little room for reaching a consensus through discussion free from domination. While the Sino-French Education Society did provide a context for unconstrained cultural and social interaction, it received minimal French official support. The work of the university in Beijing, the two institutes at Lyons and Charleroi and the journal made possible some communicative action, yet it never counterbalanced the stronger role of French Catholic education in China. The French failure to provide a reasonable amount of support through the promised Boxer Indemnity funds was just one more disappointment for an institution never whole-heartedly supported from the French side.

In the American case, a similar though less pronounced dichotomy of interests can be seen. Here it was the missionaries who provided conditions for communicative action while Dewey, for all his progressive democratic inclinations in the American context, seems to have identified closely with American political interests in his Chinese role. This is the picture that emerges from Hubert Brown's discussion of American progressivism in chapter 7. Of all the industrialized nations, the United States was most outspoken about the promotion of these political interests through educational activity. It was the first to remit Boxer Indemnity funds for the express purpose of providing for the education of a young generation of Chinese leaders who would be sympathetic towards American values and culture. Qinghua School, subsequently University, played a progressive role in many ways, yet moved more and more towards a technocratic contribution in the war years and was viewed in periods of intense Chinese nationalist sentiment as a tool of American cultural imperialism.[12] The 16 missionary colleges were certainly not exempt from such allegations either, yet the kinds of knowledge they promoted and the organization of their curriculum and student life was surprisingly supportive of Chinese progressive and even revolutionary aspirations.[13] The contrast with French missionary institutions is striking.

In the Canadian case, analyzed by Karen Minden, neither political nor economic interests were developed to a degree that affected missionary involvement. It was a pure case of cultural interaction in which Canadian missionaries consciously chose or were relegated to the great hinterland where the need for leadership in creating modern educational institutions was almost unlimited. Seeing their task as "the multiplication of themselves," the missionaries sought to educate a medical elite who could take responsibility for medical education and the diffusion of medical knowledge over a vast area. Neither political domination nor economic benefit seemed to be a part of this situation, but simply a humanitarian effort to channel applied knowledge which would better the lives of the people in a general context where Canadian churches were seen as entrusted with China's spiritual and physical welfare. Nevertheless, the missionaries came up against the increasing assertion of a Chinese approach to developing modern medical and educational systems, as Minden has shown.

Finally, the Japanese and Soviet cases are rather special in this historical discussion of the cultural policy of industrialized nations towards China. Both participated in a situation where the ruling ideology was shared, Confucianism in the late Qing and Marxism-Leninism in the fifties. In chapter 3 Hiroshi Abe has detailed in a most interesting way the process whereby China borrowed its first modern education system from Japan and the role played by Japanese teachers in China and those institutions in Japan which formed a new generation of Chinese teachers. On the Japanese side, there was a consciousness of the opportunity to extend their cultural influence and expand their power, also a sense of the possibility of a joint eastern resistance to western incursions. This view no doubt satisfied both Japanese officials and a Chinese regime that saw Japanese cultural penetration as less threatening than any other. Yet it is fascinating to notice that the majority of Chinese students in Japan studied in private institutions. There, exposure to officially approved ideology was by no means assured and considerable revolutionary thought and action was initiated. With the success of the 1911 Revolution and the growing Chinese awareness of Japan's economic ambitions, the Japanese model fell into disfavor. Its harmony with Confucian presuppositions meant that it had always been more of a facade covering persisting Confucian educational patterns than a genuine instrument of rapid educational transformation. Even with shared cultural traditions, and officially approved collaboration, communicative action was not easily realized in face of China's internal instability and Japan's economic and political ambitions.

The cooperation between China and the Soviet Union within a shared commitment to a socialist modernization guided by Marxist-Leninist thought should have been the ideal situation for forms of educational cooperation that could embody genuine communicative action. The Soviet Union had won China's trust by its unilateral relinquishing of some Chinese territory in the wake of the 1917 Revolution, and by 1949 China had finally achieved the stable and unified political conditions necessary to build socialism. Nevertheless, both Price and Orleans have shown in different ways the patterns of cultural domination established by Soviet experts and the Soviet inability to comprehend a Chinese need to assert its own approach to education. Now that China has moved away from the position of a neophyte following the correct road laid out in advance by Soviet post-revolutionary experience, and joined in eclectic educational relations with a wide variety of industrialized nations, a new set of relations seems to be emerging with the Soviet Union. These are characterized by a more balanced and critical Chinese understanding of Soviet experience and a more cautious and tenuous approach on the part of the Soviet Union. That is the picture that emerges from the details of revived Sino-Soviet cultural and educational relations given in the final sections of chapters 9 and 10. However, these are likely to remain of minor significance in comparison to China's educational relations with Japan and western industrialized countries in the near future.

Penetration or Mutuality? Contemporary Educational Interrelations

Clearly educational transfer was used to consolidate external political or economic domination in some periods of Chinese history, yet this did not characterize the broad experience of foreign educational influence in any consistent way. If transferred educational patterns were perceived as emblems of servitude in certain periods and situations, in others they were effective instruments for a liberation from tradition and for the mobilization of society towards economic or political modernity. The determining factor in all cases was the internal conditions of China, the strength and vision of the political leadership, and their ability to implement effective economic and cultural policies.

China's contemporary leadership has a wide-ranging national and international vision and has set China on a clearly defined course of modernization, as indicated in Huang Shiqi's depiction of contemporary policy on the open door in chapter 12. In this situation, perhaps more than ever before, the effects of external educational and cultural transfers will be peripheral to a social change process set in motion from within. They are, nevertheless, significant. A whole new generation of potential leaders is being educated in the advanced capitalist world, with the United States, Japan, Germany, Britain, Canada and France hosting more than 85 percent. Furthermore, various forms of educational cooperation on Chinese soil bring to mind some of the features of Chinese educational history which have been reviewed in this book. Tongji University, once again the center of Sino-German educational cooperation, is the most striking case of cultural continuity through a century of dramatic political-economic change.

The most far-reaching case of contemporary educational influence is that of the World Bank, whose eight projects, involving nearly a billion American dollars in loans, have been detailed in chapter 12. The evident American orientation of recent higher education reform noted in chapter 10 is one system-wide effect of World Bank involvement. While there may be genuine altruism in aspects of World Bank development activities, there can be little doubt about an economic penetration intended to stimulate China's greater participation in the international capitalist community, as well as a political concern for the maintenance of power balances favorable to OECD countries.

Chinese trade has a relatively minor role in the external trading interests of most OECD countries, yet there is a perceived potential for growth here that is rare elsewhere. Japan has dominated China's market, providing 35% of her imports in 1985, followed by the European Economic Community with 14.6% and the United States with 11.9%. From imports of U.S. $9.5 billion in 1978, China reached a volume of $42.3 billion in 1985.[14] The economic opportunities are thus by no means negligible.

This brings us to the question of what kind of view OECD nations have of China's future role in the global community. Do they wish to see a China that conforms to the present international status quo and that should therefore be penetrated by educational values and patterns that will bring about this conformity? Or are they prepared for the risks of a China that might bring something fresh and original to the global community and play a transformative role within global politics?[15] Policies of educational exchange and cooperation characterized by mutuality and making possible communicative action would be appropriate to the latter conception. The transfer of knowledge intended to strengthen purposive-instrumental rationality might be balanced by policies that make visible the cultural, social and philosophical underpinnings of technique in each nation. Provision could be made for dialogue between the cultural life-worlds on both sides as well as the transfer of instrumentally useful social and scientific technology.

The cultural and educational policies of industrialized nations towards China are derived from two sources. One is the constellation of political and economic goals which are consciously taken into account in the shaping of national cultural policy. The second is educational history and cultural tradition, a less conscious yet important shaping force. It makes for significant differences of approach among nations broadly similar in their political-economic goals. It is here too that historical parallels are most likely.

In this final half of the chapter I will briefly outline the contemporary educational policies of each nation, leaving the reader to make judgements on the questions that have been raised: How far do these policies hold promise for servitude or liberation? To what extent do they promote China's conformity to the status quo or open up possibilities of a transformative role?

Sino-American Educational Relations

As the nation whose educational and cultural involvement in China is the most extensive, at least in terms of participating numbers, American policies deserve close consideration. The first point that is unmistakably clear is the preponderance of political over economic motivation in American efforts to encourage China's re-integration into the global capitalist community. In an interesting parallel to the aims behind the establishment of Qinghua School in 1908, the Americans have been very open about their intention of providing educational opportunities for a young generation of Chinese whose future leadership role should ensure a China favorable to American political interests.[16] While making this general policy, the American federal government has been in the fortunate position of needing to provide very little financial subvention for the enterprise of educating Chinese students in American universities. The entrepreneurial skills of American university leaders and the diverse funding sources accessible to them, combined with a strong predilection on the Chinese side for sending their scholars and students to the United States, has meant that about 19,000 Chinese had already gone to the United States by the end of 1983. One third to one half were funded by Chinese government sources, 40% gained full or partial support from American universities, and only a handful received federal support in Fullbright scholarships.[17]

American federal funding is directed towards support for the American Sinological community and the provision of wide-ranging opportunities for American scholars at all levels to do research in China, also many projects of cooperative research in the natural and social sciences.[18] A perceived Chinese emphasis on the natural sciences, particularly applied fields, has been countered by American efforts to promote the social sciences, such as the Ford Foundation support for law, economics and international relations, which has been discussed in chapter 12. Generally American cultural and educational policy towards China has been characterized by a balance in the benefits accrued to both sides, a remarkable involvement of the American Sinological community as well as scholars in the natural and social sciences, and strong support for centers of American studies within the Chinese higher educational system.[19] This should make possible some mutuality and real opportunities for communicative action. However, parallel to it is an enormous strengthening of American intelligence about China, in both the broad and narrower senses of the word, and an undiscriminating popular Chinese fascination with all things American that may not be as conducive to mutuality.[20]

The contrast between official and individual involvement, which was noted historically in the different roles played by Qinghua and Dewey on the one hand and by the missionary colleges on the other, has an interesting parallel in the present situation. The National Center for Industrial Sciences and Technology Management Development, established through a protocol between the United States Department of Commerce and the Chinese State Economic Commission (SEC) and situated on the campus of Dalian Institute of Technology, is an interesting example of official collaboration in a cooperative institution on Chinese soil. It is providing a channel for the latest in American management theory and technology to be introduced to China and diffused throughout the whole political-economic system through the managers at senior, middle and junior levels who participate in training programs. One of its great successes has been the way in which it has cut through the rigid sectoral lines separating Chinese management and created a community of those sharing exposure to American techniques.[21] Another success has been the rapid promotion achieved by its graduates, including the accession of one of them to the headship of the Communist Youth League and subsequently to an even more responsible role within the Communist Party as head of the Central Committee's general office.[22] One American academic participating in the project even went so far as to claim that through this channel Americans have been able to contribute to Chinese policy making at the highest level, giving support to Deng's pragmatic policies.[23] The other side of this success is a strongly felt Chinese concern at the lack of an ongoing theoretical research base for this American project and the failure to create a strong and independent Chinese faculty.[24]Both political and economic penetration are clearly central to this American official effort and the Chinese are aware of both the perils and benefits involved.

On the other end of the spectrum, the burgeoning cooperative relations developing between Chinese and American universities, including a hundred or more institutions on each side, gain little official support yet are making possible a wide range of cooperative activities which may be more conducive to mutuality than official efforts. Perhaps the most interesting and ambitious effort at creating a milieu characterized by discussion free from domination is the cultural center jointly established by John Hopkins and Nanjing universities on the Nanjing campus. It provides a post-Master's program for 50 Chinese and 50 American students each year in the fields of international relations, history, politics, economics and society, and also facilitates joint research in all of these areas.[25]

Sino-Japanese Educational Relations

Next to the United States, Japan has hosted the largest number of Chinese scholars and students in recent years, a total of 3,847 by the end of 1984, with most sent under Chinese government auspices and a certain percentage supported from the Japanese side. These exchanges are organized under a general cultural agreement between the two nations, first signed in 1979, and subsequent memoranda on cooperation in the natural and social sciences. From the Japanese side, support has risen from provision for 175 scholars per year in 1983 to 225 in 1984 and a promised 500 per year by 1989.[26] The official nature of these exchanges has resulted in a situation which provides an interesting contrast to that depicted by Hiroshi Abe in the early part of the century. In 1907, 366 Chinese students of the total of 6,797 were in government institutions and the rest in private ones. In 1983 the situation was precisely opposite, with 942 out of a total of 1,038 scholars and students in national-level government institutions such as Tokyo University, and a tiny minority in local and private institutions.[27] This is likely to ensure the dominant influence of establishment ideology on Chinese scholars and students in contrast to the situation under the late Qing.

An officially funded linkage between Tokyo University and the Chinese University of Science and Technology (CUST) in Hefei has made this institution a center for cooperation with Japan in the engineering sciences and in management.[28] About 20 Japanese professors spend some time in lecturing and doing cooperative research at CUST each year and 10 Chinese faculty spend periods of time at Tokyo University. This provides an exemplar on Chinese soil of the inter-relation between science, engineering and management as expressed in Japanese intellectual life. Another Japanese official effort in the educational field has been the sending of teachers of the Japanese language and general scientific and cultural subjects for two Chinese schools preparing students for going to Japan, one at the Dalian Institute of Foreign Languages and the other at Dongbei Teachers University in Changchun. A further project which envisages a wide diffusion of understanding about Japanese culture in China is a program to educate Chinese teachers of

Japanese by providing them an intensive one-year course taught by Japanese teachers followed by a one-month period in Japan itself. Between 1980 and 1985, the Japanese government offered this program to 120 Chinese teachers each year, a total of 600 over five years.[29]

A second quite distinct level of cooperation which has so far not developed in the Sino-American context to any degree is that of technical education. Japan initiated this sort of cooperation at an early stage through the Japan International Cooperation Agency (JICA). Between 1978 and 1984, 977 Chinese trainees were invited to Japan and placed mainly in government offices in the areas of planning and administration, public works, agriculture and forestry, mining and construction, energy, tourism and commerce, health and medicine, social welfare.[30] Between 1980 and 1982, a further 471 were taken to Japan on work experience programs in Japanese industry under the Association for Overseas Technical Scholarships. All spent periods of six months to a year in Japan, with a strong focus on the technical and the practical.[31]

Complementary to its training program in Japan, JICA supports a large number of cooperative projects in China, which are linked to Japanese economic and trading interests. They include the modernization of railways in areas of key importance, the modernization of port facilities, mining projects, energy and telecommunications. There are also some educationally and socially oriented programs. The Friendship Hospital in Beijing, built by JICA, has six Japanese doctors and other Japanese staff, sends 20 Chinese doctors to Japan each year for six month periods and is making an important contribution to the fields of orthopedics and neuro-surgery.[32] The Japanese Management Center in Tianjin is one of a series of foreign-supported management institutes under the State Economic Commission, the first of which was the American-supported Dalian Center discussed above. This Japanese center is not associated with any Chinese university but is a free-standing institute in an industrial setting, focusing on the training of Chinese teachers of management.[33] Two further training institutes are planned, one under the Ministry of Communications and the other under the Ministry of Railways.[34]

This dual pattern of educational cooperation, one aspect closely linked to scholarship and the higher education system, the other integrated within the industrial-technical complex, is a pattern that started with Japan but is becoming increasingly common with other countries offering development aid to China, most notably West Germany, Canada and Australia. In the Japanese case, the links to economic interests are specific. Japan has dominated Chinese imports with a rise from 4.9 billion U.S. dollars to over 15 billion annually between 1983 and 1985.

The autumn of 1985 saw a prolonged period of student unrest, related to preparations for the 50th anniversary of the December 9th Movement, a powerful student protest against Japanese aggression in 1935. Allegations of Japanese economic imperialism were linked to perceptions of the Chinese leadership as moving into "bureaucratic capitalism" and allowing the emergence of a "princely faction" in the sons of high cadres who are lining up for positions of influence. Thus students were linking internal tendencies towards the abuse of political power to the danger of external economic domination. Their protests were probably exaggerated and the Chinese leadership succeeded in containing them through official support for patriotic commemoration ceremonies. Yet it may be significant that Japan is the only one of the six industrialized countries which has so far aroused this kind of direct social protest.[35]

Sino-German Educational Relations

West Germany has so far hosted 2,489 Chinese students and scholars on long-term programs, the highest concentration in any European country. Since the signing of an agreement on cultural cooperation in 1977, German provision has been made for Chinese scholars and graduate students to study in Germany through the Deutscher Akademische Austauschdienst (DAAD) and such semi-official foundations as the Hanns Seidel Foundation, the Alexander von Humboldt Foundation and the Friedrich Ebert Stiftung. Of a total of 1,136 in Germany in 1982, it was estimated that only 32% were financed by the Chinese government and the rest benefited from some form of German financial support.[36] The major focus of study is on the applied sciences,but some provision is made from the German side for scholarships in humanities and social sciences as well.[37]

Within China itself it was agreed that Tongji University should be made a center of Sino-German intellectual cooperation.[38] In the first instance, since Tongji is an engineering university, this cooperation focused on the engineering sciences with provision for many visiting German professors to lecture at Tongji in this area and opportunities for Tongji faculty to spend time in Germany. Gradually the focus of cooperation was extended from the sciences to include management, with the opening of a school of management at Tongji. Most recently a center for research into German problems was set up to study the West German economic and educational systems.

A large percentage of Tongji students take German as their first foreign language and an extra year of intensive study is incorporated into some programs, where German excellence in the field makes the language a valuable skill. Also Tongji has a preparatory school for Chinese university graduates intending to pursue graduate study in Germany and a German language and literature department both of which are assisted by teachers sent from Germany.[39] To a lesser degree, Wuhan Medical College, which was created out of Tongji's medical school in 1952, forms a center of cooperation with Germany in the medical sciences. In addition, about 60 other university-level linkages between Chinese and German universities, many of which are supported by the federal German government or foundations, provide a context for lively intellectual interaction.[40]

Quite distinct from this scholarly and intellectual cooperation, Germany is now giving support through the Ministry of Economic Cooperation to various forms of technical education. Through the Carl Duisberg Gesellschaft, a program has been set up which will select 120 Chinese technicians every two years and provide them with a work-experience program incorporating linguistic, academic and industrial components, with the key focus being the provision of training within German industry. Parallel to the Japanese and American management training centers, the Germans have set up a management institute at the Baoshan Steel Works north of Shanghai under an agreement between the SEC and the German Ministry of Economic Cooperation. Furthermore, German industrial involvements in China such as the Shanghai Volkswagon joint venture are planning forms of technical training as part of their activities.[41]

The German Ministry of Economic Cooperation does not limit itself to industrial-technical projects but also has broader educational interests. Through the Hanns Seidel Foundation it supports a center for Shanghai primary school teachers which is intended to disseminate new curricular and pedagogical ideas. It is also committed to supporting the establishment of a model Fachhochschule, which will probably be located in Hangzhou, with linkages to Chinese higher technical colleges in Ningbo, Nanjing and Hefei in order that materials and ideas can de disseminated.[42]

The economic motivation behind German support for technical education in China has clear parallels with the situation depicted by Francoise Kreissler in the early part of this century. The main difference is that China's internal conditions hold much greater promise for economic benefit now than then. The Germans have succeeded in dominating China's trade relations with Europe, providing 40% of China's European imports in 1984 and 1985, also absorbing between 33% and 36% of China's exports to Europe.

Sino-British Educational Relations

Britain hosted a total of 1,833 Chinese scholars and students between 1978 and 1984 under agreements for cultural and scientific-technical cooperation signed in 1978 and 1979.[43] In addition to the exchange of 25 students and scholars each year, the British government has made a special effort to attract Chinese graduate students to British programs by the provision of 260 tuition-free places each year since 1983. The Foreign and Commonwealth Office provides for sixty places in such practically-oriented social sciences as economics, law, management, project planning, international relations, education, library science and urban planning. The Overseas Development Agency provides 200 places in such applied sciences as agriculture and forestry, transport, mining, shipbuilding, offshore oil, computer technology and electronics. In these programs a clear direction is thus given to areas of practical importance where British strengths are seen to coincide with Chinese fields of priority.[44] Of all the cultural officials whom I interviewed in doing this research, the British were the only ones who had an explicit disciplinary policy in the support of Chinese students, with the ideal seen as a 70% emphasis on science and technology, 20% on social sciences and 10% on humanities.[45]

In contrast to Germany and Japan, Britain has no focused center of intellectual interaction on Chinese soil, but has adopted a more diffuse approach in a policy that has interesting parallels with the historical picture given in chapter 3. The British Council supports about 25 British teachers of English who are grouped in four or five centers within major Chinese higher institutions where they provide one-year programs for Chinese teachers of English within the higher education system. The role of the British teachers in promoting sensitive and effective language teaching methods and a depth understanding of the English language may make a real contribution to communicative action. Language forms constitute the fundamental cultural and social categories in which a people conceive their development. Therefore a greater mastery of the English language in Chinese universities would open the way to a deeper understanding of the thought and culture that underlies the technology now so attractive to the Chinese leadership. British support for the Chinese television university, both directly and through its leadership of the international advisory panel of the third World Bank project, is a further expression of this concern for the diffusion of ideas.

One British private initiative in China has been characterized by the same sensitivity to the diffusion of ideas and has made a significant contribution to cross-cultural communication. This is the support given by the Thompson Foundation to the creation of an English language newspaper, the first since 1949.[46] *China Daily* is read widely by foreign business people, scholars and tourists in China and now has direct western outlets as well. It is also watched carefully by Chinese intellectuals. Its sensitive journalistic style, scholarly approach and remarkable frankness of reporting combine features of western and eastern journalism in a way that has probably never been achieved by any other Communist country. This may be one of the most hopeful forums of communicative action that has so far been developed. In April of 1985, the Xinhua News Agency and the Thomson Foundation opened an International Journalism Training Center in Beijing with a brief to train journalists for Xinhua's English language section and for other Third World countries.[47] This is an institution which could contribute significantly to the New World Information Order, a recent concern of UNESCO that received strong support from the Chinese.[48]

Unlike Japan and Germany, Britain has no special program for technical or work-experience opportunities which are directly linked to economic and trading interests. British exports to China represented only eight percent of the European total in 1983, but they have since risen somewhat. Also official support for soft loan facilities that would enable British industry to be more competitive in the Chinese market has recently been offered.[49] However, so far cultural and educational activities are not being directly marshalled to serve economic ends, an interesting parallel with Britain's historical role in China.

Sino-French Relations

France hosted a total of 1,299 Chinese students and scholars between 1978 and 1984. A cultural accord between the two nations which goes back to 1965 has been re-negotiated every two years in the form of a detailed cultural program since 1978.[50] The fact that all university places are tuition free for foreign scholars makes French higher education attractive to the Chinese and in addition about 120 living stipends are provided by the French government each year in exchange for the provision of 60 places for French students in Chinese institutions. Chinese graduate students seeking doctoral degrees have dominated the Chinese scholarly presence in France in recent years, with 400 of an estimated total of 740 in this category in July of 1984.[51] The fields of study officially favored in exchange have been worked out between the two sides on the basis of perceived French areas of excellence and Chinese priority needs. They include medicine, biotechnology, aeronautics, space, agriculture, economics, law and mathematics.[52] There are about 50 university-level agreements between Chinese and French universities, but little French government funding is available for these linkages. This makes if difficult for them to develop substantive cooperation activities on any scale.

The French presence in China involves providing teachers and materials for a certain number of French language teaching centers in Chinese universities. There is also an official special relationship with Wuhan University as a center of intellectual cooperation which has parallels with the German presence at Tong-ji and the Japanese presence at CUST. In many ways the French project at Wuhan is the most fully developed of these in terms of a cultural vision which embraces the whole range of knowledge areas as they cohere in French intellectual culture. About 15 professors of French language and literature, basic sciences and mathematics work within Chinese departments in the university, and an inter-disciplinary center for French problems includes research in politics and history, language and literature, and economics. Plans are being made for some cooperation in the fields of engineering and management which would be introduced into a framework where the theoretical basis has already been laid. While the practical outworking of this vision has not been without serious problems, an interesting attempt has been made to create a milieu in which cross-cultural communicative action could gradually be fostered. About ten Chinese faculty at Wuhan spend time in France each year, as well as many Wuhan graduates going to France for higher degrees. A shared Chinese understanding of French intellectual life should begin to take form in these favorable circumstances.[53]

On the technological side, France has not been so quick as Japan and Germany to move into support for work-experience programs, although French economic interests in China have supported this type of activity. For example the Matra Corporation has undertaken to train 12 Chinese engineers for six month periods under an agreement for cooperation in space technology with the Chinese Academy of Space Technology of the Ministry of Aeronautics Industry. The first French government move in this area came with a program for ten Chinese trainees under an agreement between the International Agency for Technical Cooperation and the China Enterprise Management Association. A six-month language program has been provided for the trainees in the Beijing Institute of International Relations which is to be followed by nine months of work experience in French industry, interspersed with some time in a French management school. There will be some follow-up activities for each trainee on return to China.[54]

In a further economically oriented project of cooperation, the French have a strong input to the Management Institute set up by the European Economic Community (EEC) in cooperation with the Chinese State Economic Commission (SEC), another center in the series already mentioned including the American one at Dalian, the Japanese in Tianjin, the German in Baoshan. Like the German and Japanese centers, this center has no links with the Chinese higher education system. Unlike them, it offers MBA degrees which are accredited by a high-level European academic committee. The French dean of the institute is a professor from the Ecole de Commerce in Paris.[55]

French economic interests are thus not neglected in Sino-French cultural and educational relations, though the French are most proud of their political role as the first western nation to enter substantive relations with China in 1965 and to assist in China's gradual re-entry into the global community.[56] Between 1978 and 1983 France moved from an eleven to an fifteen percent share in the European community's exports to China, ahead of Britain but far behind West Germany.

Sino-Canadian Relations

Between 1978 and 1984 Canada hosted a total of 1,452 Chinese scholars and students according to the sources used by Huang Shiqi in chapter 12. This figure accords well with the results of a recent Canadian study of Sino-Canadian academic relations which estimated a total of 1,650 Chinese students and scholars spending long-term study periods in Canada between 1970 and 1983. Their fields of study had the following emphases: 24% in engineering, 21.3% in basic sciences, 9.2% in medicine, 3% in agriculture, 17% in language training, 2.2% in humanities and 16% at the secondary level. About 36% of the total were financed by the Chinese government, 12% by Canadian universities and another 22% by private citizens.[57]

1983, the last year covered by the study, marked the beginning of a new phase in Sino-Canadian relations. A development assistance agreement was signed between the Canadian International Development Agency (CIDA) and the Chinese Ministry of Foreign Economic Relations and Trade (MFERT) in October of that year.[58] The areas of cooperation were selected in relation to Canadian expertise and China's needs as an industrialized developing country which had made agriculture and light industry its priorities. These were natural resources (energy, forestry, agriculture and mining), infrastructure up-grading (power transport and communications) and the social sector (education, health, training and management). The focus was not to be so much the transfer of hardware as the multiplication of contacts among people in which both sides had something to learn and something to impart. By the end of 1984, there were 58 separate projects covering all the sectors identified and involving a range of Canadian and Chinese institutions.[59] A geographical focus on the provinces of Sichuan in the Southwest and Heilongjiang in the Northeast was agreed upon between CIDA and MFERT on the basis of broad geographical and natural similarities between these regions and Canada, though projects are by no means limited to these two provinces.

The stimulus provided by the projects for greater educational interaction was evident in the fact that applications for study visas to Canada doubled in 1984 and reached 1,300 by October of 1985.[60] Some projects involved financial support for university-level linkages in the areas of medicine, engineering, management and education,[61] while most were more closely linked to the industrial sector. The Canada-China Management Training Center in Chengdu is a free-standing institute, one of the series of foreign-assisted institutes under the SEC, which is linked on the Canadian side with the network of Community Colleges in Canada.[62] The World Universities Services of Canada administers another program for the provision of work experience to Chinese technical trainees in Canadian industry and government bureaus. It is expected that up to 367 Chinese will have spent periods of six months to a year in Canada on these programs by 1987.[63]

There are interesting parallels in the CIDA development activities in China with Canadian missionary approaches discussed in chapter 8. This is not entirely fortuitous since CIDA's approach to development aid had considerable input from Canadian missionaries in the early years.[64] However, what differs strikingly from the period described by Karen Minden is that Canada now has large and growing trade interests in China, and the desire to develop and promote these interests is clearly an important factor in Canadian development assistance.[65] Canada's exports to China grew from U.S. $442 million in 1978 to $1.259 billion in 1985, a 3% share in the Chinese market in comparison to the American 11.9% share and the German 5.8% share.

Conclusion

China has travelled a tortuous road both political and economically over the modern period. In conditions of economic weakness and political instability, it is not surprising that foreign educational inputs were seen as forms of servitude at certain times, also that they were used to marshall the unified pursuit of a particular development model at other times. In the present period there seem finally to be conditions of political stability and economic optimism which should make possible a serene and eclectic selection of educational patterns and ideas from various sources. Rather than taking one foreign model as a focal point, it may be possible to adapt attractive features from different sources to the Chinese context. This seems evident in, for example, the Chinese interest in the American teaching and research university, the German Fachhochschule, the British polytechnic and the Open University. Japanese forms of technical education also hold appeal, as does the North American community college. The adaptation of selected foreign patterns to a Chinese socialist education system that is already well developed may in turn produce new patterns of relevance elsewhere.

Nevertheless, the possibility of educational transfers again coming to be seen as forms of servitude should not be entirely discounted. All OECD countries have considerable economic and political interests at stake in China's development. Japanese, German and Canadian economic interests are being translated into technical education programs which will probably be of great value to China, as long as they are not perceived to serve economic exploitation. This appeared to be the case, briefly, in Chinese student agitation against Japan in the autumn of 1985. American political interests find expression in wide-ranging opportunities for collaboration in the social sciences. Again this collaboration should contribute greatly to the Chinese social sciences, as long as it is not perceived as a channel of political domination. In all cases there are cultural dynamics which open up the possibility of a communicative action that is mutually enriching. The British genius for the diffusion of ideas and the French ability to make accessible a whole intellectual culture are two examples of these.

During this period when China is garnering all her resources to speed up economic growth and modernization, the question of whether foreign influence in education will result in servitude or liberation is not likely to concern the leaders in Beijing. They are intent on closing the professional gap, especially that of scientists and engineers, left by the Cultural Revolution. They are therefore willingly absorbing a variety of foreign educational inputs and adapting them to China's specific needs. In the process, China is undoubtedly enhancing cross-cultural understanding and laying a foundation for Chinese participation in the global community. But whether the 1980s will be seen as a period which, once again, subjugated China to foreign influence, or liberated her from traditional constraints and transformed her into a modern nation, is a judgment which will have to be made by historians.

Notes

Notes to Chapter 1

1. *Li ji* (Book of Rites), chapter 16, paragraph 2. This work, dating from the 1st century B.C., often brought together much more ancient texts.

2. A. Thomas, *Histoire de la mission de Pékin* (Paris: Louis Michaid, 1926), Vol. 2, p. 25.

3. J. Gernet, *Chine et christianisme* (Paris: Gallimard, 1982), p. 81.

4. Thomas, *Histoire de la mission de Pékin,* Vol. 1, p. 321.

5. Teng Ssu-yu, "Chinese Influence on the Western Examination System," *Harvard Journal of Asiatic Studies,* Vol. 7, No. 4, (1942).

6. Thomas, *Histoire de la mission de Pékin,* Vol. 2, pp. 24, 31.

7. *Ibid.,* Vol. 2, pp. 86, 163. Some of these girls were Mongols, but most of them Chinese from Christian families who had fled from Peking.

8. I. T. Hyatt, *Protestant Missions in China 1877-1890, the Institutionalization of Good Works* (Cambridge, Mass.: Harvard University East Asian Research Center, Papers on China, Vol. 17, 1963), p. 77.

9. There were 564,000 pupils in 1924. See Chen Yuanhui, *Zhongguo xiandai jiaoyu shi* (The History of Contemporary Education in China) (Beijing: Renmin jiaoyu chubanshe, 1970), p. 81.

10. *Jiaoyu shijie* (The World of Education), No. 9 (September 1901).

11. *Ibid.,* No. 20 (February 1902).

12. The first survey of these schools carried out at the national level and published in official educational statistics in 1935 indicated there were still 101,027 schools with 1,767,014 pupils. The number of pupils in modern primary education at that time was 15.2 million, but in 1923 it had only been 6.6 million.

13. *Christian Education in China* (Shanghai: Commercial Press, 1922), p. 21.

14. Wu Yuan-li and Robert Sheeks, *The Organization and Support of Scientific Research and Development in Mainland China* (New York: Praeger, 1970), passim; Saneto Keishu, *Zhongguoren liuxue Riben shi* (A History of the Chinese Who Studied in Japan), Chinese translation (Beijing: Sanlian Shudian, 1983), p. 116.

15. Saneto Keishu, *Zhongguoren liuxue Riben shi,* pp. 122-123.

Notes to Chapter 2

1. Among the missionaries who went to China, the Jesuits were the most numerous and played a role of primary importance in the European understanding of the Far East. There are some exceptions, for example the Augustinian Gonzalez de Mendoza, author of *The History of the Kingdom of China*. Many travellers and merchants had gone to China before the Jesuits and also had left accounts. But these, even though sometimes intending to be "descriptive," were more like narratives of their voyage. Therefore I do not give consideration to their passing comments on Chinese society, education and the examinations.

2. For example, Father Adam Schall, born at Cologne in 1592, was appointed President of the Department of Astronomy in 1645 and mandarin in 1657.

3. The rapidity with which these works were translated into the majority of European languages at the time is surprising. I'll take as an example the Italian report by Father Ricci *Della entrata della compagnia di Giesù e Christianita nella Cina,* adapted and translated into Latin by Nicolas Trigault and published in Augsburg in 1615, republished in 1616, 1617, 1623 and 1624; translated into French as *Histoire de l'expédition Chrétienne au royaume de la Chine,* published in Lyons in 1616, republished in 1617 and 1618; translated into German in 1617, into Spanish in 1621 and again into Italian in 1622. Another example is the book by Mendoza, published for the first time in Rome in 1585, translated into Italian in 1585 and published in Rome, Venice and Genoa, translated into French in 1588 and published in Paris, in Lyons in 1609 and in Rouen in 1614; translated into English and published in London in 1588, a German edition in Frankfurt in 1589, a Dutch edition in Amsterdam in 1595.

4. Jean-Baptiste du Halde, *Description géographique, historique, chronologique, politique et physique de l'Empire de la Chine et de la Tartarie Chinoise* (La Haye: 1736), epître au Roy.

5. Joachim Bouvet, *Portrait historique de l'Empereur de la Chine* (Paris: 1697), pp. 5-6.

6. The controversy over the rites had been provoked by enemies of the Jesuits who reproached them in both Europe and China for allowing Chinese converted to Christianity to continue to show homage to Confucius and their ancestors. The Jesuits considered these rites to be primarily civil and not religious. In 1704 Pope Clement XI forbade the rites for all the Christians of China. In this way he struck a hard blow at the evangelistic methods of the Jesuits. The Roman Curia did not rehabilitate the Chinese rites until 1939. In 1700 the faculty of theology at the Sorbonne condemned the book by Father Le Comte *Nouveaux mémoires sur l'Etat présent de la Chine* (Paris: 1696) and had it burned. Le Comte appeared too admiring of the Chinese government.

7. *The Chinese Traveller,* collected from Du Halde, Le Comte and other modern travellers (London: 1775), Vol. 1, p. 61.

8. *Mémoires concernant l'histoire, les sciences, les arts, les moeurs, les usages des Chinois,* par les missionaires de Pékin (Paris: 1776), Vol. V, p. 25.

9. "Questionnaire à proposer au R. P. Couplet sur le royaume de la Chine," in Virgile Pinot, *Documents inédits relatifs à la connaissance de la Chine en France de 1685 à 1740* (Paris: Virgile Pinot, 1932), pp. 7-9.

10. A century later things had changed when in 1765 the Commissary Turgot proposed 52 questions to two Chinese who were returning to China after a stay in France. Most of the questions related to the Chinese economy, yet the existence of a ruling class whose wealth depended on a position acquired by merit rather than heredity led Turgot to say: ". . . although absolutely speaking, the public officers can get along with nothing but their stipends, yet to prepare for their positions, it is necessary in China that they undergo a long course of study, submit to several examinations, and travel. Consequently, they must be above the most elementary needs, and able to subsist during the entire time of their studies, without earning any wages by their work. It is then necessary at least, that they be born of rich parents who can provide the cost of that long education . . ." Turgot

went on to ask: 6: "this having been explained, I ask, by what sorts of men are the great positions in China commonly filled? Are they the sons of rich families, living without work from their incomes? or possibly the sons of husbandmen or craftsmen, or of tradesmen, whose fathers were rich enough to provide for them an advanced education? 7: Are there not families who from father to son have no other calling than to devote themselves to the profession of letters, and to pursue the occupations which this makes most natural. . . ?" in L. A. Maverick, *China: A Model for Europe* (San Antonio, Texas: Paul Anderson Co., 1946).

11. The first Jesuit colleges were founded at Messina and Palermo in 1548 and 1549. By 1580 there were 144 Jesuit colleges in Europe.

12. Alvarez Semedo, *Histoire universelle de la Chine divisée en trois parties* (Lyons: 1667), Chapter VIII, p. 61.

13. *Ibid.* Chapter VII, pp. 58, 68. "While they have no university nor particular schools, they nevertheless do not lack magnificent halls, beautifully furnished, for the examiners to stay in, also the incredible numbers who present themselves for the examinations. . . . In the hall at Canton, which is one of the smallest, there are over 7,500 small rooms, and on the first day of an examination up to 96,148 compositions were read there.

14. Nicolas Trigault, *Histoire de l'éxpédition chrétienne au royaume de la Chine* (Lyons: 1616), chap. V, p. 55: "In every metropolitan city one can see a grand hall, built only for the examinations and surrounded by high walls. Inside there are many rooms separated from all noise and disturbance. In addition there are 4,000 small cells in the middle of the hall which can contain only a small table, a stool and a person. . . . They are closed up in the hall, each in his own cell, so that noone can talk with anyone else over the whole time that they work on the written examinations. . . . There are guards . . . and magistrates who supervise and prevent any discussions between those who remain in the hall and those outside. . . . When the bachelors are admitted into the hall, the greatest care is taken to see that they take no book or written material with them."

15. Semedo, *Histoire universelle de la Chine,* chapter VIII, p. 67. "The newly licenced candidates go to thank the president of the examinations who receives them standing, treating them as his equals. . . . After many other ceremonies, they are splendidly regaled by the officials at three feasts. The third feast profits them, since there are three tables, the first covered with various meats, the second with fowl, game and raw flesh, the third with dried fruits, which they take back to their homes."

16. Louis Daniel Le Comte, *Memoirs and Observations made in a late journey through the Empire of China* (London: 1699), p. 279.

17. *Mémoires concernant l'histoire. . . ,* Vol. IV, p. 27.

18. Du Halde, *Description géographique. . . ,* Vol. II, p. 259.

19. *Mémoires concernant l'histoire. . . ,* Vol. IV, p. 319.

20. Joseph de Mailla, *Histoire générale de la Chine, ou annales de cet Empire* (Paris: 1777-1785), Vol. XIII, p. 631.

21. Le Comte, *Memoirs and Observations,* pp. 280-281.

22. *Mémoires concernant l'histoire,* Vol. VI, p. 203.

23. *Ibid.* Vol. VI, p. 283: "The scholars are that part of the nation which illuminates others on what is important for them to know, directs them in what they should do and establishes all the prerogatives which hold primacy. Since the Han, that is for nearly 2,000 years, they have constantly held first position in the Empire, provided its teachers for instruction, ministers to administer affairs and govern the state and magistrates to judge the people and keep them within the bounds of duty."

24. Semedo, *Histoire universelle de la Chine,* Chapter VII, p. 61.

25. *Mémoires concernant l'histoire,* Vol. IV, p. 27.

26. Leibniz, *Novissima Sinica* (Munich: 1697), cited by W. Franke, *China and the West* (Oxford: Basil Blackwell, 1962), p. 62.

27. Le Comte, *Memoirs and Observations,* p. 281: ". . . since the places are given,

the Emperor may with greater justice turn out those officers whom he shall find undeserving."

28. Du Halde, *Description géographique,* vol. II, p. 58.

29. *Ibid.*, Vol. II, p. 257.

30. Semedo, *Histoire universelle de la Chine,* Chapter VII, p. 58.

31. Voltaire, *Essais sur les moeurs et l'esprit des nations* (Paris: Garnier frères, 1963), Vol. II, Chapter CXCVII, p. 806. "Nothing in Asia resembles the European aristocracy. Nowhere is to be found an order of citizens distinguished from others because of hereditary titles, exemptions or rights merely held by birth. . . . One cannot find in India, or in China, anything comparable to this body of aristocrats which forms an essential part of every European monarchy."

32. *Ibid.,* Chapter CXCV, p. 785 and CXCVII, p. 809.

33. *Mémoires concernant l'histoire,* Commentary under a portrait of the Emperor Qian Long drawn from real life by the Jesuits, Frontspiece to the book.

34. Michel de Certeau, *L'Ecriture de l'histoire* (Paris: Gallimard, 1975), p. 164.

35. *Ibid.*, p. 164.

36. *Mémoires concernant l'histoire,* 2nd part, Vol. V, p. 26.

37. On this subject see the article by Hugues Cologan, "Quelques Lumières sur la Chine: la Chine des Lumières," *Etudes Chinoises,* No. 3, 1984, pp. 35-64. Note particularly the third part. He suggests that Montesquieu interpreted the Chinese order as a despotic order due to the tyranny of the rites, which were seen as the general spirit of the nation.

38. Trigault, *Histoire de l'expédition chrétienne,* chapter V, p. 64.

39. Soldiers at a higher level were also selected through competitive examinations. Yet the missionaries noted that their success gave them little prestige, in contrast to the scholar-officials. *Ibid.* pp. 92-93. "The point most worthy of note is that the whole kingdom is governed by scholars . . . all the military captains and soldiers defer to these philosophers with great humility and special ceremonies and are subject to them. It sometimes even happens that the military are whipped by the scholars just as among us school children are whipped by their schoolmasters. The counsel and opinions of the scholars has much more authority with the King than that of all of the military chiefs."

40. *Mémoires concernant la Chine,* Vol. I, p. 297.

41. Athanase Kircher, *La Chine illustrée de plusieurs monuments tant sacrés que profanes* (Amsterdam: 1670), chapter X, 2nd part: "I have no difficulty in believing that if there is a state highly civilized or a monarchy well regulated in the world, the Empire of China could boast of having achieved this distinction over and above all others, and that its government is the most just (according to the maxims and principles of politics and reason)."

42. Figures given by Alain Woodrow, *Les Jesuits: Histoire de pouvoirs* (Paris: J. C. Lattes, 1984), p. 193.

43. On this subject, see Jacques Gernet, *Chine et christianisme* (Paris: Gallimard, 1982).

44. See for example John Webb, *An historical essay endeavouring a probability that the language of China is the primitive language* (London: 1669).

45. Certeau, *L'Ecriture de l'histoire,* p. 137.

46. *Ibid.,* p. 169.

47. *Ibid.,* p. 153.

48. *Ibid.,* p. 155.

49. In the controversy over the rites, for example, the Jesuits were more condemned for their manner of action than their beliefs.

50. Towards the end of the 17th century, a collective Jesuit memoir declared: "In the competition between two opposing commands made to a French religious, one by the King and the other by a legitimate superior . . . it is a grievous sin against religion, fidelity and justice to obey the superior general, or the local superior, against the command of the King." This is cited by Certeau, *L'Ecriture de l'histoire,* p. 169.

51. This apologetic was reinforced by Jesuit publishers, who, in publishing Jesuit texts

did not hesitate to rework them, suppressing certain reservations which were expressed, in the fear that these would harm the Company.

52. Certeau, *L'Ecriture de l'histoire,* p. 141.

53. Michel Foucault, *Les Mots et Les Choses* (Paris: Gallimard, 1966), p. 10.

54. The Company of Jesus was suppressed in 1764 in France and dissolved by the Pope in 1773.

55. Paul Hazard, *La Crise de la conscience européenne 1680-1715* (Paris: Fayard, 1961), p. 8.

56. *Ibid.*

57. Kircher, *La Chine illustrée,* IVth part.

Notes to Chapter 3

1. A. Feuerwerker, *The Foreign Establishment in China in the Early Twentieth Century* (Ann Arbor: Michigan Papers in Chinese Studies, 1976), p. 94 and p. 17.

2. Y. C. Wang, *Chinese Intellectuals and the West 1872-1949* (Chapel Hill: University of North Carolina Press, 1966), p. IX.

3. J. W. Adamson, *English Education 1789-1902* (Cambridge: Cambridge University Press, 1964).

4. J. S. Mill, *On Liberty* (London: John W. Parker & Son, 1859), pp. 190-191.

5. Sally Borthwick, *Education and Social Change in China: the Beginnings of the Modern Era* (Stanford: Hoover Institution Press, 1983), pp. 66-7.

6. R. H. Wilkinson, "The Gentleman Ideal and the Maintenance of a Political Ideal," in *Sociology, History and Education: A Reader* ed. P. Musgrave (London: Methuen & Co., 1970).

7. The most detailed account of the schools is in Knight Biggerstaff, *The Earliest Modern Government Schools in China* (Ithaca, New York: Cornell U.P., 1961).

8. See particularly Mary Wright, *The Last Stand of Chinese Conservatism: The T'ung-chih Restoration, 1862-1874* (Stanford: Standford U.P., 1957).

9. Biggerstaff, *Modern Government Schools in China,* pp. 65-68.

10. *Ibid.,* ch. IV.

11. J. L. Rawlinson, *China's Struggle for Naval Development, 1839-95* (Cambridge, Mass.: Harvard U.P., 1967).

12. Biggerstaff, *Modern Government Schools,* p. 97, and S. Wright, *Hart and the Chinese Customs* (Belfast: Mullan, 1950), pp. 429-493.

13. W. A. P. Martin, *A Cycle of Cathay* (Edinburgh: Oliphant, Anderson and Ferner, 1897), p. 311.

14. For details, see S. Wright, *Hart and the Chinese Customs,* pp. 325-8.

15. W. E. Soothill, *Timothy Richard of China* (London: Seeley, Service and Company, 1924), p. 116.

16. S. Wright, *Hart and the Chinese Customs,* pp. 901-3.

17. Biggerstaff, *Modern Government Schools,* p. 226, and H. E. King, *The Educational System of China as Recently Reconstructed* (Washington: United States Bureau of Education, 1911), pp. 86-7.

18. See his letter in Teng Ssu-yu and J. K. Fairbank, *China's Response to the West* (Cambridge, Mass.: Harvard University Press, 1954), p. 99-102.

19. For details of Wang Tao's life and work see Lo Hsiang-lin, *The Role of Hong Kong in the Cultural Interchange between East and West* (Tokyo: Centre for East Asian Studies, 1964), Vol. 1, ch. 3.

20. B. Schwartz, *In Search of Wealth and Power: Yen Fu and the West* (Cambridge, Mass.: Harvard U.P., 1964).

21. Edgar Snow, *Red Star Over China* (London: Gollancz, 1937), p. 141.

22. Quoted in Schwartz, *In Search of Wealth and Power,* p. 147.

23. *Ibid.*, p. 242.

24. P. Cohen, *China and Christianity* (Cambridge, Mass.: Harvard U. P., 1963), p. 267.

25. See Teng and Fairbank, *China's Response,* p. 135.

26. The Reverend Lord William Gascoyne-Cecil, *Changing China* (London: James Nisbet and Co., 1910), p. 307 and Dora Russell, *The Tamarisk Tree* (London, Virago, 1977), p. 125.

27. Except when otherwise attributed, information about Fryer is taken from A. A. Bennett, *John Fryer: The Introduction of Western Science and Technology into Nineteenth Century China* (Cambridge, Mass.: East Asian Research Center Harvard University, 1967).

28. Tsien Tsuen-hsuin, "Western Impact on China through Translation," *Far Eastern Quarterly,* Vol. 13, No. 3 (May 1954), pp. 305-327.

29. A. Stanley, "Shanghai Museum," *The Educational Directory of China 1911* (Shanghai, 1917), pp. 81-82.

30. In a speech of 1893 Fryer urged the missionary educators to make more use of magic lanterns. *Records of the Triennial Meeting of the Educational Association of China,* 2-4 May 1983 (Shanghai, 1893), pp. 46-47.

31. Bennett, *John Fryer,* p. 56.

32. *Ibid.*, p. 68, and George B. Fryer "The Education of the Blind in China," in *The Educational Directory of China 1918,* pp. 49-56.

33. See *Records of the Educational Association of China May 6-9 1896* especially the address by F. L. Hawks Pott and Fryer's response. Also Fryer, "The Present Outlook for Chinese Scientific Nomenclature," in *Records of the Educational Association 1893.*

34. Bennett, *John Fryer,* pp. 42-45. For the view that the reforms were not greatly influenced by missionary scholars see Chen Chi-yun, "Liang Ch'i-ch'ao's 'Missionary Education': A Case Study of Missionary Influence on the Reformers'; in *Papers on China,* Vol. 16 (Cambridge, Mass.: East Asian Research Center, 1962), pp. 66-126.

35. Tsien Tsuen-hsuin, "Western Impact through Translation," p. 318-319.

36. Timothy Richard, *Forty-Five Years in China* (New York: Frederick Stokes and Co., 1916) and Soothill, *Timothy Richard of China.*

37. See Paul Richard Bohr, *Famine in China and the Missionary: Timothy Richard as Relief Administrator and Advocate of National Reform 1876-1884* (Cambridge, Mass.: East Asian Research Center, 1972).

38. Paul A. Cohen, "Missionary Approaches: Hudson Taylor and Timothy Richard," *Papers on China,* Vol. 11 (Cambridge, Mass.: 1957), p.39.

39. Richard, *Forty-five Years,* p. 141.

40. Soothill, *Timothy Richard,* p. 135.

41. *Ibid.*, p. 156-7.

42. *Ibid.*, p. 131.

43. *Ibid.*, p. 123.

44. Albert J. Garnier, *A Maker of Modern China* (London: The Carey Press, 1945), p. 67.

45. Soothill, *Timothy Richard,* p. 152.

46. Cohen, "Missionary Approaches," p. 49.

47. Soothill, *Timothy Richard,* p. 126.

48. *Ibid.*, p. 180.

49. *Ibid.*, p. 183. The book was: Robert Mackenzie, *The Nineteenth Century — A History* (London: T. Nelson and Sons, 1889).

50. Soothill, *Timothy Richard,* pp. 148-149.

51. Robert E. Lewis, *The Educational Conquest of the Far East* (New York: Fleming H. Revell Co., 1903), p.171.

52. Speech to missionary congress in 1911 in Kuo Ping-wen, *The Chinese System of Public Education* (New York, Teachers College, Columbia University, 1915), p. 140.

53. See *The Chinese Recorder,* XXV (1894) p. 295.

54. The best accounts of Shanxi University are Richard, *Forty-Five Years,* pp. 300-307,

Soothill, *Timothy Richard*, pp. 253-270, and Moir Duncan, "The Imperial University of Shanxi," *East of Asia,* 111 (1904), p. 102.

55. Moir Duncan, "The Imperial University," p. 102.

56. Soothill, *Timothy Richard,* p. 261.

57. See for example the suggestion by C. Middleton Smith, professor of engineering at Hong Kong University, that of all the mission universities, only St. John's in Shanghai would have been granted a charter, and that subject to strict conditions about elementary work. Professor C. Middleton Smith, "University Education in China," in *The Educational Directory of China 1916,* pp. 36-60.

58. Soothill, *Timothy Richard,* p. 261.

59. Richard, *Forty-Five Years,* p. 300.

60. Soothill, *Timothy Richard,* p. 268. Richard says it was in November, 1910, *Forty-Five Years,* p. 307.

61. Lo Hui-min (ed.), *The Correspondence of G. E. Morrison* (Cambridge: Cambridge University Press, 1976), Vol. II, p. 68-69.

62. *Educational Directories for China 1917,* p. 53, and *1918,* pp. 72-73.

63. *Educational Directory for China 1918,* p. 12.

64. *Ibid.,* p. 9 and p. 15.

65. Soothill, *Timothy Richard,* pp. 269-270. Garnier, *A Maker of Modern China,* p. 69.

66. Kenneth Scott Latourette, *A History of the Christian Missions in China* (London: Society for Promoting Christian Knowledge, 1929), p. 362.

67. *Ibid.,* pp. 362-3.

68. *Ibid.,* pp. 405-6.

69. *Ibid.,* p. 606.

70. E. Luard, *Britain and China* (London: Chatto and Windus, 1962), p. 107.

71. Evelyn Rawski, "Elementary Education in the Mission Enterprise," In Susan Wilson Barnett and J. K. Fairbank (eds.), *Christianity in China's Early Protestant Missionary Writings* (Cambridge, Mass.: The Committee on American-East Asian Relations, Harvard University, 1985), pp. 139-140.

72. E. R. Hughes, *The Invasion of China by the Western World* (London: Adam and Charles Black, 1937), p. 77.

73. Cohen, "Missionary Approaches," p. 32.

74. *Ibid.,* p. 36.

75. *Ibid.,* p. 41.

76. Latourette, *Christian Missions,* p. 442.

77. Cohen, "Missionary Approaches," p. 42.

78. Latourette, *Christian Missions,* p. 408.

79. Milton T. Stauffer (ed.), *The Christian Occupation of China* (Shanghai, 1922), p. 34.

80. See Jessie Gregory Lutz, *China and the Christian Colleges 1850-1950* (Ithaca: Cornell U.P., 1971).

81. *The Educational Directory of China, 1917,* carried a list of these schools, pp. 88-9.

82. See the regulations for Hong Kong matriculation exams in the *Educational Directory of China, 1918,* pp. 129-137.

83. *Report of the Advisory Committee together with other Documents respecting the Chinese Indemnity* (London: His Majesty's Stationary Office, 1926), p. 178.

84. See Lancelot Foster, *English Ideals in Education for Chinese Students* (Shanghai: The Commercial Press, 1936), p. 170.

85. See the section on 'Homemaking' in "The Education of Women," China Educational Commission, *Christian Education in China* (New York: Foreign Missions Conference of North America, 1922), p. 243.

86. *Educational Directory of China, 1917,* pp. 87-90.

87. *Ibid.,* and B. Harrison, *The University of Hong Kong in the First 50 Years 1911-1961,* (Hong Kong, H.K. U.P., 1962), p. 51.

88. Chen Dongyuan, *Zhongguo funu shenghuoshi* (Shanghai:Shangwu yinshuguan, 1937), p. 343.

89. Dzung Lu-Dzai, *A History of Democratic Education in Modern China* (Shanghai: The Commercial Press, 1934), pp. 145-146.

90. Paul A Cohen, *China and Christianity: The Missionary Movement and the Growth of Chinese Anti-Foreignism, 1860-70* (Cambridge, Mass.: Harvard U.P., 1963), pp. 64-8.

91. Feuerwerker, *The Foreign Establishment*, pp. 28-9.

92. Major Henry Knollys, *English Life in China* (London: Smith and Elder, 1885), pp. 205-7.

93. Lo Hsian-lin, *The Role of Hong Kong*, pp. 88-9 and p. 108.

94. Lancelot Foster, *The New Culture in China* (London: Allen and Unwin, 1936), p. 175.

95. Quoted in *Ibid.*, pp. 116-7.

96. G. B. Endercott, *A History of Hong Kong* (London: Oxford U.P., 1958), pp. 228-242.

97. Harrison (ed.), *University of Hong Kong: The First 50 Years, 1911-1961*, pp. 51, 53, and 57.

98. *Ibid.*, pp. 45-57.

99. *Ibid.*, p. 49.

100. *Ibid.*, pp. 50-51.

101. "University of Hong Kong" in *Educational Directory of China, 1916*, p. 55.

102. Professor Middleton Smith, "Technical Education in China", in *Ibid.*, p. 63.

103. *Educational Directory of China, 1917*, pp. 96-7.

104. Information on the Boy Scouts' Association is in *Ibid.*, pp. 42-48 and 69-71, Herbert Freyn, *Chinese Education in the War* (Shanghai: Kelly and Walsh, 1940), p. 107, and in *Report of the Advisory Committee, 1926*, p. 148. It is interesting to note that in Shanghai there was a separately maintained "Baden-Powell Boy Scouts" Association for boys of "British and allied nationality."

105. Foster, *The New Culture*, p. 90.

106. Lo Hui-min, *Morrison Correspondence*, Vol. I, 1976, pp. 566-7.

107. *Ibid.*, Vol. II, pp. 803-4.

108. Bertrand Russell, *The Problem of China* (London: Allen and Unwin, 1922), pp. 221-2.

109. Ronald Clark, *The Life of Bertrand Russell* (Jonathan Cape, 1976), pp. 387-388.

110. *Ibid.*, pp. 386-387.

111. *The Autobiography of Bertrand Russell* (London: Allen and Unwin, 1970), Vol. II, p. 132.

112. Dora Russell, *The Tamarisk Tree*, p. 407.

113. Clark, *Bertrand Russell*, p. 407

114. Bertrand Russell, *Education and the Social Order* (London: Allen and Unwin, 1932), p. 109.

115. Clark, *Bertrand Russell*, pp. 408-410.

116. *The Autobiography of Bertrand Russell*, Vol. II, p. 128.

117. C. H. Becker et al., *The Reorganization of Education in China, Report of the League of Nations Mission of Educational Experts* (Paris: League of Nations Institute of Intellectual Co-operation, 1932).

118. Foster, *English Ideals*.

119. Victor Purcell, *Problems of Chinese Education* (London, Kegan Paul, 1936), p. 127.

120. Gascoyne-Cecil, *Changing China*, pp. 305-309.

121. *Ibid.*, p. 218.

122. *Ibid.*, p. 305, passim.

123. Lutz, *The Christian Colleges*, pp 114-5.

124. Luo Hui-min, *Morrison Correspondence*, Vol. 2, pp. 330-1.

125. Lutz, *The Christian Colleges*, pp. 127-8.

126. *Ibid.*, pp. 215-271, and Cyrus Peake, *Nationalism and Education in Modern China* (New York: Columbia U.P., 1932).

127. *Report of the Advisory Committee*, p. 9.

128. *Ibid.*, p. 109.

129. Chu Chia-hua, "British Boxer Indemnity Fund Activities," *The China Quarterly*, V, 1941 (Shanghai: China Institute of International Relations), pp. 437-441.

130. *Ibid.*

131. See Universities' China Committee in London, *Annual Reports*, London.

132. Frances Donaldson, *The British Council: the First Fifty Years* (London: Jonathan Cape, 1984), pp. 158-9.

133. Joseph and Dorothy Needham (eds.), *Science Outpost: Papers of the Sino-British Science Co-operation Office, 1942-6* (London: The Pilot Press, 1948), p. 285.

134. See Joseph Needham, *Science and Civilization in China*, Vol. I (Cambridge: CUP, 1954), introduction.

135. *Ibid.*, 1954-1984 (to date).

136. Donaldson, *The British Council*, pp. 158-9; See also Luard, *Britain and China*, p. 57.

137. Donaldson, *The British Council*, pp. 346-7.

Notes to Chapter 4

1. Ministry of Education, Science and Culture, Japan, *Japan's Modern Educational System: A History of the First Hundred Years* (1980), p. 464.

2. Ding Shouhe, *Xinhai geming shiqi qikan jieshao* [Introduction of periodicals during the revolution period of 1911], Vol. 1 (1983), p. 123.

3. Joseph R. Levenson, *Confucian China and Its Modern Fate* (London: Routledge and Kegan Paul, 1958), Vol. I, p. 60.

4. *Zouding xuetang zhangcheng* [School Regulations of 1904].

5. *Zouding xuetang zhangcheng*.

6. "Zhongguo tixueshi dongyou fangmen jiliie" [Record of observation in Japan by Chinese Commissioners of Education], *Dongfang zazhi*, Vol. 3, No. 12 (Jan. 1907).

7. "Tai-Shin Kyoiku-saku" [Educational policy toward China], *Kyoiku Jiron*, No. 610, Mar. 15, 1902.

8. Keishu Saneto, *Chugokujin Nihon Ryugaku-shi-ko* [History of Chinese Students Studying in Japan] (draft 1939), p. 139.

9. Sakuzo Yoshino, "Shinkoku Zaikin no Nihonjin-kyoshi" [Japanese teachers working in China], *Kokka Gakkai Zasshi*, Vol. 23, No. 5 (May 1909).

10. Saishi Nakashima, *Tobungakusha Kiyo* (1908), Introduction.

11. Masahiro Kageyama, "Shin-matsu niokeru Kyoiku Kindaika Katei to Nihonjin Kyoshu" [Educational modernization in the late Qing period and the Japanese teachers], in Hiroshi Abe (ed.), *Nitchu Kyoiku Bunka Koryu to Masatsu* [The Sino-Japanese educational and cultural exchange and problems] (1983), pp. 25-27.

12. Unokichi Hattori, "Peking Kyoiku no Genjo" [Current situation of education in Beijing], *Kyoikukai*, Vol. 3, No. 13 (Sept. 1904).

13. Hiroshi Abe, "Shin-matsu ni okeru Gakudo-Kyoiku to Nihonjin-kyoshu: Chokurei-sho no Baai" [School education and Japanese teachers in the late Qing period: the case of Zhili province], in Akigoro Taga (ed.), *Ajia no Kyoiku to Shakai* [Education and society of Asia] (1983), pp. 335-52.

14. Hiroshi Abe, *Sekai no Yoji Kyoiku: I. Ajia*, [Pre-school education in the world: Asia], (1983), pp. 16-8.

15. Jiro Shirakawa, "Zai-Shinkoku Honpo Bunbu Dekasegi Kyoshi" [Japanese teachers in China], *Nihon oyobi Nihonjin*, No. 448 (Dec. 1906).

16. Toa Dobunkai (ed.), *Zoku Taishi Kaikoroku*, Vol. 2 [Memoirs in China: sequel] (1941), p. 749.

17. Zhang Zhidong, *Quanxuebian*, (1898).

18. Harry E. King, "The Educational System of China as Recently Reconstructed,"

U. S. Bureau of Education Bulletin, No. 15, Whole Number 462, (1911), p. 92.

19. Keishu Saneto, *Chugokujin Nihon Ryugaku-shi* [History of Chinese studying in Japan], (1960), p. 58.

20. *Ibid.,* p. 68.

21. Waseda Daigaku (ed.), *Kohon Waseda Daigaku Hyakunen-shi* [One hundred years of Waseda University: draft] , Vol. 2-1 (1976), p. 217.

22. Jissen Joshi Gakuen (ed.), *Jissen Joshi Gakuen 80-nen-shi* [80 years of Jissen Girls' School] (1981), p. 118.

23. Shu Xingcheng, *Jindai Zhongguo liuxueshi* [Modern Chinese history of studying abroad] (Shanghai: Zhongguo shuju, 1927), p. 68.

Notes to Chapter 5

1. K. S. Latourette, *A History of Christian Missions in China* (London: Society for Promoting Christian Knowledge, 1929), p. 253ff and p. 372ff.

2. *Ibid.,* p. 315ff.

3. *Ibid.,* p. 576.

4. For the relations between China and the German states before the end of the nineteenth century, specially the economic relations, see Yü Wen-tang, *Die deutsch-chinesischen Beziehungen von 1860-1880* (Bochum: Brockmeyer, 1983). See also D. Glade, *Bremen und der Ferne Osten* (Bremen: C. Schünemann, 1966); F. van Briessen, *Grundzüge der deutsch-chinesischen Beziehungen* (Darmstadt: Wissenschaftliche Buchgesellschaft, 1977); H. Stoecker, *Deutschland und China im 19. Jahrhundert: Dan Eindringen des deutschen Kapitalismus* (Berlin (DDR): Rütten & Loening, 1958); Walravens, ''Die Deutschlandkenntnisse der Chinesen bis 1870,'' Ph.D. thesis, University of Cologne, 1972.

5. Stoecker, *Deutschland und China im 19. Jahrhundert,* p. 211ff, and Yü Wen-tang, *Die deutsch-chinesischen Beziehungen,* p. 129ff.

6. E. Sachau, *Denkschrift über das Seminar für Orientalische Sprachen an der königlichen Friedrich-Wilhelms-Universität zu Berlin von 1887 bis 1912* (Berlin: G. Reimer, 1912). For the *Tongwenguan,* see also K. Biggerstaff, *The Earliest Modern Government Schools in China* (Ithaca, New York: Cornell University Press, 1961).

7. Yü Wen-tang, *Die deutsch-chinesischen Beziehungen,* p. 119ff.

8. *Ibid.,* p. 144ff.

9. J. E. Schrecker, *Imperialism and Chinese Nationalism — Germany in Shantung* (Cambridge, Mass.: Harvard University Press, 1971), p. 19ff.

10. *Ibid.,* p. 33ff.

11. K. Düwell, *Deutschlands Auswärtige Kulturpolitik 1918-1932* (Köln/Wien: Böhlau, 1976), p. 53ff.

12. G. Weidenfeller, *Verein für das Deutschtum im Ausland-Allgemeiner deutscher Schulverin [1881-1918]: Ein Beitrag zur Geschichte des deutschen Nationalismus und Imperialismus im Kaiserreich* (Bern: H. Lang, Frankfurt: P. Lang, 1976).

13. Düwell, *Deutschlands Auswärtige Kulturpolitik 1918-1932,* p. 53ff.

14. At this time the term propaganda did not have the pejorative connotation which it acquired after World War I.

15. *Denkschrift des Auswärtigen Amts über das deutsche Auslandsschulwesen* (Berlin: Reichsdruckerei, 1914).

16. W. Franke, *The Reform and Abolition of the Traditional Chinese Examination System* (Cambridge, Mass.: Harvard University Press, 1960), p. 48, and M. Bastid, *Aspects de la Réforme de l'enseignement en Chine au début du XXe siècle* (Paris/La Haye: Mouton, 1971), p. 10ff.

17. Zentrales Staatsarchiv Potsdam, *Deutsche Botschaft in China,* No. 642-646 (The Sino-German schools of Chengdu, Tianjin, Jinan).

18. Cai Yuanpei studied in Germany from 1907 to 1911, first at the University of Berlin,

then at the University of Leipzig. W. Duiker, *Ts'ai Yüan-p'ei: Educator of Modern China* (University Park and London: Pennsylvania University Press, 1977), p. 15.

19. *Denkscrift des Auswärtigen Amtsüber das deutsche Auslandsschulwesen.*

20. Düwell, *Deutschlands Auswärtige Kulturpolitik,* p. 90ff.

21. *Ibid.,* p. 106ff.

22. For the beginnings of technical education in Germany and its evolution, see K. H. Manegold, *Universität, Technische Hochschule und Industrie* (Berlin: Duncker & Humblot, 1970).

23. For a discussion of the history and the ideas associated with the Hankou School, see Zentrales Staatsarchiv Potsdam, *Deutsche Botschaft in China,* No. 3434 (Deutsche Ingenieurschule Hankou, 1921-1933).

24. Otto Franke, "Die deutsch-chinesische Hochschule in Tsingtau, ihre Vorgeschichte, ihre Einrichtung und ihre Aufgaben," *Marine-Rundschau,* 12, 1909, pp. 1-16.

25. Zentrales Staatsarchiv Potsdam, *Deutsche Botschaft in China,* No. 1258, fol. 237-262.

26. *Ibid.,* fol. 215-219.

27. "Statut für die Hochschule von Tsingtau vereinbart zwischen der Kaiserlichen Deutschen und der Kaiserlichen Chinesischen Regierung," Zentrales Staatsarchiv Potsdam, *Deutsche Botschaft in China,* No. 1258, fol. 193-195.

28. There were three publications: *Deutsch-Chinesische Rechtszeitung (Zhongde fabao),* a law journal published by the section of law and political science beginning from 1911; a monthly started in October of 1913, entitled *Der west-östliche Bote (Zi xi cu dong)* which was intended to "assist in diffusion of the German language and culture;" and finally, five special reports published by the section of agronomy on agricultural questions (*Berichte aus der land- und forstwirtschaftlichen Abbteilung der deutsch-chinesischen Hochschule).* See *Verzeichnis der Veröffentlichungen der deutsch-chinesische Hochschule Tsingtau* (Qingdao, Autumn, 1912) and W. Wagner, *Die chinesische Landwirtschaft* (New York and London: Garland, 1980), p. Vff.

29. Wagner, *Die chinesische Landwirtschaft,* p. Vff. This information was collected in an interview with an alumnus of the school in Shanghai, September, 1981.

30. For the history of the hospital, see *Jahresbericht der Tungchi Medizinischen Hochschule* [1922-1923], pp. 10-16, and *Festschrift anlässlich des 25 jährigen Bestehens der staatlichen Tung-Chi Universität zu Woosung* (Shanghai: ABC Press, 1932), pp. 1-15.

31. M. Linde, "Die Tungchi Medizinische Hochschule in Schanghai," in F. Schmidt, and O. Boelitz, (eds.), *Aus deutscher Bildungsarbeit im Auslande: Erlebnisse und Erfahrungen in Selbstzeugnissen aus aller* (Langensalza: J. Beltz, 1927-1928), vol. 2, pp. 214-224.

32. von Schab, "Entwicklung und Zukunft der Medizinschule in Schanghai," *Asien* (January, 1914).

33. *Denkschrift aus Anlass der feierlichen Einweihung der Tungchi Technischen Hochschule in Schanghai-Woosung* (Berlin: Meisenbach Riffarth & Co., 1924).

34. *Ibid.,* pp. 10-11; Ding Wenyuan, "Guoli Tongji daxue" (The National Tongji University), in Zhang Qiyun (ed.), *Zhongguo minguo daxue zhi* (Record of the Universities of the Republic of China) (Taibei: Zhongguo xinwen chuban gongsi, 1953), p. 120.

35. *Denkschrift aus Anlass der feierlichen Einweihung der Tungchi Technischen Hochschule in Schanghai-Woosung,* p. 11.

36. *Guoli Tongji daxue biye jiniankan* (Yearbook of the Graduates of National Tongji University) (Shanghai, 1949), chapter one.

37. These two schools were the College of Law and Commerce of Wusong [*Wusong Zhongguo gongxuexiao*], created by Liang Qichao, and unoccupied since 1911, and the naval school [*Haijun xuexiao*] situated not far from the former school.

38. Ding Wenyuan, "Guoli Tongji daxue," p. 123.

39. See the account of C. du Bois-Reymond, "Geschichte der Flucht von Prof. Claude du Bois-Reymond vor der Deportation durch die Engländer am 10. März 1919," Zentrales Staatsarchiv Potsdam, *Fonds Marie du Bois-Reymond,* No. 4., among other sources.

40. *Traité de Versailles: Texte définitif du Traité de Paix signé par les Plénipotentiaires allemands le 28 juin 1919*, s.l., s.éd., s.d. [1919], p. 29.

41. *Journal de Pékin* (August 20, 1920).

42. *Politique de Pékin*, Oct. 12, 1919, and "Eine französische technische Schule in Schanghai," *Ostasiatische Rundschau*, Feb. 1, 1921.

43. *Denkschrift aus Anlass der feierlichen Einweihung der Tungchi Technischen Hochschule in Schanghai-Woosung*, p. 19.

44. *Guoli Tongji daxue biye jiniankan* [Yearbook of the Graduates of National Tongji University], Shanghai, 1950, p. 27ff.

45. *Ibid.*

46. Chen Chi, *Die Beziehungen zwischen Deutschland und China bis 1933* (Hamburg: Mitteilungden des Instituts für Asienkunde, 1973), pp. 179-180.

47. Ding Wenyuan, "Guoli Tongji daxue," pp. 118-119; *Guoli Tongji daxue biyue jiniankan*, 1950, p. 27ff.

48. Ding Wenyuan, "Guoli Tongji daxue," p. 126.

49. Probst, "Denkschrift über die Tung-Chi Universität und Deutschlands technischen Schulwesen in China," Shanghai, Feb. 2, 1941, Politisches Archiv, Auswärtiges Amt Bonn, *Nachlass des Konsuls, Heinrich Betz*. It should also be mentioned, to complete this history of Tongji during the war, that after the university moved inland a German medical academy remained in Shanghai (*Shanghai Deguo yixueyuan*) directed by the Germans and given financial support by the German government representation in Shanghai. Hu Junyin, "Zhongde xuehui yu zhongde wenhua" (The German Institute and Sino-German Cultural Relations), *Zhongde xuezhi* (The Sino-German Annals), 51 (1-2), May 1943.

50. R. Hayhoe, "Chinese-western Scholarly Exchange: Implications for the Future of Chinese Education," in R. Hayhoe (ed.) *Contemporary Chinese Education* (London and Sydney: Croom Helm, 1984), p. 215.

51. See the interview given by the German Consul Schwamm in the Magazine *Das neue China*, April/May, 1980, pp. 21-22, and the article "Als Partner willkommen," which appeared in *Die Zeit*, September 27, 1985, following the visit of the Governor of Baden-Württemberg to China.

Notes to Chapter 6

1. Robert Lewis, *The Educational Conquest of the Far East* (New York: Fleming H. Revell Co., 1903), p. 11.

2. For example, Robert Nisbet, *Social Change and History* (New York: Oxford University Press, 1969) shows that the notion of an internal dynamic of change within societies is rooted in Aristotelian thought and identifies the roots of all major social change in the diffusion of ideas and technologies across cultures.

3. Joseph Levenson, *Confucian China and Its Modern Fate*, Vol. III (London: Routledge and Kegan Paul, 1965), p. 49ff insists on the fundamental importance of outside ideas and patterns to the Chinese historical process and analyzes the ways in which they combined with Chinese values in China's modernization process.

4. Sun Yat Sen, *San min chu i: The Three Principles of the People* (Shanghai: Commercial Press, 1929).

5. Mao Zedong, "On New Democracy," in *Selected Works of Mao Tse-tung*, Vol. II (Beijing: Foreign Languages Press, 1975), pp. 339-384.

6. Jack Gray and Gordon White, *China's New Development Model* (London: Academic Press, 1982). This analysis of the post-1978 political economy in China suggests close links between present policies and the ideas that lay behind the new democracy period of Mao's schematization of China's development.

7. John Cady, *The Roots of French Imperialism in Asia* (New York: Cornell University Press, 1954), chapter 1.

8. *Ibid.,* p. 7.

9. J. B. Piolet, *La France en dehors: les missions catholiques francaises au XIXe siècle,* Vol. III (Paris: Librairie Armand Colin, c. 1900), p. 70.

10. See Paul Cohen, *China and Christianity: The Missionary Movement and the Growth of Chinese Anti-Foreignism, 1860-1870* (Cambridge, Mass.: Harvard University Press, 1963), for a comparative discussion of French and British differences in mission policy.

11. Cady, *The Roots of French Imperialism in Asia,* p. 72ff.

12. Kenneth Latourette, *The History of Christian Missions in China* (London: Society for the Propagation of Christian Knowledge, 1929), chapter XXVIII.

13. Jeffrey Barlow, *Sun Yat Sen and the French 1900-1908* (Berkeley: University of California Center for Chinese Studies, 1979).

14. William Tung, *China and the Foreign Powers: The Impact of and Reaction to the Unequal Treaties* (New York: Oceania Publications, 1970), pp. 256, 257, 272.

15. Cady, *The Roots of French Imperialism in China,* chapter 1.

16. Piolet, *La France en dehors,* Tome III, Chapter 3.

17. *Ibid.,* chapter 7.

18. P. Pacifique Chardin, *Les Missionaries Franciscains en Chine* (Paris: Auguste Picard, 1915).

19. R. Schwickerath, *Jesuit Education: Its History and Principles* (St. Louis, Missouri: B. Herder, 1904). This book tries to refute charges against the reactionary curricula of Jesuit colleges yet succeeds in illustrating the appeal of their classicism which gave them such a lasting influence over French secondary education. A Jesuit observer described the Collège St Ignace of Shanghai in 1875 as "prenant de plus en plus la forme d'une collège de la Compagnie." See J. De la Servière, *Histoire de la Mission du Kiangnan,* Tome II (Zi-ka-wei, près de Chang-hai: Imprimerie de l'Orphelinat de T'ou-se-wei, 1914), p. 277.

20. Piolet, *La France en dehors,* Tome III, p. 318.

21. See for example Ralph Covell, *W. A. P. Martin: Pioneer of Progress in China* (New York: Christian University Press, 1978).

22. See for example the account of the Taipings in Shanghai in De la Servière, *Histoire de la Mission du Kiangnan,* Tome 1, pp. 262ff.

23. Cohen, *China and Christianity,* chapter five, illustrates this point.

24. Latourette, *The History of Christian Missions in China,* p. 500.

25. Piolet, *La France en dehors,* Tome III, p. 272.

26. Latourette, *The History of Christian Missions in China,* chapter XXIV.

27. For a Chinese account of the history of the university, which was merged with Beijing Teachers University in 1952, see Beijing Shifan Daxue xiaoshi bianxiezu, *Beijing Shifan Daxue xiaoshi* (A History of Beijing Normal University) (Beijing: Beijing Shifan Daxue chubanshe, 1982), pp. 216-265. See also *Missions de Chine,* Vol. 6, p. 513, Vol. 8, pp. 693-4.

28. In the Chinese context, of course, it had a far less prestigious position than the *grandes écoles* in France.

29. This point is strongly emphasized in Jesuit accounts of their return such as that of De la Servière, also in Piolet's chapter on the Kiangnan Mission. However these same accounts cannot avoid dealing with the conflicts that arose between the Jesuits with their authoritarian ways and a local Chinese Christianity that had become highly independent in the 60 odd years of Jesuit absence.

30. "Le Musée d'Histoire Naturelle de Zi-ka-wei et le nouveau Musée Heude," *Relations Chine* (Janvier, 1933).

31. I have written elsewhere on the life of Ma Xiangbo and his vision for a modern

university that would be truly Chinese in its spirit and ethos. See "Towards the Forging of a Chinese University Ethos: Zhendan and Fudan 1903-1919," China Quarterly, No. 92 (June, 1982), pp. 323-341.

32. Photocopies of Ma's original endowment in his own handwriting in Chinese and French were published by the Jesuits in the Bulletin de l'Université l'Aurore, Tome 4, No. 4, (1943), p. 953, at a time when the Ma family was using legal means to seek to recover the property.

33. De la Servière, Croquis de Chine (Paris: Gabriel Beauchesne and Cie, 1912), p. 45.

34. J. D. la Servière, "Une Université Francaise en Chine," Relations de Chine, No. 2 (Avril, 1925), p. 16.

35. This incident is described in detail in Hayhoe, "Towards the Forging of a Chinese University Ethos."

36. The evolution of the curriculum and full details on its contemporary state are described in greatest detail in the annual university bulletins of 1934 and 1935.

37. "L'Aurore: Une Université Catholique en Chine," leaflet published by the university in 1936.

38. "Reception de S. Ex. M. Cosme à l'Aurore," Bulletin de l'Université l'Aurore, No. 39, (1939-40), p. 52.

39. Sili Zhendan Daxue, Bulletin published by the university in 1935.

40. Ibid., p. 71. For details on some of the secondary schools, see Relations de Chine (July-October, 1918), p. 84; (Oct., 1921), pp. 598-602; (July, 1925), pp. 173-175; (Oct. 1925), pp. 230-236; (April, 1930), pp. 115-120; (April, 1936), pp. 317-318.

42. Ibid., p. 76, Gu Zhangsheng, Chuanjiaoshi yu jindai Zhongguo (Missionaries in Recent Chinese History) (Shanghai: Remin chubanshe, 1981), pp. 364-7.

43. "Le Rayonnement de l'Aurore en Chine et à l'étranger," Bulletin de l'Université l'Aurore, No. 33 (1936), pp. 8-11; Liu Maisheng, "Wo suo zhidao de Shanghai Zhendan Daxue," pp. 76ff.

44. Liu Maisheng, "Wo suo zhidao de Shanghai Zhendan Daxue," pp. 80-82.

45. Footnote 37 above notes the article reporting Cosme's visit. An article by one of the Jesuit leaders, Father Germain, entitled "L'Aurore et le Guerre," Bulletin de l'Université l'Aurore, Tome 6, No. 3 (1945), pp. 569-77, stresses the humanitarian service of the university under war-time conditions and also its role in protecting numerous library collections and museum artifacts from destruction. Still its strong condemnation of the Japanese had the tone of "protesting too much" far too late.

46. Liu Maisheng, "Wo suo zhidao de Zhendan Daxue," p. 87, documents the support given by Father Germain and some of the Law School graduates and students to the Japanese authorities in Shanghai in 1938.

47. Considerable research was done, however, in the areas of medicine, law and engineering and was published in such outlets as the Bulletin de l'Université l'Aurore [bilingual], La Revue Juridique [in Chinese], and Le Bulletin Medical [bilingual].

48. For brief comments on Teilhard's not very happy connections with the institution, see Robert Speaight, Teilhard de Chardin: A Biography (London: Collins, 1967). For the history of the institution, see Zhang Qiyun (ed.), Zhonghua minguo daxue zhi (A Record of Universities in the Chinese Republic) (Taiwan: Zhonghua wenhua chuban shiye weiyuanhui, 1956), Vol. 2, pp. 425-8. Fang Hao, the Catholic educationist who wrote this small article and who had been dean of the college of arts set up there after the war, bemoaned this separation of research and teaching.

49. Piolet, La France en dehors, Tome III, pp. 175ff.

50. See particularly Missions de Chine, Vol. 6, pp. 586-590, Vol. 7, pp. 79-91 and Vol. 8, pp. 686-692, where Catholic horror at the collapse of educational authority and discipline in Protestant and government schools is given expression.

51. Robert Smith, The Ecole Normale Supérieure and the Third Republic (Albany: State University of New York, 1982).

52. Teng Ssu-yu, "Chinese Influence on the Western Examination System," Harvard

Journal of Asiatic Studies, Vol. 7, No. 4 (1942-3).

53. Howard Boorman (ed.), *Biographical Dictionary of Republican China* (New York: Columbia University Press, 1968), Vol. 2. Some of these details were given by Marianne Bastid in her lecture "Li Shizeng and Chinese Non-Proletarian Internationalism," given to the Contemporary China Institute, School of Oriental and African Studies, University of London (June 14, 1984).

54. The best contemporary account of the evolution of these projects is given in a small volume published by their own publishing house in 1916: *Lü Ou jiaoyu yundong* (Paris: Shijie she, autumn 1916). For a retrospective view of the whole movement from the Taiwan perspective, see Peter Chu, *Bali binfen lü* (Mon Souvenir à Paris) (Hong Kong: Nanyang bianyisuo, 1969).

55. Huang Liqun, *Liufa qingong jianxue jianshi* (A Short History of the Worker-Student Movement in France) (Beijing: Jiaoyu kexue chubanshe, 1982), p. 18.

56. A recently published diary by one of these worker-students from August of 1920 to August of 1921 gives a fascinating insight into their daily life experience. See Jia Peizhen, *Liufa qingong jianxue riji* (Changsha: Hunan renmin chubanshe, 1985).

57. The idea of providing a national exemplar comes across clearly in the first issue of *Zhongfa daxue banyue kan,* which came out in 1925, and which gives a detailed description with photographs of each of the institutions forming the new university. Both the introductory article by a "reporter," and the following two articles by Li Shizeng expound the virtues of the French university model, and made it clear that this is an experiment in emulating that model.

58. Huang Liqun, *Liufa qingong jianxue jianshi,* pp. 17-20.

59. Numerous documents detailing the constitutions, curricular emphases and organizational style of these schools can be found in some of the recently published collections on the movement in Chinese. See for example Zhang Yunhou, Yin Xuyi, Li Junshen, *Lifa qingong jianxue yundong* (The Work-Study Movement in France), Vol. 1 (Shanghai, Renmin chubanshe, 1980); Qinghua daxue Zhonggong dangshi jiaoyuzu (ed.), *Fufa qingong jianxue yundong shiliao* (Historical Materials on the Worker-Student Movement in France), Vol. 1-5 (Beijing: Beijing chubanshe, 1979).

60. In Hunan there was both a society and a school explicitly for women. See Zhang, Yin, Li, *Liufa qingong jianxue yundong,* pp. 198-204.

61. *Ibid.,* pp. 79-99, provides constitutions and other documents relating to the national "Huafa jiaoyu hui" as well as its provincial branches.

62. Missionary comments on the Chinese worker students in France and the opposition they faced within their own ranks if any converted to Catholicism highlight these conflicting social ideals. See *Missions de Chine,* Vol. 6, pp. 691-692, and Vol. 8, pp. 691-692.

63. See Zhang, Yin, Li, *Liufa qingong jianxue yundong,* pp. 161-168, for documents on the various schools in the Beijing region.

64. *Ibid.,* p. 105, gives the constitution of Comte lower and higher primary school and girls' higher primary school as drafted in 1917.

65. *Université Franco-Chinoise de Pékin* (University leaflet, Na-Che-Pa, 1926). This document details the *Comité de Patronage* as having three French and seven Chinese members with the French Ambassador to China, Comte D. de Martel as Honorary President. The *Comité Exécutif* was composed of the same three French persons and eight Chinese. The rector was Cai Yuanpei, but this was an honorary role actually filled by Li Shuhua.

66. A useful brief history of the university from the perspective of 1933 is found in Zhongguo xuesheng she (ed.), *Quanguo daxue tujian* (A Handbook of Universities in the Whole Nation) (Shanghai: Liangyou tushu yinshua gongsi, 1933), pp. 107-110.

67. About U.S.$75,000.00 was provided yearly to the university from Boxer Indemnity money from 1926, far less than had been hoped for and expected. For a detailed discussion of the problems surrounding the use of French Boxer Indemnity funds in China, see Daniel Bouchez, "Un défricheur méconnu des études extrême-orientales: Maurice Courant

(1865-1935)'' *Journal Asiatique,* Tome CCLXXI, Nos. 1-2 (1983), pp. 43-150. See also *Missions de Chine,* Vol. 8, p. 690, which records a contribution of U.S.$150,000.00 to the Sino-French University in Beijing from Boxer Indemnity money in 1926.

68. *Beijing Zhongfa Saxue Kongde Xueyuan ji Kongde Xuexiao* (University leaflet, September, 1926), provides details on the primary and secondary curriculum. This and other publications of the university, together with a complete set of all its journals and many of the library holdings of the Lyons institute are held in the Bibliothèque Municipale of Lyons. For details on the upper secondary and university curriculum, see *Zhongfa jiaoyu jie,* No. 32, 1930.

69. *Université Franco-Chinoise de Pékin* (University leaflet, Na-Che Pao, 1926).

70. This figure is given in Zhongguo xuesheng she (ed.), *Quanguo daxue tu jian,* p. 110. A detailed list of students and graduates published by the university in 1934, *Sili Zhongfa Daxue ji fushu gebu tongxuelu,* lists 93 current students of Voltaire College (by this time Comte College had been closed and its economics department combined with Voltaire), 46 at Curie College and 48 at Lamarck College, which focused mainly on pre-medical studies. It also lists the names of 111 graduates of Voltaire College, 127 of Comte College, 16 of Curie College and 69 of Lamarck College, a total of 208 graduates up to that time.

71. *Zhongguo jiaoyu nianjian* (Shanghai: The Commercial Press, 1948), p. 654.

72. A brief review of the contents of the journal is found in R. Hayhoe, "A Comparative Approach to the Cultural Dynamics of Sino-Western Educational Cooperation," *China Quarterly,* No. 104 (December, 1985), pp. 693-695. From 1926 to 1931 the journal was entitled *Zhongfa jiaoyu jie* (L'Education Franco-Chinoise), and from November, 1931 to 1937, it was called *Zhongfa daxue yuekan* (La Revue de l'Université Franco-chinoise).

73. Bouchez, "Maurice Courant," gives valuable insights into the establishment of this institution from the French perspective. Its activities were also constantly reported in the journal and can be studied in some detail through the archives preserved at Université de Lyons III.

74. *Zhongfa daxue banyuekan,* Vol. 1, No. 3 (1925), pp. 10-13.

75. The provincial distribution was roughly as follows: 126 from Guangdong, 73 from Hubei, 52 from Jiangsu, 45 from Zhejiang, 35 from Hunan, 32 from Sichuan, 17 from Fujian, 14 from Henan, 12 from Anhui, 11 from Hubei, 6 from Shandong, 6 from Shanxi, etc. All this information is provided in the valuable list, based on archival sources, compiled by Li Lusheng, "1926-1946 nian Li'Ang Zhongfa Daxue haiwaibu tongxuelu," *Ouhua xuebao,* No. 1 (May, 1983), pp. 127-150.

76. *Zhongfa jiaoyu jie,* No. 34 (August, 1930), pp. 58-62.

77. Chinese worker-students were fully aware that the initial intention had been for an institution providing for 2,000, or approximately the number they represented, but that lack of funding from either the French or the Chinese side had made this impossible. See Bouchez, "Maurice Courant."

78. Perhaps the most clear and concise account of this can be found in the lengthy introduction to Zhang, Yin, Li, *Liufa qingong jianxue yundong,* pp. 1-63. A detailed study has been done drawing on French archival sources for the period by Geneviève Barman at the Centre Chine, Ecole des Hautes Etudes en Sciences Sociales, Paris.

79. Emile Durkheim, *The Evolution of Educational Thought* (London: Routledge and Kegan Paul, 1977).

80. Smith, *The Ecole Normale Supérieure and the Third Republic,* p. 9.

81. *Antoine Prost, L'Enseignement en France 1800-1967* (Paris: Armand Colin, 1968).

82. *Ibid.,* chapter 7.

83. F. Artz, *The Development of Technical Education in France* (Cambridge, Mass. and London, England: Society for the History of Technology and M.I.T. Press, 1966). Artz makes the point that in the early 19th century, France was the only country in the

world where engineering was clearly established as a learned profession, having high prestige.

84. Prost, *L'Enseignement en France*, pp. 305ff.

85. Smith, *The Ecole Normale Supérieure and the Third Republic*, pp. 141ff.

86. Xiong Qingyun, "Faguo jiaoyu gaikuang," *Jiaoyu zazhi*, Vol. XV, No. 4 (April, 1923), pp. 1025.

87. Huang Zhongsu, "Bali daxue," *Xin jiaoyu*, Vol. 7, No. 1 (1923), pp. 35-45, Vol. 8, No. 3 (1924), pp. 367-383.

88. Fowler Brooks, "Falanxi zhi gongmin jiaoyu," translated by Xia Chengfang, *Xin jiaoyu*, Vol. 6, No. 5 (1923), pp. 687-695.

89. Pan Zhiguang, "Faguo xiaoxue kecheng de xingge," *Jiaoyu zazhi*, Vol. XVI, No. 6 (June, 1924), pp. 12-23.

90. Huang Zhongsu, "Faguo gaodeng Shifan xueyuan," *Xin jiaoyu*, Vol. 8, No. 3 (1924), pp. 355-359.

91. In the section entitled "Shijie jiaoyu xinchao," *Jiaoyu zaxhi*, Vol. XV, No. 9, Sept., 1923, pp. 8-11.

92. Champenois, Julien, "Falanxi daxue gaige yundong," *Jiaoyu zazhi*, Vol. XIV, No. 1 (Jan., 1922), pp. 11-17.

93. William Duiker, *Ts'ai Yüan-p'ei: Educator of Modern China* (University Park and London: Pennsylvannia State University Press, 1977).

94. Cai Yuanpei, "Jiaoyu duli yi," *Xin jiaoyu*, Vol. 4, No. 2 (March, 1922), pp. 317-319.

95. Cai Yuanpei, "Hunan zixiu daxue de jieshou yu shuoming," *Xin jiaoyu*, Vol. 5, No. 1-2 (Aug., 1922), pp. 81-89.

96. Mao also linked this university with the *shuyuan* tradition in the inaugural manifesto he wrote for the university. See Zhang Liuquan, *Zhongguo Shuyuan Shihua* (Beijing: Jiaoyu kexue chubanshe, 1981).

97. The politics of this educational initiative and its failure are clearly analyzed in Allen Linden, "Politics and Education in Nationalist China: The Case of the University Council 1927-8," *Journal of Asian Studies*, Vol. XXVIII, No. 4 (August, 1968), pp. 763-776.

98. Discussion of the subject by contemporary historians provide valuable insights. See Chen Qingzhi, *Zhongguo jiaoyu shi*, Vol. 2 (Shanghai: Commercial Press, 1936), pp. 758ff., and Zhou Yutong, *Zhongguo xiandai jiaoyu shi* (Shanghai: Liangyou tushu yinshua gongsi, 1934), pp. 48-50, 202-203.

99. C. H. Becker, P. Langevin, M. Falski, and R. H. Tawney, *The Reorganization of Education in China* (Paris: League of Nations Institute of Intellectual Cooperation, 1932). Ernst Neugebauer, *Anfänge pädagogische Entwicklungshilfe unter dem Völkerbund in China 1931 bis 1935* (Hamburg: Mittelungen des Instituts für Asienkunde, No. 39, 1971). This study provides invaluable details on every aspect of the mission's work, including both the internal debates among members, with the Chinese and with the Americans, who deeply resented their own exclusion and the strong criticism of American influence on Chinese education in the report.

100. *Zhongguo jiaoyu faling huibian* (Shanghai: Commercial Press, 1935).

101. *Jiaoyu faling* (Shanghai: Zhonghua Shuju, 1947), p. 143.

102. *Ibid.*, pp. 156-7.

103. Neugebauer, *Anfänge pädagogische Entwicklungshilfe*, pp. 232-2, describes the visit of a Chinese delegation to Europe in 1932 and their special interest in such French professional schools as L'Ecole des Arts et Metiers.

104. John Israel, *Student Nationalism in China 1927-1937* (Stanford: Hoover Institution, Stanford University Press, 1966). This booke expertly analyzes the relations between university intellectuals and the Nationalist government up to the outbreak of the Sino-Japanese war.

105. This is not to suggest that Soviet patterns did not also have some new features drawn from socialist and revolutionary principles. However, the policies effectively im-

plemented by the Communists in the early fifties were actually quite close to those which the Nationalist government had favored in the thirties, yet never successfully implemented.

Notes to Chapter 7

1. Progressive and Progressive Education will be capitalized in this paper to distinguish the proper name of the movement from the adjective and common noun. I shall also use *Pinyin* spelling of Chinese characters unless the word has a common English spelling whose modification would obscure its reference, such as "Jiang Jieshi" for "Chiang Kai-shek."

2. An excellent succinct account appears in Barry C. Keenan, "Educational Reform and Politics in Early Republican China," *Journal of Asian Studies,* XXXIII (February 1974): 225-237, and more thorough discussion of the topic in *The Dewey Experiment in China: Educational Reform and Political Power in the Early Republic* (Cambridge, Mass.: Harvard University Press, 1977), by the same author. More or less attention is given to the fate of progressivism in China by many historians of the period, some of whom will be cited later in this paper. Of particular note, Jerome B. Grieder, *Hu Shih and the Chinese Renaissance: Liberalism in the Chinese Revolution, 1917-1937* (Cambridge, Mass.: Harvard University Press, 1970), is a thorough biography of the chief exponent of Dewey's philosophy in Republican China.

3. Hu Shih, *The Chinese Renaissance: The Haskell Lectures, 1933* (Chicago: University of Chicago Press, 1934).

4. John Dewey, *John Dewey, Lectures in China, 1919-1920.* ed. Robert W. Clopton, trans. Tsuin-Chen Ou. (Honolulu: University Press of Hawaii, 1973), p. 13.

5. Chu Don-Chean, *Patterns of Education for the Developing Nations: Tao's Work in China, 1917-1946* (Tainan, Taiwan: Kao-chang Printing Company, 1966), p. 23, and Keenan, "Educational Reform," pp. 225-227.

6. Keenan, "Educational Reform," p. 236.

7. An interesting portrait of the aftermath of this incident in terms of its educational significance is drawn in Ye Shengtao, *Schoolmaster Ni Huan-chih,* trans. A. C. Barnes (Beijing: Foreign Languages Press, 1958, original Chinese edition, 1930), chapts. 20-29.

8. See Guy S. Alitto, *The Last Confucian: Liang Shu-ming and the Chinese Dilemma of Modernity* (Berkeley: University of California Press, 1978).

9. See Maurice Meisner, *Li Ta-chao and the Origins of Chinese Marxism* (Cambridge, Mass.: Harvard University Press, 1967).

10. John Dewey, "American and Chinese Education," *New Republic,* XXX (March 1, 1922), p. 16, quoted in Keenan, "Educational Reform," p. 235. Benjamin I. Schwartz, "Themes in Intellectual History: May Fourth and After," in *The Cambridge History of China, Vol. 12, Republican China 1912-1949,* Part 1, ed. John K. Fairbank (Cambridge University Press, 1983), p. 434.

12. Schwartz, "Themes," p. 434.

13. Howard L. Boorman, and Richard C. Howard (eds.), *Biographical Dictionary of Republican China, Vol. III* (New York: Columbia University Press, 1970), p. 444. On a recent visit to a major normal university in China, the author was informed that there were in the reception room graduates of Columbia representing four decades, the author being the latest, and his hosts, leading officials of the university, the other three.

14. Tao Xingzhi, *Tao Xingzhi quanji, Vol. I-VI,* (The Collected Works of Tao Xingzhi, Vols. I-VI), ed. Huazhong Shifan Xueyuan jiaoyu kexue yanjiusuo (Changsha: Hunan jiaoyu chubanshe, 1984-1985).

15. This biographical sketch is a composite drawn in large part from the following sources: The subgroup for Research on Tao Xingzhi of the Higher Education Research Association of Central China Teachers College, "Tao Xingzhi nianpu" (A Chronology of the Life of Tao Xingzhi) in *Tao Xingzhi Xiansheng danchen jiushi zhounian jinian zhuanji 1891-1981* (The Ninetieth Anniversary of the Birth of Tao Xingzhi Commemorative Col-

lection), ed. Higher Education Association of the Central China Teachers College (Wuhan, 1981); Chu Don-chean, *Patterns of Education for the Developing Nations: Tao's Work in China, 1917-1946* (Tainan, Taiwan: Kao-chang Printing Co., 1966); Barry Keenan, *The Dewey Experiment in China: Educational Reform and Political Power in the Early Republic* (Cambridge, Mass.: Harvard University Press, 1977); Philip A. Kuhn, "T'ao Hsing-chih, 1891-1946, An Educational Reformer," *Papers on China XIII* (Cambridge, Mass.: Center for East Asian Studies, Harvard University, December 1954), pp. 163-195.

16. This signature appears in Tao Xingzhi, Letter to Dean J. E. Russell, Columbia Teachers College, February 16, 1916, Columbia Teachers College Archives.

17. Wang Yi Chu, *Chinese Intellectuals and the West, 1872-1949* (Chapel Hill, N.C.: University of North Carolina Press, 1966), pp. 150-156. Tao's indebtedness to his parents was expressed in the letter to Dean Russell, Teachers College Columbia University, cited in n. 16.

18. Tao, Letter to Dean Russell.

19. Jeremiah Whipple Jenks, *The Political and Social Significance of the Life and Teachings of Jesus* (New York: The International Committee of Young Men's Christian Associations, 1906). Tao cites Jenks as his inspiration in his letter to Dean Russell noted above.

20. Kuhn, "T'ao Hsing-chih 1891-1946," p. 168.

21. Tao, Letter to Dean Russell.

22. This conclusion was arrived at by the author after an examination of Tao's transcript, and the catalogue of course offerings during the same years. Both documents are available in the Archives of Columbia Teachers College.

23. Tao Xingzhi, "Shiyan zhuyi zhi jiaoyu fangfa" (Experimentalism's Educational Method) in *Tao Xingzhi quanji*, Vol. 1, pp. 59-64. The essay is striking for its attention to nineteenth century German philosophy and education, and its slighting of American pragmatism. It is in fact difficult not to suspect that Tao derived what notions he had of experimentalism from his courses on educational research, on the one hand, and from Cai Yuanpei, who translated Paulson into Chinese, and who was quite friendly with Tao, on the other.

24. Tao Xingzhi, "Jieshao Duwei Xiansheng de jiaoyu xueshuo" (An Introduction to Mr. Dewey's Educational Thought) in *Tao Xingzhi quanji*, Volume I, pp. 102-104.

25. Keenan, for example, writes that Tao acknowledged Dewey's influence in his early reform proposals at Southeastern University, yet the essay he cites to support this, "Jiao xue zuo heyi" (The Unity of Teaching, Learning, and Doing), 1927, does not mention Dewey. It does cite an earlier version of the same article written in 1919, "Jiao xue heyi" (The Unity of Teaching and Learning), in which Tao not only fails to cite Dewey at all, but once again depends for precedent and example upon Frederick the Great, Paulson, and other personal and institutional representatives of nineteenth century German higher education.

26. Tao Xingzhi. "The Unity of Teaching, Learning, and Doing (November 2, 1927)," *Chinese Education* VIII, No. 4 (Winter 1974-75), p. 13.

27. Tao, "Unity of Teaching, Learning and Doing," p. 11.

28. Ernest P. Young, "The Hung-hsien Emperor as a Modernizing Conservative" in *The Limits of Change; Essays on Conservative Alternatives in Republican China*, ed. Charlotte Furth (Cambridge, Mass.: Harvard University Press, 1976), pp. 182-187.

29. Tao is credited with editing Zou Enyuan's translation of Dewey's *Democracy and Education*, but the profound misunderstanding of Dewey's views on the relation of schooling to society in Tao's essay "Shenghuo ji jiaoyu," 1929, indicates no more than a passing acquaintance with the work. Indeed, the metaphor for "school is society" that Tao uses against Dewey, that "it is like taking a lively little bird from the air and putting it into a cage," may have been taken from Rabindranath Tagore, another visitor to China in this period, and his famous essay, "The Parrot's Training." Chu, *Patterns of Education*, p. 24; *Tao Xingzhi quanji*, Vol. II, p. 182.

30. The original English versions of Dewey's lectures have been lost. What is available are the Chinese translations, and their recent retranslation back into English and editing by Robert W. Clopton and Tsuin-chen Ou, *John Dewey: Lectures in China, 1919-1920* (Honolulu: University Press of Hawaii, 1973). As Clopton and Ou themselves demonstrate, there has most likely been a significant loss of meaning in the process, particularly in nuance and emphasis. On the other hand, the major trends of Dewey's thought are clearly evident, and are consistent with his earlier writings on education.

31. Dewey, *Lectures in China*, p. 214. Dewey gives no theoretical account of habit in this paragraph, only the advice that good habits should be developed in children before bad habits become rooted. CF. John Dewey, *Experience and Education* (New York: Kappa Delta Pi, 1938), pp. 35-39; *Human Nature and Conduct* (New York: Henry Holt, 1922), pp. 14-88.

32. Dewey, *Lectures in China*, p. 221.

33. Dewey, *Lectures in China*, pp. 243-244.

34. Dewey, *Lectures in China*, pp. 85, 206.

35. Dewey seemed to hold to something of a similar view in his early book *School and Society*, but later explicitly argued for the legitimate pre-eminence of the teacher as an authority in the subject at hand, and therefore the teacher's rightful role as guide and judge. Tao never seemed aware of the contradiction of his egalitarian rhetoric and authoritarian practice, as for example in the "democratic" regulations at Yucai School, one of which was that students must obey all the rules imposed by the school authorities. John Dewey, *Experience and Education* (New York: Collier-Macmillan Publishing Co., 1963, first published 1938), pp. 58-59. Zhang Zaiwei (ed.), *Yu bi ying cai*; *Tao Xingzhi he Yucai Xuexiao zai Chongqing* (Chongqing: Chongqing chuban she, 1984.

36. Dewey, *Lectures on China* pp. 227, 196.

37. Subgroup for Research on Tao Xingzhi, "Tao Xingzhi nianpu," p. 57.

38. Dewey, *Lectures in China*, p. 273. To anyone familiar with Dewey's later writings on man and society, these lectures must seem out of character. Although Dewey originally intended to publish them, he apparently later thought better of it.

39. Subgroup for Research on Tao Xingzhi, "Tao Xingzhi nianpu," p. 56.

40. Tao Xingzhi, A Teaching Manual for Uniting Teaching, Learning and Doing (October 1931)," *Chinese Education* VII, No. 4 (Winter 1974-75), pp. 99-101.

41. Dewey, *Lectures in China*, pp. 100, 185.

42. Dewey, *Lectures in China*, p. 259.

43. There is an amusing anecdote in Keenan, *The Dewey Experiment in China*, p. 92, recounting how Tao chided Jiang Menglin for being the Acting Chancellor of Peking University yet having illiterate servants. Tao immediately called the servants together and began instructing them from his *Thousand Character Text*. Jiang "scratched his head and said to T'ao: you really have missionary spirit."

44. Dewey, *Lectures in China*, p. 257.

45. Dewey, *Lectures in China*, p. 219.

46. Dewey, *Lectures in China*, p. 219.

47. Dewey, *Lectures in China*, p. 219.

48. James E. Sheridan, *China in Disintegration: The Republican Era in Chinese History, 1912-1949* (New York: The Free Press, 1975).

49. Dewey, *Lectures in China*. p. 238.

50. Dewey, *Lectures in China*. p. 238.

51. Tao Xingzhi, "Shenghuo ji jiaoyu," in *Tao Xingzhi quanji*, Vol. II, pp. 182-183.

52. Boorman and Howard, *Biographical Dictionary of Republican China*, Vol. III, p. 245.

53. Grieder, *Hu Shih and the Chinese Renaissance*, p. 190. Grieder writes that the document, known as "Our Political Proposals," and signed by Cai Yuanpei, Liang Shuming, Li Dazhao, Zhu Jingnong, and Ding Wenjiang among others, "was the first systematic summary of opinions that can be identified as 'liberal', and it constituted the platform of what came to be called . . . the 'good government group.'"

54. Boorman and Howard, *Biographical Dictionary of Republican China*, Vol. 4, p. 52.

55. Tao Xingzhi, *Zhixing shuxin* (Shanghai: 1931), p. 55, quoted in Kuhn, "T'ao Hsing-chih," p. 170. This letter to Tao's younger sister also appears in *Xingzhi shuxin ji* (Nanjing: Anhui jiaoyu chuban she, 1983), pp. 28-29.

56. Thomas H. C. Lee, "Life in the Schools of Sung China," *Journal of Asian Studies*, XXXVII, No. 1 (November 1977), pp. 46-49.

57. Sally Borthwick, *Education and Social Change in China: The Beginnings of the Modern Era* (Stanford: Hoover Institution Press, 1983), pp. 35-36.

58 A description of the tactics and methods used by Yan is given in Pearl S. Buck, *Tell the People: Talks with James Yen about the Mass Education Movement* (New York: International Institute of Rural Reconstruction, 1959), pp. 33-38.

59. The Tao Xingzhi Research Group of the Central China Normal Institute Higher Education Association, "Tao Xingzhi shengping ji qi sixiang fazhan" (The Development of the Life and Thought of Tao Xingzhi) in Central China Normal Institute Higher Education Association (ed.), *Tao Xingzhi Xiansheng danchen jiushi zhounian jinian zhuanji (1891-1981)*, p. 17.

60. Merle Curti, *The Social Ideas of American Educators* (Totowa, New Jersey: Littlefield, Adams, & Co., 1968), p. 523. See also John and Evelyn Dewey, *Schools of Tomorrow* (New York: E. P. Dutton & Co., 1915), chapt. VII, "The School as a Social Settlement."

61. Ye Shengtao, for example, ascribes such a view to educational reformers from even before the 1911 revolution. Yeh Sheng-tao, *Schoolmaster Ni Huan-chih*, chapt. 1.

62. A. Biswas and J. C. Aggarwal, *Seven Indian Educationists* (New Delhi: Arya Book Depot, 1968), p. 105.

63. Buck, *Tell the People*, pp. 60-61. Buck's book is obviously propaganda intended for an American audience, but there is much that confirms the supposition of Yen's greater conservatism, from the moral if not financial support of Chiang Kai-shek, to the resistance of areas under his influence to communist control, to other accounts of his life, as in the biography of Yen in Boorman and Howard, *Biographical Dictionary of Republican China*, Vol. IV, pp. 52-54

64. Tao Xingzhi, "Teaching Manual", p. 103.

65. Tao Xingzhi, "Zhongguo xiangcun jiaoyu zhi genben gaizao" (Basic Reform of Chinese Rural Education), *Tao Xingzhi quanji*, pp. 653-654.

66. Tao Xingzhi, "Cong yeren shenghuo chufa" (Start from the Life of Primitive Man), *Tao Xingzhi quanji*, Vol. II, pp. 74-75. The translation is after Tao Xingzhi, "Beginning by Living Like Primitive People," *Chinese Education* VIII, No. 4 (Winter 1974-75), pp. 83-84.

67. Dewey, *Lectures in China*, p. 250.

68. Tao Xingzhi, "'Wei zhishi' jieji" (The 'False Intellectual' Class), *Tao Xingzhi quanji*, Vol. II, p. 88.

69. Tao Xingzhi, "Shenghuo ji jiaoyu" (Life Is Education), *Tao Xingzhi quanji*, Vol. II, 183.

70. Particularly relevant is Levenson's application of this principle in his biography of Liang Qichao: Joseph R. Levenson, *Liang Ch'i-ch-ao and the Mind of Modern China* (Berkeley: University of California Press, 1970), pp. 1-11, but see also "'History' and 'value': The Tensions of Intellectual Choice in Modern China," in Arthur F. Wright (ed.), *Studies in Chinese Thought* (Chicago: University of Chicago Press, 1953), pp. 146-194.

71. Subgroup for Research on Tao Xingzhi, "Tao Xingzhi nianpu," p. 60.

72. Zhang Jian, "Weida de renmin jiaoyujia Tao Xingzhi Xiansheng" (The Great People's Educator, Tao Xingzhi), *Journal of Central China Teachers College* 4 (August 1983), p. 91.

73. Both Kuhn and Keenan view Xiaozhuang as the climax of Tao's career, correctly in my opinion.

74. Dai Botao, "Huiyi Tao Xingzhi Xiansheng san jian shi" (Three Things in My)

Memories of Mr. Tao Xingzhi), in *Tao Xingzhi Yi Sheng,* ed., The Educational Thought Research Institute of Anhui Province (Hunan: Hunan Educational Publishing House, 1984), p. 11.

75. This was true even in the case of the most thorough of Dewey's disciples, as is convincingly argued in Jerome Grieder's biography of Hu Shi, *Hu Shih and the Chinese Renaissance,* pp. 314 ff.

Notes to Chapter 8

1. The other denominations were the Church Missionary Society of England, American Baptist Foreign Mission Society, Friends Service Council of England, and Methodist Episcopal Church of the United States.
The early history of the WCUU is detailed in *Our West China Mission* (Toronto: The Missionary Society of the Methodist Church, 1920), pp. 358-370. A complete history of the University can be found in Lewis Walmsley's *West China Union University* (N.Y.: United Board for Christian Higher Education in Asia, 1974). For an account of other missionary educational endeavours in China, see J. G. Lutz, *China and the Christian Colleges, 1850-1950* (Ithaca: Cornell, 1971).

2. Government of Canada, Department of External Affairs (DEA), File 4.1(s), Ambassador V. W. Odlum.

3. *Ibid.*

4. E. I. Hart, *Virgil C. Hart: Missionary Statesman (Founder of the American and Canadian Missions in Central and West China)* (Toronto: McClelland, Goodchild and Stewart, 1917), p. 222.

5. *Ibid.,* p. 223.

6. United Church Archives (UCA) WCUU Pamphlet, "Spend Ten Minutes in China" (1919-20).

7. UCA-WCM Pamphlet, "A Statement of Mission Plant" (Toronto: Methodist Mission Rooms, 1910).

8. UCA-WCUU Pamphlet, "Spend Ten Minutes in China."

9. The Methodist Church amalgamated in 1925 with two other Protestant denominations to form the United Church of Canada.

10. John W. Foster, "The Imperialism of Righteousness: Canadian Protestant Missions and the Chinese Revolution, 1925-1928" (unpublished Ph.D. dissertation, University of Toronto, 1977), p. 217.

11. *Forward With China: The Story of the Missions of the United Church of Canada in China* (Toronto: Ryerson, 1928), p. 261.

12. UCA-WCM Pamphlet, "Spend Ten Minutes in China," p. 8.

13. *Ibid.*

14. Hart, *Virgil C. Hart: Missionary Statesman,* p. 220.

15. O. L. Kilborn, *Heal the Sick: An Appeal for Medical Missions in China* (Toronto: The Missionary Society of the Methodist Church, 1910), p. 21.

16. *Ibid.,* p. 38.

17. UCA-WCM Pamphlet, "A Statement of Mission Plant," p. 12.

18. W. Harding Le Riche, "Seventy Years of Public Health in Canada," *Canadian Journal of Public Health,* No. 70 (May-June 1974), pp. 156-161, and George Rosen, "The Hospital: Historical Sociology of a Community Institution," in E. Friedson (ed.), *The Hospital in Modern Society* (London: Collier-Macmillan, 1963), Chapter 1.

19. V. C. Hart, *Western China* (Boston: Ticknor and Co., 1888), p. 300.

20. *Ibid.*

20. *Ibid.,* p. 299.

22. Foster, "The Imperialism of Righteousness," passim, and G. Sarvis, "Study of

Missions in Szechuan," in *Laymen's Foreign Missions Inquiry Fact-Finders Report* (N.Y.: n.p. 1933), p. 579.

23. UCA-WCM Pamphlet, "Spend Ten Minutes in China."

24. *Ibid.*, p. 12.

25. *Our West China Mission* (Toronto: The Missionary Society of the Methodist Church, 1920), pp. 267-436.

26. Richard Allen, *The Social Passion: Religion and Social Reform in Canada, 1914-1928* (Toronto: University of Toronto Press, 1973), p. 3.

27. *Ibid.*, pp. 289-292.

28. Margaret Beattie, *A Brief History of the Student Christian Movement in Canada, 1921-1974* (Toronto: SCM, 1975).

29. *Ibid.*, pp. 75-76.

30. *Ibid.*, p. 74.

31. UCA-WCM Pamphlet, "Spend Ten Minutes in China."

32. *Forward With China* (Toronto: Ryerson, 1921), pp. 228-9.

33. *Ibid.*

34. Grace Lane, *A Brief Halt at Mile "50"* (Toronto: United Church Publishing House, 1974), p. 5.

35. G. W. Skinner, "Marketing and Social Structure in Rural China, Part II," *Journal of Asian Studies,* XXIV:2, pp. 204, 225-227.

36. Hart, *Virgil C. Hart: Missionary Statesman,* p. 296.

37. O. R. Joliffe, "The Field," in *Our West China Mission.*

38. A concise study of provincial militarism in Sichuan can be found in Robert A. Kapp, *Szechuan and the Chinese Republic* (New Haven and London: Yale University Press, 1973). Additional information about Sichuan's political structure can be found in A. Doak Barnett, *China on the Eve of Communist Takeover* (New York: Praeger, 1963), Chapter 10, and Hsiao Kung-chuan, *Rural China: Imperial Control in the 19th Century* (Seattle: University of Washington, 1960). Missionary accounts include *Our West China Mission.*

39. *Our WCM,* pp. 101-102, and Kapp, *Szechuan and the Chinese Republic,* p. 34.

40. Zhou Cheng (ed.), *Weisheng xinzheng jiangyi* (Lectures on the Public Health Administration) (Shanghai: Taidong tushuqu, 1925).

41. K. Minden, "The Development of Early Chinese Communist Health Policy," *American Journal of Chinese Medicine,* VII:4 (1979), pp. 300-301. For a thorough account of Western influences on the development of China's medical system, see AnElissa Lucas, *Chinese Medical Modernization: Comparative Policy Continuities 1930s-1980s* (New York: Praeger, 1982).

42. Kilborn, *Heal the Sick,* p. 223.

43. UCA-WCM Pamphlet, "Spend Ten Minutes in China."

44. *Our WCM,* p. 396.

45. Rockerfeller Archives Collection (RAC) 1V2B7-158-1154 CMB, Inc., "Twenty-five Years of Dentistry " (1942) (also UCC-Board of Foreign Missions (BFM)-WCUU 12-18).

46. UCC-BFM-WCM 5-107, "1934 Report of Work by E. N. Meuser."

47. UCC-BFM-WCM 2-12. "Report by Wm. Band, Sino-British Science Cooperative Office of the British Council" (Chongqing, 1944).

48. UCA-WCM Pamphlet, "Spend Ten Minutes in China," p. 15.

49. UCA (uncatalogued). Report of the Special Committee on Policy (Medical Work) 1936, pp. 8-9.

50. Walmsley, *The West China Union University,* p. 9.

51. UCC-BFM-WCM 6-135, Kilborn to Arnup, 2 August 1937, p. 3. See also *Our WCM,* p. 368, "Our Contribution."

52. UCA-WCUU Pamphlet, op. cit., p. 9.

53. UCC-BFM-WCM 1-1, "West China Union University Needs." The total medical

budget was $750,000 out of a total university budget of $1,000,000. This included the Department of medicine, physics, biology, and chemistry (which taught medical students), and the hospitals.

54. UCA, "Report on Policy" 1936, p. 8.

55. *Ibid.*

56. UCC-BFM-WCM 4-95, H. B. Collier, "Annual Report of Work: 1933," p. 2.

57. UCA-China Pamphlet Series 1-29, "Mission Legislation," Chengdu, (1916). Dr. J. Endicott mentioned that one of his Chinese colleagues exclaimed there were no less than thirteen virgin births reported in Chinese history: Interview with Dr. J. Endicott.

58. For example, see UCC-BFM-WCM 5-121, "Report of Work for the Year 1935," Spooner (Department of Chemistry), p. 2, and *Ibid.*, 4-92, Collier to Endicott, 30 August 1933, p. 3.

59. K. Minden, "Missionaries, Medicine and Modernization: Canadian Medical Missionaries in Sichuan, 1925-1952," unpublished Ph.D. dissertation (Toronto: York University, 1981), Chapter 2.

60. G. W. Sarvis, *Laymen's Foreign Missions Inquiry, Factfinders' Reports: China* (New York, n.p., 1933); Vol. 5, sup. 2, p. 601.

61. This standard was adopted after the Flexner Report was published in 1910. (It has been referred to as "The Hopkins Model" after Johns Hopkins Medical School in Baltimore.)

62. RAC IV2B9-158-1154, W. P. Fenn, General Secretary, 17 September 1963.

63. *Ibid.*, "Replies to Questionnaire from Dr. Claude Forkner," Director, China Medical Board, 1943.

64. RAC IV2B9-158-1156, Kilborn to Gregg, 1 July 1946. Also see University of Toronto Faculty of Medicine Calendars, 1933 to 1946.

65. *Ibid.* See University of Toronto Faculty of Medicine Calendars, 1933-4, p. 39.

66. UCC-BFM-WCM 4-83, Report of Work, 1932, L. G. Kilborn. This may have been an attempt to adapt the Rockefeller Peking Union Medical College system of 8 years of training. The PUMC goal was to train medical researchers who would staff university medical schools. It was not practical for WCUU to follow this model, which depended on generous funding and adequate staff.

67. RAC IV2B9-158-1154, West China Union University College of Medicine and Dentistry (1937-39), p. 1.

68. RAC RG 4-9-2109, Stevenson, May 1926.

69. *Ibid.*

70. UCC-BFM-WCM 3-66, Report of Work of the United Church of Canada West China Mission, 1931, p. 15.

71. *Ibid.*

72. RAC IV 2B9-158-1154, "Answers by the Department of Pharmacy of the West China Union University," 14 August 1944, p. 5.

73. Kilborn, *Heal the Sick,* p. 224.

74. UCC-BFM-WCM 3-51, Report of Work, 1929, A. E. Best.

75. UCC-BFM-WCM 3-51, Report of Work, 1930, L. G. Kilborn, p. 2.

76. UCC-BFM-WCUU 3-12, The China Colleges, 5:2 (November 1938), p. 2.

77. UCA-WCUU Pamphlet, The West China Union University, 1910-1939, p. 22. See also UCC-BFM-WCM 2-28, Bell to Arnup, 10 Sept. 1928, and Hayward correspondence, 11 August 1935.

78. UCA-MCC-GBM-WCM 2-36, A. Sutherland to O. L. Kilborn, 31 August 1908.

79. UCA-WCUU Pamphlet, "Spend Ten Minutes in China," p. 22.

80. Interview with Dr. Ian Hu, graduate of WCUU College of Medicine.

81. Personal papers, L. G. Kilborn, note from E. R. Cunningham (1945?).

82. RAC IV2B9-158-1154, United Board for Christian Colleges in China, Preliminary Data on Mission Medical Schools in China, 15 June 1954.

83. UCC-BFM-WCUU 1-13, Kilborn to Endicott, 7 August 1931, p. 2.

84. UCC-BFM-WCM, Report of Work for 1934, p. 7.

85. *Ibid.*

86. UCC-BFM-WCM, 3-66, Report of the UCC-WCM, 1931, L. G. Kilborn.

87. UCA-WCUU Pamphlet "Spend Ten Minutes in China," p. 24.

88. *Ibid.* Bell to Endicott, 26 June 1935, p. 4.

89. UCC-BFM-WCM 5-111.

90. UCC-BFM-WCUU Box 30, American Board of China Christian Colleges Committee on Medical Education, 24 March 1944, Appendix A.

91. DEA 6048-40C, Encl. McClure to Penfield re: Condition of Chinese Military Medical Services, 27 September 1943, p. 2.

92. Li Dingan, "Speech to Graduating Class of 1944," *Huaxi yixun,* (West China Medical Bulletin) 1:2 (June 1944), pp. 93-95. Dr. Li was affiliated with the National Health Administration and editor of the *Medical Society Journal* (Wong, K. Chimin and Wu Lien teh, *History of Chinese Medicine* (Shanghai: National Quarantine Service, 1936), pp. 706-722.

93. *Ibid.,* p. 94.

94. *Ibid.*

95. Li Dingan, "Control of Contagion and the Medical System," *Huaxi yixun,* 1:4 (December 1944), pp. 153-157.

96. *Ibid.,* pp. 155-6. See also Lucas, *Chinese Medical Modernization.*

97. DEA 7988-40C, Office of Strategic Services, R & A. No. 951, "China's Destiny," 15 July 1943, p. 10. This document is an analysis of Zhang Jieshi's book of the same title.

98. *Christian Higher Education in Changing China 1880-1950* (Grand Rapids, Michigan: Wm. Eerdmans, 1976), pp. 203-208.

99. Spooner, R. C., "In West China," *United Church Record and Missionary Review* (November 1938).

100. *Ibid.,* also UCC-BFM-WCUU 12-4, Kilborn to Arnup and Amstrong, 7 June 1938.

101. UCC-BFM-WCM8-185, Kilborn to Arnup: 8 January 1941, p. 3.

102. This was also the opinion of the Medical Education Committee of the American Board for China Christian Colleges. See UCC-BFM-BOM Box 30, Minutes of Subcommittee, 19 April 1944, and Minutes of Meeting of Committee on Medical Education, 25 September 1944.

103. UCC-BFM-WCM 10-238, Bell to Arnup, 31 March 1944.

104. RAC IV2B9 159-1156, Forkner to Lobenstine, 24 January 1945.

105. RAC IV2B9-159-1155, Chang to Balfour, 20 September 1945.

106. See UCC-BFM-WCM 11-264, G. Cunningham to Arnup, 8 November 1946 and 11-270, Kilborn to Bell, 3 July 1946.

107. *Ibid.,* 11-284, Kilborn to Arnup, 19 February 1947. Also 10-256, Kilborn to Arnup 20 August 1945, and 10-239, Kilborn to Bell, 17 October 1944.

108. UCC-BFM-WCM 4-95, Annual Report of Work: 1933, Collier, 5 February 1934, p. 2.

109. UCA Personal Papers, A. W. Lindsay, "West China Union University," 21 March (1937?).

110. *Ibid.,* Lobenstine to Arnup, 10 December 1943.

111. *Ibid.,* p. 1.

112. UCC-BFM-WCM 11-284, Kilborn to Arnup, 30 December 1947.

113. UCC-Board of Overseas Missions (BOM)-WCM 13-331, G. Cunningham to Arnup, 7 September 1950.

114. UCC-BOM-WCM 13-341, Arnup, 6 February 1951.

115. UCC-BOM-WCM 13-339, Li Yuan, "American Imperialist Missionaries In The Service of God," *Chengdu Industrial and Commercial Guide Daily Paper,* 25 November 1950.

116. RAC RG4 Ser. 1-90-2108, Beech to Greene, 7 February, 1925, p. 2.

117. UCC-BFM-WCUU 1-3, Registration with the Government, October 1927.

118. *Ibid.*, and UCC-BFM-WCUU 1-3, Speech to Board of Governors, WCUU, 15 Feburary 1928.

119. UCA-WCUU Pamphlets, "West China Union University." The University was also granted absolute charter by the Regents of the University of the State of New York in 1934.

120. UCC-BFM-WCM 5-107, WCM Report of Work for 1934.

121. *Ibid.*, 5-119, Dickinson to Endicott, 22 July 1935.

122. UCC-BFM-WCUU 12-18, "25 Years of Dentistry."

123. Interview with Mrs. J. J. (Bea) Mullett.

124. UCC-BFM-WCM 6-140, Report of Work for 1927, T. H. Williams, p. 2.

125. *Ibid.*

126. UCC-BFM-WCUU 9-230, WCUU Report, 1943, p. 3.

127. DEA 19-CR-2-40 Dr. E. S. W. Cheo, National Dental Health Board to T. C. Davis, Canadian Ambassador to China, 5 January 1949.

128. *Ibid.* Embassy of the Republic of China, to Lester Pearson, Secretary of State for External Affairs, Ottawa, 11 January 1949.

129. *Ibid.*, 22 April 1949, att.

130. *Ibid.*, 24 July 1948, and 12 March 1951.

131. *Ibid.*, 18-161, "First Report of the Szechuan Provincial Health Administration," May-December 1939, p. 1.

132. *Ibid.*

133. *Ibid.*, " State and Local Health Services," 1 November 1940.

134. *Ibid.*, 18-162, "Report of Public Health Training in Chengtu," C. C. Chen, June 1944, p. 2.

135. Interview with Dr. C. C. Chen, Toronto, 5 November 1979.

136. UCC-BFM-WCM i-175, Bell to Arnup, 9 July 1941.

137. *Ibid.*, 9-196, Bell to Arnup, 24 February 1942.

138. Interview with Dr. Chen.

139. UCC-BFM-BOM Box 30, Minutes of Meetings of Committee on Medical Education, 24 March 1944, p. 2.

140. Interview, Dr. A. S. Allen, and documents on his imprisonment in UCC-BFM-WCM 14-359; DEA 3051-40, and Allen's personal correspondence.

141. UCC-BFM-WCM 13-345, J. H. Arnup, "China and Missions," 24 January 1951.

142. For an excellent account of the PUMC experience, see Mary B. Bullock, *An American Transplant; The Rockefeller Foundation and Peking Union Medical College* (Berkeley: University of California, 1980).

143. Interviews with C. C. Chen, and William Small.

Notes to Chapter 9

1. E. H. Carr, *Socialism in One Country,* 3 vols. (Harmondsworth: Penguin, 1970), 3:747, note 5.

2. J. Guillermaz, *A History of the Chinese Communist Party,* trans. Anne Destenay (London: Methuen, 1968), p. 203.

3. R. F. Price, *Marx and Education in Russia and China* (London: Croom Helm, 1977), p. 224.

4. *Biographical Dictionary of Republican China,* ed. Howard Boorman, 3 vols. (New York: Columbia University Press, 1968), 1:475-479.

5. Mao Zedong, *Selected Works of Mao Zedong,* 5 vols. (Beijing: Foreign Languages Press, 1977), 5:17-18.

6. The question of Mao's opposition to the Soviet model and the degree to which the Cultural Revolution suggested an alternative is the subject of a considerable literature.

7. Bill Brugger, *China: Liberation and Transformation 1942-1962* (London: Croom Helm, 1981), pp. 89-108.

8. Jerome A. Cohen, *The Criminal Process in the People's Republic of China 1949-1964* (Cambridge, Mass.: Harvard University Press, 1968).

9. Stuart Schram, *Mao Tse-tung Unrehearsed: Talks and Letters 1956-71* (Harmondsworth: Penguin, 1974), p. 98. The Cultural Revolution document "Chronology of the two-road struggle on the educational front in the past seventeen years," translation in *Revolutionary Education in China: Documents and Commentary,* ed. Peter Seybolt (White Plains, New York: International Arts and Sciences Press, 1973), claims that Mao earlier laid down that the "new educational experience of the old Liberated Areas should form the basis," but they give no source. They are, however, correct in citing the First National Educational Work Conference of December 1949 for having employed this formulation. See *Revolutionary Education in China: Documents and Commentary,* p. 7, and *Zhonghua Renmin Gongheguo jiaoyu dashi ji 1949-1982 (A Record of Educational Events in the Chinese People's Republic, 1949-1982)* (Beijing: Jiaoyu kexue chubanshe, 1983), p. 8. Significantly the wording in the two sources is different, the former leaving out the words "specially" and "advanced" in the sentence "should specially draw support from the advanced experience of the Soviet Union in educational construction."

10. This he described as "our first modern university in China," complaining that those "adopted" from countries other than the USSR had all taught capitalist values. Liu Shaoqi, *Collected Works of Liu Shaoqi 1945-1957* (Hong Kong: Union Research Institute, 1969), p. 236.

11. Alexander Korol, *Soviet Education for Science and Technology* (Cambridge, Mass.: M.I.T. Press, 1957), pp. 10-11.

12. Biographical details of officials listed in the *Jiaoyu dashi ji* have been checked in *Biographical Dictionary of Republican China* ed. H. Boorman and in D. W. Klein and A. B. Clark, *Biographic Dictionary of Chinese Communism* (Cambridge, Mass.: Harvard University Press, 1971).

13. *Chinese Communist Education: Records of the First Decade,* ed. S. Fraser (New York: Wiley and Sons, 1965); R. F. Price, *Education in Communist China* (London: Routledge and Kegan Paul, 1970), pp. 103-4.

14. *Jiaoyu dashi ji,* p. 71.

15. *Ibid.*

16. *Ibid.,* p. 80.

17. *Ibid.,* p. 279.

18. Cheng Chu-yuan, *Scientific and Engineering Manpower in Communist China, 1949-1963* (Washington: National Science Foundation, 1965), p. 194; *Education and Communism in China: An Anthology of Commentary and Documents,* ed. S. Fraser (Pall Mall Press, 1971), p. 500.

19. For a brief biography, see *Pedagogicheskaya Entsiklopediya,* 4 vols. (Moscow: Sovetskaya Entsiklopediya, 1964-1968), 2:335-6.

20. *Jiaoyu dashi ji,* p. 64.

21. *Ibid.,* p. 142.

22. *Ibid.,* p. 151.

23. *Ibid.,* pp. 185, 215, 238, 262, 335, 372.

24. *Ibid.,* pp. 286, 302.

25. Cheng Chu-yuan, *Scientific and Engineering Manpower in Communist China,* pp. 196-9, 237.

26. *China aktuell,* (December, 1984), p. 705, (July 1985), p. 415.

27. *China aktuell,* (December, 1984), pp. 726-28. The following newly elected members of the CCP 12th Central Committee are reported to have studied in the USSR: members of the Politbureau and Secretariat, one out of eight: Li Peng (Moscow Power Institute); members of CC, 6 out of 56: He Zhukang (Moscow Economics College); Li Guixian

(Mendelev Chemical Technology Institute, Moscow); Ruan Chongwu (Moscow Motor Vehicle Machinery College); Song Jian (Moscow Bauman Polytechnical Institute and Moscow University); Wei Jianxing (Moscow, institute not given); and Zhou Guangzhao (Moscow, United Institute of Nuclear Physics); alternate members of the same, 1 out of 35: Keyum Bawudun (physics, USSR). See *China Aktuell* (September, 1985) pp. 627-644.

28. Articles on Soviet education in the *Remin jiaoyu were as follows:*

1950	16 items	occupying 77 pages	in 6 issues.
1951	21 items	occupying 56 pages	in 8 issues.
1952	35 items	occupying 127 pages	in 12 issues.
1953	34 items	occupying 112 pages	in 12 issues.
1954	34 items	occupying 132 pages	in 12 issues.
1955	23 items	occupying 125 pages	in 11 issues.
1956	? items	occupying 147 pages	in 10 issues.
1957	7 items	occupying 28 pages	in 6 issues.

Of these materials the following pages were by Kairov or about his textbook, *Pedagogy:* 1951: 20 pp; 1953: 6 pp; 1954: 11 pp; 1955: 12 pp; and 1957: 8 pp; a total of 57 pp or 7.8% of the total of 727 pages.

29. *Waiguo jiaoyu dongtai, Waiguo jiaoyu* and *Waiguo jiaoyu ziliao* are published by Beijing Teachers University, the Central Institute for Educational Research and Huadong Teachers University in Shanghai respectively.

30. Cheng Chu-yuan, *Scientific and Engineering Manpower in Communist China,* p. 205.

31. *Ibid.,* p. 202.

32. *Ibid.,* p. 203.

33. *Ibid.,* p. 204.

34. Michel Klochko, *Soviet Scientist in China* (London: Hollis and Carter, 1964).

35. Cheng Chu-yuan, *Scientific and Engineering Manpower in Communist China,* pp. 192, 205.

36. The doctrine of the Party is best studied in the lectures Stalin delivered at the Sverdlow University in April, 1924, *The Foundations of Leninism,* and *Concerning Questions of Leninism,* a pamphlet published in January, 1926. There also is the doctrine of "democratic centralism" expounded: "the principle of the minority submitting to the majority, the principle of directing Party work from a centre." See pp. 6, 8, 34, 39.

37. Mao Zedong, *Quotations from Chairman Mao Tse-tung* (Peking: Foreign Languages Press, 1966), chapter 11.

38. *Jiaoyu dashi ji,* p. 68.

39. Korol, *Soviet Education for Science and Technology,* pp. 147-148.

40. In 1952, China had 191,147 tertiary students and 635,609 students of specialized secondary schools. See *Zhongguo jiaoyu nianjian 1949-1981* (Chinese Education Yearbook) (Beijing: China Encyclopedic Press, 1984), pp. 966, 982. In 1951-2 the Soviet Union had 845,100 tertiary students and 1,297,600 students of specialized secondary schools. See Korol, *Soviet Education for Science and Technology,* pp. 107, 132.

41. The structure of the Ministry of Education in 1906 and 1912 is given in Yin Chi-ling, *Reconstruction of Modern Educational Organizations in China* (Shanghai: Commercial Press, 1926), pp. 8-9, 30-35. The structure is similar to that of the Ministry of Education as established in 1952, which had: a General Office (*Bangongting*); a Tertiary Teacher Training Department (*Gaodeng shifan jiaoyu si*); a Secondary Teacher Training Department (*Zhongdeng shifan jiaoyu si*); a Secondary School Education Department (*Zhongxue jiaoyu si*); a Primary School Education Department (*Xiaoxue jiaoyu si*); a Worker-Peasant Spare-time Education Department (*Gongnong yeyu jiaoyu si*); a National Minorities Education Department (*Minzu jiaoyu si*); an Educational Guidance Department (*Jiaoxue zhidao si*); a Planning & Finance Division (*Jihua caiwu chu*); a Pre-school Education Division (*You'er jiaoyu chu*); Division for Education of the Deaf, Dumb & Blind (*Mangya jiaoyu chu*); a Physical Education Guidance Division (*Tiyu zhidao chu*); a Translation Office (*Fanyi shi*); an Advisors Office (*Canshi shi*); a Textbook Editing Committee (*Jiaokeshu*

bianshen weiyuanhui); and an Office for *People's Education (Renmin jiaoyu shi)*. See *Jiaoyu dashi ji*, p. 68.

42. Nicholas DeWitt, *Education and Professional Employment in the USSR* (Washington: National Science Foundation, 1961), p. 223.

43. Examples of joint responsibility are the Beijing College of Architectural Engineering, jointly under the Ministry of Building and the Ministry of Education, the Nanjing College of Post and Telecommunication, jointly under the Ministry of Post and Telecommunications and the Ministry of Education and the Xi'An College of Highway Research, jointly under the Ministry of Highways and the Ministry of Education. See Surveys and Research Corporation, *Directory of Selected Scientific Institutions in Mainland China* (Stanford: Hoover Institution Press, 1970).

44. Surprisingly, it is difficult to discover the details of Soviet Ministerial functioning. It is not described in the obvious works on Soviet education, either English or Russian. The *Pedagogicheskaya Entsiklopediya* describes the various functions of the different Ministeries without giving their divisions (1965, 2:832-34). The collection of documents, *Narodnoye Obrazovaniye v SSR: Sbornik Dokumentov, 1917-1973 gg.* (Moscow: Pedagogika, 1974) is also strangely silent on the subject. Wasyl Shimoniak, *Communist Education: Its History, Philosophy and Politics* (Chicago: Rand McNally, 1970), p. 128, gives a table of departments for a Union Republic Ministry of Education. The particular topic of joint responsibility is inadequately explored where it is mentioned in Zaleski et al., *Science Policy in the USSR* (Paris: OECD, 1969), pp. 53, 64, 299, 375.

45. Y. C. Wang, *Chinese Intellectuals and the West 1872-1949* (Chapel Hill: The University of North Carolina Press, 1966), p. 363. The translation "middle school" which Chinese and American writers give for *zhongxue* ignores this U.S. origin. It is also misleading for at least British and Australian readers since in those countries middle school has a different, restricted meaning. With the variety of the USA itself perhaps junior and senior secondary school is the best translation, i.e. one which gives the closest agreement in the target language.

46. *Zhongguo jiaoyu nianjian 1949-1981*, pp. 150-151.

47. R. Hayhoe, "The Evolution of Chinese Educational Institutions," in *Contemporary Chinese Education*, ed. R. Hayhoe (London: Croom Helm, 1984), pp. 44, 235, note 69.

48. Cited in Price, *Marxism and Education in Russia and China*, p. 157.

49. C. H. Becker et al., *The Reorganization of Education in China* (Paris: League of Nations Institute of Intellectual Cooperation, 1932), p. 108.

50. Chen Qingzhi, *Zhongguo jiaoyu shi* (Taibei: Shangwu Yingshuguan, 1963).

51. Becker et al., *The Reorganization of Education in China*, p. 107.

52. *Jiaoyu dashi ji*, p. 48.

53. *Ibid.*, p. 173.

54. *Ibid.*, p. 242.

55. One example of this is the *Modern Chinese Reader* compiled by the Chinese Language Special Course for Foreign Students in Beijing University, published in 1963 by the "Epoch" Publishing House, Beijing. The grammar notes are particularly noteworthy.

56. One informant complained that equal time was given to new material whether it was easy or difficult. Whether this was because of fear of deviating from the Russian model, or because the Chinese method of teachers of the same grade planning their lessons together is uncertain. The latter would certainly constrain teachers to try and keep in step.

57. Theodore Chen Hsi-En, *Teacher Training in Communist China* (Washington: U.S. Department of Health, Education and Welfare, 1960), pp. 25-26.

58. Hu Shiming and Eli Seifman, *Towards a New World Outlook: A Documentary History of Education in the People's Republic of China 1949-1976* (New York: Ams Press, 1976), p. 65.

59. Chen, *Teacher Training in Communist China*, p. 26.

60. *Ibid.*, p. 18.

61. DeWitt, *Education and Professional Employment in the USSR*, pp. 181-182, 623;

G. Bereday et al., *The Changing Soviet School* (London: Constable, 1960), pp. 292-302.

62. Percentage figures were calculated from Chen, *Teacher Training in Communist China*, p. 18, Sun Banzhang, *Liushi nian laide Zhongguo jiaoyu* (Chinese Education over the Past Sixty Years) (Taibei: Zheng zhong shuju, 1971), pp. 552-554, and DeWitt, *Education and Professional Employment in the USSR*, p. 623. Since Sun gives neither the number of weeks in the year nor the total length of the course in hours, the calculations are approximate. In addition to the subjects given there were, in 1935, compulsory courses in primary school methods (5.5%), primary school administration (1.85) and education surveys & statistics (1.85), giving a total for professional subjects of 15.7% of time. In addition time was allotted for optional courses in English, literature, history of education, and others concerned with mass education or village education. One must remember, however, that these are programs which do not necessarily reflect the realities of particular schools.

63. Albert Pinkevitch, *The New Education in the Soviet Republic*, trans. Nucia Perlmutter, ed. George Counts (New York: John Day Co., 1929), p. 164.

64. N. K. Krupskaya, *Pedagogicheskiye Sochineniya v Desyati Tomakh* (Educational Works) (Moskva: Akademii Pedagogicheskix Nauk, 1959), esp. vol. 4; Price, *Marxism and Education in Russia and China*, chapter 5.

65. Two volumes of articles on education before Liberation have appeared so far: *Jiefang qu jiaoyu gongzuo jingyan pianduan* (An Evaluation of Educational Work and Experience in the Liberated Areas) ed. Renmin jiaoyu she (Shanghai: Shanghai jiaoyu chubanshe, 1959, 1979) and *Lao jiefang qu jiaoyu gongzuo huiyilu: Zhongguo xiandai jiaoyu ziliao zhiyi* (Recollections of Educational Work in the Old Liberated Areas: Selections from Contemporary Chinese Educational History) (Shanghai jiaoyu chubanshe, 1970, 1979). A collection of some 12 volumes has been prepared for internal circulation only (*neibu*) at the Shaanxi Normal University where a special collection of materials from the Yan'an period is held. In the first of the above published volumes, 6 of the 39 articles are specifically about linking education with production. Three by Liu Aifeng date from 1946, 1947, and 1949 respectively. One by the Laiyuan Xian Government is from 1944. One by Yan Wu and Li Dongchun is from 1946 while the final one by Jie Ping is from 1946. Further access to Yan'an materials is necessary before the significance of these dates can be estimated.

66. *Jiefang qu jiaoyu gongzuo jingyan pianduan*, p. 118.

67. *Ibid.*, p. 17.

68. *Ibid.*, p. 23.

69. Mark Selden, *The Yenan Way in Revolutionary China* (Cambridge, Mass.: Harvard University Press, 1971), pp. 270-274. In this brief account of the educational debate of 1944, Selden does not bring this out clearly enough, perhaps because he was anxious to stress the element of grass-roots democracy involved.

70. Korol, *Soviet Education for Science and Technology*, p. 27. The full text of this document is translated in *Soviet Education Documents, 1918 and 1931-2*, trans. and ed. R. Price (Melbourne: Centre for Comparative and International Studies in Education, La Trobe University, 1981).

71. Krupskaya in a letter to M. P. Malyshev of the Department of Schools of the CC CP(B). Krupskaya, *Educational Works*, 4:562-565, cited in Price, *Marxism and Education in Russia and China*, p. 191. Accounts of the changes in the early thirties can be found in Sheila Fitzpatrick, *Education and Social Mobility in the Soviet Union 1921-1934* (Cambridge: Cambridge University Press, 1979), chapter 10 and Oskar Anweiler, *Geschichte der Schule und Paedagogik in Russland vom Ende des Zarenreiches bis zum Beginn der Stalin-Aera* (Berlin: Quelle und Meyer, 1964). Beatrice King, *Changing Man: the Education System of the USSR* (London: Victor Gollanz, 1937), chapter 5, gives an account of the content of "polytechnization" as viewed by an enthusiastic visitor of the time.

72. Korol, *Soviet Education for Science and Technology*, pp. 31-32. These sentiments are repeated in the article by Kairov which was translated in the November 1954 issue of *Renmin jiaoyu* (People's Education), pp. 16-23.

73. M. N. Shatkin (ed.), *Voprosi Poltexnicheskogo Obranzovaniya* (Moskva: Akademii Pedagogicheskikh Nauk RSFSR, 1963), pp. 329-341.

74. *Ibid.,* p. 12.

75. Hu and Seifman, *Toward a New World Outlook,* pp. 9-11.

76. These laws are published in translation in S. G. Shapovalenko (ed.), *Polytechnical Education in the USSR* (Paris: UNESCO, 1963). The original Russian text of the basic law, but not the statues for the individual school types is available in *Narodnoye Obrazovaniye v SSSR: Sbornik Dokumentov, 1917-1973 gg.,* pp. 53-61.

77. The contrast between Kruschev's proposals and the final laws is made in Joel Schwartz and William Keech, "Group Influence and the Policy Process in the Soviet Union," *The American Political Science Review,* 62 (1968): 840-851.

78. Shapovalenko, *Polytechnical Education in the USSR,* p. 385, Articles 21-26.

79. *Ibid.,* pp. 383-385.

80. *Ibid.,* p. 405, Article 13. Vocational training is referred to in the Act as vocational and technical education (*professional'noe i tekhnicheskoe obrazovaniye*). Elsewhere the terms vocational preparation (*professional'naya podgotovka*), production education (*proizvodstvennoe obucheniye*), or using a term for education with moral implications, labor education (*trudovogo vospitaniye*). One is often uncertain whether these are synonyms or distinguish meaningfully different teaching-learning processes.

81. The Chinese text is now available in *Zhongguo jiaoyu nianjian, 1949-1981,* pp. 688-90. An English translation appears in Fraser, *Education and Communism in China, 1971,* pp. 554-566.

82. N. Bukharin and E. Preobrazhensky, *The ABC of Communism,* introduction by E. H. Carr (Harmondsworth: Penguin, 1969).

83. *Selections from the China Mainland Press (SCMP),* No. 4935, 13 July, 1971 (taken from *Renmin ribao* 27 June, 1971), discussed in Price, *Marxism and Education in Russia and China,* pp. 213-217. See also the account of Tongyi Road Primary School, Tianjin, in *Ibid.,* p. 210.

84. R. F. Price, "Labor and Education," *Comparative Education* 30 (1) (March, 1984): 81-91.

85. DeWitt, *Education and Professional Employment in the USSR,* pp. 239-244.

86. Information is hard to understand in part because outside observers do not make a clear distinction between spare- and part-time education. The Chinese would have attributed this, perhaps rightly, to their class stand! Deineko, in a vaguely-worded passage describing the situation after 1958, talks about theoretical studies alternating with work in "factory higher technical schools." But he appears to be referring to shift schooling, Troitsky gives a clear account of regulations granting time off for the preparation and taking of examinations by spare-time students before 1957. "The Fundamentals of Legislation of the USSR & Union Republics on Public Education" make no mention of part-work (or sandwich course) schooling, but refer to "evening (shift) vocational schools" and unspecified "other forms of training and advanced training directly at places of work." See *Narodnoye Obrazovaniye v SSSR,* p. 99, article 33; translation in *New Steps in Soviet Education: Materials of the Sixth Session of the USSR, Supreme Soviet, July 17-19, 1973* (Moscow: Novosti Press Agency Publishing House, 1973). See also M. Deineko, *Public Education in the USSR* (Moscow: Progress Publishers, probably 1964), p. 205; D. N. Troitsky, *Training Technicians in the Soviet Union* (London: Soviet News Booklet No. 6, 1957).

87. D. I. Chambers, "Adult Education in Urban Industrial China" in *Contemporary Chinese Education,* ed. R. Hayhoe (London: Croom Helm, 1984), p. 188. DeWitt, *Education and Professional Employment in the USSR,* p. 241.

89. Philip Stewart, "Soviet Interest Groups and the Policy Process," *World Politics,* 22 (1) (October, 1969): 29-50; Mervyn Matthews, *Education in the Soviet Union: Policies and Institutions since Stalin* (London: Allen and Unwin, 1982), pp. 29-33.

90. *Renmin jiaoyu,* 1 (January, 1983), p. 27.

91. *Renmin jiaoyu,* 4 (April, 1983), pp. 14-16.

92. See Price, "Labour and Education," for a discussion of a relevant article in the book *Lun jiaoyu he rende quanmian fazhan* (Beijing: Renmin jiaoyu chubanshe, 1982).

93. Specialist education is *zhuanmen rencai peixun;* vocational education is *zhiye xunlian.*

94. Cyrus Peake, *Nationalism and Education in Modern China* (New York: Howard Fertig, 1970); Samuel C. Chu, "The New Life Movement, 1934-1937" in J. E. Lane (ed.), *Researchers in the Social Sciences in China* (New York: Columbia University Press, 1957), pp. 1-17).

95. I am indebted to Tom Fisher for drawing my attention to W. F. Meyer's lectures on "Imperial Confucianism" in *The China Review* (March 6, 1878). I plan to treat these continuities in more detail in a forthcoming book.

96. Price, *Marxism and Education in Russia and China,* pp. 156-161; Matthews, *Education in the Soviet Union,* p. 48.

97. *Jiaoyu dashi ji,* p. 20.

98. *Ibid.,* pp. 32, 47, 65.

99. *Ibid.,* pp. 47, 66, 73.

100. The only study of Soviet school textbooks I know is that by Arthur S. Trace, Jr., *What Ivan Knows that Johnny Doesn't* (New York: Random House, 1961). More recently Felicity Ann O'Dell analyzed *Socialization Through Children's Literature* (Cambridge: Cambridge University Press, 1978). For China, C. Ridley, P. Godwin and D. Doolin, *The Making of a Model Citizen in Communist China* (Stanford: The Hoover Institution, 1971) provides a splendid selection of translations to back an analysis unnecessarily burdened with dubious computations. See also Roberta Martin, "The Socialization of Children in China and on Taiwan," in *China Quarterly,* 62 (June, 1975): 242-262; R. Price, "Chinese Textbooks: Fourteen Years On," *China Quarterly,* 83 (September, 1980): 535-550; Arai Kumiko, "Political Education in China: a Study of Socialization through Children's Textbooks," *Journal of Northeast Asian Studies,* 3 (Fall, 1984), pp. 30-47.

101. Ridley et al., *The Making of a Model Citizen in Communist China,* pp. 102-104, 137-138; Price, "Chinese Textbooks."

102. I. A. Kairov, N. K. Goncharov, B. P. Esipov, and L. V. Zankov, *Pedagogika* (Moskva: Gosudarstvennoye Ychebno-Pedagogicheskoye Izdatel stvo, 1956), p. 202.

103. *Ibid.,* pp. 203-204.

104. *Ibid.,* pp. 234-246. These themes date from the early period after the revolution, but in the twenties were subject to wider and different interpretations. Two valuable introductions to the period are Oskar Anweiler, *Geschichte der Schule und Paedagogik in Russland vom Ende des Zarenreiches bis zum Beginn der Stalin-Aera,* and F. F. Korolev, T. D. Korneichik, and Z. I. Ravkin, *Ocherki po Istorii Sovetskoi Shkoloi i Pedagogiki 1921-1931* (Moskva: Akademii Pedagogicheskikh Hazulc RSFSR, 1961).

105. This seems to ignore the late Stalin period when every important invention was claimed as Russian, and the more difficult problem that some nations can claim few such famous inventions or people! Does this make them less human?

106. *Jiaoyu dashi ji,* pp. 22, 41.

107. Price, *Marxism and Education in Russia and China,* pp. 233-238.

108. I am indebted to Jane Orton for reminding me of the influence of Makarenko. John Fyfield, *Re-educating Chinese Anti-Communists* (London: Croom Helm, 1982) deals critically with one example of re-educating prisoners.

109. *Important Labour Laws and Regulations of the PRC* (Beijing: Foreign Languages Press, 1961), p. 4.

110. Chambers, "Adult Education in Urban Industrial China," p. 190.

111. Price, *Marxism and Education in Russia and China,* pp. 278-279.

112. *Waiguo jiaoyu,* 4 (April, 1981): 7-10, 5 (May, 1981): pp. 26-31.

113. *Waiguo jiaoyu ziliao,* 5 (May, 1982).

Notes to Chapter 10

1. See, for example, Leo A. Orleans, "Soviet Perceptions of China's Economic Development," in U.S. Congress, Joint Economic Committee, *Chinese Economy Post-Mao* (Washington: U.S. Government Printing Office, November 9, 1978).

2. N. V. Franchuk, "Higher Education" in *Politika v Oblasti Nauki i Obrazovaniya v KNR (Politics in the Fields of Science and Education in the PRC)* (Moscow: Nauka, 1980), pp. 84-180. Unless otherwise noted, many of the Soviet views on Chinese higher education are from this excellent review by a specialist from the Institute of Far Eastern Studies.

3. Hsin chiao-yu she (New Educational Society), ed. *Wen-pau kai-ke kao-teng chiao-yu* (Steady Reform of Higher Education) (Shanghai: 1950), pp. 4-6, As cited in Immanuel C. Y. Hsu, "The Reorganization of Higher Education in Communist China, 1949-61," *China Quarterly* (July-September 1964), p. 137.

4. *Kuang-ming jih-pao* (Enlightenment daily), September 2, 1954, as cited in C. T. Hu, "Higher Education in Mainland China and Its Implications for World Affairs," Report prepared for the Committee on the University and World Affairs, 1960, p. 8.

5. Yang Hsiu-feng, "China's Educational Enterprise Goes through the Process of Great Revolution and Great Evolution," *People's Daily,* October 8, 1959, in Stewart Fraser, *Chinese Communist Education, Records of the First Decade* (Nashville: Vanderbilt University Press, 1965), p. 324.

6. Tseng Chao-lun, "Higher Education in New China," *People's China,* No. 12, June 16, 1953, pp. 6-10, in Fraser, *Records,* p. 192.

7. Detailed year-by-year statistics on enrollment, entrants, and graduates, by duration and field of study, are given in *Achievement of Education in China: Statistics 1949-83* (Beijing: People's Education Press, 1985), pp. 56-87. I would like to thank Ruth Hayhoe for calling my attention to this source.

8. L. N. Kutakov, *Ot Pekina do N'yu Yorka* (From Beijing to New York) (Moscow: Nauka, 1983), from a review by F. F. Lappo in *Problemy Dal'nego Vostoka* (Problems of the Far East), No. 4, (October-December 1984), p. 196.

9. Mikhail A. Klochko, *Soviet Scientist in Red China* (New York: Praeger, 1964), pp. 22-23.

10. For example, Filatov uses the lower figure (L. V. Filatov, *Ekonomicheskaya Otsenka Nauchno-Tekhnicheskoy Pomoshchi Sovetskogo Soyuza Kitayu 1949-66)* (Economic estimate of scientific-technical assistance by the Soviet Union to China 1949-1966) (Moscow: Nauka Press, 1980), p. 55, while Franchuk (p. 119) uses only the higher figure. The distinction is provided in Borisov, pp. 176-177.

11. See, for example, Filatov, p. 87.

12. Huang Shiqi, "On Some Vital Issues in the Development and Reform of Higher Education in the People's Republic of China," Paper presented at the Fifth World Congress on Comparative Education, Paris, 2-6 July, 1984.

13. "Soviet Economic, Educational Aid to China 1949-1962 Recalled," *Far Eastern Affairs* (Moscow), No. 4 (October-December 1984), p. 143.

14. Filatov, *Ekonomicheskaya otsenka,* p. 55.

15. A. Sergeenkov, "Izdaniye Uchebnikov i Pedagogicheskoy Literatury" (Publication of Textbooks and Pedagogical Literature), *Shkola i Prosveshcheniye v Narodnom Kitaye* (School and education in Peoples' China) (Moscow: 1957) p. 152.

16. O. B. Borisov, B. T. Koloskov, *Sovetsko-Kitayskiye Otnoshenaiy 1945-77* (Soviet-Chinese Relations 1945-77) (Moscow: Mysl' Publishers, 1977), p. 180.

17. "Soviet Economic, Educational Aid to China 1949-1962 Recalled," p. 143.

18. *Kuang-ming Daily,* September 2, 1954, as cited in C. T. Hu, "Higher Education in Mainland China and Its Implications for World Affairs." Report prepared for the Committee on the University and World Affairs, 1960, p. 31.

19. O. B. Borisov, *Soviet-Chinese Relations*, p. 184.

20. Ministry of Education: *Shen-hsueh chih-tao* (Guide to entrance into institutions of higher education), Peking, 1958, as cited in the C. T. Hu, Report, p. 32.

21. *Chiao-shih pao* (Teacher's Journal), August 9, 1957; translated in Joint Publications Research Service (JPRS) (NY), Report No. 753, October 16, 1958.

22. Chen Po-ta, "Speech before the Study Group of Research Members of the Academica Sinica" (Peking: Foreign Languages Press, 1953), in Fraser, *Records*, p. 184.

23. Lu Ting-yi, "Let a Hundred Flowers Blossom, Let a Hundred Schools of Thought Contend" (Peking: Foreign Languages Press, 1956), in Fraser, *Records*, p. 234.

24. See, for example, Chang Chung-lin, "Strive to Improve the Low Quality of Higher Education," *Jen-min jih-pao*, June 30, 1955, in Fraser, *Records*, p. 213.

25. *Kuang-ming jih-pao*, July 4, 1957; translated in JPRS, No. 753, October 16, 1958, p. 108.

26. Yen Chi-ts'u, "Close Cooperation between Chinese and Soviet Scientists," *Jen-min jih-pao*, February 13, 1960, in Fraser, *Records*, p. 344.

27. A. Arnol'dov and G. Novak, *Kul'tura Narodnogo Kitaya (Culture of New China)* (Moscow: Academy of Sciences of the USSR, Moscow, 1959) p. 42.

28. V. Ragazhkin, "Five Weeks in China," *Narodnoye Obrazovaniye (People's Education)* (No. 10, October 1959), p. 91.

29. Franchuk, "Higher Education," p. 107.

30. *Ibid.*, Franchuk discusses the relationship between the Party and the institutions of higher education on pages 104-7.

31. *Ibid.*, p. 122.

32. *Ibid.*, p. 122.

33. The mentality of Chinese leadership can be judged from the following item: In 1958 the schools had switched away from a grading system based on 100 per cent. Instead, China adopted the format used in Russia, where grades are from one to five, with a "three" the passing mark. The argument favoring this switch was that the Russian system was less competitive, since the distinctions in grades could not be nearly as fine as under the percentage system. But as the dispute with the Soviet Union heated up during the 1960s, the schools reverted to the one hundred per cent system, on the excuse that the 5-grade system was revisionist(!).
Jonathan Unger, *Education Under Mao* (New York: Columbia University Press, 1982), p. 168.

34. Franchuk, "Higher Education," p. 144.

35. *Ibid.*, p. 140.

36. In a letter commenting on the draft of this chapter, Marianne Bastid makes the following important observation:
The appeal of the American model of higher education as a pattern of adjustment to local needs is as firmly rooted in Chinese tradition as the appeal of the unifying Soviet model. Unity and local adjustment (*tongyi* and *yin di zhi yi*) are two closely interrelated principles in traditional government. But historical practice shows that they are applied alternatively rather than together.
I thank Marianne for this and for her other valuable comments.

37. Huang Shiqi, "On Some Vital Issues," pp. 13-14.

38. *Hongqi (Red Flag)*, No. 23, December 1, 1984; JPRS-CRF-85-003, January 31, 1985.

39. *Zhongguo jiaoyu bao* (Chinese Educational News), October 27, 1984; JPRS-CST-85-005, February 20, 1985.

40. "Decision of the CPC Central Committee on Reform of the Educational System (27 May 1985), *Xinhua*, May 28, 1985; in Foreign Broadcast Information Service (FBIS), 30 May 1985, p. K2.

41. "Changing Educational Theory and Methods," *Beijing Review*, No. 24, June 17, 1985, pp. 19-20.

42. *Guangming ribao,* July 18, 1984; JPRS-CST-84-036, November 11, 1984.

43. Huang Shiqi, "On Some Vital Issues," p. 14.

44. "Decision of the CPC Central Committee on Reform of the Educational System," p. K8.

45. Susan Jacoby, "Toward an Educated Elite: the Soviet Universities," *Change* (November 1971), p. 33, as quoted in David Milton, "China's Long March to Universal Education," *The Urban Review* (May 1972), p. 6.

46. See, for example, Leo A. Orleans, "Education, Careers and Social Status," *Bulletin of the Atomic Scientists* (October 1984), pp. 11S-13S.

Notes to Chapter 11

1. The film "La Chinoise" by Jean-Luc Godard was presented at the Festival of Venice in 1967.

2. As early as 1971, people were already talking about "demaoization."

3. This point of view was expressed by many conservative analysts. Also by several French Ministers of the Interior.

4. J. Baby, *La grand controverse sino-soviètique (1956-1966)* (Paris: Grasset, 1966).

5. M. Ciantar, *Mille jours à Pékin* (Paris: Gallimard, 1968); J. & C. Broyelle, *Deux-ième retour de Chine* (Paris: Seuil, 1975), p. 92; E. Gordon, *Liberté, tu n'es qu'un mot* (Paris: Juillard, 1971).

6. *Pékin Information,* 31 (2 August, 1974).

7. The first French Maoist journal which started from 1963 was called *Révolution.* Then there were *Les Cahiers Marxist-Léninistes* (1966-1968) on the Great Cultural Revolution. Later academic journals of description and hermeneutic were created: *Nouvelle Chine* (by collaborateurs from *Le Monde,* 1971-1974) and *Vent d'Est* (1975-1978).

8. This debate was revived in relation to the Lyssenko affair in the Soviet Union and some important epistemological work on "the spontaneous ideology of scholars."

9. The exception were a few articles written by French Maoists living in China, such as M. Mazloff, "Luttes dans l'Enseignement, *Aujourd'hui la Chine,* 24 (Paris, 1973), "Les Stages des étudiants de francais à l'usine de machine-outils no 1," *Aujourd'hui la Chine,* No. 25 (Paris, 1974) and Xavier Luccioni, "Sur quelques évènements en Chine," *Les Temps Modernes,* 380 (1978), p. 139.

10. A. Borromee and S. Palmer, *Chine, miroir d'une éternité* (Paris: Menges, 1984).

11. G. W. F. Hegel, *Leçons sur l'histoire de la philosophie* (Paris: Gallimard, 1954).

12. Essentially, the publication of Mao's works began in 1975. For Chinese reluctance to publish them, see S. Schram, *Mao Tse-tung Unrehearsed: Talks and Letters* (Harmondsworth: Penguin books, 1974).

13. R. Duchet, *La Chine et nous* (Paris: Debresse, 1967), p. 155.

14. M. Macciocchi, *De la Chine: la porte de la dialectique* (Paris: Seuil, 1971), p. 29.

15. Han Suyin, *La Chine en l'an 2001* (Paris: Stock, 1967), p. 227.

16. Han Suyin, *Le premier jour du monde* (Paris: Stock, 1975), p. 362.

17. *Ibid.,*

18. Jack Gray, "Quaderni pacentini," no. 40, cited by M. Macciocchi, *De La Chine,* p. 242.

19. M. Macciocchi, *De la Chine,* p. 223.

20. *Ibid.,* p. 224.

21. Mao Zedong, "The United Front in Cultural Work" (1944).

22. Denis Guedj and Jean-Paul Dolle, "Science et Bourgeoisie" in "La Science en question," *Après-demain,* 145 (June, 1972), p. 26.

23. Philippe Sollers, "La lutte philosophique dans la Chine révolutionnaire," *Tel Quel* 48/49 (Spring, 1972), p. 126.

24. Circular of May 16, 1966.

25. Michelle Loi, *L'intelligence au pouvoir; un monde nouveau: la Chine* (Paris: Maspero, 1973), p. 165.

26. M. Macciocchi, *De la Chine*, p. 380.

27. *Ibid.*, p. 380.

28. René Duchet, *La Chine et nous*, p. 87.

29. M. Crozier, *The Bureaucratic Phenomenon* (Chicago: University of Chicago Press, 1964).

30. R. Aron, *18 leçons sur la société industrielle* (Paris: Gallimard, 1968); Galbraith, *Le nouvel état industriel* (Paris: Gallimard, 1962); also works of the Frankfurt School began to be published in Paris at this time.

31. J. Ellul, *Propagandes* (Paris: A. Colin, 1962).

32. J. Ellul, *L'illusion politique* (Paris: Laffont, 1965).

33. Among the political organizations there was the double schism of the Union of Communist Students, one of which was Maoist. Among the religious movements there was the schism of "la Jeunesse étudiante chrétienne," the crisis of "la Jeunesee Universitaire chrétienne" and of the group "La Lettre," the journal "Frères du Monde," the crisis within the "Mouvement des jeunes ruraux catholiques," the Maoist leanings in the rural union (CNJA and Paysans Travailleurs) or in cultural institutions such as les CLAJ (youth hostels).

34. Franz Schurmann, *Ideology and Organization in Communist China* (Berkeley: University of California Press, 1968), p. 505.

35. Wilfred Burchett, *Une autre qualité de vie: la Chine* (Paris: Maspero, 1975).

36. J. J. Servan-Schreiber, *Le défi américain* (Paris: Denoël, 1967).

37. R. Aron, *La lutte de classe* (Paris: Gallimard, 1964).

38. L. Porcher, *Le nouvel etat industriel selon Galbraith* (Paris: Hatier, 1972).

39. Hans Heymann Jr., "La structure industrielle et le progrès technique," in *Science et technologie en RPC* (Paris: OCDE, 1977), p. 169.

40. "La lutte des marxistes-léninistes pour se lier aux masses, Bilan et perspectives," *Humanité Nouvelle*, 51 (April, 1967).

41. Organizations of the "Parti Communist-Marxiste-Léniniste" in France in 1965.

42. Organization of the Union des Jeunesses Communistes (Marxistes-Léninistes) in the same period.

43. The Ecole Normale Supérieure provided the largest contingent, but there were some also in the Ecoles d'Agronomie and l'Ecole Centrale.

44. This is how it was interpreted by the majority of internal studies of the movement of May. J. Jurquet, *Le printemps révolutionnaire de 1968* (Paris: Git-le-Coeur, 1968); Lucio Magri, *Reflexions sur les évènements de mai* (Rome: De Donato, 1968); Edoarda Masi, "Le marxisme de Mao et la gauche européenne," *Temps Modernes*, 284 (March, 1970).

45. V. Lenin, *Imperialism, the State and Revolution* (New York: Vanguard Press, 1926) and *Imperialism: The Highest Stage of Capitalism* (London: M. Lawrence, 1933).

46. Michelle Loi, "De la collusion idéologique des sinophobes," *Tel Quel*, 48/49 (1972), p. 112; Macciocchi, *De la Chine*, conclusion.

47. J. Broyelle, "La Chine dans nos têtes," *Pouvoir*, 3 (Paris: PUF, 1977).

48. G. Antoine and J. C. Passeron, *La réforme de l'université* (Paris: Calmann-Levy, 1966).

49. B. Queysanne, "Les étudiants et la crise de l'université bourgeoise," *Révolution*, 4 (December, 1963). This was the first pro-Chinese journal.

50. This reform was known under the name of the 'Plan Langevin-Wallon' (1947) which encouraged an increase in personnel, allocations and investments.

51. The name of Mao never appeared in books about socialist pedagogy. See for example Dommanget, *Les grands éducateurs* (Paris: Colin, 1970), Daniel Lindenberg, *L'internationale communiste et l'école de class* (Paris: Maspero, 1972).

52. There were books with summary descriptions of the Chinese education system. But it was presented from the angle of the cultural problem (S. de Beauvoir, *La Longue Marche* (Paris: Gallimard, 1957) or the repression of the anti-rightist Movement (L. Bodard, *La Chine du cauchemart* (Paris: Gallimard, 1961). Such journalists as E. Snow and R. Guillain stressed manual labor but did not distinguish the Chinese from the Russian model.

53. "Oser, oser lutter, oser vaincre," pamphlet circulated at the beginning of the student year 1966, edited by the group "Terrel-Cusenier" in *21X27 L'Etudiant de France.*

54. "De la misère en milieu étudiant, considérée sous les aspects économique, politique, psychologique, sexuel et notamment intellectuel" (Strasbourg: AFGE, 1966).

55 'Servir le peuple' was the name of the organ of the UJC m-l, July 1, 1967. See "Contre l'anarchisme petit-bourgeois, édifions dans notre pays un parti de l'époque de Mao Zedong," *Garde Rouge,* 1 (November, 1966).

56. "La Tempête révolutionnaire de mai," *Pékin Information* (16 June, 1968).

57. J. J. Michel, *Avoir 20 ans en Chine à la campagne* (Paris: Seuil, 1978).

58. R. Linhart, *L'établi* (Paris: Minuit, 1977).

59. They paid no attention to the book by J. and T. Marsouin, *Nous avons enseigné en Chine Populaire* (Paris: La Table Ronde, 1966), nor to reports by Soviet experts and African students who had been present at political campaigns on Peking campuses. Only sarcasm greeted the book by M. Ciantar, *Mille Jours à Pékin* (Paris:Gallimard, 1969), which depicted the violence against intellectuals from 1966 to 1968.

60. Anna Louise Strong, *Letters from China* (Peking: New World Press, 1953); Agnes Smedley, *The Great Road* (New York: Monthly Review Press, 1956); *La Longue Marche* (Paris: Richilieu, 1969); E. Snow, *Etoile Rouge sur la Chine* (Paris: Stock, 1965).

61. P. Bourdieu and J. Passeron, *Les héritiers* (Paris: Minuit, 1964).

62. J. Passeron, *Conservatisme et inovation à l'université* (Paris: Calmann-Levy, 1966), p. 201-202.

63. C. Baudelot et R. Establet, *L'Ecole capitaliste en France* (Paris: Maspero, 1971).

64. *Ibid.,* p. 18.

65. *Ibid.,* p. 19.

66. Michel Tort, *Le Quotient Intellectuel* (Paris: Maspero, 1974).

67. This was the name of a principal "Mao" organization.

68. *Théorie et Politique,* 3 (1975). Interview with an underground leader of the Proletarian Left.

69. *Ibid.*

70. *Ibid.*

71. *Lettre à une maitresse d'école, par les Enfants de Barbiana* (Italy: Liberia Editrice florentain, 1967).

72. Mao Zedong, "Discours aux dirigeants du Centre," 21 July, 1962.

73. See for example M. Jakubowicz, *Si j'avais beaucoup d'argent, je quitterais l'école* (Paris: Maspero, 1973).

74. A leftist group within the French teachers' union (FEN).

75. A small teachers' union within the central union of workers (CFDT).

76. The most significant document of this social utopia was the book by Claudie Broyelle, *La Moitié du Ciel* (Paris: Denoel-Gonthiers, 1973) which had a preface by Han Suyin.

77. M. M. Macciocchi, *De la Chine,* pp. 229-230.

78. Michel Foucault, "Dialogue avec G. Deleuze," *Revue de l'Arc* (1973), p. 4.

79. A political movement in China to criticize Confucius and Lin Biao from 1972 to 1975.

80. J. Chesnaux, *Du passé faisons table rase* (Paris: Maspero, 1976), pp. 140-141.

81. *Ibid.,* p. 147.

82. *Ibid.,* p. 145.

83. Christine Glucksmann, "Ecole, Savoir et Idéologie," *La Nouelle Critique,* Special Number (May, 1972), p. 21.

84. Suzanne Citron, "Le sens de l'expérience chinois: transformation des rapports sociaux et école, *Cahiers Pédagogiques,* 137 (October, 1975), p. 2.

85. Magri, "Réflexions sur les évènements de mai; 'Il Manifesto,'" *Les Temps Modernes,* 277-278 (September, 1969), p. 39.

86. Jean Onimus, article on "Jeunesse" in *Encyclopedia Universalis* (1972).

87. G. Lapouge, *Utopie et Civilisation* (Paris: Weber, 1973), introduction.

88. This was the term used to describe students like the Maoists who never appeared in class.

89. Luc Ferry and Alain Renaud, *La Pensée Soixante-Huit* (Paris: Gallimard, 1985), p. 83. See also Regis Debray, *Modeste Contribution aux cérémonies officielles du dixième anniversaire* (Paris: Maspero, 1978).

Notes to Chapter 12

1. All statistics in this section are taken from *Achievement of Education in China 1949-1983* (Beijing: People's Education Press, 1985), pp. 126-129. See also *Zhonghua Renmin Gongheguo jiaoyu dashi ji 1949-1982* (Beijing: Jiaoyu kexue chubanshe, 1983) (Chronology of Educational Events 1949-1982), item 5918. It states that between 1950 and 1958 more than 16,000 Chinese students were sent abroad, 91% to the Soviet Union and 8% to other socialist countries. The reason this figure is so high is that it includes a significant number of trainees sent by industrial ministries and also a number of students sent by the Ministry of Defence.

2. *Chronology of Educational Events,* item 6429.

3. *Ibid.,* item 6483.

4. The two "whatsoevers" refer to the statement that "we will resolutely uphold whatever policy decisions Chairman Mao made and unswervingly follow whatever instructions Chairman Mao gave." For a further explanation see Deng Xiaoping, *Selected Works of Deng Xiaoping* (Beijing: Foreign Languages Press, 1984), p. 400, notes 13 and 14.

5. Deng Xiaoping, *Selected Works,* p. 53.

6. *Ibid.,* pp. 70-71.

7. *Ibid.,* pp. 106-107.

8. *Zhongguo jiaoyu nianjian 1949-1981* (Beijing: China Encyclopedic Press, 1984), p. 667.

9. For a full account of PRC-U.S. scientific cooperation under this agreement, see Richard Suttmeier, "US-PRC Scientific Cooperation: An Assessment of the First Two Years" (Springfield, Va.: NTIS, U. S. Department of Commerce, 1982). The executive summary of the report was published in *China Exchange News,* 10(1) (March, 1982), pp. 1-3.

10. The agreement was renewed in April of 1986 with SEDC as a signatory as well as CAS and CASS on the Chinese side.

11. *Zhongguo jiaoyu nianjin 1949-1981,* p. 676.

12. *Ibid.,* pp. 675-680.

13. See *Zhongguo jiaoyu nianjian 1982-1984* (Beijing: China Encyclopedic Press, forthcoming).

14. See *Zhongguo jiaoyu nianjian 1949-1981,* pp. 675-676.

15. The information on TOKTEN and STAR was taken from a paper presented by Dr. Wang Nai at a Workshop on Human Resources Development held in Tokyo, 2-5 April, 1986. Dr. Wang is the Vice-chairman and Secretary General of the China Association for International Exchange of Personnel. See also *Beijing wanbao* (31 March, 1986).

16. The Chinese Review Commission (CRC)is composed of 38 specialists drawn from 20 project universities. Among them six Chinese professors who are experts in their fields and also experienced in university administration were appointed by CMOE to be the Chairman and Co-chairmen of the CRC. Professor Zhang Guangdou, Vice-president of Qinghua University was appointed Chairman, and the Co-chairmen are Professor Xie Xide of Fudan University, was appointed Chairman, and the Co-chairmen are Professor Xie Xide of Fudan Xuejun of Xi'An Jiaotong University, Professor Chen Deming of Beijing University and

Professor Cha Quanxing of Wuhan University.

17. The International Advisory Panel was set up in April of 1982, consisting of one Chairman and five Co-chairmen and aided by an executive director. Professor Dale Corson, President Emeritus of Cornell University, was appointed Chairman, and the five co-chairmen were nominated by the National Academy of Sciences, the Royal Society, the Max-Planck Gesellschaft and the Chairman. They are Professor Eduard Pestel of Hanover University, Professor L. Salem of the Centre National de la Recherche Scientifique, Professor E. C. Slater of the University of Amsterdam, Professor Toshiharu Tako of the Science University of Tokyo and Professor O. C. Zienkiewicz of the University of Wales.

18. Full information about WHO programs may be found in *Zhongguo weisheng nianjian 1983* (Beijing: People's Health Press), pp 388-391.

19. A fuller account of this project can be found in *Zhongguo jiaoyu nianjian 1982-1984*, forthcoming.

20. *Zhongguo jiaoyu bao* (China Education News) (22 February, 1986).

21. *Gaojiao zhanxian* (The Higher Education Front) (September, 1985), pp. 14-21.

22. *Renmin ribao* (People's Daily) (10 March, 1986).

23. A fuller account of these projects can be found in *Zhongguo jiaoyu nianjian 1982-1984*, forthcoming.

24. This information is drawn from a paper presented by Zhang Xiaobin at the Second Beijing International Conference on Strategic Orientation of Science and Technology for National Development, 7-11 April, 1986. Mr. Zhang is President of CVIC and his paper was entitled "A Strategic Move — The Practice of Venture Capital Investment for Technological Innovation in China."

25. Fei Xiaotong, "A New Stage in the Re-establishment of Sociology," *Gaojiao zhanxian*, 3 (March, 1986), pp. 30-32. See also *Sociology and Anthropology in the P.R.C. — Report of a Delegation Visit, February-March, 1984*, ed. Alice S. Rossi (Washington, D.C.: National Academy of Sciences, 1984).

26. *Zhongguo jiaoyu bao* (22 March, 1986).

27. *Zhongguo jiaoyu bao* (4 January, 1986). 36 universities and 37 institutes of CAS and the Chinese Academy of Medical Sciences are named in the list.

28. See *Renmin ribao* (11 January, 1986) for a set of questions and answers concerning the MPRS's given by the SSTC Bureau of S & T Cadres.

29. *Bulletin of the Chinese Academy of Sciences* No. 1 (February, 1986).

30. See *Zhongguo jiaoyu bao* (17 May, 1986), p. 1, and *Renmin ribao* (14 May, 1986), p. 1, for brief coverage of the conference.

31. *China Daily* (26 March, 1986).

Notes to Chapter 13

1. For a discussion of the concept of modernization see Richard P. Suttmeier, "Politics, Modernization, and Science in China," *Problems of Communism* Vol. 30, No. 1 (1981): 22-36; "Chinese Culture: The Border within," *China News Analysis*, No. 1276 (January 1, 1985); "Understanding and Mobilizing Youth," *China News Analysis*, No. 1294 (October 1, 1985); Shigezo Kawachi, "Thoughts on the 'Chinese Way of Modernization,'" *China Newsletter (JETRO)*, No. 32 (1981) : 2-9; Thomas G. Hart, "China's Modernization in Comparative Perspective," *Issues and Studies*, Vol. 21, No. 9 (1985): 35-68; Yao Meng-hsuan, "Teng Hsiao-p'ing's Line and the Four Modernizations," *Issues and Studies*, Vol. 18, No. 1 (1982): 10-36.

2. Deng Xiaoping defined the overall goal of the four modernizations as follows: "Not long ago, during a discussion with a foreign guest I was asked 'What do those four modernizations of yours really mean?' I told him they mean that we will try to reach a per-capita value of output of US $1,000 by the end of this century, and that we can then say our society is fairly well-off. The answer was not precise, of course, but neither was

it given casually." Deng Xiaoping, *Selected Works of Deng Xiaoping* (Beijing: Foreign Languages Press, 1984), p. 144. This volume contains numerous articles which reveal Deng's views on modernization. For a critical analysis and commentary of relevant documents in 1975, see Martin Krott, *Programm für Chinas Zukunft* (Hamburg: Institut für Asienkunde, 1978).

3. See "Sige xiandaihua" (The four modernizations) in Yee-fui Lau et al., *Glossary of Chinese Political Phrases*, ed. Nancy Ma et al. (Hong Kong: Union Research Institute, 1977), pp. 400-401.

4. Li Chengrui, Zhang Zhuoyuan, "An Outline of Economic Development (1977-1980)" in Yu Guangyuan (ed.), *China's Socialist Modernization* (Beijing: Foreign Languages Press, 1984), pp. 3-69.

5. Martin Krott, *Program für Chinas Zukunft*.

6. For a discussion of education as a productive force, see Li Kejing, "Is Education a Superstructure or a Productive Force?" *Social Sciences in China*, Vol. 1, No. 7 (1980): 16-25; Li Yining, "The Role of Education in Economic Growth," *Social Sciences in China*, Vol. 2, No. 2 (1981): 66-84.

7. Deng Xiaoping, *Selected Works*, p. 49.

8. *Ibid.*, pp. 119ff.

9. *Ibid.*, p. 123.

10. Carter V. Good, *Dictionary of Education* (New York: McGraw-Hill, 1973), p. 207.

11. See Shigeru Ishikawa, "China's Economic System Reform: Underlying Factors and Prospects," *China's Changed Road to Development*, ed. Neville Maxwell, Bruce McFarlane (Oxford: Pergamon, 1986), pp. 9-20; K. C. Yeh, "Macroeconomic Changes in the Chinese Economy During the Readjustment," *The China Quarterly*, No. 100 (December 1984): 691-716.

12. Yeh "Macroeconomic Changes in the Chinese Economy," p. 698.

13. *Ibid.*

14. This discussion was documented in "Educational Investment in the People's Republic of China," *Chinese Education*, Vol. 17, No. 3 (1984): 3-102.

15. See my analysis of higher education developments "Higher Education: The Tension between Quality and Equality," *Contemporary Chinese Education*, ed. Ruth Hayhoe (London: Croom Helm, 1984), pp. 93-153; Julia Kwong, "In Pursuit of Efficiency. Scientific Management in Chinese Higher Education," Paper presented at the 30th Annual Meeting of the Comparative and International Education Society, Toronto, Canada, March 13-16, 1986.

16, See Erik Baark, *Techno-Economics and Politics of Modernization in China: Basic Concepts of Technology Policy under the Readjustment of the Chinese Economy* (Lund: Policy Research Institute, 1980).

17. "China's Keypoint School Controversy 1978-1983," *Chinese Education* Vol. 17, No. 2 (1984): 5-127.

18. For a review of the state of the art in research on efficiency in education, see Manfred Weiß, *Effizienzforschung im Bildungsbereich* (Berlin: Duncker and Humblot, 1982).

19. Stuart R. Schram, *Ideology and Policy in China since the Third Plenum, 1978-1984* (London: University of London, Contemporary China Institute, 1984), p. 31ff.

20. These developments have been described in detail in Jürgen Henze et al., *Halbjahresbericht zur Bildungspolitik und pädagogischen Entwicklung in der DDR, der UdSSR, der VR Polen, der CSSR und der VR China* (Bochum: Ruhr-Universität Bochum, Arbeitsstelle für vergleichende Bildungsforschung, 1980 passim).

21. See Stanley Rosen, "Prosperity, Privatization, and China's Youth," *Problems of Communism*, Vol. 34, No. 2 (1985): 1-28; Jürgen Henze, *Bildung und Wissenschaft in der Volksrepublik China zu Beginn der achtziger Jahre* (Hamburg: Institut für Asienkunde, 1983), pp. 146ff.; Alan P. Liu, "Opinions and Attitudes of Youth in the People's Republic of China," *Asian Survey*, Vol. 24, No. 9 (1984): 975-996. An extensive collection of relevant materials is available in "Recent Survey Data on Student Attitudes," *Chinese*

Education, Vol. 17, no. 4 (1984-85): 3-114; "The Impact of Modernization on the Socialization of Chinese Youth," *Chinese Education,* Vol. 18, No. 1 (1985): 3-120.

22. This situation became most obvious in the discussion of keypoint school issues when, in some Chinese regions, criticism was voiced against streaming and the establishment of keypoint schools in general. See my analysis "Begabtenförderung im Bildungswesen der VR China: Das System der "Schwerpunkt-Schulen," *Asien* No. 4 (July 1982): 29-58, especially pp. 50ff.

23. World Bank, *China. Long-Term Development Issues and Options.* Annex 1: *China. Issues and Prospects in Education* Washington, D.C.: The World Bank (1985), pp. 2-3.

24. *Ibid.*

25. Schram, *Ideology and Policy in China 1978-1984.*

26. See *Joint Publications Research Service* (JPRS), CPS-85-081 (August 12, 1985): 41-60 (original *Jiaoyu yanjiu,* No. 4 (April 4, 1985): 27-25); JPRS, CPS-85-068 (July 7, 1985): 35-36 (original *Guangming ribao* (April 8, 1985), p. 1); JPRS, CPS-85-064 (June 28, 1985): 9-12 (original *Zhongguo jiaoyu bao* (February 26, 1985), p. 3).

27. JPRS, CPS-84-085 (December 11, 1984): 53-57 (original *Zhongguo jiaoyu bao* (August 11, 1984), p. 3); JPRS, CPS-85-080 (August 8, 1985): 86-87 (original *Zhongguo fazhi bao* (May 22, 1985), p. 2); *Fujian jiaoyu,* No. 2 (1984): 5-7. Other relevant articles on the topic have been published in *Jiaoyu yanjiu,* No. 3 (1980): 24-32; No. 9 (1983): 17-22; No. 7 (1983): 43-47; No. 9 (1984): 47-51.

28. Concerning this issue we interviewed a number of administrative cadres as well as teachers in cities and in the countryside, mainly in the regions of Anhui province, Shaanxi province, Hebei province, Beijing and Shanghai and Zhejiang province. Information was provided during discussions at the Central Institute for Educational Research in Beijing in fall 1985 and summer 1986.

29. Most important seem to be the following ones: (1) "Temporary Work Regulations for Institutions for Higher Education Directly under the Ministry of Education (DRAFT)" (1961); (2) "Temporary Work Relations for Full-time Secondary Schools (DRAFT)" (1963), and (3) "Temporary Work Regulations for Full-time Elementary Schools (DRAFT)" (1963). The revised forms of these documents were released in April and October of 1978.

These documents are available in *Zhongguo jiaoyu nianjian, 1949-1981* (Yearbook of Chinese Education, 1949-1981) (Beijing: Zhongguo dabaike quanshu chubanshe, 1984), pp. 692-705, 736-737. See also "Encyclopedia of Education, 1980," *Chinese Education,* Vol. 14, No. 4 (1981-82): 10-11. For a translation of the major documents of 1961 and 1963 see Susan L. Shirk, "The 1963 Temporary Work Regulations for Full-time Middle and Primary Schools: Commentary and Translation," *The China Quarterly,* No. 55 (1973): 511-546.

30. M. A. Brimer, L. Pauli, *Wastage in Education. A World Problem* (Paris: Unesco, IBE, 1971); Organization for Economic Co-operation and Development (OECD), *Efficiency in Resource Utilization in Education* (Paris: OECD, 1969); Joseph Katz (ed.) *Efficiencies and Inefficiencies in Secondary Schools* (Geneva: World Council of Comparative Education, 1974) (Proceedings of the Second World Congress of Comparative Education Societies, Geneva, June 28 - July 2, 1974).

31. "Wastage in Primary Education from 1970 to 1980," *Prospects,* Vol. 14, No. 3 (1984): 348.

32. Trip notes (see note 28 above). In addition *Xuexiao guanli* (School Administration) (Beijing: Jiaoyu kexue chubanshe, 1981), pp. 192-193; *Jiaoyu jingjixue gailun* (An Introduction to the Economics of Education) (Xining: Qinghai renmin chubanshe, 1983), pp. 137 ff. Han Zongli, "Shixi Hebei Sheng putong jiaoyu zhongde 'wu lü'," *Hebei Daxue xuebao,* No. 1 (1986): 25-31.

33. *Jiaogu jingii gailun,* pp. 144ff

34. *Ibid.,* pp. 147 ff.

35. For a critical discussion see Mark Blaug, *An Introduction to the Economics of Educa-*

tion (London: The Penguin Press, 1970); John Vaizey, Keith Norris, John Sheehan et al., *The Political Economy of Education* (London: Duckworth, 1972); John Simmons, (ed.), *The Education Dilemma: Policy Issues for Developing Countries in the 1980s* (Oxford: Pergamon, 1980).

36. As an example of the situation in the Soviet Union, see Friedrich Kuebart, "Schülerleistung — Lehrerleistung. Probleme der Leistungskontrolle im sowjetischen Schulwesen," Vergleichende Bildungsforschung. DDR, Osteuropa und interkulturelle Perspektiven. *Festschrift für Oskar Anweiler zum 60. Geburtstag,* eds. Berhard Dilger, Friedrich Kuebart, Hans-Peter Schäfer (Berlin: Berlin Verlag Arno Spitz, 1986), pp. 258-376.

37. Han Zongli, "The Development of the Economics of Education in China," *Canadian and International Education,* Special Issue, forthcoming in 1987.

38. Alexander H. ter Weele, "China/World Bank: University Development," *Prospects,* Vol. 13, No. 4 (1983): 498. On World Bank project activities, see also Aklilu Habte, Stephen Heyneman, "Education for National Development: World Bank Activities," *Prospects,* Vol. 13, No. 4 (1983): 471-479.

39. A. ter Weele, "China/World Bank: University Development," p. 498.

40. Warren C. Baum, Stokes M. Tolbert, *Investing in Development* (New York: Oxford University Press, 1985), p. 333.

41. *Ibid.,* pp. 124-125.

42. World Bank, *Education. Sector Policy Paper* (Washington, D.C.: The World Bank, 1980), p. 30ff.; George Psacharopoulos, Maureen Woodhall, *Education for Development* (New York: Oxford University Press, 1985), pp. 205ff.; George Psacharopoulos, William Loxley, *Diversified Secondary Education and Development* (Baltimore-London: The Johns Hopkins University Press, 1985), pp. 65ff., 154ff., 210ff.

A general outline of the problem of quality in education is offered in Stephen P. Heyneman, Daphne Siev White (eds.) *The Quality of Education and Economic Development* (Washington, D.C.: The World Bank, 1986).

43. World Bank, *Education, Sector Policy Paper,* p. 30.

44. *Ibid.,* p. 42.

45. *Ibid.,* p. 32.

46. *Ibid.,* p. 42ff.

47. World Bank, *China. Socialist Economic Development,* Vol. III: The Social Sectors, Population, Health, Nutrition, and Education (Washington, D.C.: The World Bank, 1983), p. 190.

48. Henze, "Higher Education: The Tension Between Quality and Equality," p. 131.

49. See *Jiaoyu jingjixue gailun.*

50. The evidence for this kind of development was given by the World Bank publications on China in 1981 where first-hand information from the Ministry of Education enabled World Bank missions going to China to return with large sets of data, previously unavailable to the public. These publications were first printed for internal use (official use) only and became public in 1983 in *China. Socialist Economic Development.*

A further hint on changes in this field of governmental activities was the publication of *The Statistical Yearbook of China* since 1981, where for the first time data on provincial level education institutions and students as well as on time-series (1949-1981) for school enrollment figures (higher education, specialized secondary and general secondary education, primary education) became available.

51. Besides provincial level statistical yearbooks or economic yearbooks the most important publications in the education sector are the *Zhongguo jiaoyu nianjian 1949-1981* and the *Achievement of Education in China, 1949-1983,* ed. Department of Planning, Ministry of Education (Beijing: Renmin chubanshe, 1984).

52. Most of these publications still appeared to be classified as "internal" (*neibu*). The most outstanding result was in interdisciplinary study on "China in the year 2000" where

education projections have been described in some detail. See *Jingji ribao,* November 9, 1985, p. 5.

53. Most of the activities were carried out at the Institutes of Systems Engineering at Tianjin University and Xi'an Jiaotong University. Information supplied by Prof. Liu Bao from Tianjin University and his project report "A Brief Survey of Chinese Education Problems and the Possible Application of Systems Appproaches to Chinese Education Planning," Bochum, Ruhr-University, 1986.

Notes to Chapter 14

1. Teng Ssu-yu, "Chinese Influence on the Western Examination System," *Harvard Journal of Asiatic Studies,* Vol. 7, No. 4, 1942.

2. Max Weber, *Economy and Society,* ed. F. Roth and C. Wittich (Los Angeles: University of California Press, 1978).

3. Talcott Parsons, *The Social System* (England: Tavistock Publications Ltd., 1952). chapter II.

4. Max Weber, *The Protestant Ethic and the Spirit of Capitalism* (London: Unwin University Books, 1967).

5. Max Weber, *The Religion of China* (New York: The Free Press, 1964).

6. Herbert Marcuse, *One Dimensional Man* (Boston: Beacon Press, 1964).

7. Jürgen Habermas, "Psychic Thermidor and the Rebirth of Rebellious Subjectivity," in *Habermas and Modernity,* ed. R. Bernstein (Cambridge, Mass.: The MIT Press, 1985), p. 73.

8. Martin Jay, "Habermans and Modernism," in *Habermas and Modernity*, p. 132ff.

9. Ablrecht Wellmer, "Reason, Utopia and the Dialectic of Enlightenment," in *Habermas and Modernity*, p. 58.

10. Jürgen Habermas, *Towards a Rational Society* (London: Heinneman, 1971). This is an early yet clear and compelling presentation of Habermas' views in relation to the student crisis of the late sixties and the role of the university in society. For discussions of Habermas' two-volume *Theory of Communicative Action,* see essays by Anthony Gibbins and Thomas McCarthy in *Habermas and Modernity.*

11. *Educational Policy and the Mission Schools,* ed. Brian Holmes (London: Routledge and Kegan Paul, 1967).

12. R. Hayhoe, "A Comparative Approach to the Cultural Dynamics of Sino-western Educational Cooperation," *China Quarterly,* No. 104 (December, 1985).

13. Jessie Lutz, *China and the Christian Colleges* (Ithaca and London: Cornell University Press, 1971); Philip West, *Yenching University and Sino-Western Relations 1916-1952* (Cambridge, Mass.: Harvard University Press, 1976).

14. Deutches Institut für Wirtschaftforschung, *Wochenbericht* 29/86 (17 July, 1986), p. 474.

15. I have explored the issue of conformity/transformation more fully using ideas drawn from World Order Models Project scholarship in "China, Comparative Education and the World Order Models Project," *Compare,* Vol. 16, No. 1 (1986), pp. 65-80.

16. This intention is evident in three of the ten objectives for exchange formulated by the American Office of Science and Technology and the Committee for Scholarly Communication with the People's Republic of China. These are listed in Ralph Clough, *A Review of the U.S.-China Exchange Program* (U.S.A.: Office of Research, International Communications Agency, 1981), p. 114-116, and are cited in R. Hayhoe (ed.) *Contemporary Chinese Education* (London: Croom Helm, 1984), p. 210.

17. David Lampton, Joyce Madancy and Kristen William, *A Relationship Restored: Trends in U.S.-China Educational Exchanges, 1978-1984* (Washington, D.C.: National Academy Press, 1986). Huang Shiqi's figure of 12,022 going to the United States bet-

ween 1978 and 1984 probably reflects those who were sent with the official approval of the Ministry of Education, and not the additional number who went on private arrangements or under informal university linkages.

18. The work of the Committee for Scholarly Communication with the People's Republic of China (CSCPRC), the major coordinating agent of these activities, can be followed through its quarterly journal *China Exchange News*.

19. See CSCPRC, *American Studies in China: Report of a Delegation, October, 1984* (Washington, D.C.: National Academy Press, 1985).

20. Tani Barlowe and Donald Lowe, *Chinese Reflections* (New York: Praeger, 1985). This book gives a very sensitive depiction of the attempts of two American scholars to present a critical and analytic view of American society to Chinese students determined to preserve the utopian picture that meant so much to them in 1981-82.

21. The work of the center has been discussed in greater detail in R. Hayhoe, "Penetrations or Mutuality? China's Educational Cooperation with Japan, Europe and North America," *Comparative Educational Review*, Vol. 30, No. 4 (November, 1986).

22. Lampton et al., *A Relationship Restored*, p. 65.

23. Interview with Professor Frank Jen, Jacobs School of Management, State University of New York at Buffalo, 22 May, 1985.

24. Speech of Mr. Zhang Yanning, Vice-Counsellor of the State Economic Commission, at the 5th anniversary celebration of the Center, Dalian, April, 1985. A copy of the speech was kindly provided by Mr. Christopher Marut, Science and Technology Offer of the U.S. Embassy in Beijing.

25. Interview with Professor Lin Zibin, Chinese Academic Director of the Center of Sino-American Cultural and Social Studies, Nanjing University, 10 October, 1985.

26. Interview with Mr. Makoto Nakamura, Educational Counsellor, Japanese Embassy in Beijing, 12 Sept., 1985.

27. These figures are provided in Hiroshi Abe, "Comparative International Experiences: P.R.C. Exchanges with Other Countries — Japan," Paper presented to the Conference on Sino-American Cultural and Educational Exchanges, East-West Center, Hawaii, February 18-22, 1985.

28. *Xinhua News Agency* (London), hereafter XH, 26 June, 1982, 3 Nov., 1983, 15 Mar., 1984.

29. Abe, "Comparative International Experience," p. 29.

30. Interview with T. Yashima, Head of the JICA Office in Beijing, 16 Sept., 1985; "Dui Zhonghua Renmin Gongheguo Jishu Xiezu Shiji" (Achievements in Technical Cooperation with the P.R.C.) JICA Brochure, February, 1985.

31. Abe, "Comparative International Experience," pp. 18-19.

32. XH, 24 Oct., 1985.

33. XH, 16 Feb., 1984.

34. Interview with T. Yashima, 16 Sept., 1985.

35. These students protests were carefully monitored from Hong Kong and analyzed in detail in the Hong Kong press. For translations of these analyses, as well as more subdued Chinese press accounts, see Beijing *Xinhua* in English (18 Sept., 1985) in *Foreign Broadcast Information Services* (hereafter FBIS), No. 182 (19 Sept., 1985), p. G2; Beijing *Xinhua* in English (19 Sept., 1985), in FBIS, No. 183 (20 Sept., 1985), p. D1; Hong Kong AFP in English (3 Oct., 1985) in FBIS, No. 193 (4 Oct., 1985), p. D1; Tokyo *Kyodo* in English (23 Nov., 1985), in FBIS, No. 227 (25 Nov., 1985), p. D1; Taipei *International Service* in English (5 Dec., 1985) in FBIS, No. 235 (6 Nov., 1985), p. V1; Beijing *Zhongguo xinwen she* in Chinese (9 Dec., 1985) in FBIS, No. 240 (13 Dec., 1985), p. K1; Hong Kong *Cheng ming* in Chinese (1 Jan., 1986) in FBIS, No. 3 (6 Jan., 1985), p. W3.

36. R. Hayhoe, "A Comparative Analysis of Chinese-Western Academic Exchange," *Comparative Education*, Vol. 20, No. 1 (March, 1984), p. 46.

37. A recent German study provides rich details on both national and regional programs

of cooperation. See Erhard Louven and Monkia Schädler, *Wissenschaftliche Zusammenarbeit zwischen der Volksrepublik China und der Bundesrepublik Deutschland* (Hamburg: Mitteilungen des Instituts für Asienkunde, No. 149, 1986).

38. Detailed provisions for the Tongji project are given in the *1984-85 Kulturaustausch Programm* which articulates the main lines of scientific and cultural cooperation between the two nations.

39. Interviews with Professor Cao Zhanhua, Dean, and Professor Bi Jiaju, Head of the Academic Affairs Office, Tongji University, 16 October, 1985.

40. Interview with Dr. Albrecht von den Heyden, Cultural Counsellor, Embassy of the Federal German Republic, Beijing, 10 Sept., 1985.

41. XH, 2 Feb., 1985.

42. Interview with Mrs. Theodore, West German Consulate in Shanghai, 23 October, 1985.

43. The British Council, *Programme of Cultural, Educational and Scientific Exchanges between Britain and China 1984-1986* (London: July, 1984).

44. The British Council, *Study and Research in the U.K.: Opportunities for Chinese Scholars at Postgraduate Level and Above* (London, August, 1984).

45. Interview with Mr. Adrian Johnston, The British Embassy in Beijing, 16 Sept., 1985.

46. *Britain-China* (Newsletter of the Great Britain-China Society), No. 20, (Summer, 1982), p. 10. The historian is immediately struck by the contrast with the major English newspaper of pre-Liberation China, the *North China Herald* which was entirely foreign-controlled.

47. XH, 4 March, 1985; FBIS, No. 45, 7 March., 1985.

48. Beijing *Xinhua* in English (21 Nov., 1985) in FBIS, No. 226 (22 Nov., 1985), p.A6.

49. Beijing *Xinhua* in English (17 Dec., 1985) in FBIS, No. 243 (18 Dec., 1985), p. G1.

50. *Programme d'Echanges Culturels entre le Gouvernement de la République Francaise et le Gouvernement de la République Populaire de Chine pour les années 1984-1985.*

51. Interview with Mr. Shu Wenping, Educational Counsellor, Embassy of China in France, 4 July, 1984.

52. Interview with M. Portiche, Conseiller Culturel, Ambassade de France en Chine, 10 Sept., 1984.

53. Interview with Professor Liu Daoyu, President of Wuhan University, Shanghai, 24 October, 1985.

54. Interview with M. Francois Gipouloux, Conseiller Commercial, Ambassade de France en Chine, Beijing, 10 Sept., 1985.

55. Interview with Ms. Chen Derong, Chinese Administrator of the Center, Beijing, 16 Sept., 1985.

56. Jean-Luc Domenach, "Sino-French Relations: A French View," in *China's Foreign Relations: New Perspectives,* ed. Hsüeh Chen-tu (New York: Praeger, 1982).

57. Martin Singer, *Canadian Academic Relations with the P.R.C. 1970-1983* (Ottawa: International Development Research Agency (IDRC), 1985).

58. Jack Maybee, "The China Program of the CIDA" (Ottawa: IDRC, Association of Universities and Colleges of Canada (AUCC), December, 1985).

59. "Report on Development Cooperation Activities in the P.R.C." (Beijing: UNDP Office, Sept., 1985).

60. Interview with Dr. Diana Lary, Cultural Attaché, The Canadian Embassy in China, Beijing, 5 Sept., 1985.

61. D. Ryan and T. Fleming, *Evaluation of the China-Canada Management Education Program* (Toronto: Ontario Institute for Studies in Education (OISE), April, 1986).

62. L. McLean, *The Canada-China Enterprise Management Training Centre: Report at the Transition of Phase I to Phase II* (Toronto: OISE, February, 1986).

63. B. Burnaby, A. Cummings and M. Belfiore, *China/Canada Human Development Training Progam* (Toronto: OISE, 1986).

64. These parallels were discussed in the third session of a recent conference on Cana-

dian Missionary Models of Development, entitled "The Missionary Experience and Contemporary Issues of Aid for Development," University of Toronto, May 2-3, 1986. The conference was sponsored by the University of Toronto-York University Joint Centre on Modern East Asia in connection with the centre's research project on the history of Canadian missionary activity in China.

65. Interview with Ms. Alex Volkoff, First Secretary Development, The Canadian Embassy in China, Beijing, 5 Sept., 1986. Ms Volkoff characterized 80% of Canadian development assistance as "tied-aid."

Glossary of Chinese Terms

Chinese Term		English Translation	Page
bangong bandu	半工半读	part-working schooling	175
Bangong ting	办公厅	Educational Ministry General Office	162,164, 318
bianfa	变法	transform	59
Canshi shi	参事室	Advisor's Office	318
chasheng lu	差生率	rate of unqualified students	261
Chun Miao	春苗	*Spring Shoots*	203
daxue	大学	universities	186
Dewen zhongxuexiao	德文中学校	German language secondary school	91
duanqi zhiye daxue	短期职业大学	short-cycle vocational universities	242
Ewen jiaoxue zhidao weiyuanhui	俄文教学指导委员会	Russian Language Teaching Guidance Committee	164
Ewen zhuanke xuexiao	俄文专科学校	Russian language vocational schools	169
fang qu	防区	garrison areas	146
Fanyi shi	翻译室	Translation Office	164, 318
fuxue	府学	prefectural school	58
Gaodeng jiaoyubu	高等教育部	Ministry of Higher Education	164

Gaodeng shifan jiaoyu si	高等师范教育司	Tertiary Teacher Training Department	318
Gong nong sucheng zhongxue jiaoyu chu	工农速成中学教育处	Industrial & Agricultural Accelerated Secondary School Education Division	164
Gongnong yeyu jiaoyu si	工农业余教育司	Worker-Peasant Spare-time Education Department	318
gongu lü	巩固率	consolidation rate	260
gongmin	公民	civics	176
Gongye jiaoyu diyi (er) si	工业教育第一(二)司	Industrial Education, No.1 Department & No.2 Department	164
guojiao	國教	the national ideology	12
guoli daxue	國立大學	national university	94
Guozijian	國子監	College of the Sons of the Emperor	58
Hanlin Yuan	翰林院	Hanlin Academy	27
hanlin	翰林	menber of the Hanlin Academy	74
hege lü	合格率	qualification rate	260
Jiangsu jiaoyuhui	江苏教育会	The Jiangsu Educational Society	92
Jiaohuibao	教會報	Mission News	39
Jiaokeshu bianshen weiyuanhui	教课书编审委员会	Textbook Editing Committee	318-19
jiaoyu geming	教育革命	educational revolution	254
jiaoyu xiandaihua	教育现代化	educational modernization	254
Jiaoyu bu	教育部	Ministry of Education	85, 94
Jiaoyu shijie	教育世界	*The World of Education*	62, 80, 291

liyong xiaolü	利用效率	utilization rates	258
Mangya jiaoyu chu	盲哑教育处	Division for Education of the Deaf, Dumb & Blind	318
Minzu jiaoyu si	民族教育司	National Minorities Education Department	318
nongmin shenghuo	农民生活	farmers' lives	135
Nonglin weisheng jiaoyu si	农林卫生教育司	Agricultural, Forestry & Health Education Department	164
puji lü	普及率	universalization rate	261
quanxueyuan	勸學員	school district supervisors	72
quanxuesuo	勸學所	Educational Exhorting Offices	67, 72
Qinding xuetang zhangcheng	欽定學堂章程	School Regulations of 1902	61
Renmin jiaoyu	人民教育	*People's Education*	161, 162, 180
Renmin jiaoyu she	人民教育社	Office for *People's Education*	319
Renmin ribao	人民日报	*People's Daily*	174
ruxue	儒學	official (Confucian) schools	10
ruxue lü	入学率	enrollment rate	261
San min zhu i	三民主義	The Three Principle's of the People	302
shengxue lü	升学率	promotion rate	260
shexue	社学	village school	58
shifan daxue	师范大学	teachers universities	164

shifan xueyuan	师范学院	teachers colleges	164
shuyuan	書院	old-style academies	10, 58, 108, 117
sige xiandaihua	四个现代化	the four modernizations	330
siren banxue	私人办学	privately run schools	181
sishu	私塾	private schools	13, 48, 133
taot'ai(daotai)	道台	an official who has the brevet rank and functions of a Provincial Judge	104
tixueshisi	提學使司	Office of Commissioners of Education	66
ti-yong	体用	Chinese learning as the essence(ti), and Western learning for its utility(yong)	12
Tiyu zhidao chu	体育指导处	Physical Education Guidance Division	318
Tongwenguan	同文館	College of Languages	8, 9, 36, 37, 39, 43, 58, 83
tianxue	天学	heavenly(western) learning	4
tongzhou gongji	同舟共济	overcome all difficulties together	92
Waiguo jiaoyu ziliao	外国教育资料	*Foreign Education Materials*	180, 182, 318
Waiguo jiaoyu dongtai	外国教育动态	*Foreign Education Trends*	180, 318
Waiguo jiaoyu	外国教育	*Foreign Education*	180, 318
Wenhua jiaoyu weiyuanhui	文化教育委员会	Cultural Education Committee	161
xiandaihua	现代化	modernization	252
xianxue	縣學	county school	58

Xin jiaoyu	新教育	*New Education*	99, 115, 121
xixue	西學	western learning	4
Xiaoxue jiaoyu si	小学教育司	Primary School Education Department	164
xuebu	学部	Ministry of Education	58, 85
xuedian	學店	school store	78
xueshang	學商	school business	78
Xuesheng shixi zhidao weiyuanhui	学生实习指导委员会	Student Practice Guidance Committee	164
Xuewu gangyao	學務綱要	The Introductory Section to the School Regulations of 1904	65
Xuexiao renshi si	学校人事司	School Personnel Department	164
xuexiaosi	學校司	Office of Provincial Education	71
xueyuan	学院	specialized colleges or technical institutes	186
xuezheng	學政	provincial director of education	66
yangwu yundong	洋務運動	Westernization Movement	58
yishu	義塾	voluntary school	58
yixue	義學	voluntary school	58
youdengsheng lü	优等生率	rate of outstanding students	261
You'er jiaoyu chu	幼儿教育处	Pre-school Education Division	318
you hong you zhuan de gongren jieji zhishifenzi	又红又专的工人阶级知识份子	a red and expert working class intelligentsia	174

yubei xuexiao	预备学校	preparatory school	91
Zhongdeng shifan jiaoyu si	中等师范教育司	Secondary School Education Department	318
Zhongguo jiaoyu bao	中国教育报	*Chinese Education Newspaper*	248
Zhonghua minguo daxue yuan	中華民國大學院	University Council of the Chinese Republic	117
zhouxue	州學	regional school	58
zhuanye duikou lü	专业对口率	rate of fit to manpower needs	261
Zongli Yamen	總理衙門	the traditional Chinese Ministry of Foreign Affairs	37, 90
Zhongguo jiaoyu gaijin she	中国教育改进社	Chinese Association for Educational Advancement	132
zhongxuetang	中學堂	secondary school	88
zhongxuexiao	中学校	secondary school	88
Zhongti xiyong	中体西用	Chinese learning as the essence (ti), and Western learning for its utility(yong)	65
Zhengzhi jiaoyu chu	政治教育处	Political Education Division	164
Zhongdeng jishu jiaoyu si	中等技术教育司	Secondary Technical Education Department	164
Zonghe daxue jiaoyu si	综合大学教育司	Comprehensive University Education Department	164
zonghe jishu jiaoyu	综合技术教育	polytechnic education	175
Zhongguo Gongchanzhuyi Qingnian Tuan	中国共产主义青年团	Chinese Communist Youth League	176

Zhongguo Shaonian Xianfengdui	中国少年先锋队	Chinese Young Pioneers	176
zhuanye	专业	major, specialization	187
Zouding xuetang zhangcheng	奏定學堂章程	School Regulations of 1904	57, 61, 299

* Simplified Chinese characters are used for all modern (post-1949) terms, while classical characters are used for historical terms.

A Select Bibliography of Chinese Education and Its International Relations

This select bibliography is offered as a research guide to materials available in western languages on aspects of Chinese education and its international relations, both historical and contemporary. First, the main types of source material are listed under four headings: 1) Bibliographic guides; 2) Western language journals and other source materials officially published in China; 3) Western translations of Chinese press and journal articles, and 4) Foreign sinological journals with articles on Chinese education. Then a listing of books and articles judged to be either representative or important is provided. This listing is by no means exhaustive, but may be helpful as a starting place for research.

1. Bibliographic Guides

- For the Cultural Revolution period (1966-1972), see Fraser, Stewart, and Hsu Kuang-liang (1972). *Chinese Education and Society: A Bibliographic Guide.* White Plains, New York: International Arts and Sciences Press.
- For the post-Cultural Revolution period (1969-1977), see Dilger, Bernhard, and Henze, Jürgen (1978). *Das Erziehungs und Bildungswesen der VR China seit 1969: Eine Bibliographie.* Hamburg: Institute für Asienkunde, and Barendsen, Robert (1976). *Education in the P.R.C.: A Select, Annotated Bibliography of Materials Published in the English Language 1971-1976.* Washington: U.S. Dept. of Health, Education and Welfare.
- For the post-Mao period (1977-82), see Lo, Billie L. C. (1983) *Research Guide to Education in China After Mao.* Hong Kong: Centre of Asian Studies, University of Hong Kong.
- For more general sources, see the *Bibliography of Asian Studies* published yearly since 1971 by the Association of Asian Studies Inc., U.S.A.

• Finally, the most comprehensive and up-to-date educational bibliography is Parker, Franklin, and Parker, Betty June (1986). *Education in the People's Republic of China. Past and Present: An Annotated Bibliography.* New York: Garland Publishing Inc.

2. Chinese Published Western Language Materials:
— *Beijing Review*
— *China Daily*
— *China Pictorial*
— *China Reconstructs*
— *China Official Annual Report (from 1980)*
— *New China News Agency (London and Hong Kong)*
— *Social Sciences in China*
— *Statistical Yearbook of China*

3. Western Translations of Chinese Press and Journal Materials:
— *China Report* (Joint Publications Research Service [JPRS], Virginia)
— *Chinese Education* (quarterly, Armonk, New York, since 1968)
— *Current Background* (Hong Kong, discontinued)
— *Daily Report* (Foreign Broadcast Information Service [FBIS], Virginia)
— *Survey of China Mainland (P.R.C.) Magazines* (Hong Kong, discontinued)
— *Survey of China Mainland (P.R.C.) Press* (Hong Kong, discontinued)
— *Summary of World Broadcasts: The Far East* (B.B.C., Reading, England)
— *Translations from the P.R.C.* (Springfield, Virginia)
— *Union Research Service* (Hong Kong, discontinued)

4. Foreign Sinological Journals with Articles on Chinese Education:

— *Asian Affairs* (U.S.A.)
— *Asian Survey* (U.S.A.)
— *Asian Thought and Society* (U.S.A.)
— *Asien* (Hamburg)
— *China News Analysis* (Hong Kong)
— *China Quarterly* (Great Britain)
— *China Report* (New Delhi)
— *Current Scene: Developments in the P.R.C.* (Hong Kong, discontinued)
— *Eastern Horizon* (Hong Kong)
— *Etudes Chinoises* (Paris)
— *Extrême Orient-Extrême Occident* (Paris)
— *Issues and Studies* (Taiwan)
— *Journal Asiatique* (Paris)
— *Journal of Asian Studies* (U.S.A.)
— *Modern China* (U.S.A.)
— *T'oung-Pao* (Holland)

5. A Selected Listing of Books and Articles

Ahn Byung-Joon (1978). Higher Education Policy and Politics After the Cultural Revolution. *Korea and World Affairs,* 2(3).

Alitto, Guy (1978). *The Last Confucian: Liang Shu-ming and the Chinese Dilemma of Modernity.* Berkeley, Los Angeles and London: University of California Press.

Ayers, William (1971). *Chang Chih-tung and Educational Reform in China.* Cambridge, Mass.: Harvard University Press.

Bady, Paul (1974). L'Ecole et la Revolution, *Project* (84).

Barendsen, Robert (1979). *The National College Entrance Examinations in the P.R.C.* Washington, D.C.: Office of Education.

Bastid, Marianne (1971). *Aspects de la Réforme de l'Enseignement en Chine au début du XXe siècle d'après les écrits de Zhang Jian.* Paris: Mouton.

Bastid, Marianne (1970). Economic Necessity and Political Ideals in Educational Reform during the Cultural Revolution. *China Quarterly* (42), pp. 16-45.

Bastid, Marianne (1984). Chinese Educational Policies in the 1980s and Economic Development. *China Quarterly* (98), pp. 189-219.

Bastid, Marianne (1986). Education, Youth and Social Perspectives in the Early 1980s. In Arendup, B., et al., *China in the 1980s — and Beyond.* London and Malmo: Curzon Press.

Baum, Richard (1981). *Scientism and Bureaucratism in Chinese Thought: Cultural Limits of the Four Modernisations.* Lund: University of Lund Research Policy Institute.

Becker, C. H., et al. (1932). *The Reorganization of Education in China.* Paris: Institute of Intellectual Cooperation.

Bernstein, Thomas (1977). *Up to the Mountains and Down to the Villages: The Transfer of Youth from Urban to Rural China.* New Haven and London: Yale University Press.

Bigelow, Karl (1960). Some Comparative Relections on Soviet and Chinese Higher Education. *Comparative Education Review,* 4(3), 169-173.

Biggerstaff, Knight (1961). *The Earliest Modern Government Schools in China.* Ithaca, New York: Cornell University Press.

Borthwick, Sally (1983). *Education and Social Change in China.* Stanford, California: Hoover Institution Press.

Brown, Hubert (1982). Politics and the "Peking Spring" of Educational Studies in China. *Comparative Education,* 26(3).

Brown, Hubert (1981). Recent Policy Towards Rural Education in the P.R.C. *Hong Kong Journal of Public Administration,* 3(2), 168-188.

Bullock, Mary Brown (1980). *An American Transplant: The Rockerfeller Foundation and Peking Union Medical College.* Berkeley, California: University of California Press.

Chaffee, John (1985). *The Thorny Gates of Learning in Sung China.* Cambridge: Cambridge University Press.

Chambers, David (1977). The 1975-1976 Debate over Higher Education Policy in the P.R.C. *Comparative Education,* 13(1), 3-14.

Chambers, David (1984). Adult Education in Urban Industrial China: Problems, Policies and Prospects. In Hayhoe, Ruth (Ed.), *Contemporary Chinese Education* (pp. 178-204). London: Croom Helm, and Armonk, N.Y.: M. E. Sharpe, Inc.

Chan, Luke, and Guan Zhiang (1984). *Management Education in China with Special Reference to Recent Support Programmes by Foreign Countries.* Research Report No. 111 QSEP, Hamilton: McMaster University.

Chan, Sylvia, and Price, Ronald (1978). Teacher Training in China: A Case Study of the Foreign Languages Department of Peking Teacher Training College. *Comparative Education,* 14(3), 243-252.

Ch'en, Jerome (1979). *China and the West: Society and Culture 1815-1937.* London: Macmillan.

Chen Hsi-en, Theodore (1960). *The Thought Reform of Chinese Intellectuals.* Hong Kong and London: Hong Kong University and Oxford University Press.

Chen Hsi-en, Theodore (1974). *The Maoist Educational Revolution.* New York: Praeger.

Chen Hsi-en, Theodore (1981). *Chinese Education Since 1949: Academic and Revolutionary Models.* New York: Pergamon Press.

Cheng Chu-yuan (1965). *Scientific and Engineering Manpower in Communist China 1949-1963.* Washington: U.S. Gov't Printing House.

China Educational Commission (1922). *Christian Education in China.* New York: Committee of Referees and Council of the Foreign Missions Conference of North America.

Chou Wei-ling (1974). The "May 7" Cadre School: Rotating Instruction for Cadres in Office. *Issues and Studies,* 10(11), 35-47.

Chou Wei-ling (1976). The May 7 Cadre School: A Study of Its Recent Situation. *Issues and Studies,* 12(9), 16-27.

Chow Tse-tsung (1960). *The May Fourth Movement.* Stanford, California: Stanford University Press.

Chou Wei-ling (1976). A Study of the July 21 Workers University. *Issues and Studies,* 12(10), 54-64.

Chronology of the Two-Road Struggle in the Educational Front in the Past Seventeen Years (1968, Spring). *Chinese Education,* 1(1), 3-58.

Chu, James and Fang, William (1972). The Training of Journalists in China. *Journalism Quarterly,* 49(3), 489-497.

Chu, Don-chean (1980). *Chairman Mao: Education of the Proletariat.* New York: Philosophical Library.

Chung Shih (1953). *Higher Education in China.* Hong Kong: Union Research Institute.

Cleverley, John (1985). *The Schooling of China.* London: George Allen and Unwin.

Clough, Ralph (1981). *A Review of the U.S.-China Exchange Program.* Washington, D.C.: Office of Research, International Communications Agency.

Corrigan, Philip (1974). Socialist Construction as Thought Reform for Intellectuals. *Journal of Contemporary Asia* (4), pp. 275-296.

Covell, Ralph (1978). *W.A.P. Martin: Pioneer of Progress in China.* Washington: Christian University Press.

Dean, Genevieve C. (1974). *Science and Technology in the Development of Modern China: An Annotated Bibliography.* London: Mansell.

Dean, Genevieve (1979). *Technology Policy and Industrialisation in the P.R.C.* Ottawa, Canada: International Development Research Institute.

Deng Xiaoping (1978). Speech at the National Education Work Conference. *Beijing Review,* 21(18), 6-13.

Deng Xiaoping (1985). *Selected Works.* Beijing: Foreign Languages Press.

Dilger, Bernhard (1984). The Education of Minorities. *Comparative Education,* 20(1), 155-164.

Duggan, Stephen (1933). *A Critique of the Report of the League of Nations Mission of Educational Experts.* New York: Institute of International Relations.

Duiker, William (1977). *Ts'ai Yüan-p'ei : Educator of Modern China.* University Park and London: The Pennsylvania State University Press.

Education in China: The Past Five Years (1983). Beijing: Ministry of Education.

Education and Science (1983). Beijing: Foreign Languages Press.

Educational Policy after the Gang of Four (1978). *Chinese Education* (1), pp. 3-174.

Emerson, John Philip (1971). Manpower Training and Utilization of Specialised Cadres, 1949-1968. In Lewis, John Willis (Ed.), *The City in Communist China* (pp. 183-214). Stanford, California: Stanford University Press.

Emerson, John Philip (1973). *Administrative and Technical Manpower in the P.R.C.* Washington, D.C.: U.S. Dept. of Commerce.

Emerson, John Philip (1983). Urban School-leavers and Unemployment in China. *China Quarterly,* (93), pp. 1-16.

Fairbank, John (1964). *Chinese Thought and Institutions.* Chicago and London: University of Chicago Press.

Fairbank, John (Ed.) (1974). *The Missionary Enterprise in China and America.* Cambridge, Mass.: Harvard University Press.

Fairbank, John, and Teng Ssu-yu (Eds.) (1954). *China's Response to the West: A Documentary Survey 1839-1923.* Cambridge, Mass.: Harvard University Press.

Fairbank, Wilma (1976). *America's Cultural Experiment in China 1942-1949.* Washington, D.C.: Bureau of Cultural Affairs, U.S. Department of State.

Fenn, William Purvance (1976). *Christian Higher Education in Changing China 1880-1950.* Michigan: W. B. Eerdmans.

Fingar, Thomas (Ed.) (1980). *China's Quest for Independence: Policy Evolution in the 1970s.* Boulder, Colorado: Westview Press.

Fingar, Thomas, and Reed, Linda (1981). *Survey Summary: Students and Scholars from the P.R.C. in the U.S., August, 1981.* Washington: C.S.C.P.R.C. and the National Association for Foreign Students Affairs.

Fingar, Thomas (1981). *Higher Education in the P.R.C.* Stanford, California: Northeast Asia-United States Forum on International Policy, Stanford University.

Fingar, Thomas (1980). *Higher Education and Research in the P.R.C.: Institutional Profiles.* Washington: U.S.-China Clearinghouse.

Fitzgerald, C. P. (1958). *Floodtide in China.* London: Cresset Press.

Franke, Wolfgang (1960). *The Reform and Abolition of the Traditional Examination System.* Cambridge, Mass.: Harvard University Press.

Fraser, Stewart (1964). Notes on Sino-Soviet Cooperation in Higher Education 1950-1960. In French, E. L. (Ed.), *Melbourne Studies in Education 1961-62.* Melbourne: Melbourne University Press.

Fraser, Stewart (Ed.) (1965). *Chinese Communist Education: Records of the First Decade.* Nashville: Vanderbilt University Press.

Fraser, Stewart (1969). Sino-Soviet Educational Relations. In Paulsen, R. F. (Ed.), *Changing Dimensions in International Education* (pp. 105-120). Tucson, Arizona: University of Arizona Press.

Fraser, Stewart (1972). Sino-Soviet Educational Relations: A Recent Episode. *School and Society,* 100(2338), pp. 54-58.

Fraser, Stewart (1977). Administration et Controle de l'Education en Chine. *International Review of Education* (23), pp. 491-501.

Fraser, Stewart (Ed.) (1971). *Education and Communism in China: An Anthology of Commentary and Documents.* London: Pall Mall Press.

Furth, Charlotte (1970). *Ting Wen-chiang: Science and China's New Culture.* Cambridge, Mass.: Harvard University Press.

Galt, Howard (1951). *A History of Chinese Educational Institutions.* London: Arthur Probsthain.

Gamberg, Ruth (1977). *Red and Expert.* New York: Schocken Books.

Gardner, John (1971). Educated Youth and Urban-Rural Inequalities. In Lewis, John Willis (Ed.), *The City in Communist China* (pp. 235-286). Stanford, California: Stanford University Press.

Gardner, John, and Wilt, Idema (1973). China's Educational Revolution. In Schram, Stuart (Ed.), *Authority, Participation and Cultural Change in China* (pp. 257-289). London: Cambridge University Press.

Gardner, John (1982). *Chinese Politics and the Succession to Mao.* London: Macmillan.

Godwin, Paul (1977). The Goals of Citizenship Training: A Chinese Perspective. *Studies in Comparative Communism,* 10(3), pp. 315-327.

Goldman, Merle (1981). *China's Intellectuals Advise and Dissent.* Cambridge, Mass.: Harvard University Press.

Greenblatt, Sidney (1972). Organizational Elites and Social Change at Peking University. In Scalapino, Robert (ed.), *Elites in the People's Republic of China* (pp. 451-497). Seattle and London: University of Washington Press.

Gregg, Alice (1941). *China and Educational Autonomy: The Changing Role of the Protestant Missionary in China 1807-1937.* New York: Syracuse University Press.

Grieder, Jerome (1970). *Hu Shih and the Chinese Renaissance*. Cambridge, Mass.: Harvard University Press.

Grieder, Jerome (1981). *Intellectuals and the State in Modern China*. New York: The Free Press.

Gu Mingyuan (1984). The Development and Reform of Higher Education. *Comparative Education*, 20(1), pp. 141-149.

Gupta, Krishna Prakesh (1971). Liberal Arts Education in China. *China Report*, 7(5), pp. 18-25.

Gupta, Krishna Prakesh (1972). ''Society as a Factory'': The Maoist Approach to Social Science. *China Report*, 8(3), pp. 36-57.

Hao Keming (1984). Research on Higher Education in China Today. *Comparative Education*, 20(1), pp. 149-154.

Hawkins, John (1970). *Mao Tse-tung and Education: His Thoughts and Teachings*. Connecticut: Linnet Books.

Hawkins, John (1983). *Education and Social Change in the People's Republic of China*. New York: Praeger.

Hawkins, John (1984). Educational Exchanges and the Transformation of Higher Education in China. In Barber, Elinor, Altbach, Philip, and Myers, Robert (Eds.), *Bridges to Knowledge: Foreign Students in Comparative Perspective*. Chicago: University of Chicago Press.

Hayhoe, Ruth (Ed.) (1984). *Contemporary Chinese Education*. London and Armonk, New York: Croom Helm, M. E. Sharpe.

Hayhoe, Ruth (1984, March). A Comparative Analysis of Sino-western Academic Exchange. *Comparative Education*, 20(1), pp. 39-56.

Hayhoe, Ruth (1985). Sino-Western Educational Cooperation: History and Perspectives. *Prospects*, 15(2).

Hayhoe, Ruth (1986). Penetration or Mutuality? China's Educational Cooperation with Europe, Japan and North America. *Comparative Education Review*, 31(4), pp. 532-559.

Hayhoe, Ruth (1986). China, Comparative Education and the World Order Models Project. *Compare*, 16(1), pp. 65-80.

Hayhoe, Ruth (1984). *Chinese, European and American Scholarly Values in Interaction*. London: London Association of Comparative Educationists.

Henze, Jürgen (1982). Begabtenförderung im Bildungwesen der VR China: Das System der ''Schwerpunkt-Schulen.'' *Asien*, (4), pp. 29-58.

Henze, Jürgen (1983). *Bildung und Wissenschaft in der Volksrepublik China zu Beginn der Achtziger Jahre*. Hamburg: Institut für Asienkunde.

Henze, Jürgen (1984). Higher Education: The Tension Between Quality and Equality. In Hayhoe, Ruth (Ed.), *Contemporary Chinese Education* (pp. 93-153). London: Croom Helm.

Henze, Jürgen (1984). Developments in Vocational Education since 1976. *Comparative Education*, 20(1), pp. 117-140.

Henze, Jürgen (1983). Alphabetisierung in China. *Bildung und Erziehung*, 36(3), pp. 295-313.

Herschede, Fred (1979). Higher Education and the Expansion of Technically

Qualified Industrial Workers During China's Modernization 1976-1985. *Bulletin of Concerned Asian Scholars,* pp. 64-72.

Hinton, William (1972). *Hundred Day War: The Cultural Revolution at Tsinghua University.* New York: Monthly Review Press.

Ho Ping-ti (1962). *The Ladder of Success in Imperial China: Aspects of Social Mobility 1368-1911.* New York: Columbia University Press.

Ho, Samuel, and Huenemann, Ralph (1984). *China's Open Door Policy: The Quest for Foreign Technology and Capital.* Vancouver: University of British Columbia Press.

Holmes, Brian (1984). A Comparativist's View of Chinese Education. In Hayhoe, Ruth (Ed.), *Contemporary Chinese Education* (pp. 7-22). London and Armonk, N.Y.: Croom Helm and M. E. Sharpe.

Hong Yongfan (1982). Continuing Literacy Work in China. *Prospects,* 12(2), pp. 185-191.

Hsiao, Theodore (1935). *The History of Modern Education in China.* Shanghai: The Commercial Press.

Hsu, Emmanual C. Y. (1964). The Reoganization of Higher Education in Communist China 1949-1961. *China Quarterly,* (19), pp. 128-160.

Hu Shiming and Seifman, Eli (1976). Medical Education in China. *American Journal of Chinese Medicine,* 4(3), pp. 297-310.

Hu Chang-tu (1984). The Historical Background: Examinations and Controls in Pre-Modern China. *Comparative Education,* 20(1), pp. 7-27.

Hu Chang-tu (1962). *Chinese Education Under Communism.* New York: Teachers College, Columbia.

Hu Chang-tu (1970). *The Education of National Minorities in Communist China.* Washington, D.C.: U.S. Dept. of Health, Education and Welfare, Office of Education, Institute of International Studies.

Hu Chang-tu (1972). The Chinese People's University: Bastion of Marxism-Leninism. In Butts, R. F. and Niblett, W. B. (Eds.), *The World Yearbook of Education: Universities Facing the Future* (pp. 63-74). London: Evans Bros. Ltd.

Hu Shiming and Seifman, Eli (1975). Socialist New Things in Chinese Education. *Asian Affairs,* 6(3), pp. 307-316.

Hu Shiming and Seifman, Eli (1975). A Question of World Outlook: Interviews with Chinese Middle School Graduates. *Asian Affairs,* 6(1), pp. 30-36.

Hu Shiming and Seifman, Eli (Eds.). (1976). *Towards a New World Outlook: A Documentary History of Education in the P.R.C. 1949-1976.* New York: Ams Press.

Huang Shiqi (1985). On Some Vital Issues in the Development and Reform of Higher Education. *Higher Education in Europe,* 10(3), pp. 63-75.

Hunter, Carman St. John, and Keehn, Martha McKee (Eds.). (1985). *Adult Education in China.* London: Croom Helm.

Israel, John (1966). *Student Nationalism in China 1927-1937.* Stanford, California: Stanford University Press.

Jen, C. K. (1975). Science and the Open-Door Educational Movement. *China*

Quarterly, (64), pp. 741-747.

Joint Economic Committee (1982). *China Under the Four Modernizations.* Washington, D.C.: U.S. Gov't Printing House.

Keenan, Barry (1977). *The Dewey Experiment in China.* Cambridge, Mass.: Harvard University Press.

King, Edmund (1984). Chinese Educational Development in a Comparative Perspective. *Comparative Education,* 20(1), pp. 165-182.

Kuntze, Peter (1977). *China — Revolution in der Seele.* Frankfurt am Main: Fischer Taschenbuch Verlag.

Kuo Ping Wen (1915). *The Chinese System of Public Education.* New York: Teachers College, Columbia.

Kwong, Julia (1979). *Chinese Education in Transition: Prelude to the Cultural Revolution.* Montreal: McGill-Queens University Press.

Lamb, Malcolm (Ed.). (1984). *Directory of Officials and Organizations in China 1958-1983.* Armonk, New York: M. E. Sharpe.

David Lampton (1986). *A Relationship Restored: Trends in U.S.-China Educational Exchange 1978-1984.* Washington, D.C.: National Academy Press.

Latourette, Kenneth (1929). *A History of Christian Missions in China.* London: Society for Promoting Christian Knowledge.

Lee, H. P. (1974). Education and Rural Development in China Today. In Foster, Philip and Sheffield, James (Eds.), *World Yearbook of Education* (pp. 209-233). London: Evans Bros.

Levenson, Joseph (1958). *Confucian China and Its Modern Fate: The Problem of Intellectual Continuity.* London: Routledge and Kegan Paul.

Levenson, Joseph (1964). *Confucian China and Its Modern Fate: The Problem of Monarchical Decay.* London: Routledge and Kegan Paul.

Levenson, Joseph (1965). *Confucian China and Its Modern Fate: The Problem of Historical Significance.* London: Routledge and Kegan Paul.

Li, Anthony (1977). *The History of Privately Controlled Higher Education in China.* Westport, Connecticut: Greenwood Press Publications.

Lin Pao-tchin (1926). *L'Instruction Feminine en Chine.* Paris: Librairie Geuthner.

Linden, Allen (1968). Politics and Education in Nationalist China: The Case of the University Council 1927-28. *Journal of Asian Studies,* XXVIII(4), pp. 395-422.

Lindsay, Michael (1950). *Notes on Educational Problems in Communist China.* New York: Institute of Pacific Relations.

Liu Wenxiu (1985). Developments and Interrelationships of Higher Education in New China. *Canadian and International Education,* 14(2), pp. 59-71.

Liu Shaoqi (1969). *Collected Works.* Hong Kong: Union Research Institute.

Liu, William (1974). University Administration in Post-Cultural Revolution China. *China Report,* 10(1-2), pp. 27-35.

Liu, Adam P. L. (1971). *Communications and National Integration in Communist China.* Berkeley, Los Angeles, London: University of California Press.

Liu, Adam Yuen-ching (1981). *The Hanlin Academy: Training Ground for the Ambitious.* Connecticut: Archon Books.

Lo, Billie L. C. (1984). Primary Education: A Two-Track System for Dual Tasks. In Hayhoe, Ruth (Ed.), *Contemporary Chinese Education* (pp. 47-64). London: Croom Helm.

Lo, Billie L. C. (1984). Teacher Education in the Eighties. In Hayhoe, Ruth (Ed.), *Contemporary Chinese Education* (pp. 154-177). London and Armonk, N.Y.: Croom Helm and M. E. Sharpe.

Löfstedt, Jan-Ingvar (1984). Educational Planning and Administration in China. *Comparative Education*, 20(1), pp. 57-72.

Louie, Kam (1984). Salvaging Confucian Education (1949-1983). *Comparative Education*, 20(1), pp. 27-38.

Louven, Erhard, and Schädler, Monica (1986). *Wissenschaftlicher Zusammenarbeit zwischen der Volksrepublik China und der Bundesrepublik Deutschland.* Hamburg: Institut für Asienkunde.

Lu Xingwei (1981). Moral Education in the Schools. *Beijing Review* 24(49), pp. 21-28.

Lucas, AnElissa (1984). *Chinese Medical Modernization: Comparative Policy Continuities 1930s-1980s.* New York: Praeger.

Lutz, Jessie (1971). *China and the Christian Colleges.* Ithaca and London: Cornell University Press.

Mao Zedong (1969-1973). Comrade Mao Tse-tung on Educational Work. *Chinese Education*, 2-6.

Mao Zedong (1975). *Selected Works, Vol. 1-4.* Beijing: Foreign Languages Press.

Mao Zedong (1977). *Selected Works, Vol. 5.* Beijing: Foreign Languages Press.

Martin, Roberta (1975). The Socialization of Children in China and on Taiwan. *China Quarterly* (62), pp. 242-270.

McCormick, R. (1980). Central Broadcasting and Television University. *China Quarterly* (81), pp. 129-136.

Meskill, John (1982). *Academies in Ming China.* Tuscon, Arizona: University of Arizona Press.

Miyazaki, Ichisada (1971). *China's Examination Hell: The Civil Service Examinations of Imperial China.* New York and Tokyo: Weatherhill.

Munro, Donald (1977). *The Concept of Man in Contemporary China.* Ann Arbor, Michigan: Center for Chinese Studies, University of Michigan.

Nee, Victor (1969). *The Cultural Revolution at Peking University.* New York and London: Monthly Review Press.

Neugebauer, Ernst (1971). *Anfänge Pädagogischer Entwicklungschilfe unter dem Völkerbund im China 1931 bis 1935.* Hamburg: Institut für Asienkunde.

Ogden, Suzanne (1982). The Politics of Higher Education in the P.R.C. *Chinese Law and Government*, 11(3).

Orleans, Leo A. (1972). China's Science and Technology: Continuity and Innovation. In Joint Economic Committee (Ed.), *P.R.C.: An Economic Assessment.* Washington, D.C.: U.S. Gov't Printing Office.

Orleans, Leo A. (1980). *Manpower for Science and Engineering in China.* Washington, D.C.: Committee for Science and Technology, U.S. House of Representatives.

Orleans, Leo A. (Ed.). (1980). *Science in Contemporary China.* Washington,

D.C.: Stanford University Press.

Orleans, Leo A. (1983). *The Training of Scientific and Engineering Manpower in the P.R.C.* Washington, D.C.: U.S. Gov't Printing Office.

Orleans, Leo A. (1960). *Professional Manpower and Education in Communist China.* Washington, D.C.: U.S. Gov't Printing Office.

Parker, Franklin (1977). *What Can We Learn from the Schools of China?* Bloomington, Indiana: The Phi Delta Kappa Educational Foundation.

Peake, Cyrus (1932). *Nationalism and Education in Modern China.* New York: Columbia University Press.

Pepper, Suzanne (1970). Education and Political Development in Communist China. *Studies in Comparative Communism,* 3(3-4), pp. 132-157.

Pepper, Suzanne (1982). China's Universities: New Experiments in Socialist Democracy and Administrative Reform. *Modern China,* 8(2), pp. 147-204.

Pepper, Suzanne (1984). *China's Universities: Post-Mao Enrollment Policies and Their Impact on the Structure of Secondary Education.* Ann Arbor, Michigan: Center for Chinese Studies.

Pepper, Suzanne (1978). Education and Revolution: The "Chinese Model" Revisited. *Asian Studies,* 18(9), pp. 847-890.

Pepper, Suzanne (1980). Chinese Education After Mao: Two Steps Forward and Two Steps Back and Begin Again? *China Quarterly* (81), pp. 1-65.

Petit, Joseph (1983). *Engineering Education in the P.R.C.* Washington: National Academy Press.

Physics, Chemistry and Mathematics Education in China (1980). *Chinese Education,* 13(1-2), pp. 1-165.

Pinot, Virgile (1932). *La Chine et la formation de l'esprit philosophique en France.* Paris: P. Geuther.

Prewitt, Kenneth (1981). *Research Opportunities in China for American Humanists and Social Scientists.* Washington, D.C.: Social Science Research Council.

Price, Ronald (1970). *Education in Communist China.* New York: Praeger.

Price, R. F. (1973). The Part-Work Principle in Chinese Education. *Current Scene: Developments in the P.R.C.,* 9(9), pp. 1-11.

Price, R. F. (1976). 'Community and School' and Education in the P.R.C. *Comparative Education,* 12(2), pp. 163-174.

Price, Ronald (1984). Labor and Education. *Comparative Education,* 20(1), pp. 81-92.

Price, Ronald (1972). Making Universal Schooling Serve Proletarian Politics. In *China after the Cultural Revolution* (pp. 161-184). Brusselles: Centre d'Etudes de Sud-Est Asiatique et de l'Extrême Orient.

Price, Ronald (1976). *What Chinese Children Read About: Serial Picture Books and Foreigners.* Bundoora, Victoria, Australia: La Trobe University.

Price, Ronald (1977). *Marxism and Education in China and Russia.* London: Croom Helm.

Prybla, Jan (1974). The Life of a Chinese Professor. *The Journal of General Education,* 26(3), pp. 195-204.

Purcell, Victor (1936). *Problems of Chinese Education.* London: Kegan Paul,

Trench, Trubner and Co. Ltd.

Mary Rankin (1971). *Early Chinese Revolutionaries.* Cambridge, Mass.: Harvard University Press.

Les rapports entre la Chine et l'Europe au temps des Lumières (1980). Actes du IIe Colloque internationale de Sinologie, Chantilly, 1977. Paris: Les Belles Lettres.

Rawski, Evelyn (1979). *Education and Popular Literacy in Ch'ing China.* Ann Arbor, Michigan: University of Michigan Press.

Regulations Concerning Academic Degrees in the P.R.C. (1982). Beijing: The Chinese Education Association for International Exchanges.

Ridley, Charles, Godwin, Paul, and Dookin, Dennis (1971). *The Making of a Model Citizen in Communist China.* Stanford, California: The Hoover Institution Press.

Ridley, Charles (1976). *China's Scientific Policies: Implications of International Cooperation.* Stanford, California: Hoover Institute.

Rosen, Stanley (1984). New Directions in Secondary Education. In Hayhoe, Ruth (Ed.), *Contemporary Chinese Education* (pp. 64-92). London and Armonk, N.Y.: Croom Helm and M. E. Sharpe.

Rosen, Stanley (1985). Recentralization, Decentralization and Rationalization: Deng Xiaoping's Bifurcated Educational Policy. *Modern China,* 11(3).

Rosen, Stanley (1982). Obstacles to Educational Reform in China. *Modern China,* 8(1), pp. 3-40.

Rupert, Wolfgang (1975). *Naturwissenschaft und Technik in China.* Wien: Osterreichsches Chinaforschungsinstitut.

Scalapino, Robert (Ed.) (1972). *Elites in the People's Republic of China.* Seattle and London: University of Washington Press.

Scharping, Thomas (1981). *Umsiedllungsprogramme für Chinas Jugund 1955-1980.* Hamburg: Institut für Asienkunde.

Schram, Stuart (1977). *Mao Tse-tung Unrehearsed.* Harmondsworth, England: Penguin Books.

Schwartz, Benjamin (1964). *In Search of Wealth and Power: Yen Fu and the West.* Cambridge, Mass.: Harvard University Press.

Science and Technology in the P.R.C. (1977). Paris: O.E.C.D.

Selden, Mark (1971). *The Yenan Way in Revolutionary China.* Cambridge, Mass.: Harvard University Press.

Seybolt, Peter (Ed.) (1971). *Revolutionary Education in China: Documents and Commentary.* New York: International Arts and Sciences Press.

Seybolt, Peter (1971). The Yenan Revolution in Mass Education. *China Quarterly,* (48), pp. 641-669.

Seybolt, Peter (1975). *The Rustification of Urban Youth in China: A Social Experiment.* New York: M. E. Sharpe.

Sheringham, Michael (1984). Popularization Policies in Chinese Education from the 1950s to the 1970s. *Comparative Education,* 20(1), pp. 73-80.

Shih Ch'ing-chih (1962). *The Status of Science and Education in Communist China and a Comparison with that of U.S.S.R.* Kowloon: Union Research Institute.

Shirk, Susan (1973). The 1963 Temporary Work Regulations for Full-time Middle and Primary Schools: Commentary and Translation. *China Quarterly*, (55), pp. 511-546.

Shirk, Susan (1982). *Competitive Comrades: Career Incentives and Student Strategies in China*. Berkeley: University of California Press.

Singer, Martin (1986). *Canadian Academic Relations with the People's Republic of China Since 1970*. Ottawa: International Development Research Centre.

Singer, Martin (1971). *Educated Youth and the Cultural Revolution in China*. Ann Arbor, Michigan: Center for Chinese Studies.

Bobby Siu (1982). *Imperialism and Women's Resistance 1900-1949*. London: Zed Press.

Helen Snow (1967). *Women in Modern China*. Paris: Mouton and Co.

Spence, Jonathan (1969). *To Change China: Western Advisors in China 1620-1960*. Boston and Toronto: Little, Brown and Co.

Spence, Jonathan (1985). *The Memory Palace of Matteo Ricci*. New York: Penguin.

Stauffer, Milton (Ed.) (1922). *The Christian Occupation of China*. Shanghai: China Continuation Committee.

Sun Yat Sen (1929). *San Min Chu I: The Three Principles of the People*. Shanghai: The Commercial Press.

Suttmeier, Richard (1974). *Research and Revolution*. Lexington, Toronto and London: Lexington Books.

Suttmeier, Richard (1980). *Science, Technology and China's Drive for Modernization*. Stanford, California: Hoover Institute Press.

Swetz, Frank (1974). *Mathematics Education in China: Its Growth and Development*. Cambridge, Mass. and London: The M.I.T. Press.

Taylor, Robert (1973) *Education and University Enrollment Policies in China 1949-1971*. Canberra: Australian National University Press.

Taylor, Robert (1981). *China's Intellectual Dilemma: Politics and University Enrollment 1949-1975*. Vancouver, B.C.: University of British Columbia Press.

Ten Great Years (1960). Beijing: Foreign Language Press.

Teng Ssu-yu (1942). Chinese Influence on the Western Examination System. *Harvard Journal of Asiatic Studies*, 7(4), pp. 267-312.

Ter Weele, Alexander (1983). China-World Bank and University Development. *Prospects*, 13(4), pp. 493-502.

Thomaz de Bossiere, Madame Yves de (1982). *Francois-Xavier Dentrecolles et l'Apport de la Chine à l'Europe de XVIIIe siècle*. Paris: Les Belles Lettres.

Tsang Chiu-sam (1968). *Society, Schools and Progress in China*. London: Pergamon Press.

Tsien Tche-lao (1971). *L'Enseignement Supérieure et la Recherche Scientifique en Chine Populaire*. Paris: Librairie Générale de Droit et de Jurisprudence.

Unger, Jonathan (1980). The Chinese Controversy over Higher Education. *Pacific Affairs*, 53(1), pp. 29-47.

Unger, Jonathan (1984). Severing the Links between School Performance and Careers: the Experience of China's Urban Schools 1968-1976. *Comparative Education*, 20(1), pp. 93-102.

Unger, Jonathan (1977). Post-Cultural Revolution Primary School Education: Selected Texts. *Chinese Education,* 10(2), pp. 4-102.

Unger, Jonathan (1982). *Education under Mao: Class and Competition in Canton Schools 1960-1980.* New York: Columbia University Press.

University Administration in China (1983). England: University of East Anglia: Conference of Registrars and Secretaries and Conference of University Administrators.

Wang Feng-gang (1933). *Japanese Influence on Educational Reform in China.* Peiping: Authors Book Store.

Wang Hsueh-wen (1981). Elementary Educational Reform in the Chinese Mainland. *Issues and Studies,* (1981), pp. 32-46.

Wang Hsueh-wen (1975). *Chinese Communist Education: The Yenan Period.* Taiwan: Institute of International Relations.

Wang Hsueh-wen (1978). The "Two Estimates": A Great Debate on the Educational Front. *Issues and Studies,* 14(2), pp. 22-36.

Wang, Y. C. (1966). *Chinese Intellectuals and the West: 1872-1949.* Chapel Hill: University of North Carolina Press.

Wang Yousheng (1980). How the Work-Study System Operates in One Province. *China Reconstructs,* pp. 8-11.

Wang, Robert S. (1975). Educational Reforms and the Cultural Revolution. *Asian Survey,* 15(9), pp. 758-774.

Watson, Keith (1981). The Education of Minorities in China. In Megarry, Jacquetta (Ed.), *The World Yearbook of Education: The Education of Minorities.* London: Kogan Page.

West, Philip (1976). *Yenching University and Sino-Western Relations 1916-1952.* Cambridge, Mass.: Harvard University Press.

White, Gordon (1976). *The Politics of Class and Class Origin: The Case of the Cultural Revolution.* Canberra: The Australian National University Press.

White, Gordon (1981). Higher Education and Social Redistribution in a Socialist Society: The Chinese Case. *World Development,* 9(2), pp. 149-166.

White, Gordon (1981). *Party and Professionals: The Political Role of Teachers in Contemporary China.* Armonk, New York: M. E. Sharpe.

White, Lynn (1979). *Careers in Shanghai: The Social Guidance of Personal Energies in a Developing Chinese City.* Berkeley: University of California Press.

Whyte, Martin (1974). Educational Reform: China in the 1970s and Russia in the 1920s. *Comparative Education Review,* 18(2), pp. 112-128.

Wilson, Richard (1984). *Chou: The Story of Zhou En-lai 1898-1976.* London: Hutchinson.

Wilson, Richard, and Wilson, Amy (1970). The Red Guards and the World Student Movement. *China Quarterly* (42), pp. 88-104.

Wilson, Amy, Greenblatt, Sidney, and Wilson, Richard (1977). *Deviance and Social Control in Chinese Society.* New York: Praeger.

Wolf, Margery (1985). *Revolution Postponed: Women in Contemporary China.* Stanford, California: Stanford University Press.

The World Bank (1983). *China: Socialist Economic Development, The Social Sector, Population, Health, Nutrition and Education.* Washington, D.C.: The World Bank.

The World Bank (1985). *China: Long-term Development Issues and Options.* Baltimore and London: Johns Hopkins University.

The World Bank (1985). *China: Issues and Prospects in Education.* Washington, D.C.: The World Bank.

Wu Yuan-li and Sheeks, Robert (Eds.) (1970). *The Organization and Support of Scientific Research and Development in Mainland China.* New York: Praeger.

Yen Y. C., James (1975). *The Ting Hsien Experiment in 1934.* Philippines: International Institute of Rural Research.

Yu Bo (1982). *Experiences in Anti-Illiteracy Work.* Paris: UNESCO Surveys and Studies, Literacy, Adult Education and Development Themes, ED/WS/30.

Zhao Bao-heng (1984). Education in the Countrywide Today. *Comparative Education,* 20(1), pp. 103-106.

Index